Reason in a Dark Time

REASON IN A DARK TIME

WHY THE STRUGGLE AGAINST CLIMATE CHANGE FAILED— AND WHAT IT MEANS FOR OUR FUTURE

Dale Jamieson

OXFORD
UNIVERSITY PRESS

OXFORD
UNIVERSITY PRESS

Oxford University Press is a department of the University of Oxford.
It furthers the University's objective of excellence in research, scholarship,
and education by publishing worldwide.

Oxford   New York
Auckland   Cape Town   Dar es Salaam   Hong Kong   Karachi
Kuala Lumpur   Madrid   Melbourne   Mexico City   Nairobi
New Delhi   Shanghai   Taipei   Toronto

With offices in
Argentina   Austria   Brazil   Chile   Czech Republic   France   Greece
Guatemala   Hungary   Italy   Japan   Poland   Portugal   Singapore
South Korea   Switzerland   Thailand   Turkey   Ukraine   Vietnam

Oxford is a registered trademark of Oxford University Press
in the UK and certain other countries.

Published in the United States of America by
Oxford University Press
198 Madison Avenue, New York, NY 10016

© Oxford University Press 2014

CIP data is on file at the Library of Congress

ISBN 978–0–19–933766–8

9 8 7 6
Printed in the United States of America
on acid-free paper

For Mickey Glantz
and Rikki Kimberly and her mother

The very essence of civilized culture is that we...deliberately institute, in advance of the happening of various contingencies and emergencies of life, devices for detecting their approach and registering their nature, for warding off what is unfavorable, or at least for protecting ourselves from its full impact....

—John Dewey (1910:16)

One more word about giving instruction as to what the world ought to be. Philosophy in any case always comes on the scene too late to give it....When philosophy paints its gloomy picture then a form of life has grown old. It cannot be rejuvenated by the gloomy picture, but only understood. Only when the dusk starts to fall does the owl of Minerva spread its wings and fly.

—G.W.F. Hegel (1952:12–13)

Contents

Preface

The dusk has started to fall with respect to climate change and so the owl of Minerva can spread her wings. We can now begin the process of understanding why the global attempt to prevent serious anthropogenic climate change failed and begin to chart a course for living in a world that has been remade by human action.

We are stuck with climate change. This book is about what it is, why we are stuck with it, and what we can learn from our failures to get out of the ditch. Without intending to do so, we have committed ourselves and our descendants to a world that is qualitatively different from the one that gave rise to humanity and all of its creations. Now we hope to limit the pace and extent of the change, but despite international treaties we cannot seem to do so, even with the advice of the world's best scientists. This book is a contribution to helping us think through why this is so and what it means.

Sometimes people hear this as pessimism. I say it is realism. If we are lucky, climate change will not be worse than other things that humanity has survived. During the last century about 231 million people died in war and many more from famine and other disasters.[1] Yet the arts and culture thrived. In some places material prosperity bloomed as never before, and billions of people lived in freedom and dignity. Perhaps it will be this way with climate change. On the other hand, if we are not going to be so lucky, it would be good to start making preparations now.

I am a philosopher by disciplinary training but some of my colleagues will have a hard time recognizing this as a philosophy book. I can only say that when it comes to thinking about the real world (an exercise in what philosophers call "non-ideal theory"), the facts matter. So does history. It is important to situate the subject under investigation in the world of our shared experiences. This would not have seemed as strange to my philosophical heroes (Hume and Mill) as it does to many philosophers today. Still, readers might want to know (for reasons of attraction or avoidance) that Chapters 5 and 6 are the most traditionally philosophical chapters in the book.

Not only am I a philosopher but my roots are firmly in the "analytic" tradition. Those who keep track of such matters will find traces of internalism,

[1] Leitenberg 2006.

consequentialism, naturalism, and holism. You will also find "thought experiments" and appeals to the readers' judgments about such cases. In addition, you will be subjected to my take on commonsense morality. None of this is wildly crazy or "a prioristic," at least compared to much that goes on in philosophy, but it does deserve comment. Moral judgments cannot always be consulted as if they were written down (in the heart or in a book). The corpus of our moral judgments is incomplete, indeterminate, inconsistent, and incoherent. However, with honesty, reflection, and sincerity we can make some progress using my approach. Our behavior can often provide a guide to our moral beliefs and commitments. The law often provides helpful hints, and has the advantage of being codified and discussed. Still, there are important differences between behavior, law, and morality, and I have tried to be sensitive to them.

This book is directed mainly to my fellow citizens and to those with whom I have discussed these topics over the years. It is written from a generally "Western" point of view. More specifically, it is written from my point of view. I have lived through many of the events that I chronicle and analyze in this book and I am hyperaware of what historians often miss: the feel of the time, the specificity of events, the temperament of the participants, and in some cases even important episodes that for whatever reason have not been written down or taken up in stories that are told and then repeatedly cited. At the same time, I am very aware of my own unreliability due to the usual failings of confirmation and selection bias, anchoring, failures of memory, and so on, and also because of the particular standpoint from which I have viewed these events: always a little removed from the center of action, but never really dispassionate. Perhaps the best summary of my involvement is to say that I was an untrained participant-observer in many of the events that I describe.

I owe a huge debt to scholars whose job it is to get the facts right about all sorts of matters about which my knowledge is quite amateurish. I acknowledge some of them below and in the notes to particular chapters. While I have done my best to fairly represent the state of the discussion in various fields, I have no illusions about complete success. Research is ongoing, and our understandings about many things will change at least in their details. On every topic that I mention there is a vast and sophisticated literature with which I do not fully engage. What is new and enlightening, I hope, is the way in which I bring together into a single narrative a large array of thoughts, information, and ideas. Wittgenstein said that philosophy was about "assembling reminders" and to a great extent that is what I do in this book.

Ultimately, there are no experts on climate change, only experts on particular aspects of the problem and generalists who are skilled at integrating diverse material. Anyone who tries to tell the larger story inevitably trespasses on the terrain of specialists and some of my interpretations and mistakes are bound to enrage someone. I stand by the interpretations and I hope the mistakes are few and relatively minor.

One of the most off-putting things about the climate change discussion is the welter of confusing terms and acronyms. In order to lower the price of admission a table of acronyms has been included, following this Preface. Except for acronyms that refer to standard measures (e.g., "ppm" for "parts per million") I spell out the full term in the first use of each acronym in each chapter.

I use some words in a technical way, and as you will see in Chapter 7 the vocabulary that I use for climate change interventions is non-standard. However, I remain resolutely conventional about the use of the expression "climate change." Many who write in this field are moving away from using this expression because they think it sounds too nice or for various other reasons. They prefer instead such locutions as "climate disruption" and "climate destabilization." They have a point, but for the most part I stick with the expression "climate change" because it is descriptively accurate and relatively non-emotive. I use the term "policy-maker" in a way that is very broad. Everyone is a climate change decision-maker, and I need a term that will distinguish me, on the one hand, from a regulator, state legislator, or the President of the United States on the other. I use the terms "duty" and "obligation" indifferently, though there is good reason for distinguishing them for particular purposes. On the other hand, I distinguish contributing to climate change from causing climate change, a distinction that looms large in Chapter 5.

I began writing a book on climate change just after I had turned 40, and I sent this manuscript to the press shortly before I turned 65. I would like to say that it was a labor of love, but it was really an avocation that became an obsession. When people asked me why my first attempts to write a book on this subject failed, I would say that it was impossible to write the book until I knew how the story ended. It slowly dawned on me that this joke carried an important truth (thank you, Groucho). The real story of climate change (or at least the one that I wanted to write) is not about the destination but about the journey. It is about living with change. In this respect the concern of the book is much broader than climate. It is about what it would be like to have a science, epistemology, ethics, and politics adequate to a world of change and surprise. That is the world in which we live, but much of our politics, philosophy, and even science seem to presuppose otherwise.

My intellectual debts in this area go back to 1980 when I arrived at the University of Colorado and was told that I was going to teach a course in environmental ethics, a subject that barely existed, with an environmental scientist whom I had never met. The class was a disaster but it was the beginning of a lifelong friendship with Mickey Glantz, and an eventual appointment at the National Center for Atmospheric Research, where much of the early research on climate change was taking place. These were magic days in the "pink palace" and I learned from the likes of John Firor, Will Kellogg, Walter Orr Roberts, Steve Schneider, Warren Washington, and especially Mickey Glantz. Mickey is one of the people to whom this book is dedicated. I could not do otherwise: His fingerprints are all over it.

My colleagues in the Boulder Philosophy Department tolerated my wayward activity (at least to a point). In addition to benefiting from their grace and indulgence, I learned much from Ann Davis, John Fisher, Jim Nickel, and Chris Shields.

I also benefited from the personal support and writings of Jonathan Glover and Peter Singer, who in those days were carving out the field of practical ethics in a way that was new and exciting.

I have been fortunate to have been part of other supportive communities as well. Michael Oppenheimer and Naomi Oreskes have been my co-PIs on a National Science Foundation project that has provided ample opportunity for us to discuss many matters related to this book. I am also grateful to the NSF for the grant that allowed me to begin writing about climate change in the first place, and the University of Colorado for supporting the work with a faculty fellowship. Later I benefited from leaves and conversations with students, friends, and colleagues at Carleton College and New York University.

At NYU my colleagues in Environmental Studies, Philosophy, and Law have been an inspiration. In Environmental Studies I thank especially Tyler Volk and Zahra Ali. My colleague in the Law School, Richard Stewart, has been a source of constant support. Dick Foley in all of his guises—philosopher, dean, and university vice president—has made my life better in countless ways. Béatrice Longuenesse is a model of intellectual honesty and integrity and has always been there for me through thick and thin.

The influence of the climate ethics "gang of four" has been so profound that I no longer know how to separate my ideas from theirs, though we continue to disagree amiably and productively. My debts to Simon Caney, Steve Gardiner, and Henry Shue are deep and wide.

I cannot remember everyone who commented on the manuscript at various universities and conferences, but the following people and occasions are embedded in my memory. Bonnie Nadzam provided judicious comments on Chapter 1 on very short notice. Spencer Weart provided detailed comments on Chapter 2. Material that appears in Chapter 4 was discussed at an IPCC experts meeting in Lima, Peru, and at conferences in Graz, Austria, and Boulder, Colorado. I am especially grateful to John Broome and Simon Dietz for trying to set me straight on matters of climate economics. I had the good fortune to be a guest—it turns out the last—at the legendary colloquium run by Ronald Dworkin and Thomas Nagel. Their generous, careful, and encouraging comments on Chapter 5 helped me to bring this project to conclusion. For comments on the same chapter I also thank Aaron James and Marion Hourdequin, who commented at a Pacific APA symposium, participants in a workshop at the University of Edinburgh organized by Elizabeth Cripps and Carl Knight, and audiences at Vanderbilt, Perth, Sydney, and London. Chapter 7 was discussed with audiences at Princeton University, the University of Washington, and Stanford University, and I especially thank Melissa Lane and Jean Thomas, who were commentators on these occasions.

In addition, this material was the basis for lectures at Monash University in Australia, a summer school in Moscow, the University of Oregon where I served as Wayne Morse Professor of Law and Social Change, and at LUISS University in

Rome. At Duke, Walter Sinnott-Armstrong organized a workshop on an earlier version of the manuscript and I benefited enormously from a thorough working over at the hands of Jonathan Adler, Allen Buchanan, Simon Caney, Jed Purdy and Peter Singer, as well as Walter. Milena Wazeck gave me excellent comments on almost the entire manuscript, and two anonymous reviewers for Oxford University Press (who I now know to be Marion Hourdequin and Henry Shue) provided very constructive comments that led to significant improvements in the book's tone and structure. Amanda Zink worked heroically on the notes and bibliography and also suggested many improvements.

The work of Thomas Schelling was first brought to my attention by my dissertation supervisor, Paul Ziff, and Schelling was a major influence on my doctoral dissertation in philosophy of language. It has been a pleasant surprise to engage again with Schelling's work but in a different domain. We disagree about many matters, but I have treasured my engagements with him, and the times that we have shared platforms in San Francisco and Princeton stand out in my memory. As for Paul Ziff, his influence remains palpable on everything I say and think.

This book was largely written in Torrey Pines and in Greenwich Village, with reminders of climate change close at hand in both places. The Torrey Pine may become extinct as a result of climate change, and I submitted the manuscript during Hurricane Sandy, just before the lights went out. I want to thank the good people at UCSD, the Del Mar Public Library, and the Scripps Institute of Oceanography for making their facilities available to me during my time in California, and the Institute for Advanced Study in Princeton for the idyllic conditions under which I have seen the book through to publication. I especially thank Peter Ohlin at Oxford University Press for his patience and persistence in moving this book along, as well as his sage advice at key moments.

Finally, those who are beyond thanks will not be named but I hope they know who they are. By wrapping me in their love they make it possible for me to complete projects like this; they also make it seem that there is some point in doing so.

Dale Jamieson
Princeton, NJ
October 2013

Abbreviations

AGGG	Advisory Group on Greenhouse Gases
AOSIS	Alliance of Small Island States
CEQ	Council on Environmental Quality
CFCs	chlorofluorocarbons
CIAP	Climate Impacts Assessment Program
COP	Conference of the Parties
DICE	Dynamic Integrated Model of Climate and the Economy
DOD	Department of Defense
DOE	Department of Energy
EPA	Environmental Protection Agency
FCCC	Framework Convention on Climate Change
GARP	Global Atmospheric Research Program
GCC	Global Climate Coalition
GCM	general circulation models
GCRS	General Circulation Research Section
GDP	gross domestic product
GFDL	Geophysical Fluid Dynamics Laboratory
GHGs	greenhouse gases
GISS	Goddard Institute for Space Studies
IAM	integrated assessment models
ICSU	International Council of Scientific Unions
IMO	International Meteorological Organization
INC	Intergovernmental Negotiating Committee
IPCC	Intergovernmental Panel on Climate Change
NAPAP	National Acid Precipitation Assessment Program
NAS	National Academy of Sciences
NASA	National Aeronautics and Space Administration
NEPA	National Environmental Policy Act
NOAA	National Oceanic and Atmospheric Administration
RGGI	Regional Greenhouse Gas Initiative
RICE	Regional Integrated Model of Climate and Economy

SPD	Social Democratic Party
UN	United Nations
UNEP	United Nations Environment Programme
USGCRP	United States Global Change Research Program
WCP	World Climate Program
WHO	World Health Organization
WMO	World Meteorological Organization

1 Introduction

I did not write this book in order to save the Earth. This is not a manifesto or a call to action. You will not find lists of things to do if you want to reduce your carbon footprint or become a green consumer. These things are good—better than good—but they are not my thing.

My goal is to make you think. Environmental issues like climate change have become too wrapped up in political slogans and partisan bickering. There is too much talk that purports to be about the science or policy but is really about posturing and positioning. The climate change denialists are most guilty of this, but environmentalists are not immune. Warnings about "tipping points" seemed to have increased dramatically since the publication of Malcolm Gladwell's book of the same name in 2000. We are constantly told that we stand at a unique moment in human history and that this is the last chance to make a difference. But every point in human history is unique, and it is always the last chance to make some particular difference. Until the world or humanity comes to an end (literally), there will always be a chance to make a difference. We need to see through the fog and soberly grasp the problems that we face. As the late climate scientist Jerry Mahlman used to say, "There is no need to exaggerate the problem of climate change; it is bad enough as it is."

The climate change that is underway is remaking the world in such a way that familiar comforts, places, and ways of life will disappear on a timescale of years or decades. Over the next few centuries, climate change risks putting an end to a great deal that we value, including much of humanity and its creations. Climate change is not an isolated phenomenon but is occurring in concert with other rapid environmental, technological, and social changes.

That these changes are anthropogenic is of great importance. We are bringing about a climate change that we do not want but do not know how to stop. Human action is the driver, but it seems that things, not people, are in control. Our corporations, governments, technologies, institutions, and economic systems seem to have lives of their own. It feels as though we are living through some weird perversion of the Enlightenment dream. Instead of humanity rationally governing the world and itself, we are at the mercy of monsters that we have created.

This book is about how it came to this. The Enlightenment dream was a good one. Why has it failed in the ways that it has? Have the failures been inevitable, or could they have been avoided? What can we learn from them? What do they portend about the future? In what ways do our actions continue to have significance and meaning?

I sneak up on these questions and address them in varying degrees of indirectness. The owl of Minerva is a cagey critter. She surveys the entire scene before claiming to understand. There is a lot to know about climate change before we can fully appreciate our situation.

The next chapter is an opinionated history of how we got into this mess. For some people, this will seem like launching an exciting voyage with a dull thud. Many people are bored by history, fail to see its relevance, or even despise it. "Let's get to the issues," they say. "Who cares about the past?" This attitude is profoundly mistaken. Like many other fashionable stances, purporting to be ahistorical is phony. We are up to our ears in history, whether we acknowledge it or not. We did not have to be where we are. The story that I tell is highly contingent and path-dependent. It is better to be explicit about our starting points than to pretend that they do not exist. We cannot fully appreciate the challenges of such a slowly evolving, multidimensional problem as climate change without a sense of the history in which it is embedded.

Chapter 2 begins with the rise of climate science, takes us to the enthusiasm and energy of the 1992 Rio Earth Summit, and culminates in the debacle of the 2009 Copenhagen Climate Change Conference.

The first part of the story is in many ways unexceptional. Climate science developed like other sciences: incremental contributions by many people, punctuated by occasional new insights and perspectives that were often enabled by applications of innovative technologies. Large steps were taken; there were missteps along the way; knowledge steadily increased.

The early science of climate change was largely motivated by a desire to understand the ebb and flow of ice ages. Some thought that changes in Earth's climate were mainly controlled by physical changes in Earth's orbit; others attributed them to chemical changes in the atmosphere. As scientists learned more, they became increasingly concerned, and their voices began to be heard in the media and in government. In the 1950s climate change was discussed in newspapers and popular magazines. Many will be surprised to learn that in 1965 climate change was mentioned by the president of the United States in a message to Congress.

In 1968 we were able to see the Earth from space for the first time. Many people around the world were moved by its lack of borders and apparent vulnerability. Increasingly, scientists viewed the Earth as a single system, comparing it to other planets, marveling at its uniqueness. With the development of computerized climate models, it became possible to glimpse the consequences for the Earth of anthropogenic carbon emissions. Change was happening so quickly that the human impact on the planet was now on the same scale as that of geological forces.

The world was changing politically as well. During the 1970s the old divisions between East and West, capitalist and communist, began to break down. A new world seemed on the horizon in which the fundamental division was between the North and South, and the path to reconciliation involved addressing the twin challenges of environment and development. In 1972 the United Nations (UN) held its first conference on the environment, which led to the creation of the United Nations Environment Programme (UNEP). That same year, Nixon went to China; the following year, the Paris Accords were signed, ending American involvement in Vietnam. Robert McNamara, who had been the US secretary of defense during most of the Vietnam War, became president of the World Bank, and in 1977 he announced the creation of a commission that would make recommendations regarding North/South relations. In 1983 the UN General Assembly created the World Commission on Environment and Development, which popularized the phrase "sustainable development." Its 1987 report, *Our Common Future*, was regarded by many as a manifesto for the world to come. That same year, the Montreal Protocol was signed. Scientists had alerted the world to a global problem and governments had acted to begin phasing out the ozone-depleting chemicals that were causing it, even before serious damages had occurred. To many, this was the model for how we would solve global problems. In 1988 the Intergovernmental Panel on Climate Change (IPCC) was established to provide objective, policy-relevant information about climate change to decision-makers around the world. The IPCC published voluminous consensus reports in 1990, 1995, 2001, and 2007, reflecting the growth of scientific knowledge about the seriousness of the threat. They will complete their next report in 2014.

In 1992 the largest gathering of heads of state ever assembled met at the Rio Earth Summit and more than 17,000 people attended the alternative NGO forum. This marked the beginning of a truly global environmental movement. The air was heady with optimism. The Rio dream was that the countries of the North and South would join hands to protect the global environment and lift up the world's poor. After nearly two decades of struggle, it was clear by the 2009 Copenhagen Climate Change Conference that the dream was over. The hope that the people of the world would solve the problem of climate change through a transformation in global values had come to an end. What I want to understand is what happened in those years to bring us to where we are today. In that understanding is a key to surviving the future.

Chapter 3 identifies some of the obstacles to taking meaningful action. Some concern the lack of understanding among scientists, policy-makers, and the general public. Not only is there widespread ignorance of relevant scientific and political data, but there is a lack of mutual recognition of what it is to do science and to make policy. Many scientists dismissively apply the term "politics" to everything that is not science (including the administrative practices of their own institutions). They often use this term to gesture in the direction of the black box from which arbitrary and unintelligible decisions spring. On the other hand, politicians and other decision-makers often have little patience for scientists, the pace of their investigations, the tentativeness of their conclusions, and the arcane ways in which they express themselves. These differences run very deep, going back to early life experience in which nerds, greasers, baby intellectuals, and jocks would all sit at different tables in the high school cafeteria. Later education and experience reinforce these differences. I have heard it said that in college the main difference between kids who become doctors and those who become lawyers is whether or not they freak out at "orgo" (organic chemistry).

Ignorance of science can give rise to excessive respect, which can quickly turn to disillusionment when science does not deliver the goods or when scientists turn out to be as petty and selfish as the rest of us. Politicians and other policy-makers get an even harder ride. They are often blamed for responding to incentives provided by voters and the political and administrative systems in which decision-makers work. There are also reasons internal to the practices of science and policy-making that make it difficult for them to be mutually informing. These failures play out against a background of public apathy, dissatisfaction, and cynicism that often leads to mindless recrimination.

This is fertile soil for those who make their living by manufacturing doubt and sewing discord. Some of the world's largest corporations and richest people have organized and supported front groups whose role is to slag climate science and resist regulation, just as they did in response to the science that laid the foundation for regulating lead, asbestos, smoking, and other toxic substances and behaviors. They pursue this strategy because it works. Delayed regulation translates into greater profits, and no one goes to jail for lying to the American public about the risks of greenhouse gas (GHG) emissions, smoking, or toxic chemicals. Even if in the end there are fines to pay and reputational costs to bear, they typically amount to something more like a tax on profits rather than serious disincentives to engage in the behavior in the first place.

In the aftermath of events such as Hurricane Sandy and Hurricane Katrina, people want to know whether they were caused by climate change. These are bad questions and no answer can be given that is not misleading. It is like asking whether when a baseball player gets a base hit, it is caused by his .350 batting average. One cannot say "yes," but saying "no" falsely suggests that there is no relationship between his batting average and the base hit. For both conceptual and scientific reasons, it is difficult to attribute particular events to climate change.

We also face psychological obstacles in responding to climate change. Evolution built us to respond to rapid movements of middle-sized objects, not to the slow buildup of insensible gases in the atmosphere. Most of us respond dramatically to what we sense, not to what we think. As a result, even those of us who are concerned about climate change find it difficult to feel its urgency and to act decisively.

Overlying these difficulties is the fact that climate change has the structure of the world's largest collective action problem. Each of us acting on our own desires contributes to outcomes that we neither desire nor intend.

Climate change is unique because of its scale and complexity, but problems with this structure are familiar to us and in some cases we succeed in solving them. Consider the familiar example in which each of us grazes our animals on a commons. Since we capture the benefits individually while the costs are spread over the entire community, each of us has an incentive to increase the size of his herd. But if we all act in this way, then the commons degrades and we are all worse off in the end. We can avoid this outcome by privatizing the commons so that each of us bears the full costs of adding animals to our herds. Or we can appeal to the moral sentiment of members of the community to act in the common interest. These approaches succeed, when they do, by changing the incentive structure of individual actors. Privatizing incorporates the externalized costs into each agent's decision-making so that adding additional animals to one's herd is no longer in one's interests. Moralizing attaches the cost to the violation of a moral norm, realized through conscience, community disapproval, or the establishment of legal sanctions. Economics, which I discuss in Chapter 4, helps us to understand the first approach. Ethics, which I discuss in Chapter 5, sheds light on the second.

There is a way of looking at the problem of climate change that suggests that it should yield easily to an economic solution. The problem arises from the fact that climate-changing behavior produces a negative externality: Those who benefit from such behavior do not pay its full costs; some of the costs fall on people who do not benefit and are not adequately compensated. This creates perverse incentives to engage in climate-changing behavior. In principle a more efficient outcome is available in which less climate-changing behavior occurs and those who suffer damages are adequately compensated by those who benefit from the behavior. Yet, despite the fact that we are often moved by economic considerations, in this case we do not act to reach the more efficient outcome.

Part of the explanation for this failure mirrors the reasons that scientific consensus does not produce action. Ignorance abounds, the political system is sclerotic, people are angry and mistrustful of elites, and so on. Moreover, to the extent that denialism prevails, the economic question is moot: If there is no problem, then there is no need for solutions. Economics also suffers from an additional dollop of skepticism. Many people simply do not believe that we can solve this problem without sacrifice. Economists themselves have done a lot to obscure the basic message that it is in our interests to act on climate change.

Conflicts among economists became especially sharp and visible in 2007 with the publication of the *Stern Review*, a report to the British government on the economics of climate change. While mainstream American economists such as Yale's William Nordhaus believe that we should act on climate change, they typically favor a modest response, deferred as long as possible into the future. The message of the *Stern Review* was that we should act now and we should act aggressively. Both Stern and Nordhaus advocate a carbon tax, but Stern's is an order of magnitude greater than Nordhaus's.

At the heart of their differences are different attitudes toward the future. They agree that most people discount future benefits and costs: We think that present investments will be productive, that in any case we will be richer in the future, and often we simply prefer jam today to jam tomorrow. Nordhaus analyzes this behavior and applies it to the future costs of climate change. As a result, present benefits and costs are worth much more than future benefits and costs. Stern disagrees with this approach. The proper attitude toward the future involves an ethical question, and people can be wrong about ethical questions, just as they can make mistakes in reasoning. Stern agrees that people exhibit pure time preference, but he rejects the idea that this should be reflected in economic models. The result of their different methodologies is that Nordhaus applies a relatively high discount rate while Stern's discount rate is low. The choice of a discount rate has a hugely powerful effect over long periods of time since its effects compound. At a 1% discount rate, $1 today will be worth $2.70 in a century; at a discount rate of 10%, it will be worth $13,780.60. If the future costs of climate change are heavily discounted, then only modest investments in climate protection are warranted at present; if the discount rate is low, then aggressive policies are justified.

This dispute cannot be resolved by economic analysis alone. Nordhaus owes us an explanation for why we are justified in discounting the interests of future people. Stern owes us an argument for why he does not respect people's actual choices. They are both up to their ears in ethics.

There are other features of standard economic analysis that presuppose normative stances. Standard economic theory assumes that bundles of goods are substitutable and commensurable, but this seems outlandish. The question of what is substitutable for or commensurate with my mother's love, my dog's companionship, or the joy of catching a perfect wave is somewhere between perplexing and offensive.

Economics alone cannot tell us what to do in the face of climate change. The fundamental problem with climate economics is not that it fails to come up with the right numbers but that there is more at stake than what the numbers reveal. No number seems right because the costs of climate change damages go beyond economic damages.

Economics can recommend instruments and tools for furthering our aims. If we want to reduce poverty, smoking, or carbon emissions, economics can recommend systems of incentives that may produce these results. It can tell us how to do things, but it cannot tell us whether we should do them. Economics has much to say about incentives and costs, but little or nothing to say about the ends that we should pursue.

Chapter 5 directly confronts the ethics of climate change, focusing on conceptions of responsibility. The conclusion is that the challenges that climate change presents go beyond the resources of commonsense morality.

Climate ethicists often say that climate change at its core is a problem of rich people appropriating more than their share of a global public good, and as a result harming poor people by causally contributing to extreme climatic events such as droughts, hurricanes, and heat waves, which in turn can ramify, causing disease outbreaks, economic dislocations, and political instability. Much of this behavior is unnecessary, even for maintaining the profligate lifestyles of the rich. Reasoning in this way, John Nolt (2011a: 3) calculates that "[T]he average American is responsible, through his/her greenhouse gas emissions, for the suffering and/or deaths of one or two future people."

Even most of us who care deeply about climate change would have to admit, if we were honest, that we do not feel like killers when we fly or drive. We may feel embarrassed, ashamed, or hypocritical, but we do not really feel that we are worse than Mafia hit men (despite the fact that we kill gratuitously while they kill in order to make a living). We do not feel this way, I think, because there are important differences between clear cases of morally suspect acts and those that contribute to climate change.

A paradigm of a morally suspect act is Jack stealing Jill's bicycle. Jack intentionally harms another individual, both the perpetrator and victim are clearly identifiable, and they are closely related in time and space. This case is a clear candidate for moral evaluation, and most of us would say that what Jack did was wrong.

When we alter the case along various dimensions, its claim to be a paradigm case for moral evaluation weakens. Suppose that acting independently, Jack and a large number of unacquainted people set in motion a chain of events that causes a large number of future people who will live in another part of the world from ever having bicycles. In this case, most of what is typically at the center of a morally suspect act has disappeared. For that reason, people tend to see this case as one in which the wrongness of the acts and the culpability of the agents are greatly diminished compared to Jack stealing Jill's bicycle. Since many acts that contribute to climate change are more like this second case than they are like Jack stealing Jill's bicycle, it is not surprising that many people do not see acts such as driving and flying as presenting a moral problem. Indeed, since driving and flying, and climate change, occur at different scales, the relationships between them are more complex and indirect than the relationships between Jack's action and future people not having bicycles.

Climate ethicists are trying to get us to change our moral judgments rather than simply reporting them. They want us to come to see acts that contribute to climate change as morally wrong. But how one argues for revising concepts is quite different from how one argues that particular acts fall under existing concepts.

There are two main strategies that have been suggested by those who want to moralize actions that contribute to climate change. Some seek to collectivize responsibility, while others seek to reform responsibility so that it tracks the probability of outcomes. Both approaches have counterintuitive consequences and are in tension with classical liberal ideas. However, counterintuitive consequences should be expected from revisions of morality, and by the very nature of the project we have only glimpses of what a revised morality would involve. It is difficult to know exactly what counts for or against proposed revisions in morality.

Our failure to prevent or even to respond significantly to climate change reflects the impoverishment of our systems of practical reason, the paralysis of our politics, and the limits of our cognitive and affective capacities. None of this is likely to change soon.

Chapter 6 reflects on how to live in the face of these failures. The challenge is not (only) to reduce or stabilize the concentration of atmospheric carbon dioxide but to live meaningfully in relationship with the dynamic systems that govern a changing planet. This is a new challenge because humanity is young and now constitutes an important planetary force in a way that is unprecedented. In recognition of the increasing human domination of the planet, some scientists propose that we have entered a new geological era, the Anthropocene. Climate change may be the first challenge of the Anthropocene, but it will not be the last.

The Anthropocene presents novel challenges for living a meaningful life. In an era that is dense with population and technology, it is difficult to believe that our individual actions matter. Yet they matter both because they affect the world and because they affect ourselves. Our thoughts and actions can inspire others, change their lives, and even affect the course of history. Whatever direct impact that reducing our own emissions may have on the atmosphere, it may be a necessary demonstration of sincerity and commitment for us to be effective participants in our own communities.

An ethics for the Anthropocene would emphasize nourishing and cultivating virtues. The virtues do not provide an algorithm for solving the problems of the Anthropocene, but they can provide guidance for living gracefully while helping to restore in us a sense of agency. They are mechanisms that provide motivation to act in our various roles from consumers to citizens, in order to reduce our own impact on the planet and to some extent ameliorate the effects of others. The virtues that would be part of an ethics for the Anthropocene are not identical to classical or Christian virtues, but neither are they wholly novel. They might involve traditional virtues such as humility, reinterpreted virtues such as temperance, and new virtues such as mindfulness, simplicity, cooperativeness, and respect for nature.

Traditional views die hard, and one part of the Rio dream that remains alive is the view that anthropogenic climate change is fundamentally a problem of justice between states that can be assimilated to other issues of global justice. While this view is not wholly wrong, the model is difficult to apply. China emits more than the United States, but the United States emits more per capita than China or France, and France emits more in toto and per capita than Chile. Every country has both high and low emitters. Rather than thinking of climate change as a problem caused by some nations and suffered by others, it is more plausible to think of it as a problem with a half billion or so major contributors distributed throughout the globe.

Climate change is not a problem that conforms to our traditional models of individual morality and global justice. Indeed, it is not a single problem but a cluster of challenges. It cannot be solved, but it can be managed by people acting individually and collectively in ways that blunt its force while they continue to live meaningful lives.

For the foreseeable future, climate policy will largely reflect the motley collection of policies and practices adopted by particular countries, rather than reflecting the outcome of a global deal based in a shared conception of justice. There will be climate-relevant policy virtually everywhere, but it will be different in different countries and it will be pursued under different descriptions and with different objectives. Some countries will adopt emissions trading, others carbon taxes, and others technology-forcing policies. Some countries will alter their energy mix, others their transportation systems, and others will focus on buildings. Some countries will do a lot and others will do a little. In some countries there will be a great deal of sub-national variation, while other countries will nationalize and even to some extent internationalize their policies. These policies, in different proportions depending on the country, will reflect a mix of self-interest and ethical ideals constructed in different ways in different countries.

Chapter 7 discusses the various approaches that will be taken to climate change. Adaptation is both unavoidable and important, but I also argue for the adoption of practical policies of abatement and mitigation. Such policies will reduce costs and help to spread them; will minimize losses of animals, plants, and ecosystems; and will lower the risk of catastrophic climate change. I recommend seven policy priorities, three governing principles, and one focus of immediate action.

The first policy priority is to integrate adaptation with development. The second is to protect, encourage, and increase terrestrial carbon sinks while honoring a broad range of human and environmental values. The third is to adopt full-cost energy accounting that takes into account the entire life cycle of producing and consuming a unit of energy. The fourth is to raise the price of emitting GHGs to a level that roughly reflects their costs. The fifth priority is to force technology adoption and diffusion. The sixth priority is to substantially increase research, especially in renewable energy and carbon sequestration, particularly air capture of carbon. The seventh priority is to plan for the Anthropocene.

The first of the three principles is that every particular strategy or investment should compete against everything else, whether it is considered adaptation, abatement, mitigation, or whatever. The second is that, whenever possible, policies that address climate change should piggyback on other actions. Finally, do not let the perfect be the enemy of the good.

A focus of immediate action should be to discourage, limit, and phase out the use of coal as soon as possible. In developing countries this may mean that some new coal-fired generating plants will be built as part of a larger plan for limiting their role and eventually phasing them out. In the United States and Europe this will mean no new coal-fired plants and the phasing out of existing ones. In Australia and other countries it means planning for the end of coal mining.

The priorities, principles, and immediate action that I suggest are practical. They do not require comprehensive agreements across large diverse populations in order to implement. Even so, the list should be up for constant evaluation and revision.

Despite the unprecedented nature of the challenge, human life will have meaning as long as there are people to take up the challenge. It matters what we do and how we live. We can cope with change, even when our resources are thin. This does not mean that we will "solve" the "problem" of climate change any time soon. We will have to manage and live as best we can, and hope that the darkest scenarios do not come to pass. We will have to abandon the Promethean dream of a certain, decisive solution and instead engage with the messy world of temporary victories and local solutions while a new world comes into focus.

2 The Nature of the Problem

Since at least the dawn of the industrial revolution, people have been transforming nature in ways that affect climate.[1] Burning fossil fuels such as coal and oil emits carbon dioxide (CO_2). This results in increasing the atmospheric concentration of CO_2, which in turn affects climate. In 1750 (the pre-industrial baseline) atmospheric concentrations of CO_2 were about 280 parts per million (ppm). In May 2013 the concentration reached nearly 400 ppm, the highest level in at least 3 million years, and continues to increase at a rate of about 2 ppm per year.[2]

These changes are irreversible, relative to almost any timescale of human interest.[3] The fires that medieval peasants huddled around in order to keep warm affect our climate today. Our CO_2 emissions, caused by such apparently innocent actions as driving to the farmer's market or the recycling center, will affect the lives of people in the next millennium. As a result of climate change, there will be massive extinctions of plants and animals, rising seas will engulf major cities and entire nations, and "natural" disasters including droughts, heat waves, and storms will raise havoc with virtually all aspects of life. The landscape in which people live will be remade by climate change. This is all documented in the scientific literature, reported in the popular press, and portrayed in popular media.[4] Yet thus far we have done little to address this problem.

It still matters what we do. Failures can be greater or lesser, and we can live more or less successfully with the changes we are bringing about. We can also learn from

[1] Some think longer. William Ruddiman (2005) claims that humans have been affecting climate since the beginning of agriculture.

[2] As measured at Mauna Loa Observatory, Hawaii, posted by the National Oceanic and Atmospheric Administration (NOAA), available at http://co2now.org/. Retrieved July 10, 2013. Other climate-changing gases that people are responsible for emitting include methane, nitrous oxide, and various fluorinated gases not otherwise found in nature. For a description, visit http://www.epa.gov/climatechange/emissions/. Retrieved July 10, 2013.

[3] Unless of course there is some dramatic technological intervention. See Section 7.4 for further discussion.

[4] For the standard scientific account see the various reports by the Intergovernmental Panel on Climate Change, available on the web at http://www.ipcc.ch/. Retrieved July 10, 2013. For a relatively popular account, see Archer and Rahmstorf 2010. In 1958, the Hollywood director Frank Capra made a remarkably prophetic film about climate change, available at http://www.youtube.com/watch?v=0lgzz-L7GFg (thanks to Andy Revkin for this reference). Retrieved July 10, 2013.

our mistakes, and widely apply the lessons to our societies and ourselves. Although we cannot prevent climate change, abating emissions would lessen impacts and reduce risks. Planning for adaptations that will in any case be inevitable would help to minimize damages and moderate the body count.

My task in this book is to explain why we have failed to address climate change and to provide some guidance about what we might learn from our failures that will help us to live well in the new world that we are creating. The story begins in the past, with what we knew, and when we knew it. This chapter is devoted to telling that story. It begins with the rise of climate science, takes us to the energy and enthusiasm of the 1992 Rio Earth Summit, and culminates in the debacle of the 2009 Copenhagen Climate Change Conference.

2.1. THE DEVELOPMENT OF CLIMATE SCIENCE

Climate is different from weather. Climate is an abstraction, based on weather. As Mark Twain is supposed to have said, "Climate is what you expect, weather is what you get." When I walk along the beach, feeling the sun on my back and the wind in my face, I am experiencing weather. When I say that this is unusual for this time of year, I am talking about climate.

As long as people have conceived of themselves as embedded in places that are governed by natural cycles, they have thought about climate, not only weather. As long as they have thought about climate, they have thought about climate change.[5]

Many societies have long historical memories relating to weather and climate. In Europe, grape harvests have been tracked since at least the fourteenth century. In the Arctic, traditional Inuit knowledge of ice and snow goes back centuries. In Japan, cherry blossom records have been kept for more than a millennium.[6] While traditional ways of understanding weather and climate continue to be important, our modern experience of weather and climate is deeply affected by science.

Galileo Galilei devised the first thermometer in the late sixteenth century. Although beautiful, it only roughly marked differences among temperatures and was not calibrated to a scale. Daniel Fahrenheit's invention of the sealed mercury thermometer in 1714 and his development of the scale that bears his name created a system for measuring temperature. Weather stations were soon established all over Europe, and by the mid-nineteenth century 80% of the globe was being monitored.[7] There was now an empirical basis for developing a science directed toward understanding the climate system.

---

[5] Neumann 1985; Von Storch and Stehr 2006; and Fleming 1998. For a review, see Hulme 2009: 35–71.

[6] For further discussion, see the special issue of *Climatic Change* devoted to indigenous peoples' knowledge of climate and weather (100, 2, May 2010).

[7] Schmidt and Wolfe 2009: 20.

Early in the nineteenth century, Jean Baptiste Joseph Fourier was investigating what determines the temperature of terrestrial bodies such as the earth. He speculated that part of the answer was that atmospheric gases might inhibit heat from escaping, thereby warming the earth's surface. He compared the earth and its atmosphere to a box covered with a pane of glass.[8] Just as the sun warms the interior of the box and the glass inhibits the heat from escaping, so Fourier speculated that the earth's atmosphere inhibits heat from escaping the earth's surface. Because of these speculations, Fourier became known as the father of the "greenhouse effect," though he made no reference to greenhouses, and greenhouses do not actually work in the way that he described.[9]

At about the same time there was a great deal of interest in explaining geological anomalies, such as the location of boulders many miles from where they had apparently originated. Some explained these as artifacts of the great flood described in Genesis, but there was increasing interest in the idea that the explanation involved the expansion and contraction of glaciers. The Swiss scientist Louis Agassiz proposed in 1837 that the earth had experienced an ice age in which much of its surface had been covered by glaciers.[10]

The Anglo-Irish scientist John Tyndall was intrigued by this idea and began to think about what mechanisms could bring about such climatic changes. Beginning with Fourier's insight that the atmosphere might regulate the loss of heat from the earth's surface, Tyndall measured the absorption of infrared radiation by carbon dioxide and water vapor, and showed that slight changes in atmospheric composition would significantly raise the earth's surface temperature. He also suggested that methane could affect earth's temperature, but methane is so rare that it was not discovered in the atmosphere until 1948.[11] Tyndall was a great popularizer of science, and he explained his ideas with an influential metaphor: Water vapor "is a blanket more necessary to the vegetable life of England than clothing is to man. Remove for a single summer-night the aqueous vapour from the air…and the sun would rise upon an island held fast in the iron grip of frost."[12] The metaphor of the blanket is

---

[8] Fourier referred specifically to a "heliothermometer," a device invented by Saussure in the 1760s for measuring solar radiation. Fourier's original paper was published in 1824, reprinted in a slightly revised version in 1827, and published in English translation in 1837. Both the original and translation are available at http://wiki.nsdl.org/index.php/PALE: ClassicArticles/GlobalWarming/Article1; an alternative translation is available at http://www.wmconnolley.org.uk/sci/fourier_1827/fourier_1827.html. Retrieved July 10, 2013.

[9] The analogy appears to have been introduced into the literature by Woods (1909). Thanks to Milena Wazeck for this reference.

[10] This idea was developed in cooperation with Jean de Charpentier and Karl Friedrich Schimper, but it was Agassiz who developed it in a systematic and sweeping way.

[11] Migeotte 1948.

[12] Tyndall 1863: 204–205, as quoted at http://www.aip.org/history/climate/simple.htm#L_M018. Retrieved July 8, 2013.

extremely rich, and Tyndall recognized that while water vapor is the most important constituent of the blanket, it is not the only one with causal efficacy.

In the late nineteenth century the Swedish scientist Svante Arrhenius made what climate scientist David Archer calls "the most astonishing leap I have ever read in climate science."[13] In 1894 Arrhenius heard a presentation on the work of James Croll, a Scottish scientist who provided the first credible explanation for the ice ages. Croll theorized that ice ages were triggered by variations in the earth's orbit that set off powerful feedbacks relating to the earth's "albedo."[14] On this view a slight cooling would increase the earth's ice cover, which would reflect more solar radiation, which would produce more cooling, which would increase ice, which would produce more cooling, and so on.[15] As a physical chemist, Arrhenius was doubtful that the onset of ice ages could be explained solely in terms of physical processes, and this led him to investigate how the constituents of the atmosphere affect climate sensitivity. Arrhenius used data concerning infrared radiation emanating from the moon that the American scientist John Pierpont Langley had collected for a different purpose. In calculating the effects of changing CO_2 concentrations in the atmosphere, Arrhenius took into account the fact that a warming would produce more water vapor, which would trap more heat, which would produce more warming, and so on. Recognizing that the earth's surface is not a single uniform temperature, he spent two years doing tedious pencil and paper calculations of the earth's temperature on a longitude-latitude grid. What Arrhenius was doing was beginning to quantify the structure of Tyndall's blanket. His conclusion was that a CO_2 doubling would produce a warming of 2.5–4°C. As Archer observes, "[t]here have been revisions, discoveries, missteps, and wrong directions, as in any science, but on the whole not much has changed in the past century."[16]

Arrhenius considered but initially rejected the possibility that human emissions of CO_2 might cause global warming, overestimating how quickly CO_2 would be dissolved in the oceans and underestimating how anthropogenic emissions would

---

[13] Archer 2009: 19.

[14] "Albedo" refers to the reflectivity of the earth's surface.

[15] Croll was influential on the Serbian engineer Milutin Milankovitch, whose explanation of the occurrence of ice ages in terms of long-term cycles in the variation of earth's orbit was widely accepted in the first half of the twentieth century, and continued to have some influence thereafter (see, e.g., Hays et al. 1976). Croll was also influential on the line of thought that became the "snowball earth" hypothesis, associated with Joseph Kirschvink. For information about snowball earth, visit http://www.snowballearth.org/. Retrieved July 8, 2013. Since the late nineteenth century there has been an oscillation between explanations of climate change that emphasize physical processes and those that emphasize chemical processes. Claims that the observed warming is not anthropogenic because it is caused by solar flux come around regularly.

[16] Archer 2009: 20. Actually quite a lot has changed since Arrhenius in our understanding of the processes involved, but what has not changed very much is the range of the temperature increase that would result from a CO_2 doubling.

increase over time. Nevertheless, he thought that an anthropogenic warming would be desirable, for it

> …would allow our descendents, even if they only be those in a distant future, to live under a warmer sky and in a less harsh environment than we were granted.[17]

Arrhenius's carbon dioxide theory of climate change was rejected when another Swedish scientist, Knut Ångström, discovered that adding CO_2 to a pressurized tube did not appreciably increase the absorption of infrared radiation. This, when combined with the discovery that water vapor, a much more plentiful gas in the atmosphere than CO_2, also absorbs infrared radiation in the same part of the spectrum, seemed to refute Arrhenius's view that changes in atmospheric concentrations of CO_2 could dramatically affect climate.[18] Thus the standard view into the 1950s was that the carbon dioxide theory of climate change is false. Still, Arrhenius was a respected scientist who had won the Nobel Prize in Chemistry in 1903 for his earlier work on electrolyte conductivity. His ideas about CO_2 and climate were well-known, even though widely rejected.

In the 1930s the British engineer Guy Callendar began to look anew at Arrhenius's ideas. European and North American winters had been mild for some time, and there was discussion about whether climate was changing.[19] Using whatever data he could find, Callendar claimed that there had already been a 10% increase in atmospheric CO_2 and that an observable, anthropogenic warming had already begun. What became known as the "Callendar Effect" was the claim that the combustion of fossil fuels would lead to increases in the atmospheric concentration of carbon dioxide, which would warm the earth.[20] Callendar speculated that a CO_2 doubling could raise global temperatures by 2°C over several centuries, a prospect he greeted with enthusiasm, for "the return of the deadly glaciers should be delayed indefinitely."[21] In some circles Callendar was viewed more as an eccentric amateur than as a serious scientist, and the same objections that had sunk Arrhenius's account were hurled at him as well. His responses, which appealed to the lack of a full understanding of the climate system and the incomplete and inadequate nature of spectral measurements, turned out to be right, but they did not sway his critics.

---

[17] As quoted in Christianson 1999: 115. In a later book, noting the increase in the combustion of coal, Arrhenius speculated that a warming could occur over a matter of centuries. My discussion of Arrhenius has benefited from the work of another great Swedish scientist, Bert Bolin (2008).

[18] Ångström 1900.

[19] E.g., Kincer 1933.

[20] According to James Fleming, Suess and Revelle coined the phrase "Callendar Effect" to refer to this phenomenon (1998: 118). For more on Callendar, see Fleming 2007.

[21] Callendar 1938: 236.

In the late 1940s and early 1950s the perception of a warming became more widespread both in the scientific community and in the popular mind. Articles speculating about a warming appeared in such magazines as *The Saturday Evening Post, Time Magazine,* and the *New York Times Sunday Magazine.*[22] Research on infrared spectroscopy was advancing as a result of cold war research on heat-seeking missiles and other advanced weaponry. As more of the structure of Tyndall's blanket was revealed, it became clear that the absorption spectrum of CO_2 and water vapor do not entirely overlap, and that water vapor occurs mostly in the lower layers of the troposphere while CO_2 is more evenly distributed even high into the stratosphere. Thus, radiant heat that is not absorbed by water vapor in the lower troposphere can still be absorbed by the CO_2 above it. Ångström's mistake was in supposing that the atmosphere was no more complex than a tube of pressurized gas.

In the 1950s, the Canadian physicist Gilbert Plass used new, detailed measurements of the infrared absorption bands and created an early computerized model of infrared radiative transfer. He calculated that a CO_2 doubling would increase temperature by 3.6°C. Assuming that CO_2 emissions would continue at their current rate, he expected that human activity would raise the average global temperature "at the rate of 1.1°C per century."[23] He warned that "temperature rise from this cause may be so large in several centuries that it will present a serious problem to future generations."[24]

Most of the basic elements of the CO_2 theory of climate change were now in place, but two important lacunae remained. First, Arrhenius and many scientists who came after him believed that anthropogenic CO_2 emissions would rapidly be taken up by the oceans, and thus would not significantly affect climate. However, this was largely speculation, and was denied by both Callendar and Plass. Second, there were no reliable measurements of carbon dioxide concentrations in the atmosphere.

Roger Revelle, the charismatic oceanographer and science entrepreneur who was also Al Gore's professor at Harvard, was central to answering both questions. In an obscure but influential 1957 paper, Revelle and Hans Suess addressed the role of the oceans in storing carbon.[25] Employing new carbon-14 dating techniques pioneered by Suess and developed by Willard Libby (for which he would win the 1960 Nobel Prize in Chemistry), their paper provided new estimates of carbon sequestration in the atmosphere, oceans, biosphere, and lithosphere. While taking the claims of

[22] See Fleming 2007: 78 for references and discussion.

[23] Plass 1956a.

[24] Plass 1956a. Plass considered nuclear power to be the main option to fossil fuels, and wrote that "[i]t is difficult to say which of these effects would be the less objectionable after several centuries of operation." Plass 1956b: 385. Plass died in 2004 and as far as I know never wrote or commented on climate change after this early work, though he did attend the 1963 meeting sponsored by the Conservation Foundation discussed in Section 2.2.

[25] Revelle and Suess 1957. There is a great deal of controversy over the scientific importance of this paper. Fleming (1998) sees it as largely a retreat from what was already known, while Weart (2008) argues for its scientific importance.

Callendar and Plass seriously, the bulk of the paper is directed toward showing that "most of the CO_2 released by artificial fuel combustion since the beginning of the industrial revolution must have been absorbed by the oceans."[26] However, after concluding that "[i]t seems therefore quite improbable that an increase in the atmospheric CO_2, concentration of as much as 10% could have been caused by industrial fuel combustion during the past century, as Callendar's statistical analyses indicate," they went on to say that "[i]t is possible…that such an increase could have taken place as the result of a combination with various other causes."[27] In a paragraph that was apparently taped into the manuscript shortly before the paper was submitted, the authors identify what in their view may be one of the causes, a mechanism that came to be known as the "Revelle Effect": the chemical buffering of seawater that limits how quickly the oceans can take up CO_2.[28] Because of this effect, only about one-tenth as much carbon dioxide is needed in order to reach equilibrium than would otherwise be the case. As a result, when CO_2 is absorbed by the ocean, a chain of chemical reactions occurs that results in expelling CO_2 back into the atmosphere. In light of this and other factors, including the supposition that there will be a "large increase in CO_2 production by fossil fuel combustion in coming decades," the authors concluded "[that]…a total increase of 20 to 40% in atmospheric CO_2, can be anticipated."[29]

Throughout the paper the authors emphasized how little was known about the oceans and the carbon cycle, and it is easy to feel them groping their way along in real time, speculating when knowledge gives out. In a memorable and oft-quoted passage, the authors claimed that an experiment is in progress that "could not have happened in the past nor be reproduced in the future." They seemed eager to find out the results of the experiment, saying that the expected increase of carbon dioxide in the atmosphere "should certainly be adequate to allow a determination of the effects, if any, of changes in atmospheric carbon dioxide on weather and climate…."[30] The paper ends by proposing that the International Geophysical Year of 1957 be used as an opportunity to begin gathering data for "an accurate base line for measurement of future changes in atmospheric CO_2."[31] The next year, due in part to the support of Revelle but also to the persistence of Charles Keeling, a station for monitoring atmospheric CO_2 was established in Mauna Loa, Hawaii. This station is the most important single source for documenting the buildup of carbon dioxide

---

[26] Revelle and Suess 1957:18.

[27] Revelle and Suess 1957: 25.

[28] Visit http://www.aip.org/history/climate/Revelle.htm#M_27_ for Spencer Weart's claim about the late addition of the paragraph to the paper. Retrieved July 10, 2013.

[29] Revelle and Suess 1957: 26. A paper by Bolin and Eriksson (1959) that appeared only two years later provided a much clearer and more explicit account of the role of the oceans in determining atmospheric concentrations of CO_2.

[30] Revelle and Suess 1957: 26.

[31] For this reason in particular, Mark Bowen reads this paper as "basically a grant proposal," a view that he claims was confirmed in an interview with Charles Keeling (Bowen 2005: 110–111).

in the atmosphere, showing a steady increase of about ½% per year, from about 315 ppm in 1959 to 394 ppm in 2012.[32]

A significant corner was turned with the work of Plass and Revelle. The carbon dioxide theory of climate change proposed by Arrhenius, championed by Callendar, and rejected for most of the first half of the twentieth century came to life in post–World War II America. Plass did not shrink from discussing his views in popular articles and with reporters, and Revelle was an influential public figure. Largely because of them, the possibility of an anthropogenic warming began to be discussed as a potential threat in the press and among opinion leaders. A 1956 *New York Times* article quoted Plass as "warning" that "the amount of carbon dioxide released in the atmosphere will be so large that it will have a profound effect on our climate."[33] The next year Revelle testified before congress that the rise of CO_2 might turn Southern California and Texas into "real deserts," and that the Soviet Union might become a maritime power in the twenty-first century as a result of the melting of Arctic ice.[34] Climate change had arrived in Washington.[35]

2.2. CLIMATE CHANGE AS A PUBLIC ISSUE

While climate science was developing, the environmental movement was germinating. The 1962 publication of Rachel Carson's *Silent Spring* is often regarded as marking the origin of the modern environmental movement. Carson was a trained scientist who brought her views directly to the public, in her case first in the pages of *The New Yorker* magazine.[36] Carson's concern was with the widespread use of pesticides, especially DDT. She repeatedly compared the effects of pesticides to those

---

[32] http://co2now.org/images/stories/data/co2-atmospheric-mlo-monthly-scripps.pdf.   Retrieved October 24, 2013. At various times the National Science Foundation threatened to defund the Mauna Loa observatory on the grounds that collecting such observational data was not a priority for an agency whose mission is funding basic scientific research. This conflict brings out the fact that the science that is useful for policy may not be the science that is seen as most important by the research community, a topic that is explored in the next chapter. Despite what is commonly believed, NSF's mandate is actually much broader than support of basic research. See the National Science Foundation Act of 1950 (Public Law 81-507), available on the web at http://www.nsf.gov/about/history/history-publications.jsp. Retrieved July 10, 2013.

[33] http://www.nytimes.com/packages/pdf/weekinreview/warm1956.pdf. Retrieved July 10, 2013.

[34] United States Congress (85:2) House of Representatives, Committee on Appropriations. Report on the International Geophysical Year. Washington, DC: US Government Printing Office; 1957, 104–106; as quoted in Weart 2008.

[35] For more on the development of climate science, see Weart 2008 and Fleming 1998. Many classic articles are available at http://wiki.nsdl.org/index.php/PALE:ClassicArticles/GlobalWarming (retrieved July 10, 2013), and reprinted in Archer and Pierrehumbert 2011.

[36] Carson was vilified for presenting scientific concerns directly to the public, but this pattern of communication has become characteristic of environmentalism. The list of prominent scientists who have tried to convey their environmental concerns in popular writing is very long, but any such list should certainly include Harvard biologist E. O. Wilson and National Aeronautics and Space Administration scientist James Hansen.

of radiation, even declaring that pesticide use was "the central problem of our age" along with "the possibility of the extinction of mankind by nuclear war."[37]

The anti-nuclear movement of the 1950s was an important source of the modern environmental movement.[38] In the eyes of many, the bombing of Hiroshima and Nagasaki was qualitatively different from other acts of mass destruction that were carried out in World War II, such as the bombing of Dresden. What was different was the scale of the impacts. The effects of nuclear weapons were felt by people who were remote in space and time from the explosions. Many people who were not affected by the blast suffered slow painful deaths from radiation sickness. Even the next generation, the offspring of the bombings' immediate victims, was subject to elevated rates of cancer and birth defects. For many, the message of Hiroshima and Nagasaki was that humankind now had the power to cause mass destruction on geographical and temporal scales that had never before been imagined.

Throughout the 1950s the United States, the Soviet Union, and other countries conducted frequent tests of nuclear weapons in the atmosphere. It became increasingly clear that these tests were having an effect on people very far removed from the sites of the explosions. Strontium 90 was taken up in the fatty tissue of nursing mothers and lodged in the bones of their offspring. While we still do not know the full consequences of these tests, it is clear that they caused at least tens of thousands of deaths and hundreds of thousands of cancers.[39] These tests demonstrated that invisible forces could cause great destruction thousands of miles from any sensible point of impact. People also learned that once contaminants were released into the environment, they could be active for a very long time, cycling through various systems. President Kennedy had supported a ban on nuclear testing since his days in the Senate, and made this a priority of his presidency. On October 10, 1963, a little over a month before he was assassinated, the "Treaty Banning Nuclear Weapon Tests in the Atmosphere, in Outer Space and Under Water" went into effect.[40]

Several months before the ban went into effect, in March 1963, the Conservation Foundation convened the first conference organized by an environmental group to discuss climate change.[41] The Washington meeting brought scientists such as Plass,

---

[37] Carson 1962: 18.

[38] Barry Commoner, another leading environmentalist of the 1960s, came to the environmental movement directly from his work with the St. Louis Committee for Nuclear Information. His 1971 book devoted a chapter to the nuclear threat. While Roger Revelle was not involved in the anti-nuclear movement, he was in charge of the geophysical measurements taken during the atomic bomb tests at Bikini Atoll, and was involved with nuclear-related issues his entire life, including nuclear disarmament; see Revelle 1978 and Munk 1997.

[39] For US impacts of nuclear testing in the atmosphere, visit http://www.cdc.gov/nceh/radiation/fallout/RF-GWT_home.htm. Retrieved July 10, 2013. For a good review, see Simon et al. 2006.

[40] However, France would continue atmospheric nuclear tests until 1974 and China continued such tests until 1980.

[41] There would not be another meeting sponsored by an American environmental group until 1987 when the Environmental Defense Fund co-sponsored meetings in Villach and Bellagio (see Section 2.3 for further discussion).

Keeling, and Eriksson together with representatives of the environmental community. The Conservation Foundation was an organization at the heart of the establishment. It was founded by Laurance Rockefeller, had close links to the New York Zoological Society, and was supported by many prominent Republicans and Democrats. Rockefeller himself was close to several presidents, including Lyndon Johnson, Richard Nixon, and George Herbert Walker Bush.

In 1965 an American president spoke for the first time about climate change. In his February 8 "Special Message to the Congress on Conservation and Restoration of Natural Beauty," President Johnson said, "[t]his generation has altered the composition of the atmosphere on a global scale through radioactive materials and a steady increase in carbon dioxide from the burning of fossil fuels."[42] The main point of the President's message was to announce a White House Conference on Natural Beauty, under the chairmanship of Laurance Rockefeller. It is hard not to see Rockefeller's influence on Johnson's speech.[43]

Later the same year the President's Science Advisory Committee, Panel on Environmental Pollution, published a report entitled "Restoring the Quality of Our Environment."[44] This report included a section on "climatic effects of pollution" that is notable for treating CO_2 as a pollutant. It also includes an appendix on "Atmospheric Carbon Dioxide," written by a committee chaired by Roger Revelle that also included Wallace Broecker, Joseph Smagorinsky, Harmon Craig, and Charles Keeling. This appendix discusses consequences of increases in atmospheric carbon dioxide such as the melting of the Antarctic ice cap, sea level rise, ocean warming, increasing acidity of fresh waters, and increased photosynthesis. The appendix notes that "[t]he climatic changes that may be produced by the increased CO_2 content could be deleterious from the point of view of human beings." The only response it suggests is geoengineering, stating that "[t]he possibilities of deliberately bringing about countervailing climatic changes…need to be explored." Specifically, it mentions the possibility of scattering small, reflective particles over large oceanic areas.[45] What is strikingly omitted is the possibility of reducing CO_2 emissions or moving toward decarbonizing the economy.

While climate change was discussed in this report, the emphasis was on more immediately threatening forms of environmental pollution. The 1960s was the decade of the Santa Barbara oil spill, the fire in the Cuyahoga River, and two separate

---

[42] Available at http://www.lbjlib.utexas.edu/johnson/archives.hom/speeches.hom/650208.asp. Retrieved July 10, 2013. In mentioning "radioactive materials" Johnson was presumably referring to the impacts of nuclear testing in the atmosphere.

[43] For more on Laurance Rockefeller's role in conservation policy, see Winks 1997.

[44] Available on the web at http://dge.stanford.edu/labs/caldeiralab/Caldeira%20downloads/ PSAC,%201965,%20Restoring%20the%20Quality%20of%20Our%20Environment.pdf. Retrieved July 10, 2013.

[45] http://dge.stanford.edu/labs/caldeiralab/Caldeira%20downloads/PSAC,%201965,%20 Restoring%20the%20Quality%20of%20Our%20Environment.pdf: 127.

air pollution events that killed hundreds of New Yorkers.[46] Even these environmental concerns were competing with more pressing issues such as the civil rights revolution and the war in Viet Nam. By comparison, climate change did not seem very urgent. Climate change had arrived in Washington, but it was far from center stage. One influential scientist reported that after telling Washington policy-makers that in 50 years there would be a CO_2 doubling that would have major impacts on the planet, he was told that he should come back in 49 years.[47]

Still, climate change did have a way of popping up in unexpected places. In a memo dated September 17, 1969, Daniel Patrick Moynihan, then Counselor to President Nixon for Urban Affairs, later Ambassador to the United Nations (UN) and US Senator from New York, explained the science of change to Nixon's Chief Domestic Advisor, John Ehrlichman, and warned that sea levels could rise "by 10 feet. Goodbye New York. Goodbye Washington…" Moynihan then went on to say that "it is possible to conceive fairly mammoth man-made efforts to countervail the CO_2 rise (e.g., stop burning fossil fuels)," but that "in any event…, this is a subject that the Administration ought to get involved with."[48] The first report of the Council on Environmental Quality (CEQ), published in 1970, devoted an entire chapter to climate change, including a section entitled "Energy output—A disappearing icecap?"[49]

The 1960s also brought changes in the culture of science. Rather than seeing nature as stable and equilibrium-seeking when disturbed, scientists became increasingly sensitive to contingency, chance, change, instability, and even the possibility of indeterminism in nature.[50] In 1961 MIT meteorologist Edward Lorenz discovered that ever so slightly tweaking the initial conditions of a simple weather model resulted in radically different results over a month-long simulation. All it took was truncating a single value from six decimal places to four to make storms appear

---

[46] Reitze 1999: 696–702.

[47] As reported in Oreskes and Conway 2010: 173.

[48] The Nixon Presidential Library no longer makes these memos available online, at their previous address. For an account of these memos, visit http://lawprofessors.typepad.com/environmental_law/2011/08/the-nixon-administration-and-climate-change.html. Retrieved July 31, 2013. Electronic copies are in my possession.

[49] http://www.slideshare.net/whitehouse/august-1970-environmental-quality-the-first-annual-report-of#text-version. Retrieved July 10, 2013. The presence of this discussion was probably due to Gordon McDonald, who was the only scientist on CEQ who also served on President Johnson's PSAC, and had a strong interest in weather modification. This may also help to explain why geoengineering is the only approach to countering global warming that is mentioned in either report. Curiously, climate was not discussed in subsequent CEQ reports until the Carter administration in 1977. For more on McDonald, visit http://www.nap.edu/openbook.php?record_id=10992&page=225. Retrieved July 10, 2013.

[50] The possibility that there is indeterminacy in nature had been under serious discussion since at least the 1920s with the development of the Copenhagen interpretation of quantum mechanics. For an introduction to the issues, see http://plato.stanford.edu/entries/qm-copenhagen/. Retrieved July 10, 2013. It is important to recognize that it does not follow from a system's unpredictability that indeterminacy prevails; the system may be deterministic but chaotic.

or disappear from weather forecasts. Lorenz later dubbed this sensitivity to initial conditions the "Butterfly Effect."[51] Imagine the world as it is at this instant and then imagine a world exactly like this one, but an additional butterfly is flapping its wings. Such a small difference can cascade so rapidly that the gross states of these worlds relevant to determining weather quickly diverge. This sensitivity to initial conditions severely limits the predictability of weather.

By the late 1960s it was beginning to be widely accepted that humans could destabilize climate, but there was disagreement about what, if anything, was actually going on. Norman Bryson, a distinguished University of Wisconsin meteorologist, thought that natural cycles were causing a warming trend, but that it was being overwhelmed by a cooling caused by overgrazing, slash and burn agriculture, and other human land use changes that were injecting aerosols into the atmosphere that were cooling the planet by affecting albedo. He expressed these views in popular magazines and newspapers, warning of the "human volcano" that was changing the climate.[52] Bryson speculated that this would lead to the suppression of the Indian monsoon, resulting in widespread starvation. That a global cooling was underway was never a dominant view in the scientific community, but it caught the imagination of some popular writers and journalists.[53] It even attracted the attention of the US Central Intelligence Agency.[54]

Scientists were beginning to glimpse the complexity of the climate system and grasp the importance of various feedback loops, but not enough was known about the structure of Tyndall's blanket to make very precise predictions with much confidence. It was one thing to know that a CO_2 forcing would lead to global warming; it was another thing entirely to know how this might affect particular regions, unfold through time, and be expressed in seasonal, diurnal, and other cycles.

---

[51] In his classic 1963 paper Lorenz seems to accept as a consequence of his theory an objection that he attributes to a meteorologist whose identity he can't recall: "…if the theory of atmospheric instability were correct, one flap of a sea gull's wings would forever change the future course of the weather" (431). In his 1969 paper Lorenz returns to this objection, but writes that "[i]t thus appears that our method of treating the nonlinearity greatly overestimates the growth rate when the initial errors are concentrated at a point…" (306). In a 1972 lecture entitled "Predictability: Does the Flap of a Butterfly's Wings in Brazil Set Off a Tornado in Texas?," delivered at the annual meeting of the American Association for the Advancement of Science, Lorenz writes that "[w]e must therefore leave our original question unanswered for a few more years, even while affirming our faith in the instability of the atmosphere" (as quoted in Merchant 1994: 362). Shortly before his death, Lorenz told me that he considered this to be his last word on the subject. For Lorenz, the most fundamental question was whether the climate system was deterministic, but he thought that this was a question that we probably would never be able to answer (see Lorenz 1968).

[52] See, e.g., Bryson 1967.

[53] See, e.g., Peterson et al. 2008. One influential scientific article that speculated about a cooling was Rasool and Schneider 1971. The book that had the most influence in putting the idea of global cooling into circulation was Lowell Ponte (1976), *The Cooling: Has the Next Ice Age Already Begun? Can We Survive It?*, with a foreword by US Senator Claiborne Pell, a preface by Reid A. Bryson, and an endorsement by Steve Schneider.

[54] The CIA report is available on the web at http://www.climatemonitor.it/wp-content/uploads/2009/12/1974.pdf. Retrieved October 9, 2013.

In 1946 John von Neumann began advocating for the creation of a computer model that would forecast weather.[55] Von Neumann was interested in weather prediction because he was interested in weather modification, and he was interested in weather modification mainly because he thought that it could be used as a weapon against the Soviet Union.[56] In 1948 von Neumann brought Jule Charney to the Institute for Advanced Study in Princeton, and in 1950, working with Norman Phillips who designed the prototype, they ran the first computerized weather forecasting model.[57] Von Neumann, Charney, and others convinced the Weather Bureau and several research and forecasting agencies of the Air Force and Navy to establish the Joint Numerical Weather Prediction Unit, which opened in Suitland, Maryland in 1954. The next year, at von Neumann's urging, the US Weather Bureau created a General Circulation Research Section (GCRS) dedicated to creating a three-dimensional, general circulation model of the atmosphere. Joseph Smagorinsky, whom Charney had recruited to the Institute for Advanced Study and then to the Joint Numerical Weather Prediction Unit, was chosen to direct it. After several moves and name changes, the GCRS returned to Princeton in 1968 as the Geophysical Fluid Dynamics Laboratory (GFDL).

As director of the world's premier climate modeling center from 1955 until his retirement in 1983, Smagorinsky was enormously influential on the development of climate science. His vision was that the increasing power of computers would permit going beyond simulating the evolution of the atmosphere for a few days, which is what is required for weather prediction, to simulating the evolution of the atmosphere for much longer periods of time. This would allow the study of how climate is controlled by atmospheric composition, features of the earth's surface, and ocean circulation. Among the many breakthroughs that occurred under Smagorinsky's leadership at GFDL were the first computerized simulation of a CO_2 doubling and the development of the first coupled, ocean-atmosphere general circulation model.[58]

---

[55] Von Neumann was one of the great geniuses of the twentieth century, making foundational contributions in set theory, game theory, and quantum mechanics, as well as to computer science. He was also a dedicated cold warrior, describing himself in confirmation hearings in the US Senate as "violently anti-communist…and a good deal more militaristic than most" (as quoted in Edwards 2010: 113). Von Neumann was involved in the target selection for the first two atomic bombs and argued for bombing the Japanese cultural capital of Kyoto, even though he agreed that it had no military significance. He was overruled by a general.

[56] Von Neumann 1955. He writes presciently in this paper that "[t]he carbon dioxide released into the atmosphere by industry's burning of coal and oil…may have changed the atmosphere's composition sufficiently to account for a general warming of the world by about one degree Fahrenheit" (108).

[57] At the time it was joked that they could predict today's weather by running the model for 48 hours.

[58] For the latter, see Manabe and Bryan 1969; for the former, see Manabe and Wetherald 1967. Manabe was one of a dozen or more gifted Japanese scientists who emigrated to the United States in the 1960s and were important contributors to the development of climate modeling. For historical background, see Lewis 1993. For the contributions of Akio Arakawa in particular, see Randall 2000.

Climate science was a new field, without an acknowledged place at the table or its own dedicated funding streams. It was emerging from meteorology, a traditionally low-status field, but it relied on computer modeling, a new, expensive, potentially high-status endeavor, but one that was not well understood outside the community. In a world in which disciplinary research is prized, climate science was an interdisciplinary field that relied on collaborative work from physicists, chemists, oceanographers, agricultural scientists, and others. Rather than being conducted in every university, research in climate science was concentrated in a handful of specialized centers, at least one of which had the reputation for being "monastic," "reclusive," and "snobby."[59] Climate science was the new kid on the block, often viewed as threatening established fields and disciplines by exorbitant resource demands that it justified in terms of its own importance. Indeed, some of the contrarian hostility to climate science has its source in this birthing process.[60]

In a quest for colleagues and in search of a lever to free up domestic resources, the American climate science community quickly became international. Many European countries, especially Russia, the Nordic countries, and the United Kingdom, had distinguished traditions in meteorology, and the turn toward climate modeling was emerging there as well; in addition, supercomputers were becoming faster, cheaper, and more powerful.[61] International meetings became more frequent, and new journals were established. While international meetings and conferences were held under the auspices of various organizations, the World Meteorological Organization (WMO) soon emerged as the single most important player in developing an international climate science community.[62]

The origins of the WMO go back to the International Meteorological Organization (IMO), which was founded in 1873. The IMO was an international scientific organization, but it had no official status as an intergovernmental organization. In 1951 the IMO was transformed into the WMO, a specialized UN organization whose charge was to promote both research and the use of meteorological information throughout the world. Although the WMO is not a rich and powerful organization compared to many others, its budget increased rapidly during the first two decades of its existence and it very effectively capitalized on its advantages. The WMO was one

---

[59] This was the reputation of GFDL according to Lewis 2008. Other leading climate research centers in the 1960s were located in the Meteorology Department at UCLA and at the National Center for Atmospheric Research.

[60] The MIT meteorologist Richard Lindzen, who is the most prestigious of the climate change deniers, was quoted as saying: "This is a field that was in a primitive state when it assumed a policy importance a few years ago....Suddenly we've declared thousands of people in a primitive field as world experts, and they're trying to have their day." (http://www.nytimes.com/2000/09/10/weekinreview/10REVK.html). Retrieved July 10, 2013.

[61] For a family tree of climate models, visit http://www.aip.org/history/climate/xAGCMtree.htm. Retrieved July 10, 2013.

[62] Schneider 2009 gives a good account of the importance of these early international meetings in forging an international climate science community.

of the few institutions that bridged the gaps between East and West during the cold war, and the North and South during the anti-colonial struggles of the 1950s and 1960s. The WMO allied early with the International Council of Scientific Unions (ICSU) to jointly organize the International Geophysical Year of 1957. In 1963 the WMO established World Weather Watch, aimed at creating a "world-wide operational system to which virtually every country in the world contributes, every day of every year, for the common benefit of mankind."[63] In 1968 the WMO and ICSU jointly created the Global Atmospheric Research Program (GARP), whose mission was to study the general circulation of the atmosphere in an effort to improve long-range weather forecasts.

In order to manage American participation in GARP, the National Academy of Sciences (NAS) set up a US Committee for the GARP. This gave the American climate science community its own seat in the Academy. The US Committee advocated for the creation of a National Climate Research Program, and in 1975 and 1977 published reports emphasizing the importance of climate research. In 1975 Wally Broecker published an influential paper correctly predicting a twentieth-century warming of 0.8°C, and worrying about the consequences for agriculture and sea level.[64] In 1978 Congress passed the National Climate Act, establishing a National Climate Program Office, with the National Oceanic and Atmospheric Administration (NOAA) as the lead agency.

The environmental movement was also beginning to pick up steam. In 1970 the United States celebrated the first Earth Day. The Clean Air Act was passed, and so was the National Environmental Policy Act (NEPA), which established both the US Environmental Protection Agency (EPA) and the White House CEQ. These actions were followed by the passage of a series of other environmental laws throughout the 1970s. Similar events were occurring internationally. In 1972 in Stockholm the UN held its first conference on the environment, which led to the creation of the United Nations Environment Programme (UNEP). A series of international environmental agreements quickly followed on such topics as transboundary pollution, endangered species, and wetlands.

During this turbulent period the interrelations between climate and society were coming increasingly into focus. The El Niño of 1972–1973 brought worldwide devastation and was followed by other climate anomalies. Drought-related famine killed hundreds of thousands of people in the African Sahel and in India. Drought struck other countries as well, including the United States. Crop failures brought the Soviet Union into the world grain market at the same time that global food supplies were low, resulting in a doubling of the price of some grains and causing additional hardship in poor countries.

---

[63] http://www.wmo.int/pages/prog/www/wwwinfo.html. Retrieved July 10, 2013. See Edwards 2010: ch. 9 for more on this system.
[64] Broecker 1975.

The Arab oil embargo of 1973–1974 brought price controls, rationing, and long lines to gasoline stations in the United States. Oil prices shot up throughout the 1970s before declining in the 1980s, only to go even higher in the new millennium. There was also growing concern about dependence on foreign oil.

Shortly after taking office in 1977, President Carter addressed the energy crisis, calling it "the moral equivalent of war." The Carter energy plan emphasized conservation and renewables, but also advocated increased use of coal and the development of synthetic fuels, which stoked concern about climate change. Carter had created the Department of Energy (DOE) to manage the energy crisis, and DOE pushed hard for an aggressive climate research program. However, NOAA, the National Aeronautics and Space Administration (NASA), and other agencies that were already engaged in climate research resisted, and they were supported by (what had become) the NAS Climate Research Board. Many scientists and environmentalists distrusted DOE because it had been pieced together from previously existing agencies involved with nuclear weapons, nuclear power, and various cold war projects, and did not have much of a track record with respect to energy policy.

In the midst of this controversy DOE asked JASON, an independent group of elite scientists closely associated with the Department of Defense (DOD), to review DOE's research plans. JASON took the opportunity to examine the relationship between carbon dioxide and climate more broadly, even building its own climate model. JASON concluded that climate change could cause the world's food supply to shrink and sea levels to rise surprisingly quickly, and either of these could lead to large-scale displacement of populations.[65]

The JASON report caught the attention of the President's science advisor, Frank Press, and he asked Philip Handler, President of the NAS, to review the climate models, including the one that JASON had built. Handler asked Jule Charney to chair the review, and Charney turned to climate modelers Syukuro Manabe from GFDL and James Hansen from the Goddard Institute for Space Studies (GISS) for help, although they were not formally members of the committee. Charney's committee concluded that the models were generally consistent and reliable, and that "if carbon dioxide continues to increase, the study group finds no reason to doubt that climate changes will result and no reason to believe that these changes will be negligible." More importantly, the Charney report was the first to fully grasp the logic of the problem: "A wait-and-see policy may mean waiting until it is too late."[66]

Even before Charney's study had been published, another request came to the Academy from the White House. According to Thomas Schelling (who would later win a Nobel Prize in Economics):

> President Carter was to attend a "summit" in Venice. The Chancellor of Germany had submitted, for the agenda, the "carbon dioxide problem." The White House asked the

---

[65] The declassified version of their report was later published as MacDonald 1982.
[66] Suomi 1979: viii.

National Academy of Sciences for advice on what to do with that item. I was invited to
chair a committee that would do a quick study and prepare advice.[67]

27 The Nature of the Problem

The German Chancellor who had submitted the "carbon dioxide problem"
for the agenda was Helmut Schmidt from the center-left Social Democratic Party
(SPD). The Green Party had just been formed, and the SPD was losing control of
its youthful supporters, in part because it had not been responsive enough to environmental concerns. Indeed, after ruling since 1969 the SPD would lose the 1983
elections, primarily because of the rise of the Greens.[68]

In response to the White House request, Schelling's committee produced a modest report, really only a letter, but it is important for three reasons. First, the fact that
the "carbon dioxide problem" was on the agenda of a G-7 summit showed that it was
becoming a matter of international concern. Second, the fact that the White House
was requesting information about the economic and social dimensions of anthropogenic warming showed that they were beginning to think of climate change as a
policy issue. Finally, inviting an economist into the discussion resulted in refram-
ing the discussion, shifting the questions asked, the methodologies employed, and
the assumptions made. Economists often bring views to the table that are foreign
or alienating to natural scientists. Economists often assume, for example, that any
decision involves winners, losers, and trade-offs; that for any good there is an equally
valued substitute; and that benefit-cost considerations are the foundation of public
decision-making.

The Energy Security Act of 1980, which enacted a compromise version of the
Carter energy plan, created the Synthetic Fuels Corporation, and mandated the NAS
to study the impacts of these technologies on the buildup of carbon dioxide in the
atmosphere, specifically requiring "an assessment of the economic, physical, climatic,
and social effects of such impacts."[69] The study was led by William Nierenberg, a distinguished physicist and later climate change contrarian. The resulting report was
a peer-reviewed collection of papers by climate scientists and economists including
Thomas Schelling and William Nordhaus. The report also included a collectively
endorsed executive summary and synthesis.[70] The summary asserted the reality of
climate change, predicted a doubling of atmospheric carbon dioxide in the next
century, acknowledged that benefits and costs would fall unequally on the people
of the world, and expressed "deep" concern that there might be surprises that we
cannot anticipate. However, it concluded by recommending a "balanced program

---

[67] http://nobelprize.org/nobel_prizes/economics/laureates/2005/schelling-autobio.html. Retrieved
July 10, 2013.

[68] In that election the Greens won 5.6% of the vote, which under the West German rules for proportional representation resulted in 27 seats in the Bundestag. The SPD's share of the vote declined
by 4.7% and they lost 25 seats.

[69] Board on Atmospheric Sciences and Climate et al. 1983: 492.

[70] There is controversy about how the executive summary was produced and who exactly was
responsible for it. See Oreskes et al. 2008 and Nierenberg et al. 2010.

of research," and specifically asserted that "[w]e do not believe…that the evidence at hand about CO_2-induced climate change would support steps to change current fuel-use patterns away from fossil fuels."[71]

A fault line was beginning to emerge among those studying climate change. Some warned against a "wait and see" approach while others advocated exactly that. Some saw the science as primarily supporting a case for additional research and funding, while others saw it as supporting a case for policy action. There was a tendency for economists to favor research over action since, from a purely economic perspective, delaying action until the last possible moment means acting when more of the uncertainties are resolved, abatement costs are lower, and there is less risk of over-shooting the target.[72] However, this perspective does not take into account political and institutional obstacles to turning an entire energy system on a dime, and moving from research to action at the optimal moment. Nor does it take seriously the huge time-lag in the climate system, which is what Suomi had in mind when he wrote in the introduction to the Charney report that "[a] wait-and-see policy may mean waiting until it is too late."[73]

The arrival of the Reagan administration in 1981 was a wake-up call for people in both camps. Reagan's initial environmental appointees were radical anti-environmentalists such as Anne Gorsuch (EPA Administrator), Bob Burford (Bureau of Land Management Director), and James Watt (Interior Secretary), all drawn from the hothouse of right-wing Colorado politics.[74] James Edwards, a South Carolina dentist, was made Secretary of Energy, with the mandate of abolishing the agency. Edwards cut the budget of DOE's CO_2 program and dismissed its leader. A typical story from that time is that when GISS scientist James Hansen's research showing that the world had warmed was reported on the front page of the *New York Times*, DOE responded by canceling promised research funding.[75] Climate policy was not going to be made on Reagan's watch, and research money was not going to be wasted on the environment when it could be spent on the military.

---

[71] National Academy of Sciences 1983: 4.

[72] However, the fault line was not entirely disciplinary. While this is to some extent speculative, I believe that both Revelle and Smagorinsky were primarily interested in more research, while some economists such as Ralph D'Arge were more closely aligned to some scientists in favoring policy action. For a hint from D'Arge, see D'Arge and Kogiku 1973.

[73] "…the study group point out that the ocean, the great and ponderous flywheel of the global climate system, may be expected to slow the course of observable climatic change. A wait-and-see policy may mean waiting until it is too late." Suomi 1979: viii.

[74] Gorsuch and Burford served in the Colorado state legislature, where they both were members of a group that called itself the "House crazies." Watt was Executive Director of the Mountain States Legal Foundation, which specialized in suing the government to restrict enforcement of various environmental laws including the Endangered Species Act, the Clean Water Act, the National Environmental Policy Act (NEPA), the National Forest Management Act, the Antiquities Act, the Multiple Use Sustained Yield Act, and the General Mining Law.

[75] Weart 2008: 139.

In little more than two years most of these appointees were gone. In November 1982, Edwards decided that being President of the Medical University of South Carolina was a job more to his liking. In March 1983 Gorsuch was forced to resign after being cited for contempt of Congress for her political manipulation and mishandling of the Superfund Program. Watt resigned in November 1983 after numerous controversies, the last of which was a speech in which he (perhaps jokingly) implied that while a coal-leasing panel included blacks, Jews, women, and "cripples" as members, there was in addition "talent" on the board.

A few months after Gorsuch's resignation the EPA issued a report saying that "a rapid increase in the earth's temperature and climate now seems inevitable and its effects will begin to be felt by the turn of the next century."[76] While focusing on adaptation rather than mitigation, the report stated that we should approach the problem with a "sense of urgency."[77] A few days later the NAS released the Nierenberg report, calling for more research.[78] The administration, now under pressure to choose between policy and research, grabbed on to the Academy report like a life raft. George Keyworth II, Reagan's science advisor, denounced the EPA report as "unwarranted and unnecessarily alarmist," praising the Academy report for asserting that "at this time there is no action recommended other than continued research."[79]

Meanwhile, climate models were becoming more sophisticated and data sets were getting better, in part because of progress in remote sensing.[80] In the broader global community, confidence was growing in the reality and risks of anthropogenic climate change. Pressure for action was building.

In 1979 the WMO and UNEP organized the first World Climate Conference. This led to the creation of the World Climate Programme (WCP), in collaboration with ICSU. In 1980, 1983, and 1985 the WCP held a series of increasingly high-profile meetings in Villach, Austria. The 1985 meeting, involving experts from 29 developed and developing countries, concluded that "the rate and degree of future warming could be profoundly affected by governmental policies" and that "scientists and policymakers should begin active collaboration to explore the effectiveness of alternative policies and adjustments."[81] This meeting gave birth to the Advisory Group

[76] http://news.google.com/newspapers?id=Kv4SAAAAIBAJ&sjid=5u4DAAAAIBAJ&pg=6942,3 421802&dq=history+of+epa+reports+on+climate&hl=en. Retrieved July 10, 2013. Cf. Hoffman, et al. 1983.

[77] http://news.google.com/newspapers?id=e-8aAAAAIBAJ&sjid=RkcEAAAAIBAJ&pg=5441,4518 512&hl=en. Cf. Seidel and Keyes 1983.

[78] National Academy of Sciences 1983: 492.

[79] http://news.google.com/newspapers?id=Kv4SAAAAIBAJ&sjid=5u4DAAAAIBAJ&pg=6942,34 21802&dq=history+of+epa+reports+on+climate&hl=en. Keyworth was a cold warrior who had come to the administration from Los Alamos.

[80] See Edwards 2010: ch. 8 ff for discussion of the standardization and improvement of data sets.

[81] Bolin et al. 1986: x–xii; Long and Iles 1997. The conference statement is reprinted in Abrahamson 1989, ch. 4.

on Greenhouse Gases (AGGG), whose mandate was to "initiate if necessary, consideration of a global convention." The AGGG was composed of six experts, two nominated by each of the three participating bodies.[82] Gordon Goodman, Executive Director of the Beijer Institute (later the Stockholm Environment Institute), working with Michael Oppenheimer of the Environmental Defense Fund and George Woodwell of Woods Hole Research Center, obtained funding from several sources, including the Rockefeller Foundation and the Rockefeller Brothers Fund, to support two workshops, the first in September 1987 in Villach, focusing on science, and the second in November 1987 in Bellagio, focusing on policy.[83] These conferences were intended to be a bridge between the 1985 Villach conference, which recommended that a global convention be considered, and "the actual elaboration of specific measures to limit or adapt to warming."[84]

Other events contributed to a sense of urgency about environmental challenges and to the feeling that this was a moment in which decisive, even transformational action was possible. In 1983 the General Assembly of the UN created the World Commission on Environment and Development, which published its report in 1987, popularizing the phrase "sustainable development."[85]

In Europe, especially, environmental consciousness was growing rapidly, partly in response to concerns about acid rain and fears generated by the 1986 Chernobyl nuclear disaster.[86] Green political parties were forming all over, and since most European countries have some system of proportional representation, these parties were gaining parliamentary seats. The European Community was becoming progressively stronger, and its institutions were acting increasingly independently of individual states. Greens entered the European Parliament in 1984 and have been continuously represented since then. Greens were also becoming increasingly influential in Eastern Europe and the Soviet Union through the emerging social movements that were challenging the power of the state and the Communist Party.

Gorbachev's rise to power in the Soviet Union in 1985 seemed to create new political possibilities for addressing global environmental problems. In his bold and wide-ranging speech to the UN in 1988, Gorbachev indicated that the reformed

[82] The membership included Gordon Goodman, Bert Bolin, Ken Hare, Gilbert White, G. Golitsyn, Sukiyoro Manabe, and M. Kassas.

[83] These meetings were the first climate change meetings sponsored by an American environmental group since the Conservation Foundation meeting in 1963. Perhaps the hand of Laurance Rockefeller was at work in these meetings as well.

[84] Oppenheimer 1989: 3. See Jaeger 1988 for the report of the Bellagio workshop.

[85] World Commission on Environment and Development 1987. Gordan Goodman, who served on the AAAG, was a "special advisor" to the Brundtland Commission (as it was popularly known) and has been credited with drafting the Commission's text on climate change, which draws heavily from the Villach reports. For discussion, see Torrance 2006.

[86] Keleman and Vogel 2010; Knill and Liefferink 2007: ch. 1. For an example of how these issues were treated in the popular press, see the 1981 cover story in *Der Spiegel* 47/1981 "Der Wald stirbt. Saurer Regen über Deutschland" ("The Forests Are Dying. Acid Rain over Germany").

Soviet Union would play an aggressive role in protecting the global environment.[87] It seemed that there was a real possibility that the East and West would join in trying to heal the North/South division, and would address the linked problems of global environmental destruction, poverty, and underdevelopment.

In 1987 the Montreal Protocol was signed, the first in a series of international agreements leading to the phase-out of ozone-depleting chemicals. While the possibility that human action could deplete stratospheric ozone had been discussed and debated since the early 1970s, the 1985 discovery of the Antarctic ozone hole, which no model had predicted, shocked people around the world. This discovery showed how subtle changes in the atmosphere can produce surprising, unintended consequences that can threaten the prospects for life on earth. The next year UNEP and the WMO joined to produce an international scientific assessment of the threat posed by chlorofluorocarbons (CFCs) and other compounds, while expeditions led by Susan Solomon showed that CFCs were indeed implicated in causing the Antarctic ozone hole. The adoption of the Montreal Protocol was a great achievement, and international scientific cooperation was essential to its realization. This success, which had occurred very quickly by the standards of international diplomacy, led to a sense of optimism that, with the help of the scientific community, the nations of the world could successfully address the problem of climate change.[88]

In 1988 climate change moved from an issue of public concern to a global project.[89] Much of the United States spent the summer in the grip of extreme heat and serious drought. Fires raged in Yellowstone National Park, agricultural production declined dramatically, and water levels in the Mississippi River system dropped precariously, resulting in channel closings and ship groundings. On the Eastern seaboard demand for electricity to run fans and air conditioners hit an all-time high, and air conditioners were even in short supply. On June 23, 1988, a sweltering day in Washington, DC, climate modeler James Hansen testified before a US Senate Committee that it was 99% probable that global warming had begun. Hansen's testimony was front-page news in the *New York Times*, and was extensively covered in other media as well. One week after Hansen's testimony, a WMO-sponsored conference in Toronto, following up on the 1987 Villach and Bellagio workshops, called for a 20% reduction in greenhouse gas (GHG) emissions by 2005. On July 28 Senator Tim Wirth of Colorado, along with 18 co-sponsors from both political parties, introduced the National Energy Policy Act of 1988, calling for a 20% reduction in US carbon dioxide emissions from 1988 levels by the year 2000.[90] In a September speech to the Royal Society, British Prime Minister

---

[87] http://www.writespirit.net/inspirational_talks/mikhail_gorbachev_talks/united_nations_address/. Retrieved July 10, 2013.

[88] For more on the ozone story, see Dotto and Schiff 1978; Roan 1990; Parson 2004; Benedick 1991.

[89] Chakrabarty (2009) points out that throughout the 1980s and 1990s discussions of global climate change, and economic, social, and political globalization occurred in parallel universes, and did not begin to connect until the new millennium. Perhaps the connection can be traced from Singer (2002).

[90] *Congressional Record*, Washington, Thursday, July 28, 1988, vol. 134, no. 110.

Margaret Thatcher expressed concern about climate change, ozone depletion, and acid rain, echoing Roger Revelle's language about the global experiment that was now underway, noting that the five warmest years in a century had all been in the 1980s, and reminding her audience of the vulnerability of the Maldives to sea level rise.[91] It was an election year in the United States, and the Democratic Party promised in its platform to "address...the 'greenhouse effect.'"[92] George Herbert Walker Bush, the Republican candidate, promised to counter the greenhouse effect with "the White House Effect," and declared that he would be the "environmental president."[93] What seemed like a bidding war over emissions reductions continued in November in Hamburg, Germany, when the World Congress on Climate and Development called for a 30% reduction in emissions by 2000. The year ended with *Time Magazine* forgoing its usual "man of the year" in favor of the "Endangered Earth" as "planet of the year," depicting the planet as wrapped in plastic and bound in rope.

The Reagan administration was still in power in 1988 and, having been forced to back down from the aggressive anti-environmentalism of its first term, was still on the defensive. It had shifted its strategy from opposing both policy and research to supporting research while continuing to oppose policy. At the end of 1987 the President signed the Global Climate Protection Act of 1987 (actually a provision of the Foreign Relations Authorization Act, Fiscal Years 1988 and 1989), which, among other things, directed the President "to develop and propose to the Congress a coordinated national policy on global climate change."[94] During fiscal year 1988 the administration spent $200 million on climate-related activities and proposed $232 million for FY 1989, while slashing the overall EPA budget by $600 million. Despite its attempts to market climate research as if it were policy, the administration was under growing pressure, both domestically and internationally, to actually act on climate change.

UNEP's Executive Director was the charismatic and controversial Egyptian scientist Dr. Mostafa Kamal Tolba, who had won accolades for brokering the Montreal Protocol and was eager to burnish his legacy. Since the 1985 Villach workshop he had been in active consultations with the WMO and ICSU about a possible climate convention. In 1986 he wrote to US Secretary of State George Schultz, urging the United States to initiate an international process to address climate change. This proposal went to that elephant burial ground in the American government known as "an interagency process," which predictably engaged various competing interests, each trying to protect its own turf and promote its own influence. The White

---

[91] http://www.margaretthatcher.org/speeches/displaydocument.asp?docid=107346. Retrieved July 14, 2013.

[92] http://www.presidency.ucsb.edu/ws/index.php?pid=29609. Retrieved July 14, 2013.

[93] *Los Angeles Times*, December 30, 1988.

[94] http://thomas.loc.gov/cgi-bin/bdquery/z?d100:HR01777:@@@D&summ2=m&. Retrieved July 12, 2013. It was obligations under this act that led to the EPA studies that the administration did its best to downplay.

House and DOE wanted to do nothing on climate change, while the EPA and the State Department were receptive to some kind of action. The NAS wanted more research but was not interested in policy. All the parties felt threatened by policy pressures arising from international conferences, academy committees, and other self-selected groups of scientists. They all agreed that these independent actors had to be brought under state control. What emerged from the interagency process was a lowest common denominator proposal for an intergovernmental panel to study climate change. Final statements would be crafted by people who participated not only as experts but also as official representatives of their governments, and all statements would have to be adopted by consensus. After further negotiations with and between various agencies of the US government, WMO, and UNEP, the WMO sent a letter to the governments of the world inviting participation in the formation of the Intergovernmental Panel on Climate Change (IPCC). Twenty-eight countries responded, and after further negotiations the WMO and UNEP created the IPCC. The distinguished Swedish scientist Bert Bolin would be its chair. There would be three working groups. Working Group I would focus on physical science and be chaired by the United Kingdom. Adaptation would be the charge of Working Group II and would be led by the USSR. An American would lead Working Group III, which would be concerned with policy responses.[95]

On December 6, 1988, the UN General Assembly passed Resolution 43/53 on the "Conservation of climate as part of the common heritage of mankind." This resolution, proposed by Malta and specifically referencing the 1985 Villach meeting, recognized the IPCC, set a timeline for its first report, and provided a framework for moving to a convention. Specifically, the resolution

[e]ndorses the action of the World Meteorological Organization and the United Nations Environment Programme in jointly establishing an Intergovernmental Panel on Climate Change to provide internationally co-ordinated scientific assessments of the magnitude, timing and potential environmental and socio-economic impact of climate change...Urges Governments, intergovernmental and non-governmental organizations and scientific institutions to treat climate change as a priority issue...Calls upon Governments and intergovernmental organizations to collaborate in making every effort to prevent detrimental effects on climate...Requests the Secretary-General of the World Meteorological Organization and the Executive Director of the United Nations Environment Programme, through the Intergovernmental Panel on Climate Change, immediately to initiate action leading, as soon as possible, to a comprehensive review and recommendations with respect to: (a) The state of knowledge of the science of climate and climatic change; (b) Programmes and studies on the social and economic impact of climate change, including global warming; (c) Possible response strategies to delay, limit or mitigate the impact of adverse climate change; (d) The identification

---

[95] For more on the origins of the IPCC, see Agrawala 1998 and Bolin 2008.

and possible strengthening of relevant existing international legal instruments having a bearing on climate; (e) Elements for inclusion in a possible future international convention on climate....

The resolution

Further requests the Secretary-General to report to the General Assembly at its forty-fourth session on the implementation of the present resolution...

and

Decides to include this question in the provisional agenda of its forty-fourth session....[96]

Climate diplomacy had begun.

2.3. THE AGE OF CLIMATE DIPLOMACY

Resolution 43/53 left the IPCC only about 18 months to produce its first report. Initially its work was supported and cheered on by virtually every country in the world. In January 1989, newly appointed US Secretary of State James Baker spoke at the first meeting of Working Group III, declaring that the time had come for political action.[97] In February 1990, President George Herbert Walker Bush told the IPCC that "[t]he US is strongly committed to the IPCC process of international cooperation on climate change."[98] However, in August 1990, at the IPCC meeting in Sundsvaal, Sweden, which had been called to approve the texts of the three working group reports along with a synthesis statement, competing political interests and ideologies were on display. Greenpeace International was present, and so were climate denial NGOs such as the Global Climate Coalition and the Global Climate Council, as well as various fossil fuel interest groups. Under pressure for revisions from the United States, Saudi Arabia, the Soviet Union, and some developing countries, the meeting nearly collapsed.[99] Finally, however, a text was accepted, and after one more round of ministerial review, it was submitted to the UN General Assembly in October 1990.

In response, the General Assembly created the Intergovernmental Negotiating Committee (INC) whose charge was to prepare a proposal for a framework convention on climate change, which would be acted on at the UN Conference on Environment and Development that would meet in Rio de Janeiro in June 1992. Remarkably, with only 18 months to act, the INC was able to agree on a text. The

---

[96] http://www.un.org/documents/ga/res/43/a43r053.htm. Retrieved July 15, 2013.

[97] Bolin 2008: 53–54.

[98] Bolin 2008: 58.

[99] Gorbachev's grip on power was steadily weakening and by the end of 1991 the President of the Soviet Union was no longer a president, and there was no longer a Soviet Union of which one could be president.

Framework Convention on Climate Change (FCCC) was opened for signature in Rio on May 9, 1992, and entered into force on March 21, 1994.

This cheery story masks conflicts that began before the Sundsvaal IPCC meeting.[100] The March 1989 Hague Summit, initiated by France, the Netherlands, and Norway, attended by 24 developed and developing countries, including 17 heads of state, called for the development of a "new institutional authority" to preserve the earth's atmosphere and combat global warming.[101] By May 1989 several European countries, along with Canada, were calling for negotiations to begin on a climate convention. This call was resisted by the United States, Japan, Australia, and New Zealand, ostensibly because they wanted to wait until the IPCC report had been submitted.[102] However, by the summer of 1989 the members of the European Community had agreed that they would act collectively and individually to combat climate change.[103] In November 1989 environment ministers from 67 countries and representatives from 11 international organizations and the European Commission met in Noordwijk, Netherlands. Following the precedent of the ozone regime, most European countries supported a convention that would include targets and timetables for stabilizing, then reducing, GHG emissions. The United States, supported by Japan and the Soviet Union, adamantly opposed such an agreement.[104] Throughout the negotiating process American rejectionism was consistently on display. Indeed, the policies of Reagan and both Bushes were remarkably consistent: do as little as possible on climate change, rationalized by casting doubt on the science and exaggerating the costs of action. The division between the United States and Europe on the urgency of taking strong action on climate change, with binding commitments, continues to this day.

Another conflict that has persisted since these early negotiations is between developed and developing countries. Developing countries are represented in the UN by the G-77, an organization that was founded in 1964 to further the economic aims of developing countries. On two core issues, the G-77 displays remarkable unity in the climate negotiations: demanding technology transfer and economic assistance from developed countries, and refusing to take on binding commitments for its own

[100] Here my account has benefited greatly from Bodansky 2001.

[101] However, neither the United States nor Great Britain participated. For the Hague Declaration, visit http://www.jstor.org/pss/20693363. Retrieved July 12, 2013.

[102] Cass 2006: 85.

[103] Key to the establishment of aggressive European climate change policy was the transformation of German policy led by the center-right Chancellor, Helmut Kohl. Kohl was moved by domestic political considerations, and the impending unification of the Federal Republic with the German Democratic Republic provided ample opportunities for cheap emissions reductions. For further discussion, see Oberthür and Pallemaerts 2010 and Jordan and Rayner 2010.

[104] However, there were divisions within the Bush administration, especially between a faction led by White House Chief of Staff John Sununu, who was a climate change denier, and a faction led by EPA Administrator William Reilly, who (reportedly) was willing to accept a convention with targets and timetables.

members. However, within the G-77 there is a broad range of interests. For example, the Alliance of Small Island States (AOSIS) is the strongest advocate for binding emissions reductions for developed countries, while the oil-producing states often question the underlying science and oppose any significant action at all (indeed, they often work very closely with climate change deniers in the United States). Large developing countries such as Brazil, China, and India typically focus most on issues that they see as affecting their national sovereignty.[105]

The Rio Earth Summit, technically known as the United Nations Conference on Environment and Development, was supposed to produce agreements on a wide range of issues, including an "earth charter" that would guide the global transition to sustainable development. In the end, only two legally binding treaties were concluded: The Convention on Biological Diversity, and the FCCC. The document of most interest to developing countries, Agenda 21, was adopted only as an "action plan," and has subsequently been ignored.[106]

Despite the conflicts, the FCCC has won nearly universal acceptance (there are 194 parties to the convention, while the UN has 192 member states). The parties to the FCCC committed themselves to the following:

> … to achieve…stabilization of greenhouse gas concentrations in the atmosphere at a level
> that would prevent dangerous anthropogenic interference with the climate system.[107]

They would achieve this objective by assuming "common but differentiated responsibilities." The developed countries would lead the way by reducing their own emissions and transferring technology and financial assistance to developing countries. Instead of the mandatory targets and timetables favored by the European Union, AOSIS, and most developing countries but opposed by the United States and the oil-producing states, the FCCC incorporated highly ambiguous language regarding the responsibilities of developed countries to reduce their emissions. In Article 4.2. a of the Convention, each developed country committed itself to

> … adopt national policies and take corresponding measures on the mitigation of cli-
> mate change, by limiting its anthropogenic emissions of greenhouse gases and protect-
> ing and enhancing its greenhouse gas sinks and reservoirs. These policies and measures

---

[105] China coordinates its climate change policy with the G-77 but is not a member; rather, it is a "special invitee" of the G-77. There are other divisions among parties to the convention that cannot be explored here, but see, for example, Depledge 2006.

[106] Weirdly, however, in the run-up to the 2012 elections the Republican National Committee rediscovered Agenda 21, and passed a resolution denouncing it as "a comprehensive plan of extreme environmentalism, social engineering, and global political control." http://www.republicanassemblies.org/rnc-adopts-resolution-exposing-agenda-21/. Retrieved July 15, 2013. For an abridged version of Agenda 21, see Sitarz 1993.

[107] The full text of the convention is available at http://unfccc.int/essential_background/convention/background/items/1353.php. Retrieved July 12, 2013.

will demonstrate that developed countries are taking the lead in modifying longer-term trends in anthropogenic emissions...recognizing that the return by the end of the present decade to earlier levels of anthropogenic emissions of carbon dioxide and other greenhouse gases...would contribute to such modification....

In Article 4.2.c this commitment is referred to as developed countries having "the aim of returning individually or jointly to their 1990 levels these anthropogenic emissions of carbon dioxide and other greenhouse gases." The ambiguity of the language is indicated by the fact that shortly after the United States signed the convention, a Bush policy advisor wrote to a US congressman that "there is nothing in any of the language which constitutes a commitment to any specific level of emissions at any time," while the chief British negotiator was quoted about the same provision as saying that it is "indistinguishable" from an absolute guarantee.[108]

The FCCC is a framework convention. What mattered was the way forward, and from the beginning there were two distinct visions about how it ought to go. The Europeans and environmentalists were willing to accept the FCCC because they saw it as the first step in a process in which the parties would take mutually reinforcing positive actions. Developed countries, which were responsible for 75% of CO_2 emissions from 1860 to 1990 despite having only 20% of the world population, would demonstrate the seriousness of their commitment by voluntarily stabilizing their emissions at 1990 levels by 2000. They would also transfer technology and other resources in order to enable developing countries to produce GHG inventories, take climate change into account in their planning processes, educate their citizens about climate change, and promote sustainable management. These initial steps would begin to bend the curve on CO_2 emissions and build confidence among the parties. During the next period, developed and developing countries would share the burdens of emissions reductions according to the principle of "common but differentiated responsibilities."

The problem with this approach is that it assumed goodwill and a common purpose on all sides. However, not everyone wanted global action on climate change. Most of the oil-producing states were opposed, and so were many influential actors in the United States who were motivated by ideology, self-interest, or the calculus of political advantage. The policies of some nations were unstable (e.g., Canada, Australia), while other important actors were not committed to either scenario, but were poised to follow a pragmatic or opportunistic policy. The logic of the optimistic scenario was such that it was extremely vulnerable to those who were opposed to taking action. If the naysayers could prevent developed countries from acting in a way that inspired confidence and trust on the part of developing countries (for example by casting doubt on the fairness of the bargain or the willingness of developing countries ever to do their part), then they would be able to prevent the

---

[108] Bodansky 1993: 516–517.

virtuous circle of mutually reinforcing positive actions from ever taking hold. Even if the transition to a carbon-free economy could not be prevented but only delayed, this would still result in enormous economic benefits for some of the interest groups involved.[109]

In the United States 1992 was an election year, and the Bush administration had a difficult time finding a consistent message regarding the environment. Bush was the self-declared "environmental president," but he could not decide whether he would join 106 other heads of state and government in Rio for the UN Conference on Environment and Development. After a great deal of waffling he went, but once there refused to sign the Convention on Biological Diversity and declared that the American way of life was not up for negotiation.[110] Bush was relentlessly attacked by environmentalists and Democratic Party politicians for hypocrisy, and also by many conservatives who thought that he was too soft on green issues. Presidential candidate Bill Clinton gave a speech on Earth Day, April 22, 1992, in which he said that "our addiction to fossil fuels…is wrapping the earth in a deadly shroud of greenhouse gases."[111] In June 1992, Al Gore's book *Earth in the Balance* was published, certainly the most moving and knowledgeable book about the environment ever written by an American politician. The following month, Clinton chose Gore to be his running mate. Environmentalists were both relieved and ecstatic when Clinton entered the White House with Al Gore by his side.

However, the euphoria was short-lived. In his first State of the Union address in February 1993, President Clinton called for an energy (BTU) tax that would have reduced CO_2 emissions and raised revenue. This proposal was an alternative to a carbon tax that would have put more of the burden on Democratic Party constituents. However, Democratic senators rejected even this alternative, and what was enacted instead was a modest tax increase on gasoline, which raised some revenue but had little effect on CO_2 emissions. In the fall of 1993 Clinton launched a Climate Action Plan, which gathered together and expanded existing federal programs, focusing mainly on voluntary partnerships with businesses and other entities. This modest program was not significantly different from programs that had been underway in

[109] Actors with large economic interests at stake often self-consciously play the delaying game (e.g., automakers opposing seat belts, the phasing out of leaded gasoline, etc.; see Jamieson 2010a). Political actors often benefit from opposing a policy or regulation, then becoming its champion once it is enacted (e.g., Republicans and social security). And of course some developing countries (e.g., India) have been relieved by the lack of action by some developed countries, which relaxes the pressure on them to act.

[110] President Clinton signed the Biodiversity Convention in 1993 but the Senate has not ratified it. The US, Andorra, and the Vatican are the only countries that are not parties to the Convention. William Reilly, Bush's EPA Administrator, wrote a memorandum to EPA employees after his return from Rio in which he said: "We assigned a low priority to the negotiations of the biodiversity treaty, were slow to engage the climate issue, were last to commit our President to attend Rio. We put our delegation together late and we committed few resources." (As quoted in Palmer 1992: 106.)

[111] http://www.pbs.org/wgbh/pages/frontline/hotpolitics/etc/cron.html. Retrieved July 10, 2013.

the Bush administration. At its launch it was projected that over six years the federal government would spend only $1.9 billion on this program, with most of the funds reallocated from the existing budgets of federal agencies. The failure of this program is evidenced by the fact that rather than stabilizing at 1990 levels by 2000, US net emissions (sources and sinks) increased by more than 22% and carbon dioxide emissions increased by 14.6%.[112] To the disappointment of many in the environmental community, Vice President Gore prepared his campaign to succeed Clinton by focusing mainly on such projects as "reinventing government" and developing the Internet. He did not return to full-throated environmentalism until the second term of President George W. Bush.

Shortly after the FCCC came into force in March 1994, it became clear that while some European countries would meet their voluntary commitments, others would not, and the United States certainly would not. In August 1994 negotiations began in earnest at the first Conference of the Parties (COP 1) held in Berlin in 1995. After initial skirmishing, both the European Union and the G-77 signed on to the AOSIS proposal that developed countries commit themselves in a binding protocol to reducing their emissions 20% from the 1990 baseline by 2005. They were opposed by the United States, Japan, Canada, Australia, and New Zealand. The United States also argued for "joint implementation," the idea, broadly speaking, that developed countries can purchase emissions reductions offshore and count them toward fulfilling their own obligations.

Joint implementation was important to the Americans for several reasons. First, a protocol with joint implementation could produce the same outcomes as a protocol without joint implementation but at lower cost, since what would determine which emissions would be retired would be their comparative value rather than their geographical location. Second, producing a significant fraction of emissions reductions offshore would result in less social and economic dislocation in the United States, and would thus be more politically palatable than achieving all the emissions reductions at home. Finally, the Americans argued that the Europeans were already benefiting from joint implementation within the EU "bubble," with their insistence that the European Union be treated as a single entity for emissions reduction purposes, while denying this opportunity to others.

The Berlin Mandate was the compromise that emerged. Over the next two years the parties would negotiate a protocol that, for the developed countries, would "set quantified limitation and reduction objectives within specified time-frames, such as 2005, 2010 and 2020," while developing countries would be under no additional

---

[112] One ongoing controversy in the climate negotiations concerned what exactly was supposed to be stabilized at 1990 levels by 2000: net emissions including sources and sinks; net emissions including sources and sinks minus the emissions of gases regulated by the ozone regime; or simply emissions.

obligations during that time period.[113] There would be a pilot program for joint implementation projects, but they would not count toward satisfying current obligations.

Instead of winning kudos for their negotiating skills in Berlin, the Clinton administration came under increasing pressure from different directions. Toward the end of 1995 the IPCC released its second assessment report, and it was clear that the scientific case for anthropogenic climate change was continuing to build. While there were numerous controversies regarding the second assessment, in many cases mirroring disagreements that were occurring on the diplomatic track, the report largely confirmed and elaborated the major findings of the first assessment, declaring that "the balance of evidence suggests that there is a discernible human influence on global climate."[114] Many scientists continued to press for immediate action, culminating in the "World Scientists' Call for Action at Kyoto," a statement signed by a majority of the living Nobel Prize winners in science.[115] Meanwhile, coming out of Berlin, the climate change denial industry went into high gear. A series of op-ed pieces in the *Wall Street Journal* accused American climate scientist Ben Santer of secretly altering text in the IPCC report in order to exaggerate the case for anthropogenic climate change, an absurd claim denied by Santer, both chairs of Working Group I, and IPCC Chair Bert Bolin. Nevertheless, the charges attracted an enormous amount of attention and continue to circulate on the Internet.[116] A wide range of American business interests also mobilized after Berlin and they almost universally opposed any agreement that would restrain their behavior while failing to restrain the behavior of their competitors in developing countries. The Clinton administration responded by producing economic analyses that showed that controlling emissions would be relatively inexpensive or would even result in economic benefits. They were countered by private sector and partisan analyses that showed devastating costs to the American economy as a result of emissions reductions.[117]

In the midst of all this heat the American public remained remarkably apathetic. Surveys showed that most people believed in the reality of climate change and thought that something should be done about it, but it did not rank high

---

[113] http://unfccc.int/resource/docs/cop1/07a01.pdf. Retrieved July 15, 2013.

[114] Houghton et al. 1996: 4. This and other IPCC reports are available on the web at http://www.ipcc.ch/publications_and_data/publications_and_data_reports.shtml. Retrieved July 10, 2013.

[115] http://www.ucsusa.org/global_warming/solutions/big_picture_solutions/world-scientists-call-for.html. Retrieved July 10, 2013.

[116] I discuss this case more fully in Section 3.5.

[117] In the midst of the controversy Robert Repetto and Duncan Austin (1997) examined 162 cost estimates from 16 different economic models and found that 80% of the variation in their results could be explained by differences in assumptions that were made in order to resolve uncertainties. The disagreements were mainly based on speculations rather than facts. For more on climate economics, see Chapter 4.

among their concerns and they rejected any action that would result in higher energy costs.[118] President Clinton was facing reelection in 1996, and after having lost the fight over the energy tax he wanted to make sure that this issue caused him no further political damage, while ensuring that environmentalists who were allied with the administration were not alienated. The result was that the administration neutralized the climate change issue by pursuing a low-profile, incoherent policy. Internationally, the administration resisted fulfilling the Berlin Mandate to which it had agreed and which was to be the foundation for any international agreement; domestically, the administration argued (rather halfheartedly) for the importance of an international agreement on climate change.

Congress was not impressed. In July 1997, the Senate unanimously adopted the Byrd-Hagel resolution, which stated:

(1) the United States should not be a signatory to any protocol to, or other agreement regarding, the United Nations Framework Convention on Climate Change of 1992, at negotiations in Kyoto in December 1997, or thereafter, which would--

(A) mandate new commitments to limit or reduce greenhouse gas emissions for the Annex I Parties, unless the protocol or other agreement also mandates new specific scheduled commitments to limit or reduce greenhouse gas emissions for Developing Country Parties within the same compliance period.[119]

One did not have to be a rocket scientist to see that any protocol consistent with the Berlin Mandate, which had been agreed to by all the parties to the FCCC including the United States, was not going to be ratified by the US Senate. Indeed, it might not get a single vote. Weirdly, Under Secretary of State Tim Wirth, who had negotiated the Berlin Mandate, welcomed the Byrd Amendment, saying that the administration was "very strongly supportive of the Resolution. We believe it strengthens our hand."[120]

In fact, the cauldron of conflicting pressures was making it very difficult for the United States to develop any coherent policy that it could take to Kyoto. The Americans resisted European proposals, with Under Secretary Wirth calling them "fuzzy" and objecting to the EU "bubble" proposal that would allow increases in emissions in some European countries (e.g., Spain and Greece) to be offset by reductions in others (e.g., Germany and the UK), while not tabling one of their own.[121]

---

[118] According to a survey cited in Cass 2006: 128. This remains largely true today. For samples of recent surveys, visit http://environment.yale.edu/climate/files/Climate-Beliefs-March-2012.pdf (retrieved July 12, 2013), and http://woods.stanford.edu/cgi-bin/focal.php?name=climate-change-action-drops (retrieved July 12, 2013).

[119] http://www.nationalcenter.org/KyotoSenate.html. Retrieved July 12, 2013.

[120] http://ces.iisc.ernet.in/hpg/envis/doc97html/globalus727.html. Retrieved July 12, 2013.

[121] As quoted in Cass 2006: 131.

Finally, on October 22, 1997, during the final preparatory negotiating session in Bonn, a little over a month before the Kyoto Conference was to begin, President Clinton announced the American position. The United States would stabilize its GHG emissions at 1990 levels, between 2008 and 2012, with unspecified cuts in the five-year period thereafter and beyond. The United States would do this without new taxes or regulations, relying on modest incentives, voluntary programs, and flexibility mechanisms such as emissions trading and joint implementation. In addition, "developing countries must participate in meeting the challenge of climate change."[122]

Clinton's speech was greeted in Bonn with emotions ranging from rage to dismay.[123] Clinton was agreeing to accomplish by 2008–2012 what the United States had already agreed to do by 2000, and then only by paying other people to reduce their emissions. By demanding developing country participation, Clinton seemed to be going back on the Berlin Mandate to which the United States had already agreed.[124] This was especially galling since the American negotiators were refusing to take seriously the EU proposal of 15% reductions from the 1990 baseline by 2010, and acting as if Clinton's proposal was a "take it or leave it" offer. Adding to the chaos, the American negotiator Timothy Wirth abruptly resigned and was replaced by Stuart Eizenstat, a veteran of the Carter administration with no particular expertise in the environment. Eizenstat immediately began to talk tough, saying that criticisms of the US position were "wrong" and suggesting that if others did not yield it might not be possible to conclude a treaty in Kyoto.[125]

Indeed, after the first week of meetings in Kyoto it did appear that the negotiations were collapsing, but then the American administration made the strategic decision that the failure of the Kyoto Conference would be worse than signing a protocol that the United States would have difficulty fulfilling and no chance of ratifying. On December 8 Al Gore flew to Kyoto, and after reiterating the US position, he said:

> After talking with our negotiators this morning and after speaking on the telephone from here a short time ago with President Clinton, I am instructing our delegation right now to show increased negotiating flexibility if a comprehensive plan can be put in

[122] http://frwebgate.access.gpo.gov/cgi-bin/getpage.cgi?position=all&page=1408&dbname=1997_public_papers_vol2_misc. Retrieved July 12, 2013.

[123] See Leggett 2001: 279ff.

[124] However, this may have been wrong, since Clinton might have had in mind a particular parsing of "developing countries must participate in meeting the challenge of climate change" that would have left the Berlin Mandate intact. After all, this is the man who, when asked whether the statement that he and Monica Lewinsky had had "no sex of any kind in any manner, shape or form" was false, replied that "it depends on what the meaning of the word 'is' is." (http://jurist.law.pitt.edu/transcr.htm). Retrieved July 17, 2013.

[125] http://www.nytimes.com/1997/11/27/us/american-negotiator-hedges-over-climate-treaty-talks.html?scp=1&sq=eizenstat&st=nyt. Retrieved July 17, 2013.

place, one with realistic targets and timetables, market mechanisms, and the meaningful participation of key developing countries.[126]

On December 11, 1997, the Kyoto Protocol was adopted. The text was awkward, vague, and indeterminate about some important matters, but the United States had agreed to reduce its emissions of a basket of GHGs by 7% by 2008–2012 from the 1990 baseline. Developed country reductions overall would be 5.2%. Various flexibility mechanisms would be allowed, and the EU countries would be able to meet their obligations under the EU bubble. Developing countries would undertake no new commitments in the first commitment period. Indeed, a proposed article on voluntary developing country commitments was deleted from the final text because of a lack of consensus.

The controversy over climate change intensified in the United States after the adoption of the Kyoto Protocol. While the almost universal opposition of the business community to mandated emissions reductions fractured, the Republican-controlled Congress became even more oppositional, attaching riders to spending bills prohibiting the use of EPA funds "to develop, propose, or issue rules, regulations, decrees, or orders for the purpose of implementation, or in contemplation of implementation of the Kyoto Protocol."[127] Facing a bleak political landscape, the Clinton administration saw the path to Kyoto ratification and domestic action on climate change as running through developing country commitments, and they worked hard throughout 1998 to secure them. In November 1998, after Argentina and Kazakhstan agreed to accept emissions reduction obligations, the United States signed the Kyoto Protocol, though the President announced that he had no intention of submitting it to the Senate for ratification during his remaining two years in office.[128]

Europe, on the other hand, was moving to the left and environmental consciousness was surging. In June 1997 in France the Socialists came to power in coalition with the Communists and Greens. The next year in Germany a center-left coalition of the SPD and Greens came to power. The French delegation in Kyoto had been led by a Green Minister of the Environment. A Green Minister of the Environment from Germany would join her in the post-Kyoto negotiations.

---

[126] http://clinton3.nara.gov/WH/EOP/OVP/speeches/kyotofin.html. Retrieved July 18, 2013.

[127] As quoted in Cass 2006: 168. After Kyoto, corporations began abandoning the leading climate change denial lobbying organization, the Global Climate Coalition, leading to its closure in 2002, though some corporations (notably Exxon/Mobile) continue to fund such organizations (see http://www.dailykos.com/story/2010/7/21/25858/1649, retrieved July 18, 2013). In 1998 the moderate Pew Center on Climate Change was formed, subsequently becoming the Center for Climate and Energy Solutions, which now includes more than 30 (mostly Fortune 500) companies on its Business Environmental Leadership Council (BELC).

[128] http://www.sunsonline.org/trade/process/followup/1998/11160498.htm. Retrieved July 18, 2013. Nothing of much significance came from either of these commitments.

After disappointing meetings in 1998 and 1999, the sixth Conference of the Parties (COP 6) meeting in The Hague on November 13–25, 2000, was supposed to resolve and clarify differences of opinion and interpretation regarding the implementation of the Kyoto Protocol. However, the political landscape, which had never been auspicious, had become even more foreboding. The American presidential election had occurred on November 7, but would not be decided until December 12, when a Supreme Court ruling awarded the presidency to George W. Bush. Not only was a lame duck administration representing the United States in The Hague, but it was one that did not have a determinate successor. In the interstices between administrations, the American negotiators were mainly concerned to preserve and create opportunities for satisfying America's Kyoto obligations without imposing significant emissions reductions at home. The EU delegation in The Hague was led by French Green Party Minister of the Environment Dominique Voynet, later a candidate for President of the French Republic. The Europeans saw themselves as protecting the hard-won victories of Kyoto, which in their eyes were belated and minimal, against American attempts to chip away at them.

The Americans pushed hard in three places. First, Article 3.3 of the Kyoto Protocol specifies that "removal by sinks resulting from direct human-induced land use change and forest activities, limited to afforestation, reforestation and deforestation since 1990" would be credited against emissions.[129] Inspired by a 1998 paper that purported to show that North America had been a very large CO_2 sink during the last decade of the twentieth century, the United States argued that one-third of their emissions reductions had already been achieved.[130] The Europeans were not going to allow the United States to evade one-third of its emissions reduction commitments simply by watching trees grow, especially on the basis of sketchy and ill-understood science. Second, the Kyoto Protocol specifies three "flexible" mechanisms by which countries may achieve their targets: joint implementation, the Clean Development Mechanism, and emissions trading. However, the Protocol fails to quantify the extent to which a country's obligations can be satisfied by employing these mechanisms, though Article 17 of the Protocol does state that allowable emissions trading is "supplemental to domestic actions for the purpose of meeting quantified emission limitation and reduction commitments…"[131] The initial US position was that there should be no limits on the extent to which a nation's obligation could

---

[129] http://unfccc.int/resource/docs/convkp/kpeng.html. Retrieved July 18, 2013.

[130] See Cass 2006: 207. The paper in question is Fan, et al. 1998. Subsequent work indicated that this paper radically overestimated the North American carbon sink. See Schimel et al. 2000. In any case there is a strong case to be made for why this provision of the Kyoto Protocol is a mistake: (1) It is extremely difficult to do these calculations in a meaningful way; (2) carbon stored in trees will return to the atmosphere much more quickly than carbon stored in fossil fuels that are not burned; (3) no credit is given for preserving trees as opposed to planting them. See Section 7.1 and Bolin 2008: 161 for further discussion.

[131] http://unfccc.int/resource/docs/convkp/kpeng.html Retrieved July 18, 2013.

be met through emissions trading. The European Union was worried that since the emissions of Russia and other Soviet states had fallen greatly since 1990 as a consequence of the collapse of the Soviet Union, this "hot air" would be purchased by the United States, thus resulting in emissions that would not otherwise occur. Finally, the United States repeatedly and insistently pressed for developing country commitments, even though this question had supposedly been settled in Berlin and Kyoto. Each attempt was forcefully rejected by the G-77 and China.[132] There were several last-minute attempts to reach a compromise, but in the end the conference collapsed in mutual recriminations.[133] However, since UN conferences never fail but only achieve success to a greater or lesser degree, the meeting was suspended rather than closed.

It is easy to feel some sympathy for all the parties at the Hague Conference. The developing countries had contributed far less to the total atmospheric buildup of GHGs than the developed countries, and proportionately their per capita contributions were even lower than their total emissions. The developing countries were still waiting for the developed countries to live up to the obligations they assumed in Rio. From their point of view there was little reason to be anything but offended by the repeated attempts of the Americans to shift responsibility to them. According to Sani Daura, the spokesman at The Hague for the G77 and China, the conference failed because of competing economic interests in wealthy countries.[134] While the developing countries saw themselves largely as bystanders, the Europeans saw themselves as the only real advocates for taking the necessary steps to address climate change. At every step along the way, through both Republican and Democratic administrations, the United States had tried to weaken agreements and evade responsibility. While it was true that it would have been more difficult for the United States than the European Union to meet the Kyoto commitments, to a large extent this was because the United States had done virtually nothing to keep its 1992 promise to stabilize emissions in 2000 at 1990 levels. The United States arrived in The Hague with its CO_2 emissions having increased by more than

---

[132] http://www.fair.org/index.php?page=1058; http://www.newscientist.com/article/dn211-climate-talks-collapse.html (both retrieved July 18, 2013); Dickson 2000.

[133] After a late-night phone call between President Clinton and Prime Minister Blair, British Deputy Prime Minister John Prescott thought that he had facilitated a deal with the Americans and the Europeans, but while Dominique Voynet initially seemed to accept it on behalf of the EU, she rejected it a few hours later after all four Nordic environment ministers refused to agree. Returning to Britain, Prescott upbraided Voynet for getting "cold feet" on the deal, saying she was "exhausted and tired and could not understand the detail and then refused to accept it." Voynet struck back, accusing Mr. Prescott of being "shabby," "pathetic," and "macho." http://news.bbc.co.uk/2/hi/uk_news/politics/1043430.stm. Retrieved July 18, 2013.

[134] http://www.nytimes.com/2000/11/26/world/treaty-talks-fail-to-find-consensus-in-global-warming.html?scp=3&sq=andrew%20revkin&st=nyt&pagewanted=2. Retrieved July 18, 2013.

14% since 1990, while the European Union had reduced its carbon emissions by .5% over the same period.[135] Rather than acknowledging their failures and pledging to redouble their efforts, the Americans were seen as aggressive and adversarial negotiators trying to game the system. As in Kyoto, the United States spent most of The Hague Conference pushing for views that were almost universally regarded as unacceptable, and then showing great flexibility as the conference was breaking up.[136] By then trust had eroded, negotiators were exhausted, and not enough time remained to put together a deal that everyone fully understood. The Europeans were convinced that the final attempt at compromise, brokered by British Deputy Prime Minister John Prescott, would have legitimated increases of up to 7% in US emissions while conforming to the letter of the mandated 5.2% Kyoto reduction.[137] The Americans, on the other hand, were incensed by what they saw as EU hypocrisy and mendacity. The European Union was able to keep its Rio promise by appropriating East German "hot air" and, in effect, engaging in emissions trading within the EU bubble. Yet the European Union self-righteously condemned the Americans when they wanted to use the same approaches in meeting their obligations. It didn't help that halfway through the meeting French President Jacques Chirac denounced the United States by saying that "each American emits three times more greenhouse gases than a Frenchman."[138] Nor did it help when Chief American negotiator Frank Loy was hit in the face with a pie by a demonstrator.[139] Keeping the United States in the regime was essential for forging an effective response to climate change, and the brutal realities of American politics meant that the United States needed concessions from the Europeans and the developing countries in order to remain. In denying the United States these concessions, these other actors were showing that they cared less about addressing climate change than political posturing, and furthering their own immediate interests. At least this is how it looked to the Americans.[140]

In January 2001, George W. Bush assumed the American presidency. Two months later he repudiated the Kyoto Protocol and reversed his campaign promise to regulate

---

[135] http://www.eea.europa.eu/pressroom/newsreleases/greenhouse_gas_emission. Retrieved July 18, 2013.

[136] As Benito Muller remarks about the American negotiating style, "a willingness to accept as little as 13 per cent of one's original demand can be interpreted not only as bending over backwards at championship limbo-dancing levels, but also as having made an initial demand which not even audacious bazaar traders would dare making for fear of affronting their counterparts. Making large concessions in this situation…are likely not to be counted as *bona fide* compromises, but simply as confirmation of having tried to 'pull a fast one' in the first place." http://www.oxfordclimatepolicy.org/publications/documents/hague.pdf. Retrieved July 18, 2013.

[137] http://www.newscientist.com/article/dn211-climate-talks-collapse.html. Retrieved July 18, 2013.

[138] http://news.bbc.co.uk/2/hi/science/nature/1033002.stm. Retrieved July 31, 2013.

[139] http://www.commondreams.org/headlines/112200-04.htm. Retrieved 31, 2013.

[140] For overviews of why The Hague Conference failed, see Dessai 2001; Buchner 2001; and Grubb and Yamin 2001.

CO_2 under the Clean Air Act.[141] It was widely believed at the time (certainly by the Bush administration) that this would doom the Protocol. In order to come into force, the Protocol had to be ratified by at least 55 countries, which together were responsible for at least 55% of 1990 carbon emissions. Since the United States was responsible for more than 36% of 1990 carbon emissions, this meant that there were only two paths by which the Protocol could come into force. One path was to induce the United States to return to the fold; the other path was to ensure that every other significant emitter ratified the Protocol. Both paths implied the same approach: loosen the rules in order to make it as easy as possible for countries to satisfy their Kyoto obligations.

When the sixth Conference of the Parties (COP 6) resumed its meeting in Bonn in July 2001, the atmosphere was quite different from the previous session. Virtually everything that the United States had demanded in The Hague was agreed to in Bonn or in the subsequent seventh Conference of the Parties (COP 7) in Marrakech, Morocco, that met October 29 to November 10, 2001. The parties agreed that there would be no quantitative limit on the credit that a country could claim from the use of flexibility mechanisms such as emissions trading. Nor would there be an overall cap on the amount of credit that could be claimed for land-use activities that increase carbon sinks.[142] These concessions were only qualified by vague language requiring that domestic action must constitute a "significant element" in each country's efforts to meet its target.

Despite being offered everything that it had previously demanded, American opposition to the Kyoto Protocol was so ideologically driven that the United States would not return. Nor was the administration moved by the third IPCC report, released in May 2001, which stated that "[g]lobally it is very likely that the 1990s was the warmest decade, and 1998 was the warmest year" since records had been kept, and that "[t]here is new and stronger evidence that most of the warming observed over the last 50 years is attributable to human activities."[143] The Bush administration tried to counter the IPCC report by requesting a study from the NAS on "the greatest certainties and uncertainties" in climate science, and also asking (rather curiously) for "your views on whether there are any substantive differences between the IPCC Reports and the IPCC summaries."[144] The NAS published its report the next

[141] For the campaign promise, visit http://web.archive.org/web/20010111035000/http://www.georgebush.com/News/speeches/092900_energy.html. For its reversal, see http://www.nytimes.com/2001/03/14/politics/14EMIT.html?ex=1236744000&en=d89b9a9875ec6e86&ei=5070. Retrieved July 18, 2013.

[142] http://www.econ.cam.ac.uk/rstaff/grubb/publications/J36.pdf. Retrieved July 18, 2013.

[143] http://www.ipcc.ch/pdf/climate-changes-2001/synthesis-spm/synthesis-spm-en.pdf. Retrieved July 18, 2013.

[144] http://www.nap.edu/openbook.php?record_id=10139&page=27. Retrieved July 18, 2013. This last request was in response to climate change deniers who since the 1990 assesssment had been claiming that a cabal within the IPCC had in the summaries willfully mischaracterized the science that was reported in the full assessment in order to spur the world to act on climate change. Interestingly, Oreskes and Conway (2010:174–183) make similar charges regarding the 1983 NAS report, only they claim that the summary downplayed the significance of the threat from climate

month, affirming mainstream climate science and the integrity of the IPCC assessment process.[145]

In retrospect it is highly unlikely that the United States would ever have ratified the Kyoto Protocol. Even if the European Union had given the United States what it wanted in The Hague instead of waiting until the more intransigent Bush administration had taken power, the question of developing country commitments would have remained unaddressed. Since Rio the developing countries had been resolutely committed to the principle that developed countries should lead in addressing climate change, and they were not going to cave on this point in order to please any American administration. Without such commitments, most Democratic senators as well as virtually all Republicans would oppose ratification, however well the European Union was behaving.[146] In light of this, the only way the Kyoto Protocol could have come into force is if the Europeans could succeed in uniting the rest of the world around it. Remarkably, this is what they succeeded in doing.

The European Union and its Member States ratified the Kyoto Protocol in May 2002. The "55 parties" clause was satisfied on May 23, 2002, when Iceland ratified the Protocol. Russia's ratification on November 18, 2004, satisfied the "55% of emissions" clause and brought the treaty into force on February 16, 2005.[147] As of May 2012, 191 countries have ratified the Protocol, representing 63.9% of 1990 emissions by Annex I countries (virtually all of the rest of the emissions were by the US).[148]

When the Kyoto Protocol was first adopted it was often said (especially in the US and Britain) that it could not successfully be implemented. This claim was even more ubiquitous after the US renounced the Protocol. Once the Protocol came into force it was commonly said that parties could not keep their commitments. It appears that this claim is also false and that the parties to the Protocol will meet their obligations. The total GHG emissions produced by industrialized countries with a Kyoto target will probably be about 16% lower than in the base year 1990, vastly exceeding their target of a 4.2% reduction. When as yet uncompleted projects involving the Clean Development Mechanism are included, the total reduction will be even greater. What largely accounts for this success in meeting the targets is the collapse in emissions in Russia and the other "economies in transition." Even so, in the 15 European countries that comprised the European Union when the Kyoto Protocol was adopted in 1997, emissions were nearly 5% lower in 2010 than they

change. There are interesting issues regarding the relations between scientific assessments and how they are summarized and reported to policy-makers. For discussion, see Glantz et al. 1985.

[145] http://www8.nationalacademies.org/onpinews/newsitem.aspx?RecordID=10139. Retrieved July 18, 2013.

[146] Americans have a deep-seated fear of being exploited by developing countries. I suspect the roots of this fear in its present form go back at least to the US failure in Viet Nam.

[147] The story of Russian ratification is interesting, instructive, and well told in Bolin 2008: 187–190.

[148] http://unfccc.int/kyoto_protocol/status_of_ratification/items/2613.php. Retrieved July 18, 2013.

were in 1990.[149] Compare this to the United States, which is not a party to the Kyoto Protocol, where emissions in 2010 were 5% greater than in 1990.[150]

It is difficult to know whether, and if so to what extent and in what way, the Kyoto Protocol was responsible for these reductions. The social, economic, and political dynamics are complex and historical counterfactuals are difficult. It is frequently said that "Climate policy, as it has been understood and practiced by many governments of the world under the Kyoto Protocol approach, has failed to produce any discernable real world reductions in emissions of greenhouse gases in fifteen years."[151] However, according to the Netherlands Environmental Assessment Agency, "…climate and energy policy has contributed to this trend in emissions. Analysis shows that without policy measures, emissions would have been 5 to 10% higher."[152] It is possible that these (or even more effective) policy measures would have been implemented without the Kyoto Protocol. However, this seems unlikely, especially when we compare the performance of the parties to the Protocol to that of the major emitter that is not a party. Whatever the efficacy of the Kyoto Protocol, it should be remembered that the share of global GHG emissions by countries with a Kyoto commitment was only 30% in 1990, and by 2005 that share had shrunk to about 20%. It is difficult for the regime to be fully effective when the world's largest emitter (China) has no emission targets under the Protocol, and the world's second-largest emitter is not even a party.[153]

During the Bush years, American climate policy remained incoherent but in a somewhat different way from the Clinton years. The Bush administration was caught between climate change deniers, who formed the backbone of its base and were well represented in the administration, and those who thought the issue was important but wanted an alternative to an international regime centered on targets and timetables. The Bush administration never succeeded in articulating a plausible alternative to the Kyoto Protocol. It wobbled between failed attempts to do so and

[149] http://www.pbl.nl/sites/default/files/cms/publicaties/C02%20Mondiaal_%20webdef_19sept.pdf. Retrieved July 18, 2013; for an update visit http://www.iccgov.org/FilePagineStatiche/Files/Publications/Reflections/12_Reflection_December_2012.pdf. Retrieved July 18, 2013.

[150] Calculated from http://www.pbl.nl/sites/default/files/cms/publicaties/C02%20Mondiaal_%20webdef_19sept.pdf. Retrieved July 18, 2013. Also visit http://www.nicholas.duke.edu/thegreengrok/kyoto/?searchterm=None. Retrieved July 18, 2013.

[151] This quotation is from the Executive Summary (p. 5) of The Hartwell Paper, A New Direction for Climate Policy after the Crash of 2009, available at http://www.lse.ac.uk/collections/mackinderProgramme/theHartwellPaper/. Retrieved July 18, 2013. A similar claim is made by Barrett (2003: 38, 399).

[152] http://www.pbl.nl/en/news/pressreleases/2007/20071211Industrialisedcountriestocollectivelymeet2010Kyototarget.html. Retrieved July 18, 2013.

[153] Aichele and Felbermayron (2012) argue that, on average, Kyoto has caused some domestic emissions savings, but that it has also caused increased net imports of carbon so that the carbon footprint of countries has not changed. Carbon leakage due to the Protocol's incomplete coverage has therefore neutralized emission savings. See also http://www.lse.ac.uk/collections/mackinderProgramme/theHartwellPaper/. Retrieved July 18, 2013.

denying the reality or seriousness of the problem, depending on who was staffing what agencies and what happened to be the pressures of the day. Like Clinton, what Bush wanted most of all was for this issue to go away.[154]

As in the previous decade and before, public attention and concern waxed and waned during the Bush years, but on the whole the American public remained relatively unconcerned about climate change. However, there were regional differences, and some states and municipalities (notably California, New York, and Seattle) began to fill some of the void left by the lack of a national climate policy.[155]

Then came 2007, which like 1988 was one of those years in which climate change became a major focus of attention. If the events of the year could be said to have a single message, it was that the seriousness of the problem could no longer be denied and quick action could still make a difference.

The IPCC released its fourth assessment report in 2007, rolling it out in installments, with major media events in February, April, May, and November. On February 2, the "Summary for Policymakers" of the first volume on "The Scientific Basis" was released at a press conference in Paris. The lead from the *New York Times* was a fairly restrained example of the sort of coverage that this event received all over the world:

> In a bleak and powerful assessment of the future of the planet, the leading international network of climate change scientists has concluded for the first time that global warming is "unequivocal" and that human activity is the main driver, "very likely" causing most of the rise in temperatures since 1950. They said the world is already committed to centuries of warming, shifting weather patterns and rising seas, resulting from the buildup of gases in the atmosphere that trap heat. But the warming can be substantially blunted by prompt action, the panel of scientists said in a report released here today.[156]

The British newspaper *The Guardian* summed up the message in a single sentence:

> The world's scientists yesterday gave their starkest warning yet that a failure to cut greenhouse gas emissions will bring devastating climate change within a few decades.[157]

On February 25 Al Gore won an Academy Award for his film *An Inconvenient Truth*. This film was the fifth-highest-grossing documentary in American movie

---

[154] For a timeline of Bush statements on climate change, visit http://uk.reuters.com/article/idUKN2321387820070924. Retrieved July 18, 2013.

[155] Some of this is surveyed in Farber 2013.

[156] http://www.nytimes.com/2007/02/02/science/earth/02cnd-climate.html. Retrieved July 18, 2013.

[157] http://www.guardian.co.uk/environment/2007/feb/03/frontpagenews.greenpolitics. Retrieved July 18, 2013.

history. At the award ceremony in Los Angeles, Gore made a brief speech that was seen by several hundred million people around the world:

> We need to solve the climate crisis, it's not a political issue, it's a moral issue. We have everything we need to get started, with the possible exception of the will to act, that's a renewable resource, let's renew it.[158]

On April 2 the US Supreme Court issued a surprising setback to the Bush administration. As we discussed earlier, in the 2000 presidential campaign George W. Bush had promised to regulate CO_2 under the Clean Air Act, only to renege on this promise after having taken office in 2001. In 2003 the administration went further when US EPA reversed a 1998 decision of the Clinton administration and declared that it had no authority to regulate CO_2 under the Clean Air Act. Bush's EPA went on to say that even if it had the authority to regulate it would refrain from exercising it. The state of Massachusetts, along with several other states, cities, and environmental organizations, went to court to challenge this decision. After several years of litigation, the US Supreme Court decided that US EPA did have the authority to regulate CO_2 under the Clean Air Act, and that the rationale it had given for why it would not regulate even if it had such authority was inadequate. The Court ordered the agency to reconsider the question of whether it should in fact regulate CO_2 under the Clean Air Act.[159]

In addition to splashing the climate change issue over the front page of American newspapers, the Court decision highlighted the political machinations of the Bush administration in their attempts to quash the climate change issue. In 2003 a memo from political consultant Frank Luntz outlining a Republican strategy for dealing with climate change was leaked to the press. According to Luntz,

> **The scientific debate is closing [against us] but not yet closed. There is still a window of opportunity to challenge the science.**... Therefore, **you need to continue to make the lack of scientific certainty a primary issue in the debate.**[160]

Subsequent administration actions seemed to be right out of the Luntz playbook. There were reports going back to 2004 of Bush political appointees attempting to censor or silence James Hansen and other government scientists. In 2005 a story had broken about Phillip Cooney, Chief of Staff of the President's CEQ, editing scientific

[158] http://thecaucus.blogs.nytimes.com/2007/02/25/gore-wins-hollywood-in-a-landslide/. Retrieved July 18, 2013.

[159] http://www.supremecourt.gov/opinions/06pdf/05-1120.pdf. Retrieved July 18, 2013. Other relevant documents are available at http://web.law.columbia.edu/climate-change. Retrieved July 18, 2013.

[160] The bold is in the original memo which can be viewed at http://www.motherjones.com/files/LuntzResearch_environment.pdf. Retrieved October 24, 2013. I discuss this memo in the context of organized denial in Section 3.5.

reports from government agencies in order to cast doubt on climate science and to minimize the potential impacts of climate change. Cooney had come to the White House from his position as a lobbyist for the American Petroleum Institute, and after being forced to resign he joined Exxon/Mobil.[161]

In September 2007, UN Secretary-General Ban Ki-moon brought together representatives from nearly 160 countries, including more than 70 heads of state, in order to jump-start discussions regarding the successor agreement to the Kyoto Protocol. Ban Ki-moon told his audience that the time for doubt was past and that the failure to act would be devastating.[162]

On October 12 the announcement came from Norway that the 2007 Nobel Peace Prize would be awarded jointly to the IPCC and Albert Arnold (Al) Gore Jr. "for their efforts to build up and disseminate greater knowledge about man-made climate change, and to lay the foundations for the measures that are needed to counteract such change."[163] The prize was presented in Oslo on December 10, midway through the COP 13 meeting in Bali, which was convened to launch negotiations for a new post-Kyoto climate change treaty.

The news from Bali was all too familiar. Officials from the UN, backed by the European Union and many developing countries, offered a plan for talks over the next two years, including a statement that dangerous warming can be avoided only if by 2020 industrialized countries cut emissions by 25–40% from 1990 levels. The United States rejected any language implying targets and timetables. According to Chief US negotiator Harlan Watson, deciding such matters is "what the negotiations are going to be for." Secretary-General Ban Ki-moon tried to inject a sense of urgency into the conference, saying that "[t]he situation is so desperately serious that any delay could push us past the tipping point, beyond which the ecological, financial and human costs would increase dramatically." He went on to say that countries have a choice between a comprehensive agreement or "oblivion."[164] For the first time, developing countries committed to "nationally appropriate mitigation actions...in the context of sustainable development, supported and enabled by technology, financing and capacity-building, in a measurable, reportable and verifiable manner." American representative Paula Dobriansky responded by telling delegates that the United States was "not willing to accept" language calling on industrialized nations to deliver "measurable, reportable and verifiable" assistance. Her statement sparked boos and hisses from the audience, sharp rebukes from representatives of developing countries, and no expressions of support from any allies.[165] The United States finally yielded on this point, and the Bali Road Map was adopted by consensus.

[161] Bowen 2007.

[162] http://www.nytimes.com/2007/09/25/world/25nations.html. Retrieved July 18, 2013. President Bush only showed up for dinner, even though the meeting was in New York.

[163] http://nobelprize.org/nobel_prizes/peace/laureates/2007/. Retrieved July 18, 2013.

[164] http://www.nytimes.com/2007/12/12/world/12climate.html. Retrieved July 18, 2013.

[165] http://www.washingtonpost.com/wp-dyn/content/article/2007/12/15/AR2007121500471_2. html?sid=ST2007121500591. Retrieved July 18, 2013.

However, the Bali Road Map was little more than an acknowledgment of the scientific realities with which the IPCC had confronted political leaders and a general agreement about what would have to be done, including "quantified emission limitation and reduction objectives, by all developed country Parties."[166] Nothing was said about the scale of the effort required or about who was committed to what by when. Like the Berlin Mandate, the Bali Road Map was essentially an agreement to come to an agreement with respect to some vaguely stated goals by a stipulated deadline. The Bali Action Plan, part of the Road Map, specified a two-year negotiating process that would proceed on two tracks. One track would discuss "long-term cooperative action" under the FCCC and the United States would participate as a party to the Convention. The other track would discuss the second commitment period under the Kyoto Protocol in which the United States would participate only as an observer. Negotiations would be concluded at the UN Climate Conference–COP 15 meeting in Copenhagen, December 7–18, 2009.

Ironically, in the wake of all of this activity and the release of the fourth IPCC report, Americans became more uncertain about the facts of climate change. From January 2007 through April 2008 the fraction of people who said that there is "solid evidence" of global warming declined from 77% to 71%, while the size of the minority who said that there is such a warming and that it is due to human activity remained the same at 47%. Apparently, in 2007 Americans came to see global warming increasingly as a political issue and much of the decline in belief in climate change occurred among Republicans (though there were small declines among Democrats and independents as well). What Republicans and Democrats shared was the belief that climate change is a low-priority issue. Republicans ranked it dead last on a list of 21 issues, independents ranked it 18th, and for Democrats it was 15th behind middle-class taxes, crime, and the budget deficit.[167]

In January 2009 a new American administration took office. It was committed both to engaging constructively in the international negotiations to establish a post-Kyoto climate regime, and to reducing emissions domestically through various policy interventions including the establishment of a cap and trade system. The lesson that it took from the Clinton administration's failure with the Kyoto Protocol was the importance of linking international and domestic policy. The Obama administration was not going to make international commitments that it could not ratify or achieve at home.

---

[166] unfccc.int/files/meetings/cop_13/application/.../cp_bali_action.pdf. Retrieved July 18, 2013.

[167] http://people-press.org/report/417/a-deeper-partisan-divide-over-global-warming. Retrieved July 18, 2013. The 2009 survey indicates an uptick in belief both in global warming (85%) and that it is caused by humans (49%). See http://people-press.org/report/?pageid=1550. Retrieved July 18, 2013. How questions are asked is extremely important. For discussion, see http://woods.stanford.edu/research/polls-underestimate.html. Retrieved July 18, 2013. See Section 3.7 for further discussion of the partisan divide in American politics over climate change.

Expectations were high for the new American administration, and became higher still when on October 9 the Nobel Committee announced that it was awarding the Nobel Peace Prize to President Obama for "for his extraordinary efforts to strengthen international diplomacy and cooperation between peoples," noting in particular that "[t]hanks to Obama's initiative, the USA is now playing a more constructive role in meeting the great climatic challenges the world is confronting."[168] Despite (or perhaps partially because of) the Peace Prize, the United States went to Copenhagen in December 2009 with several disadvantages. Besides electing a new president who spoke about the challenge of climate change in a different way, the Americans had done little to convince the world beyond Oslo that it was serious about addressing the problem. The administration had had less than a year to engage with the international process before Copenhagen, and the negotiations that did occur appear to have been badly managed. Furthermore, the previous summer Obama had identified health care reform as his highest legislative priority, and it is difficult for an American government to engage more than one large issue at a time.

Making things worse, the climate change denial campaign escalated once again. Less than three weeks before the Copenhagen meeting opened, e-mails were hacked from the Climate Research Unit at the University of East Anglia in the United Kingdom and posted on a climate change denial website. The *New York Times* quoted prominent climate change deniers, including Patrick Michaels, who said, "this is not a smoking gun; this is a mushroom cloud."[169] The story was picked up by all the major media and was quickly dubbed "climategate."[170] Prominent climate scientists were charged with fabricating research results, misrepresenting data, and trying to destroy the careers of scientists who disagreed with them. Death threats spiked against climate scientists. Even some advocates for aggressive action on climate change announced their disappointment, and endorsed some of the charges that were being made.[171] Finally, months later, after nine separate investigations, the scientists were exonerated. No one who was involved in stealing the e-mails, making them public, or threatening the scientists has been brought to justice. One lesson of climategate is that scientists can behave like mean-spirited little boys engaging in black humor, but the denialists play for keeps. Some in the media acknowledged that

---

[168] http://www.nobelprize.org/nobel_prizes/peace/laureates/2009/press.html. Retrieved July 18, 2013.

[169] http://www.nytimes.com/2009/11/21/science/earth/21climate.html. Retrieved July 18, 2013.

[170] There is now a climate denial website, http://www.climategate.com/ (retrieved July 18, 2013) whose goal is to "provide a daily dose of information regarding the world's greatest scam, climategate, and other information and news to help you in your battle against the Religion of Settled Science to dispute their views on Anthropogenic Global Warming, and in addition, to battle the one-world socialist agenda, which is the movement's leaders' real goal." We are also helpfully told that "[t]his site/domain name will entertain offers for sale in the low to mid $xx, xxx range" (see http://www.climategate.com/about). Retrieved July 18, 2013.

[171] http://www.guardian.co.uk/environment/georgemonbiot/2009/nov/25/monbiot-climate-l eak-crisis-response. Retrieved July 18, 2013.

this had been a "highly orchestrated, manufactured scandal," but the damage had already been done.[172] Climategate was not the bullet that killed Copenhagen, but it was one of the thousand cuts.[173]

The divisions that have haunted climate change negotiations from the beginning hardened, and they fractured even further in Copenhagen. The United States was at odds with the European Union, and the North was in conflict with the South. AOSIS, led by Tuvalu, demanded rigorous, legally binding commitments that almost no one was willing to accept. Rifts occurred between large developing countries such as China and Brazil and others in the G-77. Countries such as Venezuela, Nicaragua, and Bolivia became increasingly rejectionist. The two negotiating tracks were never successfully brought together, with many developing countries demanding that any agreement had to be within the purview of the Kyoto Protocol, a condition that could not be satisfied by the United States. New disputes broke out about how to verify national claims about emission reductions, and about the transparency and inclusiveness of the negotiating process.

President Obama remained non-committal about whether he would go to Copenhagen until November 25, when the White House issued a statement confirming his attendance and stating the US position. The United States would reduce emissions 17% by 2020 from a 2005 baseline, and also affirm as "goals" and "provisional targets" reductions of 30% by 2025, 42% by 2030, and 83% by 2050.[174]

The President arrived on the morning of the final day of the conference, going immediately into negotiations with a select group of world leaders, and then emerging for a plenary address. His speech seemed mainly addressed to Americans rather than to the conference delegates, who remained skeptical of American good faith. Obama began by acknowledging American responsibility, but in a way that seemed grudgingly tautological: "As the world's largest economy and the world's second largest emitter, America bears our share of responsibility in addressing climate change." He went on to boast of a record that many find altogether lacking if not downright pathetic, mentioning "our leadership within international climate negotiations," and claiming that "bold action" had been taken at home. All this, he said, was "ambitious," and he went on to restate the commitment to the emissions

[172] http://www.newsweek.com/blogs/the-gaggle/2010/06/25/newspapers-retract-climategate-claims-but-damage-still-done.html. Retrieved July 18, 2013. See also http://www.cjr.org/the_observatory/wanted_climate_frontpager.php. Retrieved July 18, 2013.

[173] http://environment.yale.edu/climate/publications/climategate-public-opinion-and-the-loss-of-trust/?utm_source=effects+of+climategate&utm_medium=email&utm_campaign=effects+of+climate+gate. Retrieved July 18, 2013. For a full account see Pearce 2010. For the story by one of the protagonists, see Mann 2012. An academic literature has begun to unfold regarding climategate. See, e.g., Wiley Interdisciplinary Reviews: Climate Change, Volume 3, Issue 3 (May/June 2012), available on the web at http://wires.wiley.com/WileyCDA/WiresIssue/wisId-WCC_3_3.html, and Lahsen 2013.

[174] http://www.whitehouse.gov/the-press-office/president-attend-copenhagen-climate-talks. Retrieved July 18, 2013.

reductions that had been made in the White House statement.[175] The speech was not well received. A 17% emissions reduction by 2020 from a 2005 baseline is equivalent to a 4% reduction from the 1990 baseline, by far the weakest offer of any developed country (except Canada, which offered a 3% reduction). By contrast, the European Union was offering a 20–30% reduction.

After his speech Obama went back to negotiations and shortly before midnight, the Copenhagen Accord was unveiled. Draft texts of hundreds of pages negotiated over two years were replaced by a declaration of two and a half pages that went through several drafts, each thinner and vaguer than the one before. References to emission cuts in developed countries of 50% by 2050 and 80% were dropped, reportedly at the insistence of China.[176] The final text was an agreement negotiated behind closed doors by the United States, China, Brazil, South Africa, and India, and supported by about 20 other countries including Ethiopia and the European Union. After the press conference announcing the Accord, Obama flew back to the United States, while the Accord received a tumultuous reception from angry delegates. Rather than adopting or rejecting the Accord, the Convention finally agreed to "take note" of it. The Accord was denounced by most environmental organizations, except those based in the United States. The executive director of Greenpeace UK declared that "the city of Copenhagen is a crime scene tonight, with the guilty men and women fleeing to the airport."[177]

The Copenhagen Accord is a short document that begs even more questions than has been the norm in the climate negotiations.[178] It "recogniz[es] the scientific view that the increase in global temperature should be below 2 degrees Celsius." Developed countries are required to submit their 2020 emissions targets by January 31, 2010. Developing countries "will implement mitigation actions" and report on them in national communications every two years. There are provisions for "international consultations and analysis under clearly defined guidelines that will ensure that national sovereignty is respected." Developed countries have a "collective commitment" to provide "new and additional resources…approaching USD 30 billion" to support mitigation and adaptation in developing countries, and have "set a goal of mobilizing jointly $100bn a year by 2020 to address the needs of developing countries." The Accord will be reviewed in 2015.[179]

---

[175] http://www.huffingtonpost.com/2009/12/18/obama-in-copenhagen-speec_n_396836.html. Retrieved July 18, 2013.

[176] http://www.guardian.co.uk/environment/2009/dec/22/copenhagen-climate-change-mark-lynas. Retrieved July 18, 2013. For more on the process, see Dimitrov 2010.

[177] http://news.bbc.co.uk/2/hi/science/nature/8421910.stm. Retrieved July 18, 2013. For a humorous but just as chilling account, visit http://www.youtube.com/watch?v=3_RlKxz_ymQ. Retrieved July 18, 2013.

[178] The text can be found at http://unfccc.int/home/items/5262.php. Retrieved July 18, 2013.

[179] For commentary on the provisions, see Bodansky 2010.

Thus far, 141 countries have agreed to the Accord, including many developing countries.[180] For them the main incentive is access to the promised pots of money in return for assuming only vague obligations. Developed countries have registered their emissions targets. They are in different forms and it is not easy to understand their full effects even if implemented. Some commitments are contingent on legally binding global agreements while others are contingent on various kinds of credits, in many cases relating to land management and forestry. Current analyses suggest that even if all commitments are kept, there is very little chance that global warming will be kept under 2°C and a very good chance that it will be greater than 3°C, and a 20% chance that it will be greater than 4°C.[181]

After the breakup of the Copenhagen Conference there were competing narratives about who was to blame: China, the United States, or even the Danes. As always in the climate negotiations, each side had a case to make. From the perspective of China and India, global limits on emissions without aggressive, mandatory reductions on the part of developed countries risk locking them into their relatively low per capita emissions. They fear that developed countries will continue to evade significant reductions in emissions, but the global target will be taken seriously and so developing countries will increasingly bear the burden. From their perspective the developed countries have from the beginning attempted to shift the burden of reducing emissions to developing countries. Without commitments to significant emission reductions by the United States, it is understandable that India and China were not willing to agree to targets. Without domestic legislation, President Obama had little to bring to the negotiating table. The Chinese case looks even more reasonable if we compare the pledges that China and the United States have made under the Copenhagen Accord. As Figure 2.1 shows, China has historically emitted less

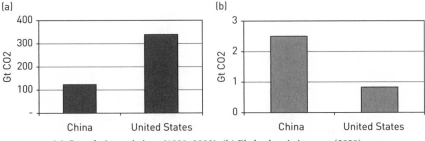

FIGURE 2.1 (a) Cumulative emissions (1900–2009); (b) Pledged emissions cut (2020).

[180] http://www.usclimatenetwork.org/policy/copenhagen-accord-commitments. Retrieved July 18, 2013. For details, visit http://unfccc.int/meetings/copenhagen_dec_2009/items/5262.php. Retrieved July 18, 2013.
[181] http://www.climateactiontracker.org/; http://www.pik-potsdam.de/news/press-releases/4-degrees-briefing-for-the-world-bank-the-risks-of-a-future-without-climate-policy. Both retrieved July 18, 2013.

than the United States, and yet it has pledged to cut more emissions than the United States under the Copenhagen Accord.[182]

President Obama's commitment to going no further internationally than he can go domestically is in many ways both wise and admirable. However, the fact is that the domestic American politics of climate change are quite different from the international politics of the issue. Climate change denial has increasingly become a core commitment of the Republican Party, and when this is combined with the difficult regional politics of GHG mitigation and the peculiarities of the American political system, Obama's approach risks making progress on global climate hostage to the worst 34 members of the US Senate (a dishonor for which there is a great deal of competition).[183] The centerpiece of Obama's domestic climate policy, an economy-wide cap and trade system, died without coming to a vote in the US Senate, even though it had passed in the House of Representatives. The prospects for any federal climate legislation are bleak for the foreseeable future. What is left is a "glorious mess": federal regulations, court decisions, state and local actions, consumer boycotts, acts of civil disobedience, and so on.[184] No one can say how effective this jerry-rigged system will be for reducing carbon emissions.

Internationally, the result is further erosion of confidence in America's ability to engage meaningfully with climate change. This further endangers relationships that need to be built and nurtured, yet are already fraying. Copenhagen showed how many and deep are the fissures within the human community on this issue. Even agreements that were once accepted are increasingly being questioned.

With the United States crippled by its lack of an effective domestic policy, international climate negotiations will increasingly resemble the protracted trench warfare of the Doha talks on world trade.[185] Diplomats will diplomatize and talking heads

---

[182] This graph is taken from "After Copenhagen: On being sadder but wiser, China, and justice as the way forward," available at http://www.ecoequity.org/2010/01/after-copenhagen/. Retrieved July 18, 2013. Since China has been aggressively reducing energy intensity in recent years, it is not entirely clear how much of the pledged emissions reductions are departures from business as usual, or even how we should assess them if they are not.

[183] Compare the bland statement from the 2008 Republican platform quoted below with recent climate change denial comments by Republican leaders: "The same human economic activity that has brought freedom and opportunity to billions has also increased the amount of carbon in the atmosphere. While the scope and long-term consequences of this are the subject of ongoing scientific research, common sense dictates that the United States should take measured and reasonable steps today to reduce any impact on the environment." http://www.conservapedia.com/Global_warming. Retrieved July 18, 2013.

[184] One of the arguments for cap and trade was to create a systematic approach to reducing carbon that would create stable expectations for business. Congressman Dingell from Michigan, who supported cap and trade after opposing action on climate change for many years, warned that a "glorious mess" would be the result of the failure to act; see http://e360.yale.edu/content/feature.msp?id=2299. Retrieved July 18, 2013. At least lawyers should be happy with the result. For a snapshot of the legal environment, visit http://www.climatecasechart.com/. Retrieved July 18, 2013.

[185] The Doha Round has been in progress since 2001 and has been stalled since 2008.

will talk, and all of this will seem very important to those whose job it is to track very important events, but will have little effect on anyone else or on the atmosphere. Diplomacy will continue because the climate regime is too big to fail and because the UN only has successes (though they come in different sizes). Climate diplomacy will increasingly become a zombie exercise. Bodies and mouths will move, but the real action will be elsewhere. Some countries will reduce emissions, largely due to domestic political or economic considerations. Bilateral relationships, such as that between the United States and China, will continue to be important, but increasingly concerns about climate change will be subordinated to negotiations over trade, currency, security, and so on.

After 20 years of climate diplomacy, the undeniable fact is that the three main factors that have reduced GHG emissions are, in increasing importance: global recession, the collapse of communism, and China's one child policy. The Rio dream is over.

2.4. CONCLUDING REMARKS

In this chapter I have told the story of the development of climate science, the rise of climate change as a public issue, and the age of climate change diplomacy.

In many ways the first part of the story is unexceptional. The development of climate science has been similar to the development of other sciences: incremental contributions from many people, punctuated by occasional new insights and perspectives, often enabled by the applications of innovative technologies.

In some ways the second part of the story is unexceptional as well. Climate becomes an issue of public concern because science reveals looming threats to humanity. When it becomes increasingly apparent that these threats originate in human behavior, science collides with economic and political power. This creates opportunities for scientific entrepreneurs who are eager to promote the science and to display its relevance. Men such as Roger Revelle, Joseph Smagorinsky, Gordon McDonald, and others provide the sinews of the story, threading themselves through various committees and agencies, wrapping themselves in ever greater authority as they make the case for the importance of their field. This too is normal, and similar stories can be told about the rise of nuclear physics, genetics, and other fields.

What is important for our purposes is that this story does not have a happy ending. By the 1960s scientists had expressed concerns about the possibility of an anthropogenic climate change to presidents of both parties. At the Rio Earth Summit in 1992 the industrialized countries seemed to agree that by 2000 they would stabilize their GHG emissions at 1990 levels. Yet global emissions are still increasing, the atmospheric concentration of carbon dioxide is now almost 10% greater than it was in 1992, we have already experienced a warming of .8°C, and there is no end in sight.[186] The underlying drivers continue to increase and intensify: population, consumption, and land transformation. We are already committed to changes that for all practical purposes are irreversible.[187] Each day we act so as to make these changes deeper, and increase their velocity and the risks they impose.

In the next chapter we will consider some of the reasons that we have failed to address climate change. However, it is sobering to be reminded that this failure was anticipated more than a half century ago:

> Two reporters who spoke with scientists in 1957 sketched out some striking implications of the greenhouse effect. If it ever became certain that CO_2 was warming the planet, they wrote, we would see "a type of control regulation, law, interstate compact, and international agreement which could scarcely help clashing with some of our cherished notions of free enterprise. Industry, which might blossom in some directions…would be hamstrung in others.…Further, in view of the global nature of the problem, ordinary international agreements might prove inadequate for effective regulation." But an international regime that imposed actual penalties would be "sure to foster great heat and controversy."[188]

---

[186] CO_2 concentrations are calculated from data provided by the Mauna Loa Observatory, and the latter number is an extrapolation from IPCC's *Climate Change 2007: Synthesis Report Summary for Policymakers*, p. 2 which says the earth has warmed. 72°C over the last century.

[187] See a pair of recent papers by Susan Solomon and colleagues (2009 and 2010).

[188] http://www.aip.org/history/climate/Govt.htm#M_24_. Retrieved July 18, 2013. Weart references Yeager and Stark 1958.

3 Obstacles to Action

As we saw in the previous chapter, much has been known about climate change for quite a long time. The President of the United States first spoke about this issue nearly half a century ago, yet little meaningful action has been taken. This chapter discusses the reasons for this failure.

One explanation, urged by the historians Naomi Oreskes and Erick Conway and the anthropologist Myanna Lahsen, appeals to political and cultural divisions both within the scientific community and in the larger society.[1] While this is surely part of the story, there are also features of the problem that make it extraordinarily difficult to address. Climate change poses threats that are probabilistic, multiple, indirect, often invisible, and unbounded in space and time. Fully grasping these threats requires scientific understanding and technical skills that are often in short supply. Moreover, climate change can be seen as presenting us with the largest collective action problem that humanity has ever faced, one that has both intra- and inter-generational dimensions. Evolution did not design us to deal with such problems, and we have not designed political institutions that are conducive to solving them.

In this chapter I explore these factors. I begin by discussing scientific ignorance and the politicization of science. Next I discuss the relations between facts and values, the interface between science and policy, and organized denial. I go on to highlight systemic failures in our political systems, focusing in particular on the problems of American democracy. I conclude with a discussion of what I consider to be the most difficult obstacle of all—the fact that our biological endowment makes it difficult for us to solve or even to recognize this kind of problem.

3.1. SCIENTIFIC IGNORANCE

In 1956 the British scientist and novelist C. P. Snow published an article called "The Two Cultures," in which he argued that the British educational system had produced a political and cultural elite, educated in the humanities, that was quite ignorant and even contemptuous of science.[2] This sparked a discussion that has never quite abated.

---

[1] Oreskes and Conway 2010; Lahsen 1999, 2005, 2008.
[2] The article was later expanded into a book, Snow 1960.

There is no question that the "two cultures" are alive and well in the United States. There are self-confessed science nerds who seem never to have read a book (except perhaps a science fiction novel), and there are brilliant humanities scholars who shiver at the sight of numbers.

The "two cultures" problem is especially dramatic when it comes to the world of policy. In the 113th Congress (in session from 2013–2015), there were only three Ph.D. scientists among the 435 members of the US House of Representatives and none in the United States Senate (no sitting US Senator has earned a Ph.D. in any subject). By comparison, 57% of senators (57) and nearly 40% of representatives (169) have law degrees, this in a country in which .003% of the general population has law degrees.[3]

Scientists and policy-makers have different educational backgrounds and paths to success and survival. For scientists it is tenure, grant proposals, and peer-reviewed publications. For policy-makers it is winning elections or functioning well in bureaucratic settings. People with different skills are attracted to each profession, and these differences are accentuated through experience.

This often leads to a lack of mutual understanding and respect. While scientists tend to view themselves as the voice of reason in an irrational world, policy-makers often see scientists as naïve and narcissistic, fixated on their own parochial issues and oblivious to everything else. From a policy-maker's perspective, scientists are another interest group: disproportionately white, affluent, and primarily residing in Democratic zip codes.

One result of the "two cultures" problem in the United States is that it is easy to find scientific ignorance among both the plain and powerful.

A revealing example of elite scientific ignorance was on display in the Supreme Court during the oral arguments in *Massachusetts versus EPA*.[4] After being gently corrected for confusing the troposphere with the stratosphere, Justice Scalia replied, "Troposphere. Whatever. I told you before I'm not a scientist." As laughter swept the courtroom, Scalia added, "That's why I don't want to have to deal with global warming, to tell you the truth."[5] Justice Scalia's scientific ignorance is sad but not surprising. What is truly disturbing was his indifference to his ignorance, and his stated desire to ignore an important problem because it has a scientific dimension. Even worse, Scalia was correct in surmising that his attitudes would be widely and sympathetically shared among his audience of lawyers, students, journalists, and others. Imagine a Supreme Court justice expressing comparable ignorance and attitudes

---

[3] http://www.fas.org/sgp/crs/misc/R42964.pdf. Retrieved July 18, 2013. The three Ph.D. scientists in the House included two physicists (Holt, Foster) and one mathematician (McNerney); all were Democrats.

[4] This was the case in which the Supreme Court ruled that US EPA had the authority to regulate CO_2 under the Clean Air Act, and that the rationale EPA had given for why it would not regulate, even if it had such authority, was inadequate.

[5] http://www.oyez.org/cases/2000-2009/2006/2006_05_1120/argument. Retrieved July 18, 2013.

toward problems centering on religion, politics, or economics: "Supply and Demand. Whatever. I told you before, I'm not an economist. That's why I don't want to have to deal with monopolies, to tell you the truth." Were a justice to say that, I doubt that it would be viewed as a charming eccentricity.

But then, Scalia is a public official in a country that is remarkably ignorant of science. Less than one in four Americans know what a molecule is, more than half think that a laser is focused sound, and only a little more than half know that the earth orbits the sun once per year and that antibiotics do not kill viruses. As bad as this is, experts tell us that Americans are less ignorant of science than they were a generation ago, and that in some respects they are no more ignorant of science than people in other countries. [6]

This ignorance about science can lead people both to overestimate what science can do and to feel betrayed when it fails to live up to these pretensions. We tend to see science as a source of unimpeachable authority that will save us from all of our problems or as another interest group battling for money and prestige. We drown in our contradictions, sometimes behaving like jilted lovers when forced to acknowledge reality.

In fairness, one does not actually have to know scientific facts in order to be able to read popular accounts of science, to find scientific information, to understand how science works, and to know when and under what circumstances one should (and should not) defer to scientific authority.[7] Just as there is a difference between a good lawyer and Lexis/Nexis, so there is a difference between being a scientifically literate citizen and a science geek.

However, the problems of scientific illiteracy go deeper than factual ignorance. Only 28% of the American public is science-literate enough to read the science section of the *New York Times*.[8] There is little understanding of such basic scientific practices as peer review, and little awareness of the fact that scientific authority comes in degrees and that science generally advances incrementally.

---

[6] Miller 2010: 241–255. While Americans' self-professed understanding of global warming has increased over time—from 69% saying they understand the issue "very well" or "fairly well" in 2001, to 74% in 2006 and 80% in the current poll—their concern about global warming across several measures is generally in the lower range of what Gallup has found historically. http://www.gallup.com/poll/146606/Concerns-Global-Warming-Stable-Lower-Levels.aspx. Retrieved July 18, 2013. Generally on climate literacy among Americans, see http://environment.yale.edu/climate/publications/knowledge-of-climate-change/. Retrieved July 18, 2013.

[7] I suppose another way of being fair to Scalia would be to echo Senator Roman Hruska, who when making the case for the nomination of Harold Carswell to the Supreme Court said on the Senate floor: "[T]here are a lot of mediocre judges and people and lawyers. They are entitled to a little representation, aren't they...? We can't have all Brandeises, Frankfurters and Cardozos." As quoted in http://query.nytimes.com/gst/fullpage.html?res=9D03E6D7173DF934A15757C0A96F958260. Retrieved July 18, 2013.

[8] Miller 2010: 241.

The origins of peer review go back to the dawn of the scientific revolution.[9] Once we accept that scientific investigation can produce knowledge, then we need some procedures for distinguishing cases in which knowledge has been produced from those in which it has not. Scientific societies such as the Accademia dei Lincei, the Royal Society, and the Académie des Sciences were founded in the seventeenth century in part to play such a role. Peer review as it is practiced by professional journals and funding agencies descends from these centuries-old practices, but it did not take its modern form until the second half of the twentieth century.[10]

There are variations in how peer review functions in different areas of science, but its basic role is to qualify a study for inclusion in the authoritative literature. Passing through peer review to publication does not mean that the conclusions drawn in a study are correct, nor even that the study does not have significant limitations, flaws, or defects. What it does mean is that the report is presumptively reliable and can be used as evidence for scientific claims.

Many of those who deny mainstream science do not grasp the significance of peer review, often treating non-peer-reviewed or even vanity publications as equally authoritative. Former Congressman John Doolittle, when asked in a 1995 congressional hearing to specify the peer-reviewed science supporting his claim that there was no scientific basis for ozone depletion, replied: "I consulted Dr. Singer, who is a very authoritative source, and I will stand with the Doctor."[11] What Doolittle seemed to be suggesting was that a designated "authoritative source" can trump the peer-reviewed literature, and that there is not much more to designating an "authoritative source" than deciding with whom to "stand."

This is confused in a number of ways. What gives the peer-reviewed literature its authority is that it has survived the evaluation of experts. But no one is an expert in everything, and not all doctors are created equal. Some speak with greater authority than others, and their authority is evidenced (and perhaps constituted to some degree) by their own contributions to the peer-reviewed literature. A 2010 study showed that 97–98% of the most actively publishing climate researchers support mainstream views on climate change, and that the relative scientific prominence and climate expertise of those who reject mainstream views are substantially below that of the overwhelming majority of researchers.[12]

---

[9] For the standard historical account, see Zuckerman and Merton 1971. Raymond Spier (2002) finds precursors in the ancient and medieval Islamic world. For an especially sophisticated discussion, see Biagioli 2002.

[10] Burnham thinks that the histories of editorial and grant review diverge in important ways (1990).

[11] As quoted in Lahsen 2005: 157. Doolittle retired from Congress in 2009 after numerous ethics charges had been brought against him. Singer is one of the three or four most influential climate change deniers (see Section 3.5 for further discussion).

[12] Anderegg et al. 2010. See also Cook et al. 2013.

Climate change is such a large and complex subject that no one can be an expert in all of its dimensions. There are experts in various domains relevant to climate change, but it may be that an expert in climate change is someone whose expertise is in absorbing, assessing, assimilating, and synthesizing relevant information from a broad range of areas in which she is not expert. This brings out another reason that the peer-reviewed literature is so important. It represents the collective wisdom of many experts, rather than the deliverances of a single doctor, however wise he might be.

Sometimes the indifference to peer review is defended on the grounds that peer review is nothing more than a "highfalutin'" form of cronyism. Critics say that establishment scientists scratch each other's backs by accepting each other's papers, giving each other prizes, awarding each other grants, and generally singing each other's praises.[13]

This picture of corruption bears little relation to reality. Papers are typically subjected to multiple, anonymous reviews, often "blind," and rejecting papers by friends and colleagues is part of the culture of science.

Of course, scientists are human, and the broad social forces that affect people and society affect scientists as well.[14] Moreover, there are failures in any system of evaluation, especially one that relies on the goodwill and ethical behavior of large numbers of people who are freely giving their time. There is an active literature discussing weaknesses in the peer review system and suggesting ways of addressing them. Among the problems most frequently mentioned are the conservatism of peer review, the difficulty in some areas (e.g., genetics) for reviewers to tell whether the work was actually done and the results obtained, and the fact that peer review is expensive and time-consuming.[15] While it is difficult to be sure, it appears that peer review is more likely to fail in some areas (e.g., medical research) than in others.

It is hard to imagine doing without peer review. If we were assessing the quality of popular music or ten-dollar bottles of wine we would want the judgments of qualified experts, even if we thought that this was not the end of the matter. The Academy Awards are given on the basis of peer review rather than box office receipts. Even the American Association of Political Consultants presents its awards for "the

---

[13] Climate change denialists tried to use "climategate" as evidence for this. See Section 2.3 for a discussion of this episode.

[14] For example, scientists are subject to the "Matthew effect" in which greater recognition tends to go to those who already have greater recognition (Merton 1968). This phenomenon will be familiar to anyone who has ever had a job or gone to high school.

[15] See, for example, http://www.nature.com/nature/peerreview/debate/. Retrieved July 18, 2013. And http://www.realclimate.org/index.php/archives/2011/02/from-blog-to-science/. Retrieved July 18, 2013. There are links in this latter post to criticisms of peer review, but see especially *Peer Review: the challenges for the humanities and social sciences: A British Academy Report*, September 2007. Retrieved July 18, 2013. For a thoughtful discussion of peer-review in climate science see Parkinson 2010, ch. 11. For a general study of peer review, see Lamont 2009.

best, the most creative, the most effective, and the most unique political communication tools" on the basis of blind peer review rather than election results.[16] In most human endeavors, not only in science, the judgment of peers is an ultimate standard of quality.

The most serious problem with peer review is not that authoritative contributions are excluded from the literature, but rather that much that is of little value winds up being published. Drummond Rennie amusingly exaggerated this concern when he wrote about medical research:

> There seems to be no study too fragmented, no hypothesis too trivial, no literature citation too biased or too egotistical, no design too warped, no methodology too bungled, no presentation of results too inaccurate, too obscure, and too contradictory, no analysis too self-serving, no argument too circular, no conclusions too trifling or too unjustified, and no grammar and syntax too offensive for a paper to end up in print.[17]

Each year more than one million peer-reviewed papers are published in 21,000 journals, and the numbers are increasing each year.[18] The text of the 2007 Intergovernmental Panel on Climate Change (IPCC) report cited approximately 18,000 peer-reviewed articles. In 2009 alone more than 8,000 research papers were published on climate science.[19] Perhaps the best way to think of peer review is as a soft filter, sort of like the spam filter on your computer. What fails to make it through peer review does not count for scientific knowledge, but it is a long way from a single peer-reviewed finding to a credible scientific belief. The challenge of forming credible scientific beliefs is like detecting a signal in a massive wall of sound. While each peer-reviewed scientific publication has some presumptive authority, it is easy to overestimate how much, and it is uncommon for a single paper to establish much on its own.

This helps to bring out another common misunderstanding about science. Many people believe that science normally progresses by great men writing landmark papers that provoke scientific revolutions. In fact, most science is incremental, and even revolutionary science is often far more incremental than it is commonly portrayed. Doing science is usually more like piling twigs than stacking logs.[20]

---

[16] For details, visit http://www.theaapc.org/downloads/Pollies/2013/2013%20FINAL%20JUDGING%20HANDBOOK.pdf. Retrieved July 25, 2013.

[17] Rennie 1986: 2391.

[18] http://www.senseaboutscience.org/data/files/resources/16/IDontKnowWhatToBelieve_web2011.pdf. Retrieved July 18, 2013.

[19] http://e360.yale.edu/feature/despite_attacks_from_critics__climate_science_will_prevail_/2264/; http://uppsalainitiativet.blogspot.com/2010/04/swedish-television-goes-oreskes-on.html. Retrieved July 18, 2013. Given how vast the peer-reviewed literature is, the fact that so little supports the climate change denialist case is especially telling.

[20] There is a vast literature on this topic. A good place to begin is with the classic work of Kuhn 2012.

Scientific ignorance abounds, but is not the sole or even most important reason that we have failed to act on climate change. Cross-national differences in the fractions of populations that say that climate change is a serious problem are not indices of scientific ignorance.[21] Indeed, the importance of scientific ignorance has often been exaggerated and its role misunderstood.[22]

Still, scientific knowledge and attitudes toward science do matter. Understanding science is important for grasping the risks that climate change poses and for evaluating possible responses. It matters, for example, that many people see climate change as a "flow" problem involving emissions rather than as a "stock" problem involving concentrations.[23] They imagine that when emissions go down, the risk of climate change must also be abating. What they fail to recognize is that concentrations of greenhouse gases (GHGs) in the atmosphere may increase even while emissions decrease, in the same way in which the water in a bathtub may increase even while the flow of water into the bathtub is reduced. There are two other reasons to be concerned about scientific ignorance: Scientific ignorance is an invitation to manipulation; and, without science, we would not even know that the problem of climate change exists.

3.2. POLITICIZING SCIENCE

Some scholars blame scientists at least in part for why we are not motivated to act on climate change. They claim that many scientists have discredited themselves by politicizing science. On this view the politicization of science by some climate scientists has compromised the credibility of the entire enterprise. John Lanchester writes:

> [T]he scientists…are…trying to sell us something. And we the public might be under-educated, but we know not to trust entirely someone who is trying to sell us something. The impression that some scientists are consciously trying to make us more afraid is a potent aid to the sceptics.[24]

[21] 30% of Chinese, 44% of Americans, 65% of Japanese, 67% of Turks, and 68% of the French say climate change is a serious problem; visit http://www.pewglobal.org/2009/07/23/chapter-9-environmental-issues/. Retrieved July 18, 2013.

[22] As I myself have argued going back to Jamieson 1992. See also Sarewitz 2004; Pielke Jr. 2010. Indeed, a recent paper shows that people's values are better predictors of whether or not they believe that climate change is a threat than their degree of scientific knowledge. The main effect of being well-informed seems to be to polarize people. See Kahan et al. 2012.

[23] For many people this is what rationalizes the "wait and see" or "go slow" approach. See Sterman 2008.

[24] Lanchester 2007. Available online at http://www.lrb.co.uk/v29/n06/john-lanchester/warmer-warmer. Retrieved July 31, 2013.

Some claims about the politicization of climate science are part of the denial machine, and will be discussed in Section 3.5. Others, however, come from scholars who accept the broad outlines of mainstream climate science.

In a 2010 book, Roger Pielke Jr. claimed that "[c]limate science is a fully politicized enterprise, desperately in need of reform if integrity is to be restored and sustained."[25] "Climategate," the episode in November 2009 in which thousands of documents were stolen from the Climate Research Unit at the University of East Anglia, revealed scientists "who saw themselves as much as activists as researchers,"[26]... "plotting to corrupt the peer review system."[27] According to Pielke Jr., the theft exposed a "clique of activist scientists" engaged in a "coup against peer review."[28] He went on to accuse a broad range of scientists and public figures of trying to scare people into taking action on climate change or advocating such scare tactics. This unlikely group includes Al Gore, Thomas Schelling, and 20 other Nobel Prize winners in physics, chemistry, economics, peace, and literature; Australian professor of public ethics Clive Hamilton; anyone who tries to show that there has been "dangerous interference" with the climate system; and whoever decided to open the Copenhagen Climate Change Conference with the film *Please Help Save the World*. Pielke Jr. goes on to claim that "influential and activist leaders of the [climate science] community have sought to achieve political outcomes...by using and shaping science as a tool to defeat their political enemies."[29] Those guilty of this charge include Princeton scientists Steve Pacala and Rob Socolow, Nobel Prize winner Paul Crutzen, Carnegie scientist Ken Caldeira, and Pennsylvania State scientist Michael Mann. According to Pielke Jr., scientists' political ideology makes them "susceptible to politicizing their science." He cites a 2009 poll in which 62% of geoscientists identified themselves as Democrats while only 4% called themselves Republicans.

One remarkable feature of Pielke Jr.'s discussion is its shrillness. "Clique," "coup," and "plotting" are the kinds of terms usually reserved for organized crime syndicates, terrorist organizations, and other conspiracies against the public good. The repeated use of the word "activist" mobilizes a characteristic trope of right-wing ideologues. The term is typically applied to judges, who like scientists are supposed to be neutral when carrying out their duties, but all too often, on this view, betray their professional responsibilities. Even someone who is sympathetic to the claim that political considerations sometimes find their way into climate science might shrink from Pielke Jr.'s characterization of climate science as "a fully politicized enterprise." He makes such institutions as the National Center for Atmospheric Research sound like an outpost of the Democratic National Committee, or perhaps something even worse.

---

[25] Pielke Jr. 2010: ch. 8.
[26] Pielke Jr. 2010: 192.
[27] Pielke Jr. 2010: 195.
[28] Pielke Jr. 2010: 195.
[29] Pielke Jr. 2010: 263.

What is most troubling about Pielke Jr.'s account is its lack of balance. As we will see in Section 3.5, the politicization of science by a handful of climate change deniers and their patrons is extremely well documented, and continues to be a major obstacle to the United States adopting effective climate policy. Yet in a 26-page chapter on the politicization of science, Pielke Jr. devotes only one paragraph to the behavior of those "opposed to action on climate change."[30] Their worst offense seems to be "[blowing] out of proportion papers at odds with the views of most other scientists."[31] If only.

Throughout the chapter, Pielke Jr. confuses scientists' motivations with their science. For example, he quotes Pacala, reflecting on a paper that he published four years previously:

> The purpose of the stabilization wedges paper was narrow and simple—we wanted to stop the Bush administration from what we saw as a strategy to stall action on global warming by claiming that we lacked the technology to tackle it.[32]

This passage shows that Pacala wanted to bring science to bear on what he regarded as a bad argument against policy action, not that the science itself was "politicized" or that Pacala was "shaping science as a tool to defeat...[his] political enemies." Pacala's science, like all science, stands or falls on its own merits; the intentions, purposes, motivations, or background beliefs of the scientist are irrelevant to the soundness of the science. In this case not only did the paper in question survive peer review (which, as we've seen, Pielke Jr. values greatly), but it was published in an extremely prestigious journal, *Science*, and is one of the most widely cited papers in climate science and policy.[33]

The confusion of scientists' motivations with their science is an important mistake. If we were to fault all the science that is motivated by a desire to produce some extrascientific result, there would not be much that escapes criticism. Newton claimed that in writing the *Principia*, "I had an eye upon such Principles as might work with considering men for the belief of a Deity."[34] Maxwell, in a letter to his wife, mused that "the scientist in union with Christ has an obligation to do such work as will benefit the body of Christ."[35] Darwin's interest in human origins was apparently motivated at least in part by his passionate anti-slavery convictions.[36]

---

[30] Pielke Jr. 2010: 205.

[31] Pielke Jr. 2010: 205.

[32] http://environmentalresearchweb.org/cws/article/news/34156. Retrieved July 18, 2013. The paper in question is Pacala and Socolow 2004.

[33] By May 7, 2013, it had been cited 1,636 times, according to Google Scholar.

[34] Newton to Richard Bentley, December 10, 1692, available at http://www.newtonproject.sussex.ac.uk/view/texts/normalized/THEM00254 (retrieved October 25, 2013).

[35] As quoted in Graves 1996: 150–153.

[36] Desmond and Moore 2009.

Einstein's failed quest for a unified theory was deeply affected by his belief in a certain kind of God. He wrote in a famous letter to Max Born,

> Quantum mechanics is certainly imposing. But an inner voice tells me that it is not yet the real thing. The theory says a lot, but does not really bring us any closer to the secret of the "old one." I, at any rate, am convinced that *He* does not throw dice.[37]

What motivates much of the concern with politicizing science is the thought that scientists are supposed to tell us what is the case, not what we ought to do. When they cross the line from description to prescription, they are guilty of politicizing science.[38]

While there is truth in this thought, it is much too simple.[39] Scientists, like doctors, lawyers, and teachers, are not only professionals, they are also citizens, parents, neighbors, friends, and lovers. In these roles and as individuals they have moral and political beliefs, religious attitudes, and cultural commitments. Navigating these complex responsibilities poses questions of professional ethics. But whatever the correct way of integrating or balancing these diverse dimensions of responsibility, it is certainly not the case that climate scientists must remain silent about climate policy, any more than that economists must refrain from providing policy advice about the economy. On the contrary, we want those with scientific expertise to actively participate in policy debates to which their science is relevant. Some climate scientists have strong views about climate policy, and this may contribute to motivating their work on particular problems. But neither this, nor expressing these views in correspondence, conversation, or even in manifestos is any sort of ethical lapse, much less evidence that they are "politicizing science."[40] Conforming to the canons of professional ethics does not mean forfeiting one's right as a citizen.

Indeed, some people think climate scientists should be more active in policy debates. Evelyn Fox Keller writes about scientists that:

> They need to redouble their efforts to make their arguments, their doubts, and the reasons for both their confidence and their concerns intelligible to the non-specialist citizen. They need to combat, piece by piece, the misrepresentations brought in support of attacks on their scientific integrity, and to show readers why the popular accounts and

---

[37] Letter to Max Born (December 4, 1926), Born 2004.

[38] Pielke Jr. 2010: 197–198. Oreskes and Conway (2010) give various examples of scientists politicizing science in order to make environmental threats seem less serious than they are.

[39] See the following two sections of this chapter as well as some of my earlier papers; e.g., Jamieson 1990 and 1991.

[40] Of course, Pielke Jr. thinks that climate scientists have done much more than this and perhaps he is right that in some cases they have, though I do not find his arguments very convincing. In any case it is a very long stretch from a few anecdotes about ethical lapses to his exaggerated claims.

even the naming of "Climategate" are so misleading…they are best equipped to take on the task, and their responsibility as scientists obliges them to do so….[41]

This too can be overstated. Although Fox Keller does not go there, some advocate scientists plunging headlong into the struggle to improve the world. While they may grant that science may not be able to directly solve policy problems (perhaps because of the distinction between facts and values that I discuss in the next section), they still think that scientists can solve the problems that mere mortals bungle. The thought is something like this (parodied a little perhaps). Scientists are ferociously smart people engaged in an incredibly difficult activity. They are in the business of generating timeless, universal truths that have cognitive value. Those involved in "politics" (sometimes used as a generic term for anything normative) seek to negotiate local, contingent, conflicting demands. Science is superior to politics because the timeless is better than the dated; the universal is superior to the contingent; and the cognitive should rule the non-cognitive. Because science is superior to politics, scientists are superior to non-scientists. Anyone who is skeptical about this claim needs only to compare the progress of science with the eternal conflicts of politics and morality. Mutual respect between warring peoples (for example) seems about as likely now as it did centuries ago, but scientific progress permits people's lack of respect to be expressed with ever greater firepower. For someone who sees the world in this way, it is a short step to supposing that not only can scientists solve our problems but that they have an obligation to do so.

This view commits the crude fallacy of supposing that the patina of science somehow invariably rubs off on scientists. We do not have to believe that there is a profound, unbridgeable gap between science and other human activities to think that this is a mistake and that we should distinguish the political and social pronouncements and maneuverings of scientists from their scientific work. While scientists have societal contributions to make, especially regarding the problems to which their science is directly relevant, there appears to be little reason to think that scientists have any special competence in addressing the purely normative dimensions of environmental problems.[42]

Fear of this headstrong ideology and the desire to keep scientists in their place may motivate to some extent the concern about politicizing science. It is true that some scientists are barely disguised elitists, impatient with process and politics, and apparently confident that if they could get their hands on the machinery of governance, then whatever problems we face could be solved before dinner.

In my opinion, however, scientists have largely behaved admirably in bringing climate change to public attention, and in doing what they can to motivate action

---

[41] Keller 2011.

[42] Indeed, we are learning more all the time just how limited and domain-specific expertise is. See, e.g., Kahneman 2011: ch. 22.

in ways that are consistent with their professional responsibilities. In some cases this has come at a high personal price.[43] Sure, supersized egos can be annoying and there have been stumbles and falls, but scientists are not trained to be public figures, and they have been arrayed against vastly more powerful and well-organized forces. In any case-blaming scientists doesn't go very far toward explaining why we haven't acted on climate change.

3.3. FACTS AND VALUES

In the background of concerns about politicizing science is often a simple, linear model of the relations between facts and values, and science and policy. This linear model represents the problem of climate change in the following way.[44]

We begin with a problem, in this case, increasing concentrations of GHGs in the atmosphere. These increasing concentrations cause various physical effects, which in turn cause various societal effects. Many of these effects are regarded as undesirable. The goal of policy is to prevent, mitigate, or adapt to these undesirable effects. In order to manage successfully we need information. The role of physical science is to produce information regarding the physical effects of increasing concentrations of GHGs. Physical effects include climatological effects, hydrological effects, and biological and ecological effects, including increasing global mean temperature and precipitation, rising sea levels, drier soils, species extinctions, and shifting patterns of biological activity. Once information about physical effects is developed, it is transferred to social scientists, who evaluate the effects of these physical changes on individual and social behavior and economic and political systems. These effects may involve impacts on individual lifestyles, the availability and price of food, migration patterns, economic development, the stability of national governments, and patterns of international relations. Information from both physical and social scientists is then transferred to policy-makers and their advisers. One response would be to welcome or ignore the anticipated changes. But if the effects of such changes are regarded as undesirable (and this is presupposed by calling something a problem), then some policy interventions would seem to be called for. These interventions may aim at preventing or mitigating the predicted physical or societal effects, or individual or collective adaptation. Policy interventions may be implemented by designing new institutions or institutional processes, or by redirecting existing ones.

---

[43] Climate scientists have been abused, harassed, and in some cases have even received death threats; for example, visit http://www.guardian.co.uk/science/2012/mar/03/michael-mann-climate-change-deniers. Retrieved July 18, 2013.

[44] Concern about this linear model is part of the common heritage of science studies. I first characterized and criticized this model in Jamieson 1990. Pielke Jr. (2007) also criticizes this model. There is also a linear model for technological innovation, which should not be confused with the linear model that I am discussing.

There are many problems with the linear model. First, information about the extent and physical effects of global warming is uncertain and incomplete. Second, information about societal effects is even less certain and complete because it depends on information from the physical sciences, because it involves difficult problems of its own, and because there is continuous feedback between societal and physical effects. Third, the information-transfer process cannot be as linear and sequential as the model specifies. If we face a serious problem and if policy is to be effectual, then we must make policy while we continue to investigate the physical and societal effects of climate change. But this means that policy will also enter the feedback loop, influencing societal responses and physical effects. Instead of a pyramid, with the physical sciences forming the foundation for societal knowledge and policy interventions, we have something much more like a "hermeneutic" circle with each element informing and causally interacting with every other element. For these reasons and others, the linear model is inadequate.

What I want to discuss in some detail is the sharp distinction between facts and values that the linear model enshrines. Determining the physical and societal effects of increasing concentrations of GHGs is viewed as a factual matter to be resolved empirically. This stage of the inquiry is supposed to be purely descriptive; normative considerations do not enter at all. The next stage, assessing and selecting policy options, is the normative stage. Here such notions as equity, fairness, and efficiency come into play. The difference between the two stages is this: Management and policy-making are matters of decision, while scientific inquiry is a matter of discovery. Since management involves resolving conflicts of values, interests, and preferences, it is the proper domain of democratic participation. Management and policy are matters of politics rather than expertise. Since scientific inquiry involves the determination of the way things are, it is the proper domain of scientists and other experts. Preferences are created equal, but judgments about what is the case are not.

At the heart of this model is the idea of value-free science, which brings with it supposed gaps between facts and values, and "is's" and "oughts." These are intuitive distinctions that most of us would agree should be observed, yet facts and values and "is's" and "oughts" are entangled in our minds, language, and behavior.[45]

In some cases values are so widely shared that simply stating facts conversationally implies what ought to be done. For example, there isn't much difference between a doctor saying that only an operation will save Kelly's life and the doctor saying that Kelly ought to have an operation.[46] That we all want Kelly to live goes unsaid. In this case it appears that an "ought" is following directly from an "is," but really there is another "ought" lurking in the background.

---

[45] One interesting case of entanglement that I will not discuss here is the "Knobe effect," which in its original presentation involved a case in which moral judgments about outcomes affected factual judgments about whether the outcome was produced intentionally. See Knobe 2003.

[46] Pielke Jr. (2010) also notes cases like this.

In other cases there is disagreement about what ought to be done that appears to rest on a conflict of values, yet what is really at issue is a difference of factual beliefs. For example, people often disagree about the desirability of various climate change policies and this may appear to reflect a deep difference in values. However, in some cases people disagree about these policies because they sincerely disagree about facts. They disagree about whether anthropogenic climate change is occurring, what its effects would be were it occurring, and what the consequences would be of government action taken in response to it. The strong displays of emotion in these debates can obscure the factual differences that are at the foundation of the dispute. In these cases getting the facts right is important to settling the question of what we ought to do. The IPCC was established, in part, in order to resolve such disagreements, and this is the picture of the dispute over climate change that highlights the importance of reducing uncertainties.[47] However, this approach is quite limited. People can have crazy but consistent factual beliefs that are impervious to correction. Or they can have crazy factual beliefs in one domain and quite sober, conservative beliefs in others.[48] In any case ground zero for our most divisive public disputes cannot be found in the domain of facts.

More central to disputes that mobilize great passion, such as that over climate change, is our differences in values and especially our penchant for displacing arguments about values into the language of facts.[49] For example, in the climate change debate there are disputes about abstruse questions regarding paleoclimatic reconstructions that function as proxies for debates about what we ought to do about GHG emissions.[50] This displacement of arguments about values into the language of facts has been a central feature of American political discourse for at least half a century, though naked appeals to conflicting value differences are becoming increasingly prominent, especially when they involve values that people locate in their religious beliefs.

A clear example of this displacement can be seen in the argument over whether a fetus is a human being and the role that this argument plays in the abortion debate. It is trivially true that a (human) fetus is biologically a human being and it is surprising that anyone would deny it (What else would a human fetus be? A fish?). But for an anti-abortion advocate, what is supposed to follow from a fetus being a human being is that it has a right to life. But for this to be at all plausible it must be the case

---

[47] See Section 3.5 for more on the treatment of uncertainty in climate change.

[48] I once served on a National Science Foundation review committee with a scientist who believed in alien abduction. This belief did not seem to intrude on his scientific work nor on his ability to judge the quality of grant proposals, but it did make for some strange conversation over dinner.

[49] Jamieson 1991; Sarewitz 2004; Pielke Jr. 2010. Differences in values can occur at different levels and it is an open question how deep they go in particular instances of disagreement. For example, pro-choice and pro-life advocates regarding abortion may subscribe to some different values and disagree about the force of others, yet they may generally agree about relatively fundamental values (e.g., that it is wrong to intentionally kill an innocent person).

[50] For some examples visit http://climateaudit.org/. Retrieved July 18, 2013.

that "human being" is being used in a moral rather than a biological sense. Yet in the moral sense it is not at all clear that a (biologically human) fetus is a (morally significant) human being. In fact, this is exactly what is in dispute.[51] Thus what parades as an obvious factual claim, that (human) fetuses are human beings, is actually a restatement of the controversial moral claim that fetuses are human beings in the moral sense and so have a right to life. Rather than making a factual claim, one party to this dispute is making a moral claim disguised in apparently factual language. What these examples show is that disagreements about facts can present themselves as disagreements about values, and disagreements about values can be kitted out as disagreements about facts.

It is also the case that facts are responsive to values and "oughts" are responsive to "is's" in various subtle ways. For example, whether one sees an act as child abuse or parental discipline is sensitive to one's values. How much we think we ought to donate to famine relief is related to our views about the efficacy of such aid. Only a completely mad value system would spin freely in a fact-free zone. If we acted on the basis of such a value system we would be "robotic" rather than cognitively and affectively responsive agents.[52]

Moreover, there is not always a neutral way of characterizing facts. Philippa Foot made this point half a century ago when she pointed out that someone's behavior is rude if it satisfies certain factual conditions, but in characterizing the behavior in this way one expresses an evaluation.[53] Scientists try very hard to speak in colorless, unexpressive language, but it is difficult to hear about "abrupt climate change" without feeling some trepidation.[54]

Maintaining a clear distinction between "is's" and "oughts" and facts and values may be good conceptual hygiene and may help to resolve some conflicts, but we should not get carried away with it. "Mind the gap" may be a good regulative ideal, sort of like the injunction to always tell the truth, but facts and values are not that distinct, and even the best regulative ideal should sometimes be ignored. Since the relations between facts and values and "is's" and "oughts" are so complex, it is hardly surprising that scientists, as well as their critics, often trip over the complexities.

Steve Schneider and Jim Hansen are both highly admirable climate scientists who have been very active in communicating science both to decision-makers and to the public. However, neither has a very sophisticated view about the relationship between facts and values. Schneider is sensitive to the diverse values at play in the climate change debate, but speaks as if values were entirely subjective: We

[51] However, some think that abortion is justified even if the fetus is a morally significant human being. The classic defense of this view is Thomson 1971. For discussion, see Boonin 2003.

[52] See Ziff 2004 for more on this, and generally for discussion about the difficult relationships between facts and values.

[53] See Foot 1978.

[54] For discussion of the attitudes suggested by various terms in the climate change discussion, see Villar and Krosnick 2011.

all have our own personal values and we should make them clear and put them on the table. Schneider tells us that he values equity and avoiding irreversible changes in the Earth system and there he stops.[55] However, there are a variety of different concepts masked by these words, and some people would reject these values in any form. Is there nothing further to say? The challenge is not just to announce our values, as if they were preferences for one flavor of ice cream over another, but to mobilize resources of reason, temperament, and shared perspectives to show how we can make progress in resolving our differences. Hansen often writes as if values can simply be read from the science. For example, he writes that "[t]he science demands a simple rule: Coal use must be prohibited..."[56] He often seems astonished that political leaders do not obey science's commands. In Hansen's simple world our choice is between doing what science requires or acting out of vicious self-interest. The thought that people may have diverse values that may intervene between science and policy seems foreign to him. Whatever is true about the complex relations between facts and values, we cannot simply read what we ought to do from science, any more than we can ignore science when deciding what to do about problems such as climate change. Science can show us the consequences of our actions, but ultimately we must decide, guided by our values, what to try to bring about. Facts and values are neither as distinct as Schneider supposes nor as connected as Hansen seems to think.

Historically, philosophers have often been more scientistic than scientists, seeing themselves as "under-laborers...clearing the ground...for the master-builders...such as...the incomparable Mr. Newton."[57] In the wake of work by philosophers such as Thomas Kuhn (2012) most philosophers (as well as virtually everyone in the science studies community) have abandoned the idea of the value-neutrality as a descriptive account of science. This helps equalize the playing field between science and other ways of knowing.

Some however, take the value-ladenness of science further. According to J. B. Callicott (1987: 280, 279), "from a more sophisticated post-modern epistemological point of view, all so-called facts—especially the primary, unquantifiable properties of the 'realities' recognized by modern classical science—are theory-laden....Our interests—what we value—in a sense create actual facts." Bryan Norton (1991: 195, 193) claims that "environmentalists are united by their belief that ecological science is capable of transforming worldviews and ultimate values." There is a "shared acceptance of science as a value-laden enterprise," and an underlying consensus around what he calls five "scientific axioms" (dynamism, relatedness, systematicity,

---

[55] Schneider 2009.

[56] Hansen 2010: 174.

[57] These are the words of John Locke in "The Epistle to the Reader," from *An Essay Concerning Human Understanding*, first published in 1690, available in many editions, and on the web at http://oll.libertyfund.org/?option=com_staticxt&staticfile=show.php%3Ftitle=761&chapter=80706&layout=html&Itemid=27. Retrieved July 18, 2013.

creativity, and differential fragility)." Others in the science studies community have argued that scientists create cultural and societal order when they create scientific order.[58]

A great deal can be said about these claims, but the most important point to make here is this: "[C]ommitted" science loses its claim to be a value-free, institutional truth-detector, and thus endangers its claims to epistemological privilege. If, as Callicott suggests, facts are created by interests and if the currency of science is facts, then science is fundamentally an institution for organizing, ordering, and interpreting the expressions of various interests.[59] Since science on this view is not a neutral arbiter between alternative ways of representing the world, there is little reason for people with interests that diverge from those expressed by science to defer to the authority which science claims for itself. Once scientific discourse is seen as committed, it is not relevantly different from history, philosophy, or any other value-laden way of knowing and arguing. Once it has been admitted that science is liberally laced with value commitments, there is little reason to think that it can be the epistemologically privileged "truth-detector" that can help solve environmental problems.

There is always tension between science's authority and its being mobilized to solve problems. The power of science is in its self-presentation as that value-free, institutional "truth-detector," for this is what gives it the authority to sit in judgment on the epistemological practices of other cultures and institutions. But the very characterization of states of the world as "problems" and responses to them as "solutions" inherently involves the projection of values onto the world. Thus, the power of science to solve problems such as climate change is limited and contested. Climate science, in our present social context, provokes fundamental questions about how we ought to live and organize our societies that it is powerless to answer, sometimes to the surprise and consternation of both scientists and their publics.

It is the contingent, social embeddedness of science that gives science its normative push rather than its abstract ideals. Thick value-commitments are implicit in scientific practice, scientific institutions, and in the behavior of scientists. Scientists are part of culture, and their practices express the values of the broader society as well as values that are unique to scientists as individuals and to scientific institutions. Science also shapes the broader society, in part through enabling technological innovation.[60]

Despite the tensions, there is little question that in practice science has been remarkably influential in shaping our responses to ethical and political questions. Minding the gap betweens facts and values is a good regulative ideal, but it should

---

[58] See e.g., the work of Sheila Jasanoff 1990.

[59] There is wiggle room for Callicott here. He might claim that while interests "create" facts, facts do not express interests. This view would need to be developed in detail to be made plausible. The interpretation that I have given seems consistent with the spirit of Callicott (1987), and certainly characteristic of a currently influential view.

[60] See Jassanoff 1990 for further discussion.

not be fetishized. Facts and values are more closely related than some think. In any case we should not always struggle to keep them apart.

3.4. THE SCIENCE/POLICY INTERFACE

In the previous section I rejected some simple views regarding the relations beween facts and values and "is's" and "oughts." Both the linear model and the view that science is the universal solvent that can resolve all of our problems are insensitive to the complexities endemic to science and policy-making and the relations between them. It is thus not surprising that in recent years in the United States, science and policy have become decidedly decoupled even when the stated goal is to link them. Climate change is a clear case, but this is generally true with regard to environmental issues.[61] In this section I will briefly sketch why it is so difficult to link science and policy.

Different scientific research programs play different roles in society, and most programs play multiple roles. In some cases scientific research programs are about basic research, while in other cases they are closely tied to particular policy choices. Some scientific research is meant to inform policy. In other cases a research program is supposed to build support for implementing a policy that has antecedently been chosen. In still other cases instituting the scientific research program is itself the policy response.

Consider some examples. While the IPCC plays a number of different roles, it was created largely in order to inform policy. The Strategic Defense Initiative and its successor research programs were instituted in part to liberate the United States from the network of arms control agreements that were seen by some as restricting America's ability to act unilaterally. The National Acid Precipitation Assessment Program (NAPAP) was created in part as an alternative to regulating precursors of acid precipitation.[62] These are different research programs, each with its own purposes.

The Global Change Research Act of 1990 created the United States Global Change Research Program (USGCRP). The Act mandated the USGCRP to provide policy-makers with "usable information on which to base policy decisions relating to global change"(P.L. 101-606, Sec. 104.b.1). In its more than 20 years, the USGCRP has been a bureaucratic success but a policy failure. Beginning with a modest budget of $134 million, the USGCRP received large increases in the Clinton and Obama administrations, and budgets were roughly stable during the Bush years. Today the USGCRP receives about $2.5 billion per year in public money.[63] While many of the

---

[61] It is of particular concern that environmental law has become quite detached from environmental science, in some cases even presupposing scientific views that have been rejected. For discussion of how to reform American environmental law, see Schoenbrod et al. 2010.

[62] This last point is controversial. See Herrick and Jamieson 1995.

[63] For budget data, visit http://www.whitehouse.gov/sites/default/files/microsites/ostp/2014_R& D budget_climate.pdf. Retrieved July 18, 2013.

activities it supports are important, the USGCRP has not been very successful in achieving its legislative mandate.[64] Despite hand-wringing and rhetoric about the importance of people, society, "human dimensions," or whatever the latest buzz-words are, most of the USGCRP money has gone to the National Aeronautics and Space Administration for hardware rather than in investments in providing "usable information on which to base policy decisions." This was true at the beginning of the program, and has not changed through the years.

Even when the USGCRP and other agencies indicate a willingness to involve the human sciences, it is difficult for them to find a research community with which to work. For many years social scientists and humanists have tended to ignore the natural world in which people and societies are embedded, at least in comparison to their interests in social groups and the interactions between them.[65] There has thus not been a "shovel ready" social science community that can collaborate with natural scientists. But that is just the beginning of the problem. Methods and vocabularies are so diverse among social scientists that it is often difficult for them to find common ground among themselves. It can be difficult to integrate the insights of qualitative and quantitative social scientists even when they are studying the same phenomena.

The differences between science and policy-making are even more profound. These practices have different purposes and foci. Science is centered on understanding the diversity of nature; policy is focused on the singleness of action. Science can point to trends, identify thresholds, and establish links between variables leading to probabilistic beliefs based on the accumulation of evidence. The political systems within which policy-making is embedded act on the basis of up or down votes, with no middle ground, and always with an eye to political and legal liability.

Science and policy-making are tethered to different clocks. Scientific understanding unfolds over centuries or millennia; political decisions often have to be made in a relative heartbeat. Scientists, freed from the demand of timeliness, can institute orderly, long-term research programs and incorporate strong standards of proof and evidence. But when the world is on fire and a cacophony of voices demands action or forbearance of one kind or another, decisions must be made on the basis of whatever is available.

A clash of clocks is at the center of the climate change problem. As we saw in Section 2.2, some understood this as early as the 1960s. V. E. Suomi, the father of satellite meteorology, made the point very clearly in his preface to the 1979 Charney report, when he wrote that "A wait-and-see policy may mean waiting until it is too late."[66] Since these words were written, the evidence for anthropogenic climate

---

[64] See various papers by Roger Pielke Jr. including 2000a and 2000b.

[65] For evidence that this may be beginning to change, visit http://www.eurozine.com/articles/2009-10-30-chakrabarty-en.html. Retrieved July 18, 2013.

[66] Suomi 1979: viii.

change has continued to mount. We now know that while we have been debating the uncertainties and fretting about precipitous action, our ever-increasing emissions have committed future generations to living with climate change for at least the next millennium.[67]

Scientists and policy-makers often speak different languages. Scientific vocabularies, though precise in conveying what is and is not known according to a particular conception of knowledge, are often regarded as arcane and obfuscatory by policy-makers. Policy-makers are more at home speaking in stories, anecdotes, metaphors, analogies, adages, and homilies than with abstract or probabilistic characterizations.

Scientists and policy-makers think with different concepts. The output from general circulation models (GCM) and statistical profiles of anticipated behavior are not the conceptual currency of policy-making. Policy-makers tend to think about people and how they respond to environmental changes and policy interventions; scientists tend to think about physical and biological systems, and how they respond to changes caused by people.

For these reasons and others, scientists often fail to provide the kind of information that is most useful to policy-makers. GCM output tends to focus on means and averages rather than on extremes and variability. It is more accurate with respect to temperature than precipitation, and provides more insight into global than regional climate. Yet the challenges that face policy-makers are almost entirely local and concrete.

One of the great challenges for policy-makers over the next century will be to manage adaptation to climate change. This requires understanding the diverse, local impacts of climate change. These social, economic, and political impacts of climate change will depend greatly on how the physical effects are distributed and on what form they take. If the American high plains heat up and dry out, the impacts of this will be very different than if the deserts of the Southwest become even hotter. In order to make these decisions and to balance the costs of adaptation against the costs of reducing emissions, it is much more important to understand regional climate variability than to have knowledge of global means and averages.[68]

Suppose that we want to know whether citrus groves will be an economically viable investment in central Florida in 2050. Predictions about mean or average temperatures over the next century would not be very useful. We need to be able to assess the probability of extremely cold winters and to have some idea of how extreme these winters might be. Focusing on mean temperatures does not reveal this information.

---

[67] Solomon et al. 2009 and 2010.

[68] Oreskes et al. 2010.

There are ways of thinking creatively about how to link science and policy.[69] For example, the idea that the relationship should be iterative rather than linear is a good place to start.[70]

Still, policy-makers and the public often demand too much from science. While improvements can surely be made in linking science to policy, it must be recognized that there will always be some lack of fit between these practices since they have different goals, purposes, methods, concepts, and vocabularies.

Climate science has been a success story. Whatever its failures to adequately inform policy, the larger failure has been that we have not enacted climate policy. Ultimately, the failure to take action on climate change rests with our institutions of decision-making, not on our ways of knowing.

3.5. ORGANIZED DENIAL

One reason that the United States has not taken significant action on climate change is the success of the denial industry. Influential opinion leaders, backed by large sums of money, have successfully worked to cast doubt on mainstream climate science. When scientific ignorance is so prevalent it is easy for denial to take root.

The story of organized denial has been well told and documented, and I will not repeat it here.[71] My interest is in the way in which it has interacted with other factors to produce the current state of policy paralysis. In what follows I will simply mention some central episodes, point out some salient features, and relate them to the larger background. I will focus on denialism in the United States, but denialists are now active in many countries.

As we saw in Section 2.2, 1988 was a watershed year for interest in climate change. Scientists were speaking out, bills were introduced in Congress, the IPCC was formed, and the first steps were taken toward an international agreement. This threatened those who were making billions in profits from fossil fuel-related activities and so they began to strike back. In 1989 the leading oil and automotive companies, along with the Chamber of Commerce and the National Association of Manufacturers, formed the Global Climate Coalition (GCC). Shortly after, the Western Fuels Association, a cooperative that supplies coal to Western utilities, also became active in climate change denial. They produced a film, *The Greening of*

---

[69] Michael Glantz has done important and interesting work on this topic, mostly organized around the idea of "usable science:" http://www.ilankelman.org/glantz.html#usable. Retrieved July 18, 2013.

[70] For different versions of this idea see discussions of "mode 2" (Gibbons et al. 1994, Nowotny et al. 2001), "post-academic science" (Ziman 1995; Ziman 2000), "post-normal science" (Funtowicz and Ravetz 1993), "academic capitalism" (Slaughter and Leslie 1997), and the "triple helix" model of university-government-industry relations (Etzkowitz and Leydesdorff et al. 1997).

[71] See Leggett 2001; Gelbspan 1998; Oreskes and Conway 2010, ch. 6; Hoggan 2009; Lahsen 1999, 2005, 2008; Dunlap and McCright, 2011; Monbiot, 2006, ch. 2.

Planet Earth, which sang the praises of a doubling in atmospheric carbon dioxide. The result would be a greener, more verdant world, with large increases in agricultural productivity, and greater happiness for all. The film was widely distributed and was very influential on members of Congress.

In response to the 1995 IPCC report, the GCC produced a document entitled "The IPCC: Institutionalized Scientific Cleansing" (a reference to the "ethnic cleansing" then underway in Bosnia). On the basis of this document, retired physicist Fred Seitz wrote an "op-ed" piece for the *Wall Street Journal* in which he claimed that one of the chapters of the IPCC report had been changed in such a way as to "deceive policy makers and the public into believing that the scientific evidence shows human activities are causing global warming." Ben Santer, the chapter's lead author, bore the "major responsibility" for the most "disturbing corruption of the peer review process" that Seitz claimed to have "witnessed" in his "more than 60 years as a member of the American scientific community, including service as president of both the National Academy of Sciences and the American Physical Society."[72] Actually, Seitz had not "witnessed" anything very relevant to this chapter; he had only read the GCC report, and discussed it with like-minded friends. He did not even discuss his charges with anyone who had been involved in writing the chapter. Immediately after Seitz's article appeared, Santer, his co-authors, and the IPCC leadership publicly refuted the charges. Nevertheless, this manufactured controversy continued to sprawl though the pages of the *Wall Street Journal* and spilled over into other publications. It lives on in the Internet, where every day someone new is shocked to discover Santer's deception, along with the facts about President Obama's alien origins and the revelation that the moon landing was a hoax.[73]

After the Kyoto Protocol was signed in 1997, multinational corporations began to leave the GCC. They thought that in the wake of Kyoto they would have to accommodate themselves to a carbon-constrained world and they were becoming increasingly uncomfortable with the GCC's "slash and burn" tactics. In 2002 the GCC became dormant, but only after spending tens of millions of dollars attacking climate science and policy.

A small group of scientists, mostly associated with the George C. Marshall Institute, got on the denialist bandwagon early on. Several of these, notably Fred

---

[72] *Wall Street Journal*, June 12, 1996, available widely on the web, including at stephenschneider. stanford.edu/Publications/PDF.../WSJ_June12.pdf. Retrieved July 18, 2013. Actually this op-ed was only the tip of the iceberg. There were even attempts to get Santer fired from his job at Lawrence Livermore National Laboratory (Oreskes and Conway 2010: 3). For detailed discussion of this episode see Oreskes and Conway 2010: ch. 6, and Lahsen 1999, 2005. For Santer's own account, see http://www.realclimate.org/index.php/archives/2010/02/close-encounters-of-the-absurd-kind/. Retrieved July 18, 2013.

[73] Just after writing these words on June 2, 2011, I googled "Ben Santer, chapter 8" and the second link was to a website vilifying him (http://www.greenworldtrust.org.uk/Science/Social/IPCC-Santer. htm). Even *Forbes* magazine continues to circulate the falsehoods (http://www.ucsusa.org/news/ press_release/forbes-fails-to-correct-ben-santer-0506.html). Retrieved July 18, 2013.

Seitz and Fred Singer, had previously been involved in tobacco industry denial campaigns.[74] Seitz later went on to send thousands of letters to scientists asking them to sign a petition rejecting the Kyoto Protocol, since there was "no convincing scientific evidence" supporting concern about anthropogenic climate change, and "there is substantial scientific evidence" that increases in atmospheric concentrations of carbon dioxide produce many beneficial effects.[75] Accompanying the letter was a 12-page "summary" of climate science written by two astrophysicists, a chemist, and someone without an advanced degree. The document was formatted in such a way as to appear as if it were reprinted from the *Proceedings of the National Academy of Sciences*, a prestigious peer-reviewed journal published by the Academy. Actually the paper had not been peer-reviewed at all, and it contained numerous errors and inaccuracies.[76] The NAS issued a statement in response, disavowing the petition campaign, pointing out that "[t]he petition does not reflect the conclusions of expert reports of the Academy" and expressing its concern about the confusion the petition had engendered.[77]

The *ad hominem* attacks pioneered by the GCC have become even more vicious as denialism has spread to Washington "think tanks," lawyers, public relations hacks, and Internet sites. Distinguished scientists are treated as scammers and frauds, accused of peddling the climate change "theory" for their own economic benefit. On the day that renowned climatologist and Stanford professor Steve Schneider died, an important climate denial website, after duly noting his death, called Schneider a "propagandist" and a purveyor of "crap science."[78] I checked the website as I was writing this paragraph (on June 3, 2011), and discovered that the target *du jour* was Pennsylvania State University professor Donald Brown. The home page had a picture of him with the caption "wacko warmist ethics prof." There were links to six articles variously attacking Brown as "unhinged," "a liar who is stealing lots of U.S. dollars from the U.S. taxpayer by saying…things that…he knows, are lies," and as someone who **"states usual religious insanities**…. [boldface in the original]" One post goes after his university: "Penn State University should be stripped of the status of a university and only regain this privilege once it starts from scratch and

[74] Oreskes and Conway 2010: chs.1, 5.

[75] To see the petition, visit http://www.petitionproject.org/. Retrieved July 18, 2013.

[76] The paper was, however, eventually published in two journals, one the official publication of the American Association of Physicians and Surgeons, which declares on its website that it was "founded in 1943 to guard against the intrusion of government into the practice of medicine," and the other a climate journal edited by a well-known climate change denier.

[77] http://www8.nationalacademies.org/onpinews/newsitem.aspx?RecordID=s04201998. Retrieved July 18, 2013.

[78] This has apparently since been taken down in favor of some kinder sentiments. Visit http://www.climatedepot.com/a/7404/Shock-News-RIP-Stephen-H-Schneider-of-Stanford-University-19452010-Died-of-a-heart-attack-today-as-a-flight-he-was-on-was-landing-in-London. Retrieved July 18, 2013.

proves that the breathtaking intellectual weeds similar to Mr. Brown have been safely removed from the institution in a way so that they can never return again."

The main aim of the climate change denial campaign has been to prevent the formation of a consensus for political action on climate change. The strategy has been to suppress both belief in the science and belief that there is a consensus about the science. As we saw in Section 2.3, in the run-up to the 2002 elections, Republican pollster and political consultant Frank Luntz identified the issues for his clients in a memo that was leaked to the press.

> Should the public come to believe that the scientific issues are settled, their views about global warming will change accordingly. Therefore, **you need to continue to make the lack of scientific certainty a primary issue in the debate.... The scientific debate is closing (against us) but not yet closed. There is still a window of opportunity to challenge the science.... You need to be even more active in recruiting experts who are sympathetic to your view....**[79]

There are fallback arguments for those who do not want to take action. The most important are that climate change is good for you, it's too expensive to reduce emissions, and nothing can be done about it. However, the brute response of denying the facts has thus far been quite successful.

Research has shown that frequent viewers of Fox News, a network that writes skepticism about climate change into its scripts, are less likely to accept the scientific consensus than those who do not watch Fox News.[80] Another study shows that "balancing" a scientist expressing the consensus view about climate change with a denier reduces the audience's belief both in the consensus view and that there is a consensus view.[81] Several scholars have discovered a link between climategate and both reduced trust in scientists and diminished belief in the consensus view.[82]

There are differences of opinion about what the various studies conducted over the last two decades have revealed. Public opinion about climate change can be remarkably sensitive to various factors, including the wording of particular questions, the use of particular survey instruments, local weather conditions, and so on.[83] Still, there are some robust results.[84] First, a significant majority of Americans

[79] The bold is in the original memo, which can be viewed at http://www.motherjones.com/files/LuntzResearch_environment.pdf. Retrieved October 24, 2013.

[80] This result is consistent with both persuasion and selective exposure; the authors of the study suspect that both are at work (visit http://woods.stanford.edu/docs/surveys/Global-Warming-Fox-News.pdf). Retrieved July 18, 2013.

[81] http://woods.stanford.edu/research/global-warming-skeptics.html. Retrieved July 18, 2013.

[82] Leiserowitz et al. 2013; Maibach et al. 2011.

[83] Schuldt et al. 2011; Joireman et al. 2010.

[84] http://www.washingtonpost.com/blogs/the-fix/wp/2013/04/22/how-americans-see-global-warming-in-8-charts/; http://climatechangecommunication.org/sites/default/files/reports/Climate-Beliefs-April-2013.pdf. Retrieved July 18, 2013.

believe that climate change is occurring.[85] Second, about half of those who believe that climate change is occurring think that it is at least partly caused by humans.[86] Third, Americans tend to see climate change as relatively unimportant compared to other problems.[87] In one recent survey 43% said that the risks of climate change are exaggerated in the news, while 29% said that they are underestimated.[88] Fourth, overwhelming majorities reject both cap and trade, and carbon taxes. According to one recent survey, 41% of Americans are unwilling to spend a single dollar to address climate change, up from 22% in 2008.[89] Fifth, Americans are less likely to believe in climate change and to support action than citizens of most other industrial countries.[90] Finally, Americans believe that the scientific community is quite divided about whether anthropogenic climate change is occurring.[91]

Climate change denialists are often pictured as healthy skeptics or charming contrarians, while scientists who express consensus views are portrayed as betraying the scientific ethos by trying to enforce a party line.[92] Scientists are supposed to follow ideas wherever they lead. It is not their job to sing with the choir. However, it is possible to agree with your colleagues and believe that a particular view is true, while maintaining a healthy skepticism both about the view and the supporting evidence.[93] This kind of healthy skepticism reminds us that we could be wrong in believing some proposition even though the best evidence that we have at a particular time supports it. This general attitude follows from the fallibilism that is

---

[85] http://environment.yale.edu/climate/publications/americans-global-warming-beliefs-and-attitudes-in-may-2011/. Retrieved July 18, 2013.

[86] http://www.gallup.com/poll/147242/Worldwide-Blame-Climate-Change-Falls-Humans.aspx, http://www.gallup.com/poll/126560/americans-global-warming-concerns-continue-drop.aspx, http://www.gallup.com/poll/146606/Concerns-Global-Warming-Stable-Lower-Levels. aspx. Retrieved July 18, 2013.

[87] http://www.gallup.com/poll/153653/Americans-Worries-Global-Warming-Slightly.aspx, http:// www.gallup.com/poll/126560/americans-global-warming-concerns-continue-drop.aspx. Retrieved July 18, 2013.

[88] http://www.gallup.com/poll/1615/Environment.aspx. Retrieved July 18, 2013.

[89] The good news is that they are willing to pay something. Visit http://closup.umich.edu/policy-reports/15/climate-compared-public-opinion-on-climate-change-in-the-united-states-and-canada/, http://www.brookings.edu/~/media/Files/rc/papers/2011/04_climate_change_opinion/ 04_climate_change_opinion.pdf. Retrieved July 18, 2013.

[90] http://www.gallup.com/poll/147242/Worldwide-Blame-Climate-Change-Falls-Humans.aspx. Retrieved July 18, 2013.

[91] http://environment.yale.edu/climate/publications/americans-global-warming-beliefs-and-attitudes-in-may-2011/. Retrieved July 18, 2013.

[92] Indeed, no one has a monopoly on virtue, and scientists sometimes go too far in trying to protect received opinions. An example of this, in my opinion, was when some scientists asserted that Bjorn Lomborg's 2001 book should never have been published. The suppression of even very bad books is against the ethos of both science and democracy (personally, I'm glad no one has tried to suppress my book!). For discussion, see Harrison 2004.

[93] I am using "skepticism" in a particular sense (which I am calling "healthy skepticism") in which I think it is a scientific virtue. There are, of course, many kinds of skepticism and not all of them are virtuous. Visit http://plato.stanford.edu/entries/skepticism-ancient/for the beginnings of the rich philosophical discussion regarding skepticism. Retrieved July 18, 2013.

characteristic of science and, some would say, of any plausible epistemology.[94] Just as healthy skepticism can be an important virtue, so there is also a place for contrarians both in science and in our broader public discourse. Contrarians force defenders of received views to consider alternative views and counter-arguments.

A denialist is neither a skeptic nor a contrarian. Rather than being skeptical about some widely believed and well-supported claim, a denialist asserts its contrary and tries to explain away the evidence for the claim on the basis of conspiracy, deceit, or some rhetorical appeal to "junk science."[95] Denialists, unlike both skeptics and contrarians, are dogmatists. They persist in espousing some particular view despite the evidence against it. Contrarians, on the other hand, may assert outlandish views but they are as skeptical about the views they propose as the ones they attack. Unlike the denialists, they argue on the basis of evidence rather than engaging in *ad hominem* attacks. The scientists enlisted by the denial machine like to portray themselves as skeptics or contrarians, but really they are denialists.

Climate change denial often exploits public ignorance about science and scientific language. Scientists are epistemologically conservative, and speak in terms of uncertainties and probabilities. From the perspective of a scientist, virtually every assertion is surrounded by a cloud of uncertainty. However, in our everyday lives we tend to see acknowledgments of uncertainty as discrediting. For if we say that something is uncertain, we often mean that there is no fact of the matter about it, no way of knowing whether it is true, or that there is no reason to believe one thing rather than another. For example, if I am uncertain about whether I paid the water bill, then it is natural to think that there is no reason to suppose that I did. So it is easy to see an acknowledgment of the fact that there are uncertainties about the climate models, for example, as an invitation to ignore what the models are telling us (especially since they are usually telling us something that we don't want to hear). These differences between ordinary and scientific uses of language create a niche that climate change deniers can exploit: They comb the scientific literature for uncertainties, then restate them in a dismissive way in popular fora in which they have different meaning and significance. Unsophisticated audiences predictably take a scientist's acknowledgment of uncertainty as a confession that there is no reason to take her claims seriously.[96]

Another difference in the way that uncertainty is treated in science and in everyday life concerns its relation to the extremity of possible impacts. When a scientist

---

[94] Fallibilism is associated with the pragmatist tradition. The concept was introduced by the late-nineteenth-early-twentieth-century philosopher Charles Sanders Peirce.

[95] Herrick and Jamieson 2001.

[96] MacKenzie (1990: ch. 7) talks about the normal arc of scientific knowledge as involving a "certainty trough." The primary producers of knowledge highlight uncertainties, but these caveats are typically ignored when knowledge is retailed. If these knowledge claims bear on controversial matters, then those seeking to discredit the science will often highlight the uncertainties identified by the primary producers. See also Jamieson 1996a.

says that she is uncertain that a particular effect will occur, she leaves open the possibility that an even more extreme effect will occur. However, in ordinary language we typically attach the uncertainty to the most extreme effect that we can reasonably envision. Thus, in everyday discourse saying that we are uncertain about whether a given atmospheric concentration of carbon dioxide will produce a 2°C warming conversationally implies that the warming will be no more than 2°C, while in scientific discourse there is no such implication.

The denial industry has exploited these confusions on an industrial scale. It has developed strategies for systematically producing misinformation and misunderstanding. The denial industry has marketed climate change denial as if it were a product. Strategies have been deployed that systematically produce misinformation and misunderstanding. What is surprising is how little outrage there is about it from the mainstream media and "responsible" press.

In 1957 there was a national uproar when Vance Packard showed that advertisers were manipulating people into buying products in ways that bypass rational responses and decision-making capabilities.[97] Advertisers angrily (and ironically) denounced Packard's work as "propaganda that walks around hidden in the trusted and respected apparel of a book."[98] Packard also warned that advertisers were marketing politicians in the same way as products. In the 1956 election President Eisenhower's image had been carefully crafted by Batton, Barton, Durstine, and Osborn, then the nation's third-largest advertising agency. His opponent, Adlai Stevenson, grumbled that "[t]he idea that you can merchandise candidates for high office like breakfast cereal…is the ultimate indignity to the democratic process."[99] Indignity or not, Eisenhower won in a landslide.

Theodore White's *The Making of a President 1960* brought the marketing of politicians to public consciousness. It became extremely vivid in *The Selling of the President 1968*, a book by 26-year-old Joe McGinnis that remained on the *New York Times* best-seller list for 31 weeks. Neil Postman generalized the implicit critique in his 1985 *Amusing Ourselves to Death*, arguing that in the age of Reagan, news and public affairs reporting had become a branch of the entertainment industry. Not only were politicians being marketed like products, but the products that politicians had become were increasingly being trivialized.

The innovation of the last quarter century is to market epistemologies as products to be bought and sold, in the oft-requited hope that this will replace the rational appraisal of ideas and claims. This gives new meaning to the old metaphor of "the marketplace of ideas." Rather than convincing people of the truth or utility of ideas, theories, or understandings of the world, we now brand and market them, and manipulate consumers (or perhaps audiences—we certainly do not think of them

---

[97] Packard 2007.
[98] Packard 2007: 22.
[99] Packard: 187.

as citizens) into accepting or rejecting them. This is not a secret, and climate change is not unique in this regard (consider, e.g., tax policy and criminal justice). Nor is it a difference in kind. The marketing of ideas is just another step on the road from marketing products and candidates. What is missing is not an awareness of these developments, but a sense of revulsion about them. The attentive American public would once have been shocked by the commodification of epistemology. Now we are mainly interested in how well people succeed at it.

When former vice presidential candidate Sarah Palin gave a confused and garbled account of Paul Revere's midnight ride, rather than apologizing and setting the record straight, her supporters tried to change the account in Wikipedia in order to conform to her version.[100] There were attempts to find words that would not contradict whatever she was saying, and there were even attempts to incorporate her own words into the Wikipedia account on the grounds that Wikipedia is supposed to reflect what "trusted sources" say about a matter, and she of course is a "trusted source."[101] What was most revealing about this episode is that it was widely regarded as an amusing, poorly executed political ploy, rather than as an attack on the very idea of truth or an expression of a complete misunderstanding of the concept.

Part of what explains the relatively lackadaisical attitude of the public and opinion leaders is the deep cynicism that characterizes public life in contemporary America. We are no longer surprised at the depths to which others will sink. Finely attuned to their hypocrisy, we are increasingly skeptical of those who claim expertise (while, of course, exempting ourselves from the critique).[102] To some extent this is a general response to the perceived failures of expertise-driven, post–World War II industrial societies, and there is a version of this story to tell in many countries, but what follows is a sketch of what happened in my neighborhood.

Having emerged victoriously from World War II, the United States was almost immediately haunted by the specter of nuclear annihilation. The technological creation that decisively ended the war with Japan, the atomic bomb, soon threatened to end all of humanity. At the same time there was an explosion of new technology that promised "better living through chemistry."[103] As the 1950s turned to the 1960s, the price that these new technologies were exacting became increasingly obvious. Nuclear weapons, even if they were not being used in war, were killing people in peacetime through the effects of nuclear tests in the atmosphere. Pesticides such as DDT threatened to bring about a "silent spring," which would not only be

---

[100] For an account, see http://www.theatlanticwire.com/politics/2011/06/wikipedia-very-sick-sarah-palin-supporters/38535/. Retrieved July 18, 2013.

[101] For Wikipedia's policy see http://en.wikipedia.org/wiki/Wikipedia:No_original_research. Retrieved July 18, 2013.

[102] For an argument that a penchant for hypocrisy is a deep design feature of humanity, see Kurzban 2011.

[103] This is a variant of a motto that was associated with the Dupont Chemical Company.

ecologically disruptive but would put an end to a common human experience of the natural world.

These threats were the unforeseen consequences of scientific and technological innovation. The pretty picture that had been given to us in 1945 by Vannevar Bush, that a well-funded, unfettered scientific community was essential to the national welfare, was increasingly seen as only part of the story or even as a deception.[104] Some scientists defended the Faustian bargain that we had unwittingly made, while others, including some who had been involved in the development of these technologies, became critics both of their deployment and of the research trajectories that had given rise to them.

Still, the 1960s began optimistically with President Kennedy arriving in Washington with his "whiz kids," drawn from America's most prestigious universities and progressive corporations. For a while it seemed as though any problem would yield to intelligence, vigor, and a "can-do" attitude. Senator Hubert Humphrey, soon to become Vice President, singled out the social sciences as a neglected element for American progress. In an influential 1962 article, Humphrey wrote:

> At home and abroad, we as a nation confront awesome problems to which we must look to the social and behavioral sciences for inter-disciplinary answers.

With the support of Humphrey and others, the National Science Foundation began to fund social science research, and social and behavioral scientists were brought into the administration. They were influential in creating and administering Lyndon Johnson's "Great Society" programs, as well as in prosecuting the war in Viet Nam.

By the end of the 1960s both of these projects were widely viewed as failures. "The best and the brightest" had failed to win the war in Viet Nam.[105] They had been defeated by committed, disciplined, but technologically limited and often illiterate fighters, who refused to behave in accordance with the deliverances of rational choice theory. Despite the billions that were spent to address poverty and racism, there were hundreds of riots in American cities, killing more than 200 people and causing untold economic and social damage that would persist for decades.[106]

The truth is, of course, more complicated. New laws and court decisions had transformed race relations in America. In only seven years the poverty rate was nearly halved, and by 1970 it was lower than it is today.[107] As far as Viet Nam goes, whatever failures can be attributed to the "best and the brightest," they may at least have restrained the military from using nuclear weapons.[108] What is clear is this: The

---

[104] Available at http://www.nsf.gov/about/history/vbush1945.htm#ch1.1. Retrieved July 18, 2013.

[105] This was the title of a very influential 1972 book by David Halberstam.

[106] These numbers reflect riots from 1964 to 1971. For discussion, see Bean 2000; Collins and Margo 2007.

[107] http://www.washingtonmonthly.com/features/1999/9910.califano.html. Retrieved July 18, 2013.

[108] Tannenwald 2006.

Kennedy and Johnson administrations raised expectations beyond the government's ability to fulfill them.

The discrediting of the political class, which is usually seen as beginning with the Watergate scandal of the 1970s, was actually in evidence during the 1968 election campaign. President Johnson left office under a shadow, on the verge of being rejected by his own party.[109] Many Democrats refused to acknowledge his vice president, Hubert Humphrey, as the legitimate Democratic candidate. Humphrey did not run in the primaries, instead campaigning among party bosses. Robert Kennedy at the time of his assassination was the most popular politician in the country, both among Democrats and the electorate at large.[110] Had he not been assassinated, he may well have been the Democratic nominee and gone on to be president. Humphrey also had the bad luck or judgment to play "Happy Days Are Here Again" while he was being nominated and demonstrators were being beaten.

Things got worse as a result of the Watergate scandal and have only recovered fitfully, if at all. There is widespread contempt for government, and each new cohort of voters has lower participation rates than the previous one.[111] Some jurisdictions have adopted term limits, and many people have an almost pathological suspicion of government officials.[112]

One consequence of this loss of confidence has been the rise of a new culture of participation. No elite is going to decide on its own where a new dump will be sited, what punishment a sex offender should receive, or whether to raise taxes. This is most striking with the rise of the tea parties, but was also mirrored in the "occupy" movement, and also plays out in community board and city council meetings around the country.

The sociologist Ulrich Beck thinks of this as a new golden age. He thinks we now live in the "risk society" in which science is no longer seen as a neutral bearer of universal privilege, but as another important institutional player in public decision making, with its own interests and values. Instead of aspiring for certainty in the risk society, there is universal uncertainty, since "in matters of hazards, no one is an expert—particularly not the experts."[113]

It may be true that in some circumstances this confluence of forces could lead to the epistemological sophistication that Beck envisions (what he calls "reflexive modernization"). However, in the American context, it has led to epistemological

---

[109] The nadir of Johnson's job approval rating was in August 1968, when it stood at 35%. It is worth noting that both Presidents Bush, as well as Carter and Nixon, had lower job approval ratings, and the lows of Reagan, Clinton, and Obama were not much better.

[110] Converse et al. 1969.

[111] Those whose first vote was cast for Obama may be an exception. If so, it is an open question whether it indicates a reversal of a trend or a passing blip.

[112] This is indicated in many different ways but one sign is that Congress's approval rating has been mostly under 20% since 2008 (http://www.gallup.com/poll/1600/congress-public.aspx). Retrieved July 18, 2013.

[113] Beck 1992: 58.

nihilism. The loss of epistemological privilege and authority, indicated by the decline of the mainstream media, has led to the democratization of resentment, expressed in the rise and increasing power of both social media and the Internet, and in particular the influence of some of the Internet's most noxious sites.[114]

Actually, here in America we are beyond cynicism and heading toward the breakdown of some central features of Enlightenment thought.[115] Denialism is a powerful force in American society, not just with respect to climate change, but also regarding evolutionary theory. It manifests around events such as the 9/11 attacks, President Obama's citizenship, and bizarre health claims based on religion and New Age spirituality. A recent study indicated that people are more likely to accept paranormal claims as true when they believe that such claims have popular support, but knowing that scientists have rejected such claims does not make them more likely to reject them. In fact, it makes people more likely to accept such claims.[116]

One source of the resistance to science is that many people see science as threatening to their belief systems. Still, according to one survey, 67% who say that science conflicts with their religious beliefs still think that scientists contribute significantly to societal well-being. And among the public at large, scientists rate behind only two other professions in popular esteem: members of the military and teachers.[117] If we look at the data more deeply, it becomes clear that the kind of science that Americans respect is that which most resembles magic: medical science. Americans love science when it brings us miracles that affect our daily lives, but respect wanes when it is seen as remote or "curiosity-driven" (or so I hypothesize). Many of the same people who denigrate climate science are enthusiastic supporters of medical research. If they could shut down research in environmental science and shovel the money to medical research they would gladly do so.[118]

One way of understanding what is going on is to see Americans as divided between two different epistemologies.[119] Sometimes these divisions are across

---

[114] While exact numbers are hard to obtain, the Drudge Report has been reported to get more hits than the *New York Times* website (http://www.aim.org/on-target-blog/fox-news-getting-more-hits-than-new-york-times/). Retrieved July 18, 2013.

[115] Some may think this is an old story. For enlightening but depressing reading, see Hofstadter 1963, 1965.

[116] http://www.miller-mccune.com/science-environment/esp-study-suggests-lack-of-trust-in-science-14659/. Retrieved July 18, 2013.

[117] http://people-press.org/2009/07/09/public-praises-science-scientists-fault-public-media/, http://www.nsf.gov/statistics/seind02/c7/c7s3.htm. Retrieved July 18, 2013. There seems to be an inverse relation between how well members of a profession are paid and the esteem in which they are held.

[118] Senator Tom Coburn, himself a medical doctor and cancer survivor, has more or less this view; visit http://www.coburn.senate.gov/public//index.cfm?a=Files.Serve&File_id=2dccf06d-65fe-4087-b58d-b43ff68987fa. Retrieved July 18, 2013. The other elite that still carries respect in American society is the rich. Perhaps it is because we all think of ourselves as a potential rich person, or because in a society that is as culturally diverse as ours wealth is the only value on whose importance we can all agree.

[119] Here I develop a thought expressed to me by John Weiner. This division can be thought of as reflecting the centuries-old struggle between pragmatism and evangelical religion in American life.

communities and sometimes they are within the mind of a single individual. One model is procedural, evidence-based, and reflects the temper of scientific thinking. The other model focuses on outcomes, accepts beliefs based on their compatibility with other commitments, and rejects evidence if it does not support these commitments. Now to be clear, as psychologists have shown, all of us generally have a bias in favor of our existing beliefs, and in some circumstances this is justifiable.[120] The procedural model is not a description of how anyone always behaves. It describes an aspiration that we can achieve to some extent. What I am claiming is that large segments of American society reject the first model even as an aspiration. They see nothing wrong with accepting evidence based on their beliefs rather than accepting beliefs based on the evidence.[121]

This helps to explain what is otherwise puzzling. Several libertarian-leaning, pro-business "think tanks" such as the Competitive Enterprise Institute and the Cato Institute make a point of denying the facts about climate change. It is strange that anyone would think that standing up for liberty should require you to deny science. Moreover, these organizations have very little scientific expertise. They are largely staffed by lawyers and economists. One would expect them to be arguing about policy rather than trashing science. The "two epistemologies" model suggests an explanation for this behavior. These organizations accept the second rather than the first epistemological model. They sense that if science turns out a certain way then they will be under pressure to give up some of their policy views. Since they take their policy views as fixed, they reject the science that they see as threatening them. Indeed, they often attribute similar motivations to those who accept science, seeing it as a subterfuge for restricting liberty and individual rights.[122]

Scientism and denialism feed off each other.[123] Increasingly we are presented with a forced choice between two pictures of human agency. In one picture the brain moves in mysterious ways, and rationality, agency, and free will are illusions. In the other picture, rationality, agency, and free will are real, but only because they are implanted in us by a transcendent God. Since God moves in mysterious ways, we must take his existence on faith. What is missing from the popular mind is the idea that we are natural creatures of limited means, who are sometimes able to form

---

[120] See, e.g., Gilbert 1991.

[121] As the experiment cited earlier about people's acceptance of paranormal claims shows, people also endorse beliefs in order to affiliate with other people and communities. For evidence that Republicans engage in such system-justifying behavior more than Democrats, see Feygina et al. 2010: 326, 327.

[122] Another part of the explanation has to do with knowing who butters your bread. Charles and David Koch, who are some of the leading funders of right-wing causes in America and the primary owners and managers of a corporation heavily invested in extractive industries, are co-owners of Cato. They, along with an assortment of oil and tobacco companies and other corporate interests, also fund the Competitive Enterprise Institute.

[123] This is the main point that Lahsen is making in her 2013 article, though I disagree with how she makes it.

beliefs on the basis of evidence and act rationally upon them. This, along with our sympathetic and empathetic impulses, reflects our better nature. It is to be honored and encouraged, rather than dismissed or explained away.

3.6. PARTISANSHIP

Part of what feeds the fire of denialism is the increasing partisanship of American political life, and the way that this has affected environmental issues generally and climate change in particular.

Politically, environmentalism in America can be seen as having gone through three stages. Initially it was associated with Republicans. In 1864 Abraham Lincoln signed a bill setting aside Yosemite Valley and the Mariposa Grove of Giant Sequoias as a state-supervised public reserve, establishing the foundation for what later became Yosemite National Park. The year before, Lincoln had signed a bill creating the National Academy of Sciences. In 1872 President Ulysses S. Grant signed a bill designating Yellowstone as the first national park. Benjamin Harrison created Yosemite National Park in 1890, and created the first forest reserves in 1892. The environmental legacy of Theodore Roosevelt is well known. He created the United States Forest Service, established 155 national forests (two-thirds of the present system), five national parks, 18 national monuments, and 55 bird and game preserves. He also did an enormous amount in his speeches, writings, and actions to raise environmental consciousness.

The bipartisan period in environmental policy began with the rise of the progressive movement, which influenced both the Republican and Democratic parties in the early twentieth century. Woodrow Wilson was the first progressive Democratic president and he was active in conservation, founding the National Park Service. Theodore Roosevelt was an early political hero of his distant cousin Franklin Delano Roosevelt, and when it came to the environment they shared many of the same ideals.[124] Franklin Delano Roosevelt was a progressive, and he was initially undecided whether to enter politics as a Democrat or Republican. Republican President Dwight D. Eisenhower created the Arctic National Wildlife Refuge, an achievement that much of the Republican Party has been trying to undo over the past several decades. Richard Nixon signed into law four landmark federal bills: the Clean Air Act, the National Environmental Policy Act, the Environmental Pesticide Control Act, and the Endangered Species Act. He established the Environmental Protection Agency, and made many strong environmental appointments in his administration.

As we saw in Section 2.2, it was when the Reagan administration came to power in 1980 that environmental concern began to become a partisan issue. The Republican Party was becoming a more ideologically conservative party, and its base of support was shifting to the south and west. Over the last 30 years, partisan differentiation

---

[124] Woolner and Henderson 2005.

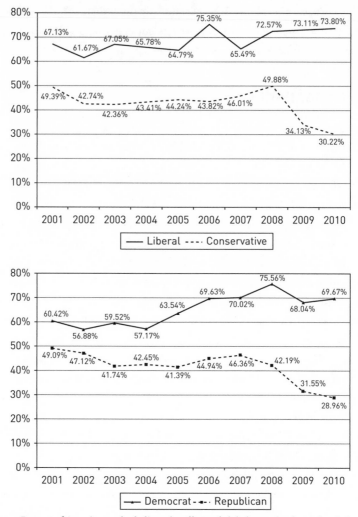

FIGURE 3.1 Percent of Americans who believe the effects of global warming have already begun to happen (2001–2010) by political ideology and party identification.

Source: From McCright and Dunlap 2011a.

has increased. Figure 3.1 is indicative of that change through time with respect to climate change.[125]

Increasingly, climate change denial is becoming part of the core Republican identity, as Figures 3.2 and 3.3 indicate.[126]

Actually, things are worse if you look at party leadership. A 2007 survey of 113 members of Congress indicated that 95% of Democrats believed that "it's been

[125] From McCright and Dunlap 2011a.
[126] Figures 3.2 and 3.3 are from http://environment.yale.edu/climate/news/the-climate-note-climate-change-by-political-party/. Retrieved October 25, 2013. The Republican commitment to denialism is to some extent a function of the large population of conservative white males who affiliate with it (see McCright and Dunlap 2011b).

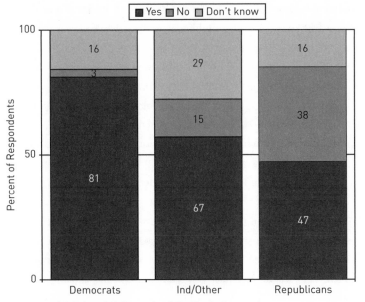

FIGURE 3.2　Do you think that global warming is happening?

Source: Yale, July 2010.

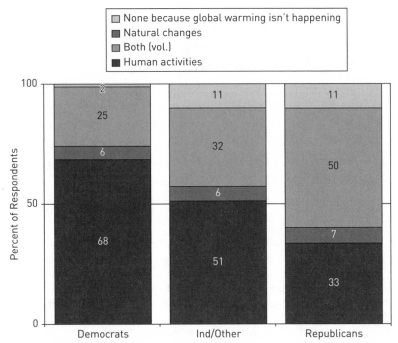

FIGURE 3.3　Major causes of global warming.

Source: Yale, July 2010.

proven beyond a reasonable doubt that the Earth is warming because of man-made problems," while only 13% of Republicans endorsed this claim.[127] Several candidates for the Republican nomination for president in 2012 had previously accepted the climate science consensus, and in some cases actively worked toward climate change solutions (e.g., Huntsman, Pawlenty, Gingrich, and Romney). After becoming presidential candidates, they retreated from their previous positions in every case. Former Governor of Minnesota Tim Pawlenty went so far as to apologize for mandating reductions in Minnesota's carbon emissions and for supporting a national emissions trading system.[128] The Republican nominee, Mitt Romney, was one of the architects of the Regional Greenhouse Gas Initiative (RGGI), which is a carbon cap and trade system for the northeastern states. However, in 2005, when he was preparing to run for the Republican nomination against John McCain, who had co-sponsored a bipartisan federal cap and trade bill in 2003, Romney abruptly took Massachusetts out of RGGI. During the 2012 campaign his statements were equivocal; he said frequently that "we don't know what's causing climate change on this planet."[129] It would be interesting to know how Romney would explain his change of heart about climate change, but I doubt that it had much to do with what he had learned about climate science.

3.7. POLITICAL INSTITUTIONS

The reasons that political leaders fail to act on climate change go beyond character defects. As we saw in Section 2.3 the eight years in which Al Gore was Vice President saw little action on climate change. When he ran for president in 2000, Gore was so reluctant to address environmental issues that a third-party Green candidate was able to take nearly 3 million votes, costing Gore a majority of the popular vote as well as the presidency.[130] The political system is supposed to be the adult in the room that prevents the clash of private interests from dragging us down to outcomes that almost none of us would prefer. However, there are facts about how our political system functions, along with some structural and conceptual features of the climate change problem, that make it difficult for political systems to arrive at solutions.

One reason that it is difficult to act on climate change is that there is not a single frame for understanding the problem. Consider the following example. Energy

---

[127] National Journal 2/3/07, pp. 6-7. For a sampling of Republican views, visit http://www.nationaljournal.com/pictures-video/congressional-republicans-and-their-differing-views-on-climate-change-pictures-20111202. Retrieved July 18, 2013.

[128] http://www.nationaljournal.com/politics/pawlenty-running-from-his-past-moves-on-environmental-policy-20110623. Retrieved July 18, 2013.

[129] http://www.politifact.com/truth-o-meter/statements/2012/may/15/mitt-romney/mitt-romney-and-whether-humans-are-causing-climate/. Retrieved July 18, 2013.

[130] Even with all this, it should not be forgotten that Gore would have been elected president had he carried his home state of Tennessee.

prices are an important dimension of the climate change problem. Higher energy prices generally mean lower emissions, while lower energy prices mean higher emissions. Yet the same edition of a newspaper might say in the science section that climate change is a serious problem that must be addressed, while the business section bemoans increases in the price of energy, as if these were completely different matters. Someone who reads only the business section may not appreciate at all the energy/climate nexus. Someone who reads both sections may simply be confused.

Matthew Nisbett has presented a table (Table 3.1), that shows some of the diverse ways that the climate change problem can be framed.[131]

There is a lot to say about each of these proposed frames, but I will not discuss them in detail. Suffice it to say that one does not have to believe that all of these frames apply or that the list is exhaustive in order to accept the main point, which is this: There are many different ways of conceptualizing the problem of climate change, each of which finds different resources relevant to its solution, and counts different responses as successes and failures. If the problem is fundamentally one of global governance, then new agreements and institutions are what are needed. If the problem is market failure, then carbon taxes or a cap and trade system is what is required. If the problem is primarily a technological failure, then we need an Apollo program for clean energy or perhaps geoengineering. If climate change is just the latest way for the global rich to exploit the global poor, then the time has come for a global struggle for justice. This problem of multiple frames is characteristic of what are called "wicked problems," and wicked problems are extremely difficult for political systems to address successfully.[132]

There are particular problems with the American political system. Governments in the United States are relatively weak, face immense problems, and are often captured by special interests. This makes it very difficult for them to act decisively in response to emerging problems that affect the public good. Constitutional design, voter initiatives, legislation, legislative rules, and case law accentuate the status quo biases that are generally characteristic of individuals and institutions. The federal system creates limits on the ability of any single government (federal, state, local, or tribal) to act, though the exact limits change through time and are often only discoverable through litigation. The separation of powers between the three branches of the federal government, with the legislative branch further divided into two independent bodies, makes it extremely difficult for innovative or proactive legislation or policy to be enacted. When this does occur, for example with the passage of the Endangered Species Act in 1973, it is usually because political actors have no idea

[131] http://www.environmentmagazine.org/Archives/Back%20Issues/March-April%202009/Nisbet-full.html. Retrieved July 18, 2013.
[132] For more on wicked problems, see http://eureka.sbs.ox.ac.uk/66/1/TheWrongTrousers.pdf. Retrieved July 18, 2013. One of the functions of a political system is to impose frames on problems and thus make them soluble. Calling something a wicked problem is in part to characterize it and in part to confess to failure in solving it.

Table 3.1 Typology of Frames Applicable to Climate Change

Frame	Defines science-related issue as...
Social progress	A means of improving quality of life or solving problems; alternative interpretation as a way to be in harmony with nature or to master it.
Economic development and competitiveness	An economic investment; market benefit or risk; or a point of local, national, or global competitiveness.
Morality and ethics	A matter of right or wrong; or of respect or disrespect for limits, thresholds, or boundaries.
Scientific and technical uncertainty	A matter of expert understanding or consensus; a debate over what is known versus unknown; or peer-reviewed, confirmed knowledge versus hype or alarmism.
Pandora's box/Frankenstein's monster/ runaway science	A need for precaution or action in face of possible catastrophe and out-of-control consequences; or alternatively as fatalism, where there is no way to avoid the consequences or chosen path.
Public accountability and governance	Research or policy either in public interest or serving special interests, emphasizing issues of control, transparency, participation, responsiveness, or ownership; or debate over proper use of science and expertise in decision-making ("politicization").
Middle way/alternative path	A third way between conflicting or polarized views or options.
Conflict and strategy	A game among elites, such as who is winning or losing the debate; or a battle of personalities or groups (usually a journalist-driven interpretation).

Sources: W. A. Gamson and A. Modigiiani, "Media Discourse and Public Opinion on Nuclear Power: A Constructionist Approach,"*American Journal of Sociology* 95, no. 1 (1989): 1–37; U. Dahinden, "Biotechnology in Switzerland: Frames in a Heated Debate," *Science Communication* 24, no. 2 (2002): 184–97; J. Durant, M. W. Bauer, and G. Gakell, *Biotechnolgy in the Public Sphere: A European Sourcebook* (Lansing, MI: Michigan State University Press, 1998); M. C. Nisbet and B. V. Lewenstein, "Biotechnology and the American Media: The Policy Process and the Elite Press, 1970 to 199," *Science Communication* 23, no. 4 (2202): 359–91; and M. C. Nisbet, "Framing Science: A New Paradigm in Public Engagement," in L. Kahlor and P. Stout, eds., *Understanding Science: New Agendas in Science Communication* (New York: Taylor & Francis, 2009).

what they are doing. In addition to supermajorities that are required by the United States Constitution, the Senate has effectively imposed a supermajority rule for both debating and passing most legislation, and 16 states have imposed supermajority requirements for tax increases. Finally, many people see the current system of financing political campaigns as discrediting or corrupt, and the Constitution, as the courts currently interpret it, makes it difficult to enforce significant reforms.[133] While it is not difficult to list problems with the American political system that make action on issues such as climate change difficult, and even to identify reforms that would make a difference, it is the question of how to get there from here that is most vexing.[134]

As we saw in Chapter 2, the most systematic attempts at climate governance have been through the international system, taking nation-states as primary agents. The crowning achievement is the Framework Convention on Climate Change (FCCC). The Kyoto Protocol, which provided mechanisms for beginning to implement the objectives of the Convention, specified a first commitment period that expired in 2012. A second commitment period has been established for 2013–2020 but has not yet come into force as I write these words in May 2013. In any case these commitments will only cover the European Union and Australia, which together produce less than 15% of annual global emissions.[135] Whatever importance the Kyoto Protocol might once have had, it is clear that it is falling apart. What is not clear is how the FCCC will be affected.

There are many specific problems with the existing governance structure (e.g. the requirement for consensus, the crude division between developed [Annex I] and developing [non-Annex I] countries, etc.). However, the heart of the problem is that climate change has many of the properties of being the world's largest collective action problem, and it is difficult for any country that is responsive to its citizens to do its fair share in securing the global public good of climate stability. In part, this is because of self-interest. People as individuals want climate to be stabilized, but they also want to benefit from their own GHG emissions while others reduce their emissions. High-emitting rich countries do not want developing countries to follow in their footsteps, but developing countries want rich countries to take the first steps in reducing emissions. Even among the rich countries there is a "you first, then me" attitude. To a great extent, this behavior simply follows from the logic of a collective action problem: For each of us, defection dominates cooperation, however others act.

---

[133] The relation between widespread public perception of corruption and campaign finance is complex, however. See http://ideas.repec.org/p/bep/upennl/upenn_wps-1033.html. Retrieved July 18, 2013.

[134] See Speth 2012.

[135] http://www.carbontrust.com/news/2013/01/doha-it-kept-the-show-on-the-road-but-only-just. Retrieved July 18, 2013.

Climate change also poses an intergenerational collective action problem. Since every generation benefits from its own emissions but the costs are deferred to future generations, they have an incentive not to control their emissions. Moreover, since each generation (except the first) suffers from the emissions of previous generations, benefiting from their own present emissions may even appear to be just compensation for what they have suffered. But of course, this reasoning leads to the continuous buildup of GHGs in the atmosphere over time.[136]

Indeed, these problems are even worse than they seem, for climate change does not involve just single, intra- and intergenerational collective action problems. Jurisdictional boundaries and competing scales cause multiple, overlapping, and hierarchically embedded collective action problems. A vast variety of behaviors by individuals, nations, and other entities affect climate, but they are governed by an equally vast array of different regimes with different mandates and even in many cases different parties. For example, decisions about trade and intellectual property affect GHG emissions, but each of these areas is governed by its own legal regimes. While this may seem abstract, we witness policy failures and dysfunctions driven by the same dynamics on a daily basis with respect to simpler problems. When a city provides services for residents who live in outlying areas and do not pay city taxes, this is an example of the sort of problem that occurs with respect to climate change.

One way of solving or softening such collective action problems is through love, sympathy, and empathy. However, these seem in short supply in diverse, fragmented, modern societies, and in their more systematized forms as ethical systems and principles of justice, they too require revision in order to be responsive to the problem of climate change, as we will see in Chapter 5.

Sadly, it is not entirely clear that democracy is up to the challenge of climate change. Well-functioning democracies act in the interests of the governed rather than on behalf of all those whose interests are affected. The benefits from the activities that cause climate change accrue primarily to those who are members of particular political communities, while the costs are borne primarily by those who are not members of those communities. Costs are borne by those who live beyond the borders of the major emitters, future generations, animals, and nature. Perhaps surprisingly, this seems relatively well understood by the American public, as Figure 3.4 indicates.[137]

If democratic institutions are to succeed in addressing climate change, they will have to be more responsive to concerns that go beyond those of the political community over which they have authority. They will have to be sensitive to where we are located in time and how we are embedded in nature. Sometimes this will mean

---

[136] For an excellent discussion of the precise nature of these problems, see Gardiner 2010, parts B and C.

[137] This figure is constructed from data found here: http://www.climatechangecommunication.org/images/files/Climate_Change_in_the_American_Mind.pdf. Retrieved July 18, 2013.

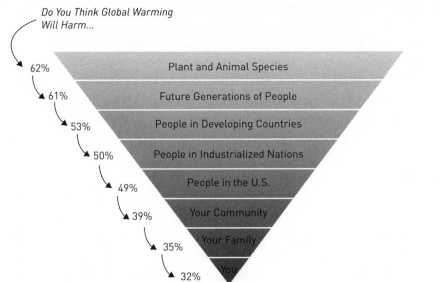

FIGURE 3.4 Harmful effects of global warming.

protecting non-citizens, future people, or even nature at the expense of present citizens and even perhaps going against their preferences. In one respect this calls for more rigidity and less responsiveness in political institutions, perhaps through such mechanisms as constitutional restrictions.[138] Yet political institutions that can successfully address climate change will also have to be intelligently flexible and responsive to new information, in many cases scientific information. It is difficult to know how to design institutions with both virtues: that are rigid when they ought to be and flexible when they need to be. What is clear is that the populist direction in which most democracies are moving is not tailored to such concerns. Indeed, it is difficult to see how to get populist democracies to accept constraints on the popular will that might help make climate stability possible.[139]

Since the end of World War II, humans have attained a kind of power that is unprecedented in history. While in the past entire peoples could be destroyed, now all people are vulnerable. While once particular human societies had the power to upset the natural processes that made their lives and cultures possible, now people have the power to alter the fundamental global conditions that permitted human life to evolve and that continue to sustain it. There is little reason to suppose that our systems of governance are up to the task of managing such threats.[140]

[138] However, some constitutional restrictions are directed toward more fully expressing populist fervor rather than restraining it, such as those requiring supermajorities for tax increases.

[139] For some hopeful reflection, visit http://www.fdsd.org/wordpress/wp-content/uploads/Democracy-and-climate-change-scenarios-final-with-foreword.pdf. Retrieved July 18, 2013.

[140] For further discussion, visit http://www.humansandnature.org/can-democracy-in-crisis-deal-with-the-climate-crisis--question-7.php, and http://www.earthsystemgovernance.org/. Retrieved July 18, 2013.

3.8. THE HARDEST PROBLEM

The most difficult challenge in addressing climate change lurks in the background. Evolution did not design us to solve or even to recognize this kind of problem. We have a strong bias toward dramatic movements of middle-sized objects that can be visually perceived, and climate change does not typically present in this way.

The onset of climate change is gradual and uncertain rather than immediate and obvious. Increments of climate change are usually barely noticeable, and even less so because we re-norm our expectations to recent experiences. Some have suggested that the strong reaction to the severe winter of 2009–2010 in Eurasia and the United States can partly be explained by the fact that as the world warms, people lose their memory of cold winters. Bizarrely enough, against the background of a warming world, a winter that would not have been seen as anomalous in the past is viewed as unusually cold, thus as evidence that a warming is not occurring. In fact, regional data from a single season is not the sort of evidence that could overturn a climatological theory like global warming.[141] Global warming does not mean that every region will become warmer, nor does it mean that every day in a warmer world will be warmer than a comparable day at present. Schneider explains this with a gambling metaphor: Global warming loads the dice in favor of increased temperatures, changes in precipitation, and extreme climatic events, but it doesn't determine the outcome.[142] A global warming increases the probability for particular regions to be affected by these changes but need not bring about such changes in every season of every year in every region. The basic problem here is that climate change is a technical, complex issue that is best represented probabilistically, and our intuitions often betray us when it comes to probabilistic thinking.[143]

Another feature of climate change that makes it difficult for us to respond is that its causes and effects are geographically and temporally unbounded. Earth system scientists study the earth holistically and think on millennial timescales and beyond, but this perspective is foreign to most people. Most of us pay little attention to events that occur beyond national boundaries, unless they are "one-off" disasters. The idea that turning up my thermostat in New York can contribute to affecting people living in Malaysia in a thousand years is virtually beyond comprehension to most of us.

Climate change will have multiple, sometimes paradoxical, indirect effects, and many of its impacts on human welfare will be relatively invisible. Effects of climate change will include sea level rises and increased frequency of droughts, storms, and extreme temperatures. In some regions these effects may also include an increased frequency of cold days. In addition to these first-order impacts, climate change

---

[141] At least part of the explanation for the winter weather of 2009–2010 involved the occurrence of an El Niño. See James Hansen, "If It's That Warm, How Come It's So Darned Cold?," available at http://www.columbia.edu/~jeh1/mailings/. Retrieved July 18, 2013.

[142] Schneider 1989.

[143] This is a theme of Daniel Kahneman's work (see e.g., 2011).

will have indirect, second-order impacts such as species extinctions and changes in agricultural patterns, as well as third-order impacts affecting social and political relationships, and human and national security. Many people will be killed or harmed by first-order effects, but many more will be affected by the second- and third-order effects that are mediated by economic status, food availability, disease burdens, and so on. However, many of these effects will be relatively invisible since they will involve "statistical" rather than '"individual" lives.[144] Climate change will cause the deaths of many people, but there will be no obituary that will say that Dale Jamieson (for example) died yesterday, cause of death: climate change. While we can be very responsive to individual victims, we have difficulty empathizing with statistical victims. We mobilize huge resources around highly publicized cases of little girls falling into wells while we do comparatively little to save children when they are the invisible victims of policy choices.[145]

There are other psychological mechanisms at work that inhibit action.[146] The scale of a problem like climate change can be crippling.[147] When we do not feel efficacious with respect to a problem, we often deny that it exists. There are deep cultural reasons that we often say of predictable disasters that we never saw them coming.[148] Climate change can seem to violate our sense that the world is just and well-ordered.[149] It has even been suggested that our denial of climate change is associated with our fear of death.[150]

Underneath these reactions are some deep truths about our animal nature. Climate change must be thought rather than sensed, and we are not very good at thinking. Even if we succeed in thinking that something is a threat, we are less reactive than if we sense that it is a threat. Consider the difference between touching a hot stove and being told that the stove is hot. Scientists are telling us that the world is warming, but we do not sense it and so we do not act. This is the hardest problem to overcome. Any approach to coming to terms with climate change must respect these facts about ourselves. As we will see, the approach that I sketch in Chapter 7 tries to do just that.

3.9. CONCLUDING REMARKS

In this chapter I have explained some of the obstacles to acting on climate change. We live in a society in which there is a cultural chasm between scientists and policy-makers. Most of us, including scientists, are largely confused about the

---

[144] Schelling 1968.

[145] For more on these concerns, see Jamieson 1991.

[146] For an overview, see Norgaard 2011.

[147] Slovic 2007.

[148] Cerulo 2006.

[149] Feinberg and Willer 2011.

[150] Dickinson 2009.

relations between facts and values, and science and policy. Many of us are scientifically ignorant, and large sums have been spent to further confuse and misinform us. This has occurred against the background of rising cynicism, eroding respect for Enlightenment values, and dysfunctional political systems. Making things worse, climate change presents us with the largest collective action problem that humanity has ever faced, one that is extended both in space and time. It is not the sort of problem that Mother Nature raised us to solve or even to notice. The economist Cameron Hepburn has succinctly summarized the difficulty of the challenge that we face by saying that if someone wanted to put an end to humanity, he would design a pill that would produce many of the effects of climate change.

The most powerful motivators that we have for solving collective action problems are economics and ethics. They ask the central questions: How much does it cost? Is it the right thing to do? Economics leads us to think in terms of rational self-interest. Ethics pushes us to think expansively, collectively, and impartially. In the next two chapters we will see how these motivators fare with respect to our problem.

4 The Limits of Economics

Climate change poses the world's largest collective action problem.[1] Each of us acting on our own desires contributes to an outcome that we neither desire nor intend. This basic structure is true of nations as well as individual people. Economics is one of the most powerful resources we have for resolving collective action problems. By providing information about economic benefits and costs, economics helps us to determine whether some action or policy is in our interest. In addition, economists have designed policy instruments that can help us to implement policies that are in our interests even when markets fail. It is no wonder that economics is extremely influential both on policy choices and implementation, and on individual decision-making.

4.1. ECONOMICS AND CLIMATE CHANGE

There is a way of looking at the problem of climate change that suggests that it should easily yield to an economic solution. The problem of climate change arises from the fact that climate-changing behavior produces an unpriced negative externality. The costs that people bear are not equal to the costs that they impose, since these unpriced costs are not compensated. As a result, those who benefit from climate-changing behavior do not pay the full cost of their behavior, while some of the costs fall on people who are not adequately compensated. This creates perverse incentives to engage in climate-changing behavior, resulting in an excess of such behavior. In principle a better, more efficient outcome is available in which less climate-changing behavior occurs, and those who suffer damages from this behavior are adequately compensated by those who benefit from it. Since some people can be made better off by moving to this more efficient, lower level of climate-changing behavior and no one would be made worse off than she would otherwise be if she were bearing the full costs of her behavior, we can address climate change without compromising anyone's interests. This is the possibility that John Broome calls "efficiency without sacrifice."[2]

---

[1] Throughout this book when I speak of climate change as having the structure of a collective action problem, I mean this generically in the sense in which I describe it in the text. There is a lot of looseness in how this term is used in the literature. Various problems are distinguished and sometimes considered instances, or near neighbors, of collective action problems. These are disputes which I do not wish to enter here.

[2] Broome 2012: 45, drawing on Foley 2009. Cf. Stern 2010a: 85.

While this is very abstract, most economists believe that in practice a relatively small investment in addressing climate change would produce a better economic outcome than "business as usual."[3] In 1997 2,600 American economists, including eight Nobel Prize winners, released a statement that declared:

> Economics studies have found that there are many potential policies to reduce greenhouse-gas emissions for which the total benefits outweigh the total costs. For the United States in particular, sound economic analysis shows that there are policy options that would slow climate change without harming American living standards, and these measures may in fact improve U.S. productivity in the longer run.[4]

The investment required to produce this better outcome is usually estimated at 1.5–2% of global gross domestic product (GDP).[5] Since this is less than a year of normal economic growth, it means that if we were to adopt this policy it would take until 2050 to reach the GDP level that we would otherwise reach in 2049 on a straight line extrapolation.[6] As Schelling (1997: 10) remarked,

> If someone could wave a wand and phase in, over a few years, a climate mitigation program that depressed our GNP by two percent in perpetuity, no one would notice the difference.

However, if we fail to make this investment, then we will be worse off in 2050 than we will be on a business-as-usual scenario.

While it may seem to disappear over a long time horizon, 1.5–2% of GDP is a lot of money. Still, it helps to put it in comparative perspective. In 2009 American

---

[3] See, e.g., Nordhaus 2010 and Parry et al. 2007; see also Krugman, http://www.nytimes.com/2010/04/11/magazine/11Economy-t.html?ref=magazine&pagewanted=all (retrieved July 18, 2013) and the Congressional Budget Office report that he cites.

[4] It is getting increasingly difficult to find this statement on the web but it can be found here: http://dieoff.org/page105.htm. Retrieved July 18, 2013. For a brief account, visit http://thomas.loc.gov/cgi-bin/cpquery/?&dbname=cp105&sid=cp1055c4Ad&refer=&r_n=sr054.105&item=&&&sel=TOC_317793&. Retrieved July 18, 2013.

[5] To put this in perspective, consider the fact that some economists believe that political choices about US fiscal policy resulted in a 1.5% GDP loss for 2012, and that budget sequestration will reduce GDP by .6% in 2013 (visit https://mm.jpmorgan.com/stp/t/c.do?i=19642-7A9&u=a_p*d_645537.html*h_-1ni8eo3 for the former and http://www.cbo.gov/publication/43961 for the latter, retrieved July 18, 2013). These are not policy choices that produce significant benefits comparable to reducing carbon emissions. Since 2007 the consulting firm McKinsey & Co. has identified a large suite of GHG-reducing actions that would return almost immediate benefits; these reports can be accessed by visiting http://www.mckinsey.com/Client_Service/Sustainability/Latest_thinking/Costcurves. Retrieved July 18, 2013.

[6] Schelling first made this point in his 1992 article. According to a 2008 study by the International Monetary Fund, the policies needed to reduce emissions by 60% from 2002 would leave the global economy about 2.6% smaller than it otherwise would be in 2040; visit http://www.imf.org/external/pubs/ft/fandd/2008/03/tamirisa.htm. Retrieved July 18, 2013.

GDP was about $14.12 trillion, so investing 2% in climate protection would have amounted to about $282 billion. Since 2001 the United States has spent $1.3 trillion on wars in Afghanistan and Iraq, and on the global war on terror. The costs of these wars are expected to rise to between $3.2 and $4 trillion.[7] The Bush tax cuts of 2001 and 2003 cost about $1.2 trillion before they were modified in 2012.[8] They have now been made permanent for 95% of all taxpayers. Various arguments can be given for and against the supposed economic benefits of the tax cuts and the wars, but similar arguments can be made for climate protection as well. When seen comparatively, it seems surprising that the smaller investment in climate protection would not have been made, especially since the aggregate economic benefits of this investment seem much less risky than military invasions or tax cuts. It is even more puzzling in light of the common presumption among economists that people are economically rational. The supposed irresistibility of economically rational action is brought out by the old joke about why an economist never bends down to pick up a dollar ("if it were really a dollar someone else would have already picked it up").

If we bring these considerations together we have something of a paradox. In principle, addressing climate change would move us to a more efficient state of the economy without sacrifice. The costs of the upfront investment are significant, but not large compared to other recent and ongoing expenditures whose benefits are less clear. People are often, perhaps invariably, moved by economic considerations, yet in this case we do not act. What is the explanation?

Part of the explanation for why economic consensus does not produce action mirrors the reasons discussed in the previous chapter for why scientific consensus does not produce action. Ignorance abounds, the political system is sclerotic, and people are angry and mistrustful of elites. We are confused about the interrelations between facts, values, science, and policy, and generally not well equipped to deal with problems that have the characteristics of climate change. Moreover, any attempt to respond to climate change activates distributional conflicts. Those who benefit from the present inefficient system might be worse off in a more efficient system in which compensation was paid, and those who lose in the present system fear that they will be hurt even more by any change, since there is no guarantee that compensation will actually be paid. Finally, to the extent to which denialism about the reality of climate change is successful, the economic question becomes moot: If there is no problem, then there is no need for action.[9]

---

[7] See Amy Belasco, The Cost of Iraq, Afghanistan, and Other Global War on Terror Operations Since 9/11, Congressional Research Service, March 29, 2011; available at www.fas.org/sgp/crs/natsec/RL33110.pdf. Retrieved July 18, 2013. Also visit http://costsofwar.org/. Retrieved July 18, 2013.

[8] http://www.cbpp.org/cms/?fa=view&id=909. Retrieved October 25, 2013.

[9] Some recent surveys indicate that more people support taking action on climate change than believe that it is actually occurring. Part of the explanation is that people favor these policies for other reasons (e.g., energy security), and that they support precautionary policies even if they are not convinced that the threat will materialize. Visit http://environment.yale.edu/climate-communication/article/

These considerations go a long way toward explaining why economic consensus has not led to action. Still, it is difficult to shake the feeling that the problems with climate economics are even deeper. Whatever people say in academic seminars, many people simply do not believe the economic projections.[10]

One reason is that the changes to our way of life that are being envisioned seem so massive and systematic that it is difficult to believe that they would not entail huge costs. A century-long project to decarbonize the global economy sounds about as world-historical as the Russian Revolution. How could that come cheap?

When we imagine in advance large-scale changes over relatively long periods of time, we think that such changes must be draconian and expensive. This is an illusion, perhaps related to the psychological mechanisms discussed in Section 3.8. Viewed retrospectively such changes may actually be relatively cheap and invisible.

Consider a homely example. One of the things that make movies from the 1970s look dated is the plethora of analogue devices that they depict, from clocks to phonographs, with hardly a computer in sight. Yet within two or three decades the analogue world almost completely disappeared, replaced by the digital world in which we now live. This change was massive, revolutionary, systematic, and even relatively rapid. Contemplating this transition in advance, it might well have seemed too daunting both in terms of resources and in the amount of social engineering that would be required. Yet, while people incurred expenses in replacing analogue devices and in reorganizing their lives, the forces driving this innovation were so powerful and the benefits so palpable that the economic and social obstacles were overwhelmed.

This illusion is related to why it is difficult for us to imagine how relatively small changes can radically alter earth systems. For example, it is difficult to imagine how adding to the atmosphere a few hundred parts per million of a trace gas such as carbon dioxide could radically change the earth's climate. Yet the last time carbon dioxide levels were as high as they are today, sea levels were 60–80 feet higher.[11] We are geared up to notice large sudden changes, but small changes over long periods of time can have profound effects through the constant repetition of incremental drivers, self-reinforcing mechanisms, paradoxical effects, path dependencies, and

PolicySupportMay2011/?utm_source=Yale+Project+on+Climate+Change+Communication &utm_campaign=1532310204- and consult other documents on this site. Retrieved July 18, 2013.

[10] There is a deep-seated mistrust of economic expertise in post-recession America. Another interesting example is that the Congressional Budget Office estimates that the Affordable Care Act will reduce the budget deficit, but the opposite belief is close to being the conventional wisdom (http://www.cbo.gov/publication/44008, retrieved July 18, 2013).

[11] http://www.nytimes.com/2013/05/11/science/earth/carbon-dioxide-level-passes-long-feared-milestone.html?_r=0. Retrieved July 18, 2013.

various other mechanisms. The paradigm, of course, is the constant drip of small amounts of water that can create the Grand Canyon or destroy your house. A different example that illustrates the same point concerns the extinction of New Zealand's flightless birds. Holdaway and Jacomb (2000) showed how, even with relatively low rates of population growth and habitat destruction, subsistence hunting by 100 newly arrived Maori in New Zealand could drive a population of 158,000 moas to extinction in little more than a century.[12]

Change that is seen upfront as extremely rapid, costly, and wrenching may not seem that way when we look back from the comfort of the new world that we have created. Imagine that someone were to say that we were going to move from typewriters, hard copy, and paper storage to computers, light displays, and digital storage in a 20-year period. Or imagine changing the modality of long-distance travel from railroads and ships to airplanes, a change that occurred in my lifetime. What is seen from one perspective as rapid and wrenching social change is often seen as irresistible and incremental from another point of view.

A second reason that many people do not believe the economic projections is a better one. Despite the fact that there is a consensus that it is in our collective economic interest to act on climate change, there are profound disagreements about what drives these conclusions. It can be quite unsettling when people who disagree about so much seem to agree on conclusions. Should this make us more or less confident about the conclusions? We could see the disagreement about premises as a kind of sensitivity analysis that should make us more confident about the conclusions. Or we could see the disagreement about premises as evidence that the economists do not know what they are doing. It is reasonable to be confused about what stance to take when the various views that converge on a policy recommendation embody such profound disagreements.

Another reason that we have not acted on the advice of economists is that they themselves have done an enormous amount to obscure the basic message that it is in our interests to act on climate change. In the United States almost every concrete measure to address climate change has been opposed by prestigious economists. Some economists went out of their way to condemn the Kyoto Protocol, even though it is the only agreement with binding emissions limits that has actually gone into effect. When cap and trade appeared to be a viable political option in the United States, some highly visible economists condemned it in favor of other policies (e.g., a carbon tax) that were not under active political consideration. Disagreements among economists about how quickly and urgently to act have often drowned out the simple consensus message that it is important to do something to slow climate change. While all economists speak in equations, they have done an enormous amount to build a tower of Babel.

---

[12] The moas were nine species (in six genera) of flightless birds endemic to New Zealand.

4.2. THE STERN REVIEW AND ITS CRITICS

The conflicts became especially sharp and visible with the publication of the Stern Review. On July 19, 2005, shortly after the Kyoto Protocol came into effect, Gordon Brown, Britain's Chancellor of the Exchequer and later Prime Minister, announced that he had asked Sir Nicholas Stern to lead a major review of the economics of climate change. The Review's purpose was to "understand more comprehensively the nature of the economic challenges and how they can be met, in the UK and globally."[13] The Stern Review was rolled out at a press conference in London on October 29, 2006, the week before 5,000 climate change negotiators, activists, and interested parties were meeting in Nairobi for the 12th Conference of the Parties to the UN Framework Convention on Climate Change (FCCC). Flanked by Gordon Brown and Prime Minister Tony Blair, Stern announced the Review's conclusions.[14]

> The scientific evidence is now overwhelming: climate change is a serious global threat, and it demands an urgent global response....Hundreds of millions of people could suffer hunger, water shortages and coastal flooding as the world warms...if we don't act, the overall costs and risks of climate change will be equivalent to losing at least 5% of global GDP each year, now and forever. If a wider range of risks and impacts is taken into account, the estimates of damage could rise to 20% of GDP or more...the costs of action—reducing greenhouse gas emissions to avoid the worst impacts of climate change—can be limited to around 1% of global GDP each year.... *The costs of stabilising the climate are significant but manageable; delay would be dangerous and much more costly.*[15]

The Review was greeted with extensive, positive media coverage in Europe, though it received much less attention in the United States. The British newspaper *The Independent* wrote that

> Climate change has been made the world's biggest priority, with the publication of a stark report showing that the planet faces catastrophe unless urgent measures are taken to reduce greenhouse gas emissions. Future generations may come to regard the

---

[13] http://webarchive.nationalarchives.gov.uk/+/http://www.hm-treasury.gov.uk/independent_reviews/stern_review_economics_climate_change/sternreview_backgroundtoreview.cfm#terms. Retrieved July 18, 2013.

[14] For video coverage of the news conference visit http://www.blinkx.com/watch-video/environment-climate-change-stern-report-new-bill-promised-by-chancellor/FB9rMc_vtxnXKFj_JCDL2w. Retrieved July 18, 2013. It is revealing that the network ITV "balanced" its coverage by featuring a climate change denier, and expressed skepticism in a voice-over about whether Great Britain could do much on its own to stem climate change.

[15] From the short version of the Executive Summary, available at http://webarchive.nationalarchives.gov.uk/+/http://www.hm-treasury.gov.uk/sternreview_summary.htm. Retrieved July 18, 2013. Bold in the original text.

apocalyptic report by Sir Nicholas Stern, a former chief economist at the World Bank, as the turning point in combating global warming, or as the missed opportunity.[16]

From the beginning, economists were sharply divided about the Stern Review. Even those who were broadly sympathetic to its conclusions were often critical about the methodology and assumptions.[17] Some critics were downright rude. For example, Richard Tol wrote:

> In sum, the Stern Review is very selective in the studies it quotes on the impacts of climate change. The selection bias is not random, but emphasizes the most pessimistic studies. The discount rate used is lower than the official recommendations by HM Treasury. Results are occasionally misinterpreted. The report claims that a cost-benefit analysis was done, but none was carried out. The Stern Review can therefore be dismissed as alarmist and incompetent.[18]

William Nordhaus wrote that "the Stern Review should be read primarily as a document that is political in nature and has advocacy as its purpose."[19] He called the Review "radical"[20] and accused it of making "extreme"[21] assumptions, and adopting the perspective of "Government House utilitarianism."[22] According to Nordhaus, the Stern Review "...takes the lofty vantage point of the world social planner, perhaps stoking the dying embers of the British Empire."[23]

What is going on here? The Stern Review commanded attention because it moved climate economics from the pages of academic journals and the orbit of partisan "think" tanks to the world of politics and government. It was conducted by a highly respected former Chief Economist of the World Bank and carried the imprimatur of the British government. Its message was loud and clear: begin immediately to reduce emissions, and go hard. This message was at odds with the prevailing view in the United States, both in the government and in the economics and policy-making establishment. The Review's style and its method of presentation probably also offended some American sensibilities.

Economists in the United States began working on climate change in the late 1960s, largely funded by government agencies and private foundations. From 1971 to 1974 Ralph D'Arge worked with the US Department of Transportation's Climate Impacts Assessment Program (CIAP), and shortly thereafter began working with

---

[16] http://www.combusem.com/STERN.HTM. Retrieved July 18, 2013.
[17] For a review, see Cole 2008.
[18] Tol 2006: 979–980.
[19] Nordhaus 2008: 167.
[20] Nordhaus 2008: 166, 168.
[21] Nordhaus 2008: 169.
[22] Nordhaus 2008: 174.
[23] Nordhaus 2008: 174.

the climate scientist Stephen Schneider at the National Center for Atmospheric Research.[24] In 1977 William Nordhaus, then serving on the President's Council of Economic Advisors, spoke to the American Geophysical Union on the economics of climate change, and shortly thereafter began publishing on the subject. In 1980 V. Kerry Smith wrote a research plan on the economics of climate change for the National Oceanic and Atmospheric Administration (NOAA), based on a workshop that involved many leading environmental economists. The same year Thomas Schelling chaired a National Academy of Sciences (NAS) committee that produced a report on climate change, and in 1983 Nordhaus joined Schelling on the NAS Changing Climate study, which was led by William Nierenberg. During the early 1990s major studies in climate economics were published by Cline (1992), Nordhaus (1994a), and others. During the late 1990s, as the politics around the Kyoto Protocol heated up, shameless partisan studies, often conducted by consulting firms whose purpose was to produce numbers in support of conclusions, became increasingly influential. Against this background, Nordhaus's RICE and DICE models emerged as the gold standard for academic work in climate economics.[25]

DICE, which is an acronym for Dynamic Integrated model of Climate and the Economy, views the economics of climate change from the perspective of neo-classical growth theory. It represents the climate system as capital stock, greenhouse gas emissions (GHGs) as degrading capital stock, and emissions reductions as investments that protect this capital stock. DICE links emissions to future economic welfare via a damage function. It calculates the optimal carbon price, which is the price on carbon emissions that balances the incremental costs of reducing emissions with the incremental benefits of reducing climate damages. DICE is a globally aggregated model. RICE, which is an acronym for Regional Integrated model of Climate and Economy, is a multiregion version of DICE. There are other integrated assessment models, but Nordhaus's are the most influential.[26]

One of Nordhaus's complaints about the Stern Review was that it was not peer-reviewed. He wrote that "the British government is not infallible in questions of economic and social analysis of global warming, any more than it was in its assessment of weapons of mass destruction in Iraq."[27] Putting aside the rather weird

---

[24] For a review of CIAP see Glantz et al. 1985. D'Arge was an interesting and important figure in the development of environmental economics; see Smith 2010.

[25] Indeed, Gary Yohe uses the phrase "gold standard" in his blurb for Nordhaus 2008. Nobel Prize–winning economist Kenneth Arrow calls the book "the standard of analysis by which the field may be judged."

[26] See Nordhaus 2008 for a description of DICE and RICE. Stern relied on the PAGE model developed by Cambridge economist Chris Hope, though the relation between model runs and Stern's conclusions is not always clear. For a critical survey of integrated assessment models, see Ackerman et al. 2009. For a wide-ranging critique of the use of general equilibrium models in climate economics see DeCanio 2003. Indeed, Stern himself in recent work emphasizes their limitations (2013 and forthcoming).

[27] Nordhaus 2008: 167.

analogy, the criticism misses the point. Peer review is very important in science, as explained in Chapter 3, but there is also a place for expert assessments and reports. Nordhaus himself knows this, having served on at least three NAS committees that produced climate change reports. The Stern Review was commissioned by the UK treasury in order to inform policy; it was not meant as an academic exercise. What the Stern Review did, in its own words, was to take

> a broad view of the economics required to understand climate change. Whenever possible we have based our Review on gathering and structuring existing research material.[28]

The staff also invited submissions, traveled widely to meet with experts, commissioned papers, and conducted some of their own research when "we found that existing literature did not provide answers."[29] The Review was a government document and did not go through the sort of formal peer review typical of professional journals, but at least much of it was reviewed by peers, and peer-reviewed publications have resulted from this work.

Nordhaus also complained that the conclusions of the Stern Review were at odds with consensus views in climate economics. This is an important criticism, since it would be surprising for a review to come to different conclusions than the material that it was reviewing. However, climate economics is an emerging area of research characterized by a great deal of uncertainty. While there are consensus views (some reported in Section 4.1), they are not very settled. It is thus not too surprising that an ambitious review might arrive at some surprising conclusions. Indeed, one worries that what Nordhaus takes to be the consensus view is largely his own view, projected onto the American climate economics community and then into the global community that studies climate economics.

Nordhaus and Stern disagree about both the shape and the extent of the optimal response to climate change.[30] Nordhaus favors a "policy ramp" that begins with a modest carbon tax of $27 per ton in 2005, then goes to $90 per ton in 2050, and then to $200 per ton in 2100.[31] A $30 per ton carbon tax would increase the price of gasoline about 9 cents per gallon and the price of coal-generated electricity by about 1 cent per kilowatt-hour. The optimal tax is global, and costs would increase to the extent that the tax was not universal, economy-wide, or was implemented in an inefficient way (e.g., through cap and trade). The optimal path would result in emissions reductions from a business-as-usual scenario of 25% by 2050 and 45% by 2100, resulting in a warming from the 1900 baseline of 2.6°C by 2100 and 3.4°C by

---

[28] Stern 2007: ix.

[29] Stern 2007: x.

[30] In the next two paragraphs I summarize the results of Nordhaus 2008 and Stern 2007. I discuss Nordhaus's more recent results in Section 4.5. The nature and shape of the disagreement between Nordhaus and Stern have not changed, though it appears to have become more constructive.

[31] Nordhaus 2008: 14.

2200. Without policy intervention, damages would reach nearly 3% of global output per year by the end of this century, mostly concentrated in tropical Africa and India, and would rise to almost 8% per year by 2200. Nordhaus's path would accept about $17 trillion in climate change–related damages. Stern favors a much more aggressive response to climate change. He advocates an immediate carbon tax of $311 per ton, an order of magnitude greater than the tax advocated by Nordhaus. Without policy interventions, Stern estimates damages at 5–20% of global GDP. He estimates the costs of stabilizing atmospheric concentrations of carbon dioxide at 550 ppm at about 1% of global GDP, which would give us a reasonable chance of the warming being less than 3°C.[32] From Stern's perspective, acting on climate change is a "no brainer": Every dollar spent on reducing emissions returns $12 in benefits.[33]

Nordhaus is more cautious than Stern about the rate and impact of technological innovation. For Nordhaus, technological change is exogenous; his models do not take into account the effect of policy interventions and changing prices on guiding investment and promoting innovation. He admits that this is a "serious limitation, particularly for carbon-saving technological change, because changing carbon prices are likely to induce research and development on new energy technologies."[34] Stern produces his emission reduction path not only through a carbon tax, but also by increased spending for research and development and on incentives to deploy new technologies.[35] While it is hard to speak definitively about the impact of technological change on the costs of emissions reduction, it is worth noting that when it comes to environmental remediation, costs generally have been lower than initial forecasts suggest. Examples include smog control in Los Angeles, the reduction of sulfur oxides under the 1990 Clean Air Act Amendments, and the ban on chlorofluorocarbons (CFCs) under the Montreal Protocol and successor agreements.[36]

There are economists who favor even less aggressive policies than Nordhaus. Mendelsohn (2011: 185) has written that "[m]ost recent estimates of the market impacts of climate change suggest much lower global damages of between 0.05% and .0.5% of GWP [Gross World Product] by 2100," with "the bulk of climate damages…felt in low-latitude countries" while "mid- to high-latitude countries will bear very little damages." He claims that many adaptations will occur without large investments, economies will reorganize in ways that limit climate change damages, and climate change will produce benefits as well as costs.[37] Mendelsohn criticizes the Stern Review for its choice of a discount rate, its assumptions about technological

---

[32] Stern 2007: 220.

[33] http://www.iie.com/publications/papers/paper.cfm?ResearchID=874. Retrieved July 18, 2013.

[34] Nordhaus 2008: 34.

[35] Stern 2007: ch. 16.

[36] For discussion, see Summers and Zeckhauser 2008.

[37] Actually costless and low-cost adaptations are accounted for in the Stern Review, and as we will see in the next paragraph and in Section 4.3, it is at best misleading to say that estimates of climate change damages have been falling.

change, and for supposing that "the probability of a large catastrophe is nonnegligible this century" (2011: 186). He thinks that adopting Stern's recommendations "could be one of the greatest follies mankind ever considered" (2011: 186).

Sterner and his colleagues, on the other hand, advocate sterner measures.[38] They argue that Stern has underestimated the non-market damages of climate change.

> If output of some material goods (e.g. mobile phone) increases while access to environmental goods and services (e.g., clean water, rainfed agricultural production or biodiversity) declines, then the relative price of these environmental amenities would be expected to rise over time. The result of these uneven growth rates in the economy would be increased economic damages stemming from climate change and, subsequently higher levels of climate change mitigation would be warranted today.[39]

The idea is that as climate change degrades the natural environment over the next century and beyond, we will increasingly value these scarce amenities much as we value more highly the remnant populations of endangered species than we do those animals who are more common. Summers and Zeckhauser (2008: 120) make the point in this way:

> We could see people in the far future paying many dozens of times as much as people would today in terms of dishwashers or televisions sacrificed for an authentic wilderness experience, or a magnificent 70° spring day in New York.

Sterner shows that if we take into account the effect of climate change on the relative prices of these goods, even with the higher discount rate that Nordhaus advocates, then we will get roughly Stern's conclusions. If we accept Stern's discount rate, as Sterner himself does, then we will get even sterner results than Stern.

4.3. DISCOUNTING

In the previous section I tried to give some sense of the diversity of views among climate economists, both in the assumptions they make and in the conclusions they draw. In this section I want to focus on a deep difference that divides Nordhaus and Stern and drives most of their disagreement. This concerns the choice of the discount rate. When Nordhaus (2007) ran his model with Stern's discount rate, it produced results that were similar to Stern's. Of course, this does not settle the matter of which of them, if either, is correct, but it does help to locate the core of the

---

[38] Sterner and Persson 2008.

[39] Sterner and Persson 2008: 2. As early as 1967 Krutilla recognized that environmental amenities would become the ultimate scarce commodities and developed the notion of "existence value" in an attempt to account for this.

dispute. Investigating this controversy dramatically exposes the limits of economics when it comes to assessing responses to climate change.

Much of our present behavior produces future benefits and costs. Saving for retirement, going to college, and starting a business are only a few of the most obvious examples. Deciding what to do in such cases presents us with the challenge of determining the present value of these future costs and benefits. In order to determine their present value, we must decide how much to discount them.[40]

Consider a simple example. Is it worth my while to borrow $10 from you now, promising to pay you $20 in ten years? If I know that I can collect 10% annual interest on the borrowed money, then in order to determine the present value of the $20 it makes sense for me to discount it at 10% per year. What I discover is that the present value of the $20 is $7.71, so it is certainly worth my while to borrow the $10 from you now. At the end of 10 years the $10 which I borrowed from you will have grown to $27.07. I will be able to pay you back and also enjoy a (cheap) night on the town.

Another factor that can affect the present value of future costs and benefits is whether I am rich or poor. For $10 is more valuable to a poor person scratching around for something to eat than it is to a rich person for whom $10 may be negligible. Everything else aside, I may prefer to have $10 now when I am unemployed rather than $10 next year when I will be back to work.

A third factor that may affect the present value of money is pure time preference. Suppose that I prefer to be given money on Wednesdays rather than on Thursdays. If I have this preference, then $10 on Wednesday is worth more to me than $10 on Thursday.

These questions about the present value of future costs and benefits arise for public as well as private decision-making: in decisions about investing in education and infrastructure, and in a big way with respect to investing in emissions reductions. When people reduce emissions they incur present costs in order to provide future benefits. In determining whether this is economically rational, it is important to calculate the present value of those future benefits.

One reason the choice of a discount rate matters so much is that discounting compounds, and so has a hugely powerful effect over long periods of time, as Table 4.1 (from Cowan and Parft 1992) indicates.[41]

---

[40] "Discounting" as used in the economics literature can be positive or negative. If the future economy will be worse than the present, then applying an appropriate discount rate to a future benefit may result in the future value of the benefit being greater than its present value. Imagine, for example, the value of a crust of bread in the future when bread is scarce, compared to the present when bread is plentiful.

[41] In the same paper in which this chart appears, Cowen and Parfit bring out the power of temporal discounting by asking us to "[i]magine finding out that you, having just reached your twenty-first birthday, must soon die of cancer because one evening Cleopatra wanted an extra helping of dessert."

Table 4.1 Estimated Number of Future Benefits Equal to One Present Benefit Based on Different Discount Rates

Years in the Future	1%	3%	5%	10%
30	1.3	2.4	4.3	17.4
50	1.6	4.3	11.4	117.3
100	2.7	19.2	131.5	13,780.6
500	144.7	2,621,877.2	39,323,261,827	4.96×10^{20}

Chichilnisky (1996: 234, as quoted in Gardiner 2010: 268) has pointed out that

[a]t the standard 5% discount rate...[a] simple computation shows that if one tried to decide how much it is worth investing in preventing the destruction of the earth 200 years from now on the basis of measuring the value of foregone output, the answer would be no more than one is willing to invest in an apartment.

Most of the differences between Nordhaus and Stern are due to the different discount rates that they adopt. Nordhaus[42] applies a discount rate of 5.5% for the first half of the century, averaging out to 4% over the century as a whole, while Stern's discount rate is 1.4%. As Table 4.1 suggests, this difference has large impacts over long periods of time. On Nordhaus's discount rate, future costs and benefits halve in less than 13 years, while it takes more than 50 years for them to halve on Stern's discount rate. Nordhaus's discount rate implies that the Indians got a good deal when they sold Manhattan for $24 in 1626.[43] Stern would not agree.

This difference in the discount rate drives their different policies in two ways. First, since the most severe damages of climate change will occur in the further future, their present value is much larger for Stern than it is for Nordhaus, thus justifying more aggressive policies to reduce emissions. Second, Nordhaus's policy ramp (i.e., a carbon tax that increases through time) is determined to a great extent by the fact that present costs are so much greater than the heavily discounted future costs, so it makes sense to delay costly emissions reductions as long as possible. Stern's low discount rate tends to flatten the cost trajectory, thus undercutting some of the rationale for a policy ramp.

Nordhaus and Stern disagree about the discount rate, but they agree on the equation that should be used to determine it. The "Ramsey equation," which follows, is standardly used by economists to determine the discount rate.[44]

[42] Nordhaus 2008: 61, 10.

[43] Nordhaus 2008: 11.

[44] Ramsey 1928: 543–549. Ramsey, a brilliant mathematician and philosopher, was Ludwig Wittgenstein's official Ph.D. supervisor. He died tragically at age 26. While the equation is widely accepted, some economists reject it, as does Gardiner 2010. For more on Ramsey, visit http://www.the-tls.co.uk/tls/public/article1327894.ece. Retrieved October 25, 2013.

$$ro = eta \times gamma + delta$$

In this equation *ro* is the social discount rate, *eta* marks the elasticity of the social marginal utility of consumption, *gamma* reflects the per capita growth rate of consumption, and *delta* is the rate of pure time preference. Nordhaus calculates the discount rate in this way:

$$5.5\% = 2 \times 2\% + 1.5\%.$$

Stern's calculation is the following:

$$1.4\% = 1 \times 1.3\% + .1\%$$

In the example we discussed earlier about borrowing $10 for 10 years, the three variables in the Ramsey equation were all present in a general way. In what follows I will discuss these variables, running roughshod over some technical details that are important for economic theory but not for understanding the larger picture.[45]

One obvious reason for discounting is that in a growing economy a present sum of money will be worth more in the future. I expressed this in my example by saying that I had an opportunity to collect 10% annual interest on the $10 I would borrow from you. This consideration roughly corresponds to what *gamma* is supposed to capture in the Ramsey equation. What exactly will be the future per capita growth rate of consumption is an empirical question, though one that no one is in a good position to answer, especially for the timescales relevant to climate change. As Weitzman and Gollier (2010: 350) observe,

> there is no deep reason of principle that allows us to extrapolate past rates of return on capital into the distant future. The seeming trendlessness of some past rates of return is a purely empirical reduced-form observation, which is not based on any underlying theory that would confidently allow projecting the past far into the future.

Nordhaus sets *gamma* at 2% and Stern sets *gamma* at 1.3%. In so doing they are agreeing that there will be decades and even centuries of increasing per capita consumption. Even at a growth rate of 1.3% per capita, consumption would triple by the end of the century. Perhaps this is consistent with an optimistic scenario in which developing countries develop while consumption levels off in developed countries. However, many people doubt that this will happen, and are even skeptical that per capita consumption will continue to increase over the next decades and centuries, especially given increases in global population. It is hard to know what to think about these questions. Since Stern and Nordhaus are so close on *gamma*, this disagreement is the least important difference between them with respect to the Ramsey equation. Though both are optimistic, this difference conforms to the general pattern of Stern's assumptions being less optimistic than Nordhaus's.

---

[45] In what follows, discount rate factors are expressed in annual rates unless otherwise noted.

If Stern and Nordhaus are right about *gamma*, then future people will be richer than we are. As I discussed in my example, $10 is worth more to a poor person than to a rich person. *Eta* is the variable that captures this concern. The higher that *eta* is, the more benefits future people must receive in order for the value of these benefits to be equivalent to a single unit of consumption by present people.

Disputes over *eta* are important. If Stern were to set *eta* at 3 instead of 1, then his discount rate would be virtually the same as the 4% discount rate that Nordhaus adopted for the century as a whole. The policy disagreements between them would shrink, and the Stern Review would not be seen as a clarion call for fast and furious action on climate change.

Dasgupta thinks that *eta* should be set between 2 and 4. He claims that

> [t]o assume an *eta* of 1 is to say that the distribution of well-being among people doesn't matter much....[46]

He runs a thought experiment that is meant to be a *reductio ad absurdum* of an *eta* of 1: Under certain conditions, this implies that "the current generation...ought literally to starve itself so that future generations are able to enjoy ever increasing consumptions levels."[47] Whatever the fate of the counterexample, Dasgupta surely overstates his point when he says that on an *eta* of 1 the distribution of well-being "doesn't matter much."[48] Existing inequalities in most countries, and in their tax systems, indicate an *eta* that is closer to 1 than to 2.[49] Setting *eta* at 2 or 3 would, according to Cline, "place the income tax on the moderately rich, such as the president of a top university, at about 90 percent."[50] This would be enough to make most Americans Republicans.

One way to understand an *eta* of 1 is to view it as saying that 1% of any consumption has the same value as 1% of any other consumption. More intuitively, an *eta* of 1 implies that Bill Gates and a welfare recipient benefit equally when they each increase their consumption by 1%. As *eta* increases, larger fractions of consumption are required for higher levels of consumption to have the same value as smaller fractions of less consumption. Looking at it from another point of view, suppose that Jack consumes three times as much as Jill. With an *eta* of 1, an additional increment of consumption would have one-third the value to Jack that it has to Jill. With an *eta* of 2, the extra increment would have one-ninth the value to Jack as it has to Jill. *Eta* is often spoken of as expressing an aversion to inequality because a positive *eta*

---

[46] Dasgupta 2007: 7.

[47] Dasgupta 2007: 7.

[48] See Quiggin 2008 for a reply to Dasgupta.

[49] Dietz et al. 2009.

[50] http://www.iie.com/publications/papers/paper.cfm?ResearchID=874. Retrieved October 25, 2013. Arrow 2007 endorses an *eta* of 2 or 3 with this laconic remark: "a value of 2 or 3 seems reasonable."

implies that, for a given increment of consumption, more utility can be produced by allocating it to those who consume less. As *eta* increases, the aversion to inequality increases in a non-linear way.

There is a great deal of disagreement about what is the correct setting for *eta*, and it is not clear how these disputes can be settled. Many cost-benefit analyses simply compare costs to benefits without comment, effectively setting *eta* at zero. The Stern Review refers to its choice of *eta* as a "value judgment" (p. 52), but goes on to say that this choice is "in line with some empirical estimates"(p. 663). Nordhaus gives no justification for his choice of *eta*. He remarks that

> [t]he assumption behind the DICE model is that the time discount rate should be chosen along with the consumption elasticity so that the model generates a path that resembles the actual real interest rate.[51]

His concern is that *ro* turns out to "resemble the actual real interest rate," and he doesn't care much about the values of particular variables.

One way of thinking about *eta* is not that it reports some fact about the elasticity of consumption, but rather that it expresses an ethical judgment about inequality. Perhaps this is what the Stern Review means when it says that the choice of *eta* is a "value judgment." Stern thinks that both pure time preference and aversion to equality must be discussed as directly ethical choices.[52] On this interpretation, one would expect most egalitarians and prioritarians to favor a high *eta*.[53] By this measure, the Stern Review is not very egalitarian.

One reason that it is difficult to know how to set *eta* is that it is a construct that employs a single number to express attitudes toward three distinct phenomena: temporal inequality, present inequality, and risk. However, these issues are conceptually distinct, and there is empirical evidence that attitudes toward them are often different. A recent paper concludes:

> Unfortunately, there is little agreement on the value of η [*eta*], partly because, in the standard model of welfare economics, it simultaneously represents preferences over risk, spatial inequality and intertemporal substitution. Our survey of over 3000 people shows that the correlations between preferences over these three dimensions are weak in the context of climate change.[54]

---

[51] Nordhaus 2008: 61.

[52] Stern 2007: 50–54. In later publications Stern explicitly acknowledges that the choice of *eta* is a value judgment and discusses how it might be set (see Stern 2010b and Dietz et al. 2009).

[53] While egalitarians and prioritarians come in different flavors, they typically support equalizing what is of value or disproportionately benefiting the worst off. For an introduction, visit http://plato.stanford.edu/entries/egalitarianism/. Retrieved July 18, 2013. For a classic discussion, see Parfit 1997.

[54] Saelen et al. 2009.

Of course, someone might argue that even though these issues can be conceptually distinguished, our attitudes toward them should be the same even if they are not.[55] We ought to revise our failures in light of our normative views rather than revising our normative views in light of our failures. I suspect that it would not be easy to make this argument plausible, but that is another matter.

What is striking is that even economists who say that identifying the value of *eta* involves a value judgment quickly retreat to discussing the value of *eta* as revealed in economic behavior or in psychological experiments. It is not clear exactly how this empirical material is supposed to bear on the value judgment. What is clear is that the value judgment is part of what forms the basis of the economic analysis, and the economic analysis that presupposes it cannot answer the value question. This is not a trivial point. The very question of whether it is economically advantageous to aggressively act now to slow climate change turns on such value judgments.

However, not all economists would agree that the choice of *eta* is a value judgment. The question of whether the Ramsey equation should capture our behavior or our values has been most explicitly discussed in arguments about the value of *delta*, and it is to this question that we shall turn. The same arguments about the role of value judgments in setting *delta* also apply to their role in setting *eta*.

Delta marks another reason for discounting: pure time preference. In the example that I gave at the outset, we supposed that I prefer to be given money on Wednesdays rather than on Thursdays. If I have this preference, then $10 on Wednesday is worth more to me than $10 on Thursday. This is an example of pure time preference.

However, the pure time preference that is relevant to an economic analysis of climate change is not about individuals scheduling their own consumption, but about consumption across generations. The question is whether it is acceptable to discount the utility of future people simply because of their location in time. Nordhaus says that it is acceptable because people do it; Stern says that it is not acceptable because it would be unethical to do so.

Stern is in the tradition of British economists such as Jevons, Pigou, and Ramsey who, influenced by utilitarian philosophers such as Sidgwick, rejected pure time preference on ethical grounds.[56] Nordhaus represents a different tradition, more influential in the United States than in Britain and influenced by broadly positivist views in philosophy of science that take behavior as the primary material for economic analysis.

---

[55] Harsanyi (1955, 1976) argued that if people were to choose between different income distributions from behind a "veil of ignorance," aversion to spatial inequality would be identical to risk aversion. Broome (1991) showed that if certain conditions are fulfilled, consistency may require that risk aversion, aversion to spatial inequality and aversion to temporal inequality must all be equal.

[56] On this point Rawls is also in this tradition. For an interesting critique of Rawls and Sidgwick, see Ziff 2004, which argues that temporal location can always be viewed as having rationally relevant characteristics because of its relational properties.

Stern sets *delta* at .1% in order to account for the possibility of human extinction. This is another one of Stern's pessimistic judgments, since it implies that *homo sapiens* is almost certainly an evolutionary failure. Setting *delta* at .1% implies that there is a 10% chance of human extinction within a century and a 50% chance of extinction within 500 years. Since humans have only been around for a few hundred thousand years, their chances of rivaling the dinosaurs who lasted well over 160 million years are pretty slim on Stern's view. Stern (2007: 53) tries to take the sting out of this by hinting that he would count catastrophes which "'took out' a significant fraction of the world's population" as extinctions even though humanity might survive. It is not clear why catastrophes that do not actually cause human extinction should provide grounds for discounting, any more than any other future events. It is a further question why *delta* should reflect the probability of extinction at all, however it is understood, since discounting for the probability of extinction is not discounting for pure time preference.[57]

Nordhaus sets *delta* at 1.5%, though, as we have seen, he is not as attached to the value of any particular variable in the Ramsey equation as he is to the idea that the discount rate should "resemble the actual real interest rate." Even if we accept Nordhaus's view that the correct discount rate should be based on behavior, there is enormous disagreement about exactly how to do the calculation and what is the correct value for *delta* that results. No one, including Nordhaus, thinks that *delta* should just be identical to the "actual real interest rate," even if we could identify this in a non-controversial way. The "actual real interest rate" would have to be cleaned up, idealized in some way, because of the distortionary effects of public goods, externalities, and various phenomena highlighted in behavioral economics.[58]

The 1995 Intergovernmental Panel on Climate Change (IPCC) report clearly distinguished these two traditions about how to set *delta*. It called the tradition that Stern represents "prescriptive," and the tradition which Nordhaus represents, "descriptive."

> The normative or ethical perspective (called the *prescriptive approach* in this chapter) begins with the question, "How (ethically) should impacts on future generations be valued?" The positive perspective, called here the *descriptive approach*, begins by asking, "What choices involving trade-offs across time do people actually make?" and, "To what extent will investments made to reduce greenhouse gas emissions displace investments elsewhere?"[59]

Many writers have followed this way of making the distinction, and the dispute between Stern and Nordhaus over the value of *delta* is often characterized as a clash between "ethicists" and "positivists."[60]

---

[57] Gardiner 2010 makes this point and several others that I make in this section.
[58] For details, see Hepburn et al. 2010.
[59] Watson et al. 1996: 129.
[60] For example by Sunstein and Weisbach 2009.

However, this is misleading. Both Nordhaus and Stern have prescriptive approaches. What should tip us off to Nordhaus's approach as prescriptive is the emotive and somewhat moralistic tone that he adopts when rejecting Stern's views about the discount rate. As we have seen, he accuses Stern of "Government house utilitarianism," of "taking the lofty vantage point of the world social planner," of "perhaps stoking the dying embers of the British Empire."[61] He reminds us that "the British government is not infallible in questions of economic and social analysis of global warming…," and tells us that "[t]he normatively acceptable real interest rates prescribed by philosophers, economists, or the British government are irrelevant to determining the appropriate discount rate to use in the actual financial and capital markets of the United States, China, Brazil, and the rest of the world."[62] What Nordhaus believes, I think, is that Stern is paternalistic and undemocratic when he substitutes his own ethical judgment for the actual decisions that people make.[63] I suspect that Nordhaus sees himself as a democratic, autonomy-respecting, "new world" liberal, in opposition to Stern's "old world" willingness to engage the power of the "nanny-state" in imposing his own values.[64]

The dispute between Stern and Nordhaus is not a dispute between a prescriptivist and a descriptivist view, but rather a dispute between two kinds of prescriptive views. What they disagree about is the sorts of reasons that are relevant to determining the prescribed discount rate. Nordhaus thinks that only suitably cleaned up behavioral data is relevant. Stern thinks that ethical arguments matter. This methodological disagreement underlies their differences about the value of *delta*. Unfortunately, neither goes very deep in explaining or justifying their methodology.

Thinking through this dispute requires us to reflect on the purposes of economic analysis. One view, which Stern, Nordhaus and most economists officially reject, is that economic analysis tells us what we ought to do. Despite officially rejecting this view, the language that economists use often suggests otherwise. Moreover, among the consumers of economic data there is often a strong presumption that the route from numbers to policy is short and swift.

A more plausible view, one with which Stern and Nordhaus agree, is that an economic analysis is supposed to tell us what is in our economic interests to do.[65] While this sounds like a simple thought, the idea of economic interest is a complex notion. Increasingly, economists build into their analyses the supposed economic value of

---

[61] Nordhaus 2008: 174.

[62] Nordhaus 2008: 175.

[63] Weitzman actually says that Stern's view is paternalistic (2007: 704–705). John Broome (2012: 106 ff) discusses this charge.

[64] Weitzman (2007: 712) accuses Stern of "relying mostly on a priori philosopher-king ethical judgements." Some would say that I've overinterpreted this dispute but I think that I have just exposed some of its unstated presuppositions. Nordhaus's implicit premises when it comes to his discussion of *delta* are very much in the spirit of the introduction to Friedman 1966.

[65] There are of course other purposes of economic analysis, including explaining the past and informing us of cost-effective means for reaching our goals.

non-market goods.[66] It is not always clear where the line is between discovering the economic value of these goods, and substituting an economic value for what is fundamentally a non-economic value.

It is true that we often express our broader values in economic behavior (e.g., by buying organic or "fair-trade" products), just as we express them in other forms of behavior. However, having noticed that markets fail with respect to these values, there is a temptation to suppose that their significance could be exhaustively represented in perfect markets. This thought, however, is a mistake. There may be values that are appropriately honored or respected in ways that markets cannot express. Ronald Dworkin, for example, points out that there are things that people hold sacred: Human beings, artworks, species, and my mother's ashes are all candidates.[67] Dworkin's point is that we honor what is sacred and treat it as inviolable. We do not view it as an incremental good, which we should produce as much of as possible in order to satisfy consumer demand. Nor do we think that there are perfect substitutes for what we hold sacred. My mother's ashes are literally irreplaceable. As economists increasingly attempt to incorporate broader and more diverse values into their analyses, suspicion grows that while the philosopher-king may be a relic of history, there is an economist-king ready to take his place.

We want to know what is in our economic interests because we want to know what we have reason to do. Economic reasons are rarely conclusive, but it is also rare when they are irrelevant to determining what we ought to do. We are interested in the economic analysis of climate change because we want to know whether and to what extent we have economic reasons for taking action. We may have other reasons for acting to slow climate change as well, but economic considerations matter. Since economic considerations are connected to reasons for action, we can ask of any economic analysis to whom it is addressed: For whom would the economic considerations be a reason for acting?

Nordhaus's analysis is addressed to everyone who is currently alive. His analysis is supposed to show us (i.e., all of us who are now alive) the optimal path for emissions reduction. The interests of future people figure in the analysis only insofar as we value their interests. What *delta* represents is the extent to which we value their interests less than we value our own. Stern's analysis is addressed to future people as well as to everyone who is now alive. Setting *delta* at 0 implies that the community whose economic interests matter directly is the temporally extended community.

Stern's argument for why we should take everyone into account who is part of this temporally extended community is, at its heart, a utilitarian consistency argument. He says that a *delta* of 2% (which he attributes to two of his critics, Nordhaus

---

[66] Sandel 2012: 84–85 documents a shift over the last half century in the way that economics textbooks characterize their subject from "the world of prices, wages, interest rates, stock and bonds, banks and credit, taxes and expenditure" to the study of "a group of people interacting with each other as they go about their lives."

[67] Dworkin 1993: ch. 3.

and Weitzman) "implies that the utility of a person born in 1995…would be 'worth' (have a social weight) roughly half that of a person born in 1960."[68] This inconsistency, Stern thinks, is ethically unacceptable. He follows Ramsey, who wrote that pure time preference "is ethically indefensible and arises merely from the weakness of the imagination," and Harrod, who said that discounting is "a polite expression for rapacity and the conquest of reason by passion."[69]

However, an economic analysis is supposed to report, aggregate, and calculate economic values. It is not supposed to assess our ethical values, except insofar as they have economic expressions. Moreover, an economist is not supposed to tell us what values we ought to have. If there is a core truth about economic value, it is that the value of widgets is what people pay for them in perfect markets under ideal conditions. Someone who tries to convince us that widgets are undervalued under such conditions may be right but she is not doing economics. This is what is behind Nordhaus's view that an economic analysis should reflect the value that we place on future generations, not the value that an economist thinks that we should place on them.[70] Nordhaus's economic analysis is addressed to us. We are the ones who want to know whether it is in our economic interests to act on climate change. Since future generations are not now in a position to act, there is no point in addressing the economic analysis to them, even if we could figure out how to put the correct number in a bottle and get it to them through the oceans of time.

While this much seems plausible, Nordhaus has a consistency problem. As Schelling (1995: 396) points out:

> The optimization models have no provision for redistributing current income. They redistribute only forward in time: contemporary Chinese get nothing from us, but future Chinese we treat as part of the family.

It is hard to see why I, whoever I am, should accept the idea that "we" are everyone who is now alive. In fact most of us discount the interests of others, whether they are people living in other countries, people who are different from us, strangers, those who are not our co-religionists, members of our tribe, or members of our family. Some people even discount the interests of everyone who are not themselves.[71]

---

[68] Stern 2010b: 52. The late climate scientist Steve Schneider used to like to ask whether your granddaughter will be less valuable than your daughter simply because she will be born a generation later (reported in Ackerman 2009: 26).

[69] Ramsey 1928: 543; Harrod 1948: 40. For a particularly persuasive statement of this view, see Cowan and Parfit 1992.

[70] Stephen Marglin (1963: 97) explicitly states, "Whatever else democratic theory may or may not imply, I consider it axiomatic that a democratic government reflects only the preferences of the individuals who are presently members of the body politic." This echoes what I said in Section 3.7, only there I was highlighting the weakness of democracy in addressing problems such as climate change, not endorsing a principle.

[71] See, e.g., Hare 2009.

It is hard to see what reason, consistent with his own methodology, that Nordhaus could give for why I (or any of us) should be interested in an economic analysis that treats the interests of everyone now alive as equally important, when we have empirical evidence that this is not a true reflection of our economic values. Moreover, in Nordhaus's analysis all future people are treated the same. Their interests are discounted for their remoteness in time but not for their remoteness in other respects from those who will put up most of the cash to protect their interests. The fact is that even on Nordhaus's preferred policy, people in the developed world will be the largest contributors to protect the interests of the progeny of people who now live in the developing world. Given current patterns of aid flows from the developed to the developing world, this does not seem consistent with prevailing preferences.[72] This result may be baked into the model for convenience, but one suspects that some liberal view about human equality is lurking in the background, or perhaps Nordhaus is just "stoking the flames" of the dying American imperium.

Stern gets the better of this argument because he is more consistent. He thinks we should count everyone equally wherever and whenever they live. Nordhaus thinks that we should count everyone equally wherever they live, but people's interests can be discounted depending on when they live. But if we're allowed to discount people's interests at all, it is hard to see why only future people should be vulnerable to such discounting.

However, Stern's view leads to implausible and perhaps unlivable conclusions. This is brought out by Nordhaus's two arguments against Stern's choice of *delta*: the wrinkle experiment, and the argument from hair-triggers and uncertainty.

The wrinkle experiment hypothesizes that scientists discover a

> wrinkle in the climate system that will cause damages equal to 0.1 per cent of net consumption starting in 2200 and continuing at that rate forever after....If we use the methodology of the Stern Review...it is worth a one-time consumption hit of approximately $30,000 billion today to fix a tiny problem that begins in 2200...in terms of average consumption levels...[T]he *Stern Review* would justify reducing per capita consumption for one year today from $6,600 to $2,900 in order to prevent a reduction in consumption from $87,000 to $86,900 starting two centuries hence and continuing at that rate forever.[73]

This result, according to Nordhaus, is "bizarre."

The arguments from hair-triggers and uncertainty begin from the assumption that rather than discovering that the wrinkle will in fact occur, scientists discover that there is a 10% chance that the wrinkle will occur in 2200 and reduce consumption by 0.1% forever. Using the Stern Review's discount rate, we should be willing

---

[72] Schelling (1995) forcefully makes this point.

[73] Nordhaus 2008: 182–183.

now to pay 8% of one year's income in order to prevent this possible reduction of consumption in the future. If we suppose that the wrinkle might occur in 2400 instead, then the fraction of annual income that we should spend now to prevent the possible future loss of consumption is 6.5%. Nordhaus (2008: 183) writes that with "conventional discount rates (and one might say, with common sense), we would ignore any tiny low-probability wrinkle two centuries ahead."

There are replies that can be made on Stern's behalf. First, these cases are so remote that it is not entirely clear what our intuitions are; and it is very clear that whatever they are, we should not invest them with a great deal of confidence. It is true that we largely ignore low-probability events in the further future, but it is not immediately obvious that we ought to do so.[74] Second, the fact that the hypothesized wrinkle is a natural occurrence that will apparently affect everyone in the same way is a significant disanalogy to the actual climate change problem that we face, which is anthropogenic in origin and will tend to damage people in inverse proportion to their contributions to bringing it about. These differences may also affect our intuitions about these examples.

However, once one sees how to play this game, it is obvious that slight adjustments in the timing and probability of the wrinkle will have dramatic consequences for present consumption, and it is this that is the problem. The troubling feature that these cases bring out is how sensitive Stern's economic calculations are about what is now in our interests, to events that occur in the further future and to small tweaks in probabilities. This is a point that Cline made about the Stern Review in a different way.

> Because of the combination of an infinite horizon, near-zero pure time preference, and unitary elasticity of marginal utility, 93 percent of the present value of total future welfare in the [R]eview arises after 2200. This means the [R]eview is vulnerable to the critique that the distant unknowable tail wags the dog.[75]

Rejecting pure time preference makes present people hostages to the future. At almost any point in time there will be good reason to believe that the number of people who will live later is vastly greater than the number who are presently alive. Thus, the interests of present people would almost always be swamped by the interests of future people.[76] Any act that would in any way, however slightly, compromise the interests of future people would have to be of earth-shaking importance for it to be economically rational for present people to do it. This also places an enormous epistemological strain on people. Should I have a cup of coffee? In order to know whether this would be economically rational, I would have to determine the

---

[74] Posner 2005.

[75] http://www.iie.com/publications/papers/paper.cfm?ResearchID=874. Retrieved July 18, 2013.

[76] It can be argued that this result comes not from the rejection of pure time preference alone, but from the conjunction of this rejection with utilitarianism. See Broome 2012: ch. 8 for discussion.

long-term effects of this action on all those who will live in the future. Virtually everyone who will ever live will have to ask these questions.[77] The really deplorable possibility is that economic analysis would tell each generation to sacrifice for a future that never arrives. For these reasons, setting *delta* at 0 does not seem plausible.

If we bring these considerations together, there seems to be no plausible value for *delta*. If the setting is 0 or extremely low, the interests of the present are swamped by the future. If *delta* is set high enough to protect the interests of present people, then the interests of those who will live in the further future lose virtually all significance.

In response, some economists have suggested that the value of *delta* should decline through time. Indeed, this is actually Nordhaus's view. For the first half century he discounts at 5½% per year but then the discount rate drops to an average of 4% over a century.

The great advantage of a declining *delta* is that it seems to conform more closely to how people think and behave than does a fixed value for *delta*.[78] Indeed, it is not only people who apply declining discount rates. According to Cole Porter, "birds do it, bees do it, even educated fleas do it." OK, I admit that he was talking about something else (falling in love), but it is true that there is cross-species evidence for declining discount rates, especially among birds.[79]

Weitzman agrees with Nordhaus that discount rates should be set on the basis of behavior, but on the timescale that is relevant to climate change there is great uncertainty about future discounting behavior. The best way to deal with this uncertainty, Weitzman thinks, is with declining discount rates. This leads to the conclusion, as he says in the title of one of his papers, that "the far-distant future should be discounted at its lowest possible rate."[80] Weitzman thinks that, given the uncertainty, we should calculate the discount rate by averaging discount factors rather than rates. Suppose that the discount rate over the next year is likely to be either 10% or 2%.[81] Instead of averaging these numbers and discounting at 6%, we should first calculate present values on the basis of each of these discount rates. $1 in ten years is now worth $.39 on the 10% discount rate or $.82 on the 2% discount rate. In order to determine present value we should average these values. When we do this, we discover that the present value of $1 is $.60, which reflects a discount rate of 5.2%. If 10% and 2% continue to be the most likely discount rates, the discount rate calculated by averaging discount factors will decline through time. For example, the discount rate in a century would be 2.7%; in a millennium, it would be 2.1%.

---

[77] This is one worry that the father in Cormac McCarthy's *The Road* does not seem to have, but even here there is some chance that humanity will survive (though perhaps not in Stern's sense).

[78] See Hepburn et al. 2010; Heal 2007.

[79] For references and discussion, see Read 2001.

[80] Weitzman 1998. For discussion and an argument that "climate policies deserve a negative discount rate," see Fleurbaey and Zuber 2013.

[81] I take this example from Revesz, from whose work I have greatly benefited. See Revesz and Shahabian 2011.

This is a clever response but it is open to criticism. First, some would say that virtually any positive discount rate has the effect of trivializing future costs. Higher discount rates do this over shorter times than lower discount rates but it happens all the same in both cases.[82] Second, it is unclear whether what drives this approach is the independent plausibility of averaging discount factors or whether its attractiveness stems from the attempt to find some reason to favor declining discount rates. Consider, for example, this response to Weitzman. Suppose that you are one of the two leading experts on the subject, and you are convinced that we should expect a discount rate of 10%, expressed in behavior, over the next century. You have arguments and data for your view that you think should be convincing to any reasonable person. However, the other leading expert on the subject, who is like you in all relevant respects, has her own arguments and data that she thinks should convince any reasonable person. She believes that the discount rate should be 2%. The decision-maker, following Weitzman, averages the discount factors and adopts a discount rate of 5.2%. You might object that this is indefensible because no expert believes that the discount rate will be 5.2%. The decision-maker is more likely to adopt the correct discount rate by flipping a coin between 10% and 2% than he is by averaging discount factors. You might also object that your judgment has not been given as much weight as that of the other expert, for the decision-maker has selected a discount rate that is closer to her favored discount rate than to yours. Whatever we think about Weitzman's proposal and these responses, it is clear that it is not responsive to the ethical arguments for rejecting pure time preference.

Gathering the threads in this section, we can say that economic theory does not have the resources for setting the discount rate in a convincing way on the temporal scale that is relevant to climate change. First, we have little idea about how per capita consumption will fare over the next century or longer. Second, *eta* masks several distinct, important values (attitudes toward temporal inequality, present inequality, and risk) that an adequate account would have to disentangle. Third, both the prescriptive and descriptive approaches to setting *delta* and *eta* are in fact prescriptive, though there is disagreement about what the correct values are and how to set them. Both approaches to setting these values find actual behavior relevant, but each approach faces its own challenges in explaining exactly what the relation is between behavioral observations and how these values are set.[83] This problem is especially severe for Stern's prescriptive approach. A persuasive account of how to set these values would have to confront fundamental questions about the methods, limits, and purposes of economic analysis that have been neglected in the climate economics literature. When it comes to the economics of climate change, we are very far from the paradigm of economic analysis, and the usual resources of economic theory

---

[82] Gardiner 2010.

[83] There are interesting analogies with the problem of the relationship between moral theory and actual moral behavior that I cannot pursue here. See Jamieson 2001a.

have little to say in answer to the most important questions about discounting. I conclude that whether or not it is economically rational to aggressively respond to climate change depends on the discount rate, which in turn depends on answering questions that standard economic theory is not prepared to address.

4.4. FURTHER PROBLEMS

The problems for climate economics go beyond discounting. In this section I will briefly sketch some of these further problems.

As I indicated earlier, most work in climate economics, including that of Nordhaus and Stern, relies on integrated assessment models (IAM). These "end to end" models are very ambitious in attempting to go all the way from GHG emissions to economic growth. In order to realize these ambitions in a way that is computationally tractable, they make simplifications that are in some cases so extreme that they endanger the significance of the results.

One simplification that we overlooked in the previous section is that they apply a single discount rate to all commodities.[84] Various economists have pointed out that we value commodities in quite different ways and apply different discount rates to them. Compare, for example, how someone might relate to a family heirloom compared to a new electronic gizmo, and how they might differently value each object's survival.[85]

A second simplification concerns the fact that integrated assessment models assume a fixed population, but climate change will surely alter both the quantity and composition of the global population.[86] There is little agreement about how to value these changes.[87]

Models by their very nature are simplifications of reality. Some of the simplifications in integrated assessment models are unavoidable or harmless. Rather than dwelling on these simplifications, I want to convey some sense of how arbitrary some of the assumptions are that are carried along by the models, and how this can lead to tenuous and implausible results.

Estimates of the potential damages of climate change are extremely important in determining whether or not it is economically rational to act aggressively to reduce emissions. As we have seen, Nordhaus and Stern have quite different views about potential damages, to a great extent driven by their views about the discount rate. Both have been criticized for understating damages by relying on out-of-date studies, supposing that damages will not vary with the rate of climate change, and

---

[84] Heal 2007 emphasizes this concern and says that it was first noticed by Ramsey.

[85] For some other examples, see Broome 1994.

[86] Schelling 1992.

[87] Broome 2012 emphasizes this point. The most important philosophical work on population ethics has been done by Derek Parfit, which mainly amounts to elucidating paradoxes that seem to resist even our most vigorous thinking.

underestimating the damages that will occur in developed countries such as the United States.[88]

Consider an example of this last point. Agriculture in the United States is one of the most well-studied areas of climate change damages. It should also be one of the most tractable areas of inquiry, given the richness and accessibility of data. Yet estimates of the effects of climate change on the value of US agricultural output vary from a loss of 25% to a gain of 20%.[89] There are many reasons that the results are so mixed. Interactions between climate and crop growth are complex, non-linear, multidirectional, and multidimensional. Climate affects crops through temperature, precipitation, carbon dioxide fertilization, ozone formation, envirotranspiration, and impacts on weeds and pests. Each of these factors has different effects on crop yields and quality. Studies focus on the effects of temperature, precipitation, and carbon dioxide fertilization on major grain crop yields and neglect most of these other factors. These effects, which are often local and episodic, are to a great extent obscured by the spatial and temporal aggregation of the models. Most of the damages to agriculture from climate change will be associated with changes in the frequency of extreme events rather than changes in average temperature.

The failure of the models to disaggregate adequately also obscures economic variation within generations. Economists typically perform benefit/cost analyses, modeling them on decisions faced by single agents with consistent and coherent preferences. Whether the agent is taken to be the human community timelessly extended, all those currently alive, a single nation or single sector, the question is the same: What actions are optimal (or at least beneficial) for the agent in question? Since Nordhaus and Stern postulate an indefinitely growing economy, it follows that future generations will be richer than the present generation. Thus, asking the present generation to reduce its emissions is asking those who are relatively poor to benefit those who will be relatively rich.[90] By treating generations as single agents, this approach obscures the reality of the situation.

Currently, about 7% of the global population is responsible for about 50% of emissions, while 50% of the global population is responsible for about 7% of emissions.[91] It is the descendants of the latter group, poor people who emit little, who will suffer most of the damages of climate change. The climate change that is now underway is not a matter of a poor generation causing damages to rich generations,

---

[88] The first two objections draw on lectures by and conversations with Michael Hanemann; the third objection is from Ackerman 2009: 93. Generally for Hanemann's views, visit http://www.eforenergy.org/toxa/papers/Invitedpapers2-MichaelHanemann-Whatiswrongwiththedamagefunctions-1.pdf. Retrieved July 31, 2013. For an overview of the issues, visit http://e360.yale.edu/feature/calculating_the_true_cost_of_global_climate_change/2357/. Retrieved July 18, 2013.

[89] From a lecture by Michael Hanemann. This paragraph is generally indebted to Hanemann.

[90] There are many responses to this concern, some of which we have already mentioned. See also Gardiner 2010; Brekke and Johansson-Stenman 2009.

[91] Chakravarty et al. 2009.

but rather it is rich people, who may be members of a relatively poor generation, causing damages to poor people, who may be members of relatively rich generations. The excessive aggregation of the models obscures this problem, thus effacing the implicit question of distributive justice.

One of the results of climate change will be the early deaths of millions of people.[92] Virtually all public decisions, from setting speed limits to regulating workplaces, affect mortality, and economists have techniques for valuing the lives that are lost. However, these techniques break down when excess mortality is widely distributed through space and time and occurs in a broad range of contexts. The 1995 IPCC report addressed this problem directly.

> The theoretically preferred approach is to value a statistical life on the basis of what individuals are willing to pay or accept for risk changes. Such values can be based on methods such as "contingent valuation," where individuals are asked directly how much they would be willing to pay to reduce risks. Other measures include finding out how much people are spending on safety and disease-preventing measures, or by how much wages differ between safe and risky jobs (the "hedonic approach").[93]

Notice that this passage talks about how to value a "statistical life."[94] There is a sleight of hand at work here.[95] If you ask someone what they would accept in return for their life they would reject any amount of compensation, since money is no good to a dead man. Thus, on the contingent valuation approach, the value of life would be infinite. However, if you shift the question to what compensation someone would accept in return for a specified increase in risk or look at the measures used in the hedonic approach, then the answer will be some finite sum. Yet over a large population we might know the number of people who will die as a result of increasing a particular level of risk. We know that there is no compensation that these people would accept in return for the loss of their lives. However, each person will accept a finite sum as compensation in return for accepting this particular level of risk because some of them falsely believe that they will not die. We know that some of these people have false beliefs. We do not need to know their names in order to know that the costs of the increased risk are actually infinite. They only appear to be finite because we are exploiting the ignorance of those who will die. The value of a statistical life is the value of a life when some people have false beliefs. There is no reason

---

[92] According to the World Health Organization, 150,000 people had already died as a result of climate change by 2000 (http://www.who.int/heli/risks/climate/climatechange/en/, retrieved July 18, 2013).

[93] Bruce et al. 2006: 196.

[94] Thomas Schelling (1968) was one of the early contributors to the development of this concept.

[95] John Broome brilliantly pointed this out years ago in his 1978 paper. See Broome 2012 for more on this issue. See also Heinzerling 2006. In what follows I put aside the fact that some people under some conditions would trade their lives to increase the welfare of those they love.

to think that we should accept such a defective measure for evaluating policies that affect mortality. This is a general problem with attempts to value life by shifting to the concept of a statistical life. While this is important in thinking about climate change economics, it is not a problem that is peculiar to this subject.

A problem that is special to climate change economics (and perhaps some related problems) occurs when these techniques for valuing lives are employed globally in a comparative way. In these cases they result in large inequalities in the value of life between nations and individuals. This is true for a number of reasons, including the fact that rich countries and people have much greater resources to spend on life-saving than poor countries and people.

In the summer of 1995, while the second IPCC report was being finalized, a dispute broke out over the methods that were used by the economists writing Chapter 6 of the Working Group III report on "The Social Costs of Climate Change: Greenhouse Damage and the Benefits of Control." Developing countries such as China, India, Brazil, Cuba, Colombia, and those from the Alliance of Small Island States objected that the analysis valued a developed world life 15 times more than a life in the developing world. India's environment minister denounced this as "absurd" and "discriminatory."[96] It also had the effect of weakening the case for limiting emissions, since most deaths caused by climate change will occur among people in the developing world whose lives are worth comparatively little. There was an international outcry from activists and academics, including some other IPCC authors. However, the economists remained adamant about their position. The chapter's lead author, David Pearce, said:

> We won't be revising it, and we have no intention of apologising for our work. This is a matter of scientific correctness versus political correctness.[97]

The result was an uneasy compromise in which the Summary for Policymakers distanced itself from the approach taken in the disputed chapter. In the 2001 IPCC report an equal value was stipulated for all human life. While this controversy has receded into history, the issues remain very much alive and much can be learned from this story.

Standard economic techniques not only have difficulty in valuing human life but also in valuing the "more than human world," including the lives of other animals.[98] Since climate change may drive 40% of all extant species to extinction, this is extremely important in assessing potential damages and in evaluating possible responses.[99] Even in standard economic terms, the value of the more than human

---

[96] As quoted in Spash 2002: 190.

[97] http://www.newscientist.com/article/mg14719910.900-global-row-over-value-of-human-life.html. Retrieved July 18, 2013. See Spash 2002: 188 for an account of the controversy.

[98] This expression is taken from Abram 1996.

[99] Parry 2007 et al.: ch. 4, sec. 4.4.11.

world is radically unstable. Think of how differently whales, dogs, pigeons, wilderness, and wetlands are valued today than they were a century ago.[100] As climate change and other human activities continue to threaten nature, we are very likely to increasingly and intensely value what remains of the natural world.[101] However, there is a more fundamental defect than simply getting the numbers wrong in valuing the more than human world solely in this way. Imagine that we were to value women and slaves solely in terms of the economic value that they had to their husbands and owners. The problem is that asking how much we value the more than human world in economic terms elicits only a shadow of its value.

This returns us to one of the fundamental questions about climate economics: What is its point and purpose? If it is only an exercise in economic valuation narrowly construed, then it may be perfectly appropriate to ignore goods that do not pass through markets, or simply to report the values that markets assign to them, even if they seem shockingly shallow, chauvinistic, or incomplete. This may, in some way, simply reflect the actual attitudes that we have. Human lives may be of equal value even if their economic value is not. What this would show is that value is more than economic value.

However, many economists seem to want their analyses to do more than reflect economic value in this narrow sense. Nordhaus (2008: 4) writes that "economic welfare—properly measured—should include everything that is of value to people, even if those things are not included in the market."[102] He seems to be suggesting that economic value should reflect the value of my mother's love, my dog's companionship, the joy of catching the perfect wave, and even the importance of my moral ideals and spiritual attachments.

One way of reading Nordhaus is as proposing to rename philosophy, calling it instead "economics." If this were all there were to it, then we would simply change the signs on the office door and reduce the salaries of the economists accordingly. However, there is more than this going on. Economics, as it is normally practiced, is procrustean. It demands that people's values fit the theory rather than shaping the theory to fit people's values. In particular, what people value must display some particular formal features.

One of these features is substitutability. As Myrick Freeman writes:

> By "substitutability" economists mean that if the quantity of one good in a person's bundle is reduced, it is possible to increase the quantity of some other good so as to leave the person no worse off because of the change. In other words, an increase in the quantity of the second good can substitute or compensate for the decrease in the first good. The property of substitutability is at the core of the economist's concept of value....[103]

---

[100] For samples, see Burnett 2012; Nash 2001; and Jerolmack 2008.

[101] This is the insight that Krutilla and Sterner attempt to capture in economic terms.

[102] This is very much in the spirit of the expansion of the economic domain discussed in Sandel 2012.

[103] Freeman 2000: 278.

Substitutability simply does not obtain for all of the goods that will be affected by climate change. It is one thing for me to agree that there are substitutes for my house or bank account, but it is another thing entirely to agree that there are substitutes for my best friend or companion. Many people would say that there are no substitutes for mountain gorillas, wild nature, stable climates, or clear skies.[104]

In order for substitutability to obtain, bundles of goods have to be commensurable. Only then can we say that "it is possible to increase the quantity of some other good so as to leave the person no worse off because of the change." One way of making bundles commensurable is to monetize them. For example, we can compare the value of a dishwasher with that of a vacuum cleaner by consulting prices. In other cases goods are commensurable even if they are not monetized. I know that the worst day surfing is better than the best day in prison, even if I don't know how to monetize either. In some cases we make choices between goods (or bads) without regarding them as commensurable. Perhaps like E. M. Forster, I would betray my country rather than my friend. I may make this choice, but it does not follow that I think that it would be better to betray my country. Forced choices between incommensurable goods can result in choices, but they may be the stuff of tragedy. There are still other cases in which goods are incommensurable and I have no idea how to choose between them. I would not know what to say if given the choice between death by lethal injection and death by firing squad. However, this does not mean that I would be indifferent between them. In still other cases we accept monetary compensation for a loss (e.g., a quantity of money for the loss of a limb) but we do not think that we have been made whole, much less that one substitutes for the other.[105]

O'Neill et al. (2008: 78) go to the heart of what is wrong with supposing that all goods must be substitutable and commensurable:

> Monetary transactions are not exercises in the use of a measuring rod. They are social acts which have a social meaning....Given what love and friendship are, and given what market exchanges are, one cannot buy love or friendship....To believe one could would be to misunderstand those very relationships.[106]

There are limitations on what can be valued in economic terms but there are also deep questions about the nature of the value that economic analysis attributes. Traditionally, this value is called "utility." Utility is a theoretical construct that is supposed to be revealed in market behavior. While virtually no one would explicitly identify utility with income or consumption, as a matter of fact they often are treated

---

[104] The rejection of substitutability is one of the insights that have led to the development of ecological economics. For discussion, see Neumayer 2007.

[105] There is a rich philosophical discussion of the varieties of incommensurabiity. For an introduction, visit http://plato.stanford.edu/entries/value-incommensurable/. Retrieved July 18, 2013. See also Kysar 2010; Ackerman and Heinzling 2005; and Sagoff 1988/2008.

[106] See also Satz 2010.

as proxies for utility. Yet we know that income, while important, maps only roughly onto other things that we care about, such as happiness, freedom, and opportunity.[107] In recent years an extensive literature has opened up about the nature of the goods that public decision-making should promote. Some have argued for notions of welfare that are psychologically richer than the abstract notion of utility.[108] Others have plumped for more objectivist notions. Rawls's "primary goods" include basic rights and liberties, freedom of movement and free choice among a wide range of occupations, the powers of offices and positions of responsibility, and the social bases of self-respect, as well as income and wealth.[109] In recent years the idea that public action should be directed toward promoting "capabilities" has become increasingly influential.[110] Climate change will affect welfare, primary goods, capabilities, and much more besides. Yet it is only goods such as income and consumption that economic models tell us about directly.

Some have been deeply skeptical about the role of traditional economic models in thinking about climate change. Schelling (1995: 396) sees little use for the optimality models that are mainly concerned with smoothing consumption over time. He says the way to think about GHG reduction is as a foreign aid program. Instead of one country aiding another, GHG reduction is one generation aiding another generation. Many factors, both psychological and moral, go into determining appropriate levels of foreign aid. However, few people would say that there is some optimal level of foreign aid that can be calculated.[111] Spash questions whether the pollution model that is intrinsic to environmental economics applies to climate change.[112] Virtually everything we produce or consume has embedded carbon. From a pollution perspective, the prices are wrong for virtually everything. It is hard to know how to begin to implement a model that begins from such a premise. From his perspective, climate change involves managing the carbon cycle, not internalizing negative externalities.

One deep cause for concern is that most economists do not share the sense of urgency that many scientists have about climate change.[113] I think there are deep, mostly tacit commitments in economics and in the earth sciences that lead them to quite different views of the world. For economists, decisions are made at the margin from where we are; there is little interest in the pathway by which we got here. Earth sciences, on the other hand, are deeply historical subjects. Generally, for scientists,

---

[107] This is a line of thought that goes back at least to Scitovsky 1976. For more recent treatments see Graham 2012, Layard 2005, and Lane 2001.

[108] For an introduction to these notions, visit http://plato.stanford.edu/entries/well-being/. Retrieved October 25, 2013.

[109] Rawls 1971.

[110] See Nussbaum 2011 and Sen 2009: Part III. This approach has been especially influential on the UN Development Programme's Human Development Index.

[111] But see Singer 1972.

[112] Spash 2007. See Section 7.1 for further discussion.

[113] Nordhaus 1994b documented this.

how pathways constrain present choices is of great and increasing interest since how planets, ecosystems, and organisms develop and evolve depend enormously on initial conditions and random events. For economists, the focus on the margin is bound up with the interest in optimality. When it comes to planetary systems there is little role for optimality. The concern for optimality leads to a focus on the distance that a choice or policy is from optimality and a relative indifference about the direction in which it deviates. Most discussion in climate economics seems tacitly to assume that acting too aggressively to reduce emissions is as bad as failing to act aggressively enough so long as the distance from optimality is the same. Scientists, on the other hand, are more likely to be impressed by the importance of precaution and think that it is worse to reduce our emissions too little than too much. Earth scientists are impressed by the tumultuous nature of our planet. They note that virtually everything we associate with human life and culture has developed during a period in which the planet was uncharacteristically quiet. Economists, on the other hand, are more likely to take calm, linear change for granted, projecting it out indefinitely into the future, and viewing abrupt change as deviant. Economists tend to value change in a world they see as largely stable; scientists tend to value stability in a world they see as constantly changing. For economists, change brings substitutes for what is lost; for scientists, losses are often irreversible. Because they see us navigating a tumultuous world, scientists are more concerned with resilience and robustness than optimality. Resilience and robustness may require multiplexing, redundancy, diversity, multiple pathways, and other features that economists may see as deviations from efficiency and optimality.[114]

Despite these limitations, economic models, thinking, and considerations are important and helpful. In almost any context it is useful to know how much something costs. However, it is important to use the resources of economics gracefully, modestly, and in recognition of their limits. It is manifestly not the case that anything worth doing is worth doing badly.[115] When our ignorance is so extreme, it is a leap of faith to say that some analysis is better than none. A bad analysis can be so wrong that it can lead us to do bad things, outrageous things—things that are much worse than what we would have done had we not tried to assess the costs and benefits at all.[116]

---

[114] Some of these points are made by DeCanio 2003: 92. For the fairly characteristic perspective of a climate scientist not given to politics or activism, see L. Thompson 2008. Also visit http://physics.ucsd.edu/do-the-math/2012/04/economist-meets-physicist/#more-894. Retrieved July 18, 2013.

[115] A distinguished economist told me that this adage was given to him by his dissertation advisor.

[116] The last two sentences in this paragraph are from a lecture I gave to the American Association for the Advancement of Science in 1989, subsequently reprinted as Jamieson 1992 and in revised form as Jamieson 2012. For more on the limits of the models employed in climate economics, see the papers that can be accessed from http://realclimateeconomics.org/reviews_of_models.html. Retrieved July 18, 2013. In Chapter 7 I discuss how some of these cautions apply to geoengineering.

Ackerman and his colleagues conclude their review of integrated assessment models with "two take-home messages."

> The first is that policy makers and scientists should be skeptical of efforts by economists to specify optimal policy paths using the current generation of IAMs. These models do not embody the state of the art in the economic theory of uncertainty, and the foundations of the IAMs are much shakier than the general circulation models that represent our best current understanding of physical climate processes. Not only do the IAMs entail an implicit philosophical stance that is highly contestable, they suffer from technical deficiencies that are widely recognized within economics. Second, economists do have useful insights for climate policy. While economics itself is insufficient to determine the urgency for precautionary action in the face of low-probability climate catastrophes, or make judgments about intergenerational and intragenerational justice, it does point the way toward achieving climate stabilization in a cost-effective manner. IAMs cannot, however, be looked to as the ultimate arbiter of climate policy choices.[117]

4.5. STATE OF THE DISCUSSION

Despite the criticism to which it has been subjected, the Stern Review has been extremely influential. In a recent paper Nordhaus's optimal path is more aggressive in reducing emissions than it was previously. This revised optimal path would hold the warming to 3°C instead of 3.4°C. Nordhaus devotes an entire section to "cautionary notes," and he explores some policy proposals for reducing emissions that are not on his optimal path. Most revealingly, instead of denouncing Stern's choice of the discount rate, he simply writes:

> Discussions about discounting involve unresolved issues of intergenerational fairness, aversion to inequality, and projections about future technological change and population growth as well as the appropriateness of the utilitarian framework used in the Ramsey model.[118]

Other influential economists who have criticized Stern's methods or assumptions have gone on to agree with his conclusions about the need for strong policy action. As we saw in the previous section, Cline criticizes Stern for locating so many of the damages that we are supposed to respond to today in the post-2200 world. He points out that this could be remedied in a way that is consistent with Stern's conclusions.

---

[117] Ackerman et al. 2009: 314.
[118] Nordhaus 2010: 4.

The overall effect of raising the elasticity of marginal utility somewhat and incorporating a shadow price on capital would be to reduce the cost-benefit ratio of aggressive abatement from about 12:1 to perhaps 3 or 5:1, in the Stern Review framework. The bottom line would still be that such action is justified but not by as wide a margin.[119]

Arrow shows that if *eta* is increased to 2 and we use various estimates for damages and mitigation costs that are within the ranges that Stern specifies, then Stern's conclusions would be relatively insensitive to the choice of *delta*.[120]

Weitzman (2007) agrees with Nordhaus on the central methodological questions but with Stern on the conclusions. This has opened up a fruitful discussion, since one may wonder what the point of sound methodology is if it leads to the wrong answers. Weitzman criticizes Stern for "optimistically low expected costs of mitigation and pessimistically high expected damages from greenhouse warming" (2007: 705), and he says that "the Stern Review dwells in a nonscientific state of limbo" (706). He calls Stern's views about pure time preference "paternalistic" (507) and calls its policy conclusions and recommendations "radical" (708, 706). Yet he concludes that Stern may have gotten it "right for the wrong reasons." The right reason, according to Weitzman, is because of the possibility of a climate catastrophe, which should lead us to look beyond the standard economic models.

> [w]e lack a commonly accepted usable economic framework for dealing with these kinds of thick-tailed extreme disasters, whose probability distributions are inherently difficult to estimate…the hidden core meaning of *Stern vs. Critics* may be about *tails vs. middle* and about *catastrophe insurance vs. consumption smoothing*. (2007: 723)

Weitzman concludes that

> … spending money to slow global warming should not be conceptualized primarily as being about optimal consumption smoothing so much as an issue about how much insurance to buy to offset the small chance of a ruinous catastrophe that is difficult to compensate by ordinary savings.

In the literature that has developed since the publication of the Stern Review, economists have increasingly backed away from the sort of benefit-cost analysis attempted by Nordhaus. The insurance model, mentioned by Weitzman, has become increasingly prominent. Frank Ackerman, who has long been skeptical of integrated assessment models, entitled a chapter of a recent book "We need to buy insurance for the planet."[121]

---

[119] http://www.iie.com/publications/papers/paper.cfm?ResearchID=874. Retrieved July 18, 2013.
[120] Arrow 2007.
[121] Ackerman 2009: ch. 3.

Robert Stavins, in the centenary symposium issue of the *American Economic Review*, wrote that

> there is considerable agreement that benefit-cost analysis based exclusively on conventional expected values is of less use in this realm than in others and that the primary (economic) argument for limiting increases in GHG concentrations is to provide insurance against catastrophic climate risks.[122]

These distinguished economists have finally caught up with the climatologist Stephen Schneider, who since at least the 1980s talked about the need for insurance against climate change. In one characteristically pithy formulation he said:

> we buy fire insurance for our house and health insurance for our bodies. We need planetary sustainability insurance.[123]

However, as early as 1992, Thomas Schelling expressed reservations about the insurance model.

> Insurance against catastrophes is thus an argument for doing something expensive about greenhouse emissions. But to pay a couple percent of GNP as insurance premium, one would hope to know more about the risk to be averted.[124]

There are important disanalogies between reducing GHG emissions and buying insurance. First, we have no actuarial tables for the climate protection market in the way that we have for accidents and fires. We have no statistics, reliable generalizations, or even much idea about the specific impacts of climate change on societies like ours, inhabiting planets like this; much less any data about how specific changes in the composition of the atmosphere are likely to produce these impacts. The disanalogies run even deeper. Insurance is typically purchased by an agent to benefit herself or, in some cases, those whom she loves or to whom she feels responsible. But in this case, we would be asking people who are now living well, who under many scenarios have adequate resources for adaptation, to buy insurance that will mainly benefit poor people who will live in the future in some other country, and to do this primarily on the basis of predictions based on climate models, expert reports and so on. Rich people do not for the most part love or feel responsible for their poor contemporaries, especially those who live across national boundaries, much less those who will live in the future. Finally, the purposes of insurance and the purposes of emissions reduction are in many ways quite different. As Weitzman suggests, we buy

---

[122] Stavins 2011: 98.

[123] Nuzzo 2005.

[124] Schelling 1992: 8.

insurance to protect against catastrophic risks, but the costs of climate change may be gradual and incremental, though quite large. Moreover, I buy house insurance so that I can replace my house if it gets damaged. I buy life insurance so that those who depend on me will be able to live decently once I am gone. However, reducing emissions does not help replace what climate change may take from us or provide for those who are damaged by climate change. The point of cutting emissions is to reduce the probability of the worst effects of climate change from occurring. In this respect it is more like contributing to the fire department or fireproofing one's house than it is like buying insurance.

Economists who are moving away from the language of benefit-cost analysis and optimal paths, toward the language of insurance, are onto something important that is implicit in the *Stern Review*. They are moving toward seeing climate change as a risk management problem rather than as a problem of optimal growth. On the surface it may appear that Nordhaus and Stern are doing the same thing, but there are important differences. Nordhaus is working toward a global benefit-cost analysis, which he takes to be an empirical exercise, about which he thinks we can be confident. Stern views climate change as involving great uncertainties and diverse values that cannot all be quantified. He sees climate change as a problem that has ethical questions at its center.[125] In any case there are limits to what the economics can do for us.

4.6. CONCLUDING REMARKS

Despite the differences between Stern and Nordhaus, we should not overlook the fact that in many ways the Stern Review is a conventional economic analysis, though one produced to inform policy rather than as an academic exercise.[126] The Review assimilates public choice to what would be in the interests of a single, rational individual, whose preferences are complete, coherent, and consistent. While it notes the limitation of this approach, it does not seriously confront the fact that communities are diverse, comprising individuals with different interests, who are not (in the economists' sense) perfectly rational or even, in many cases, aspiring to be. Despite expressing reservations, the Review monetizes preferences and treats them as commensurable, even though it is difficult to see how such diverse values as biodiversity protection, social solidarity, and increments of income can be monetized and put on the same scale.

Many economists see the Stern Review as a radical departure because of its large estimates of the damages of climate change and the benefits of aggressive action.

---

[125] In 2013 and forthcoming Stern has more fully developed this perspective.

[126] Spash (2007) argues that Nordhaus basically ignores alternative views and that the Stern Review's failure to adequately situate itself in the literature makes it appear to be more of an outlier than it really is.

But Stern's damage estimates are not that large, seen from a certain perspective.[127] Stern's estimate of a 1.3% average annual increase in real per capita consumption swamps the projected damages of climate change. It implies that in 2200 the world will be 12.3 times as rich as today. Even if Stern's worst-case scenario comes true and climate change causes a 35% drop in consumption, people in 2200 will be 8 times as rich as we are today. This hardly sounds like a catastrophe that we must act urgently to forestall.

Imagine that the economic damages of climate change were twice or four times greater than Stern's largest estimates. This implies that future people would only be 4 times or 2 times richer than we are today. These numbers would still not seem right for expressing the losses that climate change will inflict.

Suppose that we could work the sums so that climate change was actually economically neutral over the next few centuries. Climate change would cause damages but also create opportunities that would balance them out from an economic perspective. As species became rare, the value of individual plants and animals would grow, and the revenues of zoos and safari parks would increase accordingly. Disease outbreaks and epidemics would kill many people but pharmaceutical companies would become richer. Engineering firms would rake in billions protecting human settlements against rising sea levels. Suppose all this were true. What would we think about climate change?

I do not think that many of us would say that radically remaking the Earth's climate would be fine, so long as it were economically neutral. Like any change, an economically neutral climate change would produce winners and losers. The identities of winners and losers are not usually of particular concern to economists but are central to those who are concerned with justice, especially when the winners are rich and primarily responsible for causing the problem while the losers are poor.[128] Rather than using the language of harms and damages, some would condemn what they see as the oppression or domination of future generations by those who are now alive.[129] Some would say that climate change jeopardizes the rights of future people.[130] Others would focus on what they see as the wrongness of perturbing the natural order in such a profound way. They might invoke God, nature, or simply the importance of precaution for support. Still others would express a sense of mourning and loss occasioned by the disruption of the human experience of nature. They might wonder what sort of people would act in such a careless way. Others would talk about the intrinsic value of animals and nature. The list of concerns could go on. What this response brings out is that for many people the problem with climate change is more than that it affects our pocketbooks.

---

[127] The following thought is due to Frank Ackerman (2009).

[128] See, e.g., Shue 2010.

[129] Nolt 2011b.

[130] For discussion, see Kysar 2007.

The problem with the Stern Review is not that it fails to have the right numbers but that there is more at stake than what the numbers reveal. No number seems right because the costs of climate change damages go beyond economic damages. Economic damages matter but they are not all that matters. Even if climate change were economically neutral, many people would still find something deeply wrong with humans changing the global climate.

Economics alone cannot tell us what to do in the face of climate change. Not all of the calculations can be performed, and even if they could, they would not tell us everything we need to know. At its best economics is a science and therefore cannot tell us what to do. At its worst it is an ideology, a normative outlook disguising itself as a report on the nature of things.

The legitimate power of economics is in its ability to provide instruments and tools for furthering our aims. If we want to reduce poverty, smoking, or carbon emissions, economics can recommend systems of incentives that may produce these results. It can tell us how to do things but not whether we should do them. Economics has much to say about incentives and costs, but little or nothing to say about "optimal" policies.

Economic resources need to be brought to bear in our thinking about climate change but we should be both epistemologically and normatively humble. We should be epistemologically humble since there is so little we know about the future that awaits us. We should be normatively humble because the economic analysis of climate change rests on normative assumptions that it does not have the resources to justify. In the end we're thrown back onto ethics.

5 The Frontiers of Ethics

I have argued that climate change presents us with problems of utmost complexity. Considerations ranging from our biological nature to facts about our political institutions all bear on the explanation of why we have failed to act. In the face of such problems, two broad families of considerations are sometimes effective in motivating action. Economics can sometimes succeed in showing that particular solutions appeal to our interests. Ethics can sometimes show that particular responses accord with our moral ideals. In Chapter 4 I showed that climate economics is severely limited in demonstrating that aggressive responses to climate change are in our economic interests. I identified several reasons for this limitation. The most important one concerns the fact that at key moments in the analysis, climate economics relies on ethical considerations. Our hope for motivating action on climate change must therefore to a great extent turn on ethical concerns.[1] In this chapter I explain why this hope largely has been disappointed. Just as the problems of climate change overwhelm our cognitive and affective systems, as well as our ability to do reliable economic calculations, so they also swamp the machinery of morality, at least as it currently manifests in our moral consciousness. In this chapter I explain why. I begin with a broad overview of the range of issues in the domain of climate ethics.

5.1. THE DOMAIN OF CONCERN

Since the signing of the Framework Convention on Climate Change (FCCC) at the Rio Earth Summit in 1992, abating greenhouse gas (GHG) emissions has been regarded as an urgent global responsibility.[2] GHGs linger in the atmosphere for decades, centuries, and even longer. When this is coupled with the fact that their impacts are mediated through various complex systems, the result is that climate change is practically irreversible on the timescales that most of us care about.[3] Abatement matters both because it affects the total concentration of atmospheric GHGs and also because it affects their rate of increase. Both of these factors affect the rapidity and extent of climate change, which in turn affect the nature and

---

[1] Indeed, there is evidence that those who see climate change as an ethical issue are more highly motivated to engage in climate-friendly actions (Markowitz 2012).

[2] Abatement is usually called "mitigation" in the climate change literature. See Section 7.1 for discussion of why "abatement" is a better term.

[3] See Solomon et al. 2009 and 2010.

severity of the impacts. Since abating GHG emissions imposes costs on emitters, the question of how to allocate these costs fairly has been at the center of climate ethics. Questions about the fairness of various abatement strategies are complicated by the fact that land use changes such as deforestation can also dramatically affect atmospheric concentrations of GHGs, both by directly affecting emissions and by affecting the biosphere's ability to sequester carbon. Unfortunately, these processes are difficult to characterize and measure.

As it has become increasingly clear that we are in the early stages of a climate change that is likely to continue for centuries even if we pursue aggressive abatement policies, questions about the fair distribution of the costs of adaptation have also begun to receive attention.[4] Since the resources that can be brought to bear on adaptation are limited, questions about setting priorities are also becoming increasingly important. How do we decide what to save and what to give up when we cannot protect everything?

Adaptation is motivated by a concern to avoid damages. However, climate change damages have already occurred and will continue, though it is difficult to tell exactly what damages can be attributed to climate change and to assess their extent. Research in this area is ongoing, and is especially active regarding climate change impacts on human health. The World Health Organization (WHO) estimates that climate change is already causing more than 150,000 deaths per year. This estimate is controversial, but there is no doubt that climate change will cause millions of deaths, or even orders of magnitude more.[5] Compensating for loss of life raises special problems (as we discussed in Section 4.4), but there is a range of other climate change damages (e.g., property losses) that are straightforwardly compensable. This raises questions about whether compensation should be paid and, if so, who should pay it to whom and how the required compensation should be determined and delivered.[6]

There are also difficult and neglected questions of participatory justice and how it interacts with distributive concerns. Climate change will remake the world that we bequeath to our descendants and in which we live. Generally, the impacts will be greater on those who contribute little to the problem than on those who contribute a lot. The 42 members of the Alliance of Small Island States (AOSIS) emit about ½% of global GHG emissions and on a per capita basis emit one-fourth as much carbon dioxide as the global average. Yet many of them will disappear under rising

[4] See Jamieson 2005b; Baer 2010; Adger et al. 2006. The Intergovernmental Panel on Climate change (IPCC) defines "adaptation" as "adjustment in natural or human systems in response to actual or expected climatic stimuli or their effects, which moderates harm or exploits beneficial opportunities" (Parry et al. 2007: 27). I say more about adaptation in Section 7.2.

[5] See the policy brief available at http://www.who.int/heli/risks/climate/climatechange/en/. Retrieved July 18, 2013. For a taste of the controversies in this area, visit http://dotearth.blogs.nytimes.com/2009/05/29/warming-and-death/. Retrieved July 18, 2013.

[6] For discussion, see McKinnon 2012. While compensation is discussed in the academic and NGO community, and increasingly by the leaders of some African countries, it is not central to the current diplomatic discourse.

seas.[7] Sub-Saharan Africans emit about one-twelfth as much carbon per capita as Europeans, who in turn emit about one-half as much carbon as North Americans, yet Sub-Saharan Africans will suffer disproportionately from climate change and have less capacity to adapt than Americans or Europeans.[8] While 194 nations are parties to the FCCC and their diplomats fly around the world in a seemingly endless series of talkathons, most of these nations have very little power over the forces that actually affect the world's climate, and billions of their citizens have even less voice.[9] Eighty percent of global carbon emissions come from only 10 countries. Their leaders, along with the executives of the world's most powerful corporations, have disproportionate influence on the decisions that affect emissions and the resources available for adaptation.[10] While this disparity in the ability of various nations and their peoples to effectively participate in climate change negotiations is decried by some academics and NGOs, American academics and policy-makers increasingly seem to want less inclusive regimes.[11]

Finally, there are impacts on non-human nature. The 2007 Intergovernmental Panel on Climate Change (IPCC) report documented that climate change has already shifted the geographic ranges of plants, animals, and biomes around the world.[12] Climate change is occurring against a background in which human activities have already diminished the populations of many species and fragmented landscapes in ways that will reduce dispersal rates and block range shifts, and these human activities show little sign of diminishing. The ability of many species to migrate, even if dispersal corridors are available, will be slow relative to the pace of future climate change.[13] Moreover, since many species engage in mutualistic interactions, the dispersal dynamics of multiple species can affect the viability of any single species.[14] For these reasons, conservation biologists generally agree that climate change will

---

[7] Office of the High Representative for the Least Developed Countries, Landlocked Developing Countries and Small Island Developing States (UN-OHRLLS), *The Impact of Climate Change on the Development Prospects of the Least Developed Countries and Small Island Developing States*, 2009, available on the web at http://www.un.org/ohrlls/. Retrieved July 18, 2013.

[8] http://earthtrends.wri.org/searchable_db/index.php?step=countries&ccID[]=5&theme=3&variable_ID=466&action=select_years. Retrieved July 18, 2013.

[9] To get a feel for what it was like for developing world representatives in Copenhagen in 2009, visit http://www.iied.org/climate-change/media/climate-game-and-worlds-poor-documentary-film-inside-cop15-climate-change-summi. Retrieved July 18, 2013. For discussion, see Roberts and Parks 2007: 14–19.

[10] http://www.npr.org/templates/story/story.php?storyId=121240453. Retrieved July 18, 2013.

[11] There is of course reason to be frustrated by the FCCC process. See Chapter 7 for further discussion.

[12] See also Parmesan and Yohe 2003; Gonzalez et al. 2010; Young et al. 2008.

[13] This has led to questions about whether such migration should be assisted. See Schwartz et al. 2012.

[14] Baums 2008.

raise extinction rates.[15] The polar bear has already become the popular symbol of climate change–caused extinction.

Climate change poses many different kinds of problems and some of them can be seen as familiar moral problems. Powerful countries and wealthy people plunder global commons in various ways, not just by emitting carbon. Powerful nations have largely frozen the post–World War II order in place, effectively depriving billions of people and their governments from participation in much of the international system. Each year more than 600,000 people die from malaria and nearly 2 million people die from AIDS, all without the assistance of climate change.[16] The first human-caused extinctions may have occurred 50,000 years ago in Australia, Southeast Asia, and perhaps Africa.[17]

The contribution of climate change to many of these problems will challenge our existing moral commitments only at the margins, if at all. For example, hurricanes may become more intense as a result of climate change, and our attitudes may shift to some extent if they also become more frequent and we come to see them as at least partly anthropogenic. However, we already have attitudes and dispositions regarding the victims of hurricanes, and while it is easy to imagine that we might become a little more or a little less responsive, it seems unlikely that these attitudes would change dramatically.

However, the origins of our commonsense morality are in low-population, low-density societies, with seemingly unlimited access to many natural resources, so it would not be surprising if there were questions relating to anthropogenic climate change about which our everyday morality is flummoxed, silent, or incorrect. In this chapter I focus on what I think are some of the deeper challenges to commonsense morality that climate change presents. In particular, I focus on responsibility for individual actions that in some way may contribute to climate change.

First a word about "commonsense morality."[18] This is not an entirely happy expression for several reasons. There is no single precisely characterized entity that it names. Nor is commonsense morality well-defined over everything that we might think is open to moral evaluation. Finally, rather than being a fixed set of commitments, commonsense morality is a dynamic system of interrelated beliefs, ideals, attitudes, emotions, dispositions, and more besides. Nevertheless, I will assume that there is a phenomenon that we can usefully discuss under this rubric. We may disagree around the edges, but most of us know at least roughly what we are talking about. It can usefully be thought of as what we learned at our parents' knees.[19]

---

[15] Thomas et al. 2004; Cameron et al. 2004.

[16] http://www.who.int/features/factfiles/malaria/en/index.html (retrieved July 18, 2013); http://www.avert.org/worldstats.htm (retrieved July 18, 2013).

[17] http://darwin.bio.uci.edu/~sustain/bio65/lec04/b65lec04.htm. Retrieved July 18, 2013.

[18] Sidgwick (1907: xix) uses this term but I am not sure of its origins. For further discussion, see Haworth 1955.

[19] I use this florid language in order to dodge some interesting questions about our access to commonsense morality. Is it like knowing a language, as some have thought, or is it more empirically

The climate change issue can be seen at its core as centering on rich people appropriating more than their share of a global public good and, as a result, harming poor people by causally contributing to extreme climatic events such as droughts, hurricanes, and heat waves, which in turn can ramify, causing disease outbreaks, economic dislocations, and political instability. Much of this behavior is unnecessary, even for maintaining the profligate lifestyles of the rich.

There are five distinguishable claims here. First, some people appropriate a disproportionate share of a global public good. Second, the disproportionate appropriation harms other people. Third, it is rich people who are doing the disproportionate appropriation. Fourth, it is poor people who are disproportionately harmed. Finally, the rich could appropriate less of the global public good and still maintain their lifestyles.[20]

Each of these claims can be challenged, and all of them require more careful formulation. What interests me here, however, is how these claims can be explained and justified by our prevailing notions of moral responsibility. In my opinion it is a rough fit, as I will now try to explain.

Most of the time we do not subject what people do to moral evaluation.[21] This may be because we consider most of what people do to be "their business," belonging to a private sphere that is beyond the reach of morality. Or it may be because we regard most of what people do to be permissible. Generally our moral thinking only consciously engages when something strikes us as not quite right. There are also acts that come to our attention because they are morally exemplary or "beyond the call of duty," but these occur less frequently than the feeling that something is fishy. Various moral theorists would like to dislodge this way of seeing things, but nevertheless this is more or less how most of us see things most of the time. When it comes to acts, the most fundamental distinction in our prevailing moral consciousness is between those that are morally suspect and those that are not, and we see most of what people do as in some way, for some reason, outside the domain of moral evaluation.

A paradigm of an act that is morally suspect is one that has the following structure: An individual acting intentionally harms another individual; both the individuals and the harm are identifiable; and the individuals and the harm are closely related in time and space.

---

grounded? This dispute is in some ways analogous to that between Stanley Cavell, and Jerry Fodor and Jerry Katz in the early 1960s about our knowledge of language. For further discussion, see Mikhail 2011.

[20] These claims are made by various contributors to Gardiner et al. 2010. See also Gardiner 2010.

[21] As Raquelle Stiefler pointed out to me, celebrities and politicians may be the exceptions.

Consider an example.[22] Suppose that Jill has parked her bicycle on the porch of her house and then gone inside to make dinner. Jack, who has been looking for a bicycle to steal, sees Jill's bicycle on the porch, cuts the lock, and rides off. The following is an apt characterization of this case:

1. Jack intentionally steals Jill's bicycle.

In this case Jack intentionally acts in such a way as to knowingly harm another individual.[23] Both the perpetrator and victim (Jack and Jill) are clearly identifiable, and they are closely related in time and space. This case is a clear candidate for moral evaluation, and most of us would resoundingly say that what Jack did was wrong.

Consider, however, what happens when we alter the case along various dimensions. We may still see the case as a candidate for moral evaluation, but its claim to be a paradigm weakens. Consider the following examples:

2. Jack is part of an unacquainted group of strangers, each of which, acting independently, takes one part of Jill's bicycle, resulting in the bicycle's disappearance.

3. Jack takes one part from each of a large number of bicycles, one of which belongs to Jill.

4. Jack and Jill live on different continents, and the loss of Jill's bicycle is the consequence of a causal chain that begins with Jack ordering a used bicycle at a shop.

5. Jack lives many centuries before Jill, and consumes materials that are essential to bicycle manufacturing; as a result, it will not be possible for Jill to have a bicycle.

In example 2 we transform the agent who harms Jill into an unstructured collective. In 3 we reduce the amount of harm that Jack causes Jill to a minimum. In 4 we disrupt the spatial contiguity between Jack and Jill and cancel Jack's *mens rea*.[24] In 5 we also cancel Jack's *mens rea* and in this case disrupt the temporal contiguity between Jack and Jill. Each case, I claim, is less of a paradigm for moral evaluation than Case 1. Indeed, some people would not think that there is anything morally questionable about Jack's actions in 4 and 5. Examples 2 and 3 may still be seen as candidates for moral evaluation, but less obviously so than in 1. People who see Jack's action as wrong in 2 and 3 are likely to see it as less wrong than in 1.

---

[22] I introduced these cases in Jamieson 2007a, inspired by an example in Glover 1975. For an earlier investigation of some of these themes in a different genre, see Bob Dylan's "Who Killed Davey Moore," lyrics available at http://www.bobdylan.com/us/songs/who-killed-davey-moore. Retrieved October 25, 2013.

[23] There are some ambiguities about intentional action, so let me stipulate the following. When I say that an agent intentionally phis, I will mean that the agent acted intentionally and that *phi*ing would be a reasonable description of the act from the agent's point of view, whether or not the agent acted under that description.

[24] *Mens rea* is Latin for "guilty mind." In many cases it is regarded in the law as a necessary condition for criminal liability.

Now consider example 6, which incorporates all of the changes serially considered in examples 2–5.

6. Acting independently, Jack and a large number of unacquainted people set in motion a chain of events that causes a large number of future people who will live in another part of the world from ever having bicycles.

For many people this is just an abstract description of normal, everyday behavior. There is nothing suspect about it at all. For other people the perception persists that there is something morally questionable about this case. This is because what some people take to be at the center of a moral problem persists: Some people have acted in a way that harms other people. However, most of what typically accompanies this core has disappeared, and this is why some people do not see this case as presenting a moral problem. Even for those who do see this case as presenting a moral problem, the wrongness of the acts and the culpability of the agents are greatly diminished by comparison to example 1. In example 6 it is difficult to identify the agents, the victims, and the causal nexus. Nor does it appear that anyone has intentionally deprived future people who will live in another part of the world from ever having bicycles. The fact that they will not have bicycles is just a consequence of Jack and others getting on with their lives. In these circumstances it is difficult for the network of moral concepts that involve responsibility and harm to gain traction. In my opinion it is example 6 that bears the greatest resemblance to the climate change case. If I am right about this, then it is not surprising that many people do not see climate change, at least with respect to individual responsibility, as presenting a moral problem.[25]

[25] In his comments on an earlier version of the manuscript, Peter Singer claimed that 6* is closer to the climate change case than 6:

> 6*. For many years, Jack and a large number of unacquainted people have been acting in a way that is probably already causing harm to some present people who live in another part of the world, and will in future very probably cause much more harm to a larger number of future people, also mostly living in another part of the world. The benefits that Jack et al. gain from acting in these ways are much less than the harms they are probably causing, and very probably will cause, to others, most of whom are already far worse off than Jack et al. are. Jack and many of these other people have been informed, by the relevant experts, that the way they act is likely to be causing this harm, and is likely to cause more harm in future. Nevertheless, they have refused to stop acting in these ways.

Any analogy can be seen as tendentious and I do not want to enter the discussion of which of these analogies is the most tendentious. Singer and I agree that our response to an action that may contribute to climate change is highly sensitive to how it is described and conceptualized. My point is that many such actions are commonly thought of as more analogous to 6 than to 1 (or to 6* for that matter), and that it is not unreasonable to think of them in this way, at least without much more work being done. Others have also challenged this analogy, including Gardiner 2011. I reply to Gardiner in Jamieson 2013a.

The previous section, it might be said, overstates the relationship between harm causation and moral responsibility. Though harm-causation plays a central role in our conception of moral responsibility, there are many cases in which it is not sufficient.[26] For example, in the following cases I may be causally but not morally responsible:

7. A hurricane picks me up and throws me through your window, shattering the glass.

8. My roommate inadvertently substitutes aspirin for my meds; during the psychotic episode that results I deface your wallpaper.

9. The donut shop that I open drives your donut shop out of business, leading to the impoverishment of your family.

In many cases what is needed for an agent who causes harm to be morally responsible is for the agent to be at fault in some way or other.

An agent can be at fault by violating a duty that is relevant to causing the harm. For example, an agent can intentionally act in a way that produces the harm, as Jack did in example 1. Or an agent can act recklessly in "conscious disregard of a substantial risk of serious harm."[27] An agent can also act negligently in failing to take the precautions that a "reasonable person" would take, thereby imposing an unreasonable risk of harm on another person.[28]

According to some theorists, we are morally responsible only for those GHG emissions that involve fault on our part. There are various ways of marking the distinction between faultless emissions and those for which the emitter is at fault.

For some it is knowledge that matters.[29] When my grandfather was smoking his pipe, he did not know that he may have been contributing to climate change by emitting carbon dioxide. He acted from ignorance, not negligently or recklessly. I, on the other hand, know that the airplane that I am taking to the next climate change conference emits climate-changing GHGs. In acting in the face of this knowledge, some would say that I am behaving negligently, recklessly, or in some other morally defective way. I, unlike my grandfather, am at fault for my emissions.[30]

---

[26] Some think that it is never sufficient while others deny that it is necessary. For discussion, see the papers collected in Sinnott-Armstrong 2008: ch. 8. A great deal of this territory was covered from a different perspective in Hart and Honoré, 1985.

[27] This is the formulation in the Restatement of the Law of Torts. For discussion, see Rapp 2008.

[28] For discussion, see Hunter and Salzman 2007.

[29] For others it is the extent of an individual's emissions that matter. I discuss this proposal in the next section.

[30] What if I offset my emissions by paying people to plant trees or retiring emissions permissions in some emissions-trading scheme? See Chapter 7 for further discussion.

While my grandfather and I may be easy cases, others may not be so clear. About a quarter of the people in the world have never heard of global warming, much less know anything about the link between GHG emissions and climate change. Many of these people are from developing countries whose GHG emissions are low but nevertheless contribute to the stock of these gases in the atmosphere.[31] In many countries, less than half the population believes in anthropogenic climate change.[32] Of course we can say that these people are acting in bad faith; many of them willfully reject the reality of anthropogenic climate change because they do not want to see themselves as acting wrongly or to change their behavior. This, however, is too simple. Many people are not scientifically equipped to understand the rudiments of how driving a car or heating a house can contribute to climate change. Some people are confused by the mixed messages that come from the media about whether there is scientific consensus about anthropogenic climate change. Others are unwitting victims of their own ideologies. In any case, the impact on the climate of the emissions of an individual person, even one who is a high-emitter, may be inconsequential or negligible, and in any case unknown.[33] It is thus not surprising that people do not see picking up their kids after soccer practice as reckless or negligent behavior. They may be correct in thinking that this behavior does not fall under our prevailing concepts of negligent, reckless, or otherwise morally defective behavior (even if it does involve a Chevrolet Suburban).

5.4. HUMAN RIGHTS AND DOMINATION

While actions that may contribute to climate change may not obviously fall under our prevailing notions of wrongful behavior, it may be claimed that they are instances of them nevertheless. In order to see this we need to think harder, and it is the job of philosophy to help us to do this. I may not have known that a whale was a mammal until I did some science, but once stirred to study, I saw that this was true: Whales are mammals. Similarly, it might be said, it is reflection on our moral concepts, not conceptual revision or revolution, that is needed to see that behaviors that may contribute to climate change are wrong.

Reflecting on our commitment to human rights is one way to see this. Simon Caney has written that although there is no human right to a stable climate, "anthropogenic climate change violates human rights" including "the human right to life, the human

---

[31] 40–50% of Africans say they have never heard of global warming. See http://www.gallup.com/poll/124652/Awareness-Climate-Change-Threat-Vary-Region.aspx. Retrieved July 18, 2013.

[32] These include the United States, the United Kingdom, Denmark, and Norway. The fact of anthropogenic climate change is less controversial in China and India. See http://www.gallup.com/poll/117772/Awareness-Opinions-Global-Warming-Vary-Worldwide.aspx. Retrieved July 18, 2013.

[33] Sinnott-Armstrong (2005) seems to claim that the emissions from a Sunday drive in a gas guzzler (for example) have no causal effect in producing climate change. I discuss this claim in Section 5.6.

right to health, and the human right to subsistence"(2010a: 166) and perhaps also "a human right to development" and "a human right not to be forcibly evicted"(169).[34] Caney's thought is analogous to Woody Guthrie's idea that "some men rob you with a six-gun—others with a fountain pen."[35] They both rob you, but those who rob you with a fountain pen are seen as respectable while those who rob you with a six-gun are viewed as criminals (though "[you] won't never see an outlaw [d]rive a family from their home"). Similarly, it might be said that those who kill innocent people with carbon are seen as respectable citizens, while those who kill with bombs and guns are viewed as human rights violators.

But who in the climate change case are the moral equivalents of those who rob you with a fountain pen? Who are the human rights violators in the case of anthropogenic climate change?

Recent writers on human rights have tended to shy away from the language of human rights violations in favor of talk about respecting, honoring, and promoting human rights. They also emphasize that states and other institutions, rather than individuals, are the primary bearers of these duties. For example, James Nickel writes:

> human rights are political norms dealing mainly with how people should be treated by their governments and institutions. They *are not ordinary moral norms applying mainly to inter-personal conduct* (such as prohibitions of lying and violence).[36]

There are good reasons for these emphases. They help to break down the distinction between "positive" and "negative" rights and help us to see that individuals who act in human rights–compromising ways often do so as authorized agents of states or other institutions.[37] On such a view, any particular human right (or pattern of human rights violation) will imply a complicated account of duty-bearers and the contents of their duties, one that will be affected and mediated by various institutional, social, and political realties.[38] There is no guarantee that an account that is adequate for a particular human right at one moment will apply to other human rights, or even the same human right at different moments.[39] In view of these complexities and contingencies, it is not surprising that the development of specific accounts for various human rights is underdeveloped. In particular, no

---

[34] Although Caney doesn't go there, it has become increasingly common to see anthropogenic climate change as a human rights violation (see, e.g., Humphreys 2010). A landmark in the development of this idea was the 2005 petition from the Inuit Circumpolar Conference to the Inter-American Commission on Human Rights (ICHR) charging the US government with violating the human rights of the Inuit people by emitting carbon (the ICHR refused to hear the case).

[35] In his 1939 song "Pretty Boy Floyd."

[36] From the *Stanford Encyclopedia of Philosophy* entry on human rights, available at http://plato.stanford.edu/entries/rights-human/. Retrieved July 18, 2013. See also Beitz 2009 and Pogge 2002.

[37] The former theme is especially prominent in Shue 1996.

[38] See Shue 1988.

[39] John Tasioulas 2007 discusses this under the rubric "the dynamism of rights."

such account has been produced that would allow us to understand in detail who bears what duties with respect to the human rights violations that are supposed to be entailed by anthropogenic climate change.[40] Without such specific and precise accounts, there is a worry that replacing the language of moral responsibility with the language of human rights simply amounts to speaking in a louder voice.[41] This is especially important for us since we have turned to the discourse of human rights in the hope that it will help us to see moral responsibilities with respect to behaviors that may contribute to climate change as embedded in commonsense morality.

Despite the emphasis on states and institutions in most contemporary accounts of human rights, the idea that individuals are also responsible for respecting, honoring, or promoting human rights is difficult to leave behind.[42] Indeed, most theorists of human rights, including those who emphasize institutional obligations, accept this.[43] Even when states or institutions are the most important agents in promoting human rights, there are many cases in which such duties are distributed among, or entail duties for, individuals (e.g., as duties to refrain from behavior that may contribute to climate change, or as duties to obey laws that promote climate stability). Indeed, after characterizing what he calls a "hybrid" approach to upholding human rights that are jeopardized by climate change, Caney writes that "[r]ecognizing the centrality of states does not entail that one cannot apply these principles to individuals."[44] In light of these considerations, it is worth discussing what duties individuals might have with respect to human rights claims, even while recognizing that most theorists of human rights would emphasize the institutional nature of the duties. This will help to bring out the difficulties involved in seeing anthropogenic climate change as a case of human rights violations from the perspective of commonsense morality.

As we have seen, Simon Caney claims that "anthropogenic climate change violates…human rights" because of its impact on life, health, and subsistence. According to Caney, one reason that anthropogenic climate change violates human rights is that it kills people. Compare this to the claim that murder violates human rights. When someone says that murder violates human rights, what she means is that agents violate human rights by performing acts of murder. If we were to follow this lead, we would say that agents violate human rights by performing acts of

---

[40] Simon Caney and Derek Bell deserve credit for having taken the discussion this far. In addition to Caney's 2010 paper cited above, see also his 2010b and 2009. For Bell's views, see his 2013 article.

[41] This echoes Joel Feinberg's (1970) concern with what he called "manifesto rights." See also Beitz 2009: ch. 5.

[42] Judith Lichtenberg (2009) makes this point.

[43] For example, Nickel explicitly qualifies his claim with the use of the word "mainly," Griffin states that some duties grounded in human rights are owed by individuals to other individuals (2008: 181), Pogge talks about human rights "giving me a duty" (2002: 66), and Beitz (2009: 128) writes that "this does not mean that human rights impose no constraints on other agents or that only states have responsibilities.…"

[44] Caney 2009: 246.

anthropogenic climate change that kill people. But if performing an act of anthropogenic climate change means bringing about climate change in the way in which performing an act of murder means bringing about murder, then no agent violates human rights because no agent has the capacity to bring about climate change on her own, much less to kill people by bringing about climate change.[45] On the other hand, if we say that performing acts that may contribute to climate change is sufficient for committing acts of climate change that kill people, then everyone from Barack Obama to a Tibetan herder is a human rights violator.

Relations between emitting GHGs, changing climate, and killing people are quite different from and more complex than those that exist in standard cases of human rights violations. By way of comparison, consider a human rights violation such as torturing someone by water-boarding them. Water-boarding is avoidable while some GHG emissions are not—for example, those that result from human respiration. Moreover, cooking, heating, and transport are generally required in order to have decent lives and these require consuming energy, which in virtually every country in the world involves emitting carbon.[46] On the other hand, one can normally have a decent life without engaging in acts that implicate oneself in torture.[47] Finally, not only does everyone emit GHGs but virtually everyone will be affected by climate change in some way. Torturers, on the other hand, do not torture themselves and certainly do not torture themselves by torturing others (except perhaps in some attenuated psychological sense).

One way of responding to at least part of this problem is to see it as presenting the challenge of identifying a permissible threshold. On this view it is only emissions that go beyond this threshold that raise the suspicion of violating human rights. But what exactly is the threshold for permissible GHG emissions, and how can we determine what it is?

There are different views about what are the emissions to which people are entitled. Some, including myself, have argued that people are entitled to equal per capita emissions, indexed to fixed population levels. It is only permissible for people to emit more if they purchase permissions from those who would willingly emit less.[48] Others have thought that historical patterns of emissions are relevant to determining

---

[45] We can imagine a case in which a single agent would be capable of changing climate on her own, thereby killing people. Perhaps a supervillain such as James Bond's nemesis, Ernst StavroBlofeld, would be a good candidate. Various actors have aspired to such power, often with the best of intentions (see Fleming 2010).

[46] In 2010 88% of global energy consumption came from fossil fuels (see BP's Statistical Review of World Energy 2011, available at http://www.economist.com/blogs/schumpeter/2011/06/energy-statistics. Retrieved July 18, 2013.

[47] However, it may be difficult to live a middle-class lifestyle in Europe, North America, or Australasia without implicating oneself in abuses such as sweatshop labor. Still, there is a distance between these cases and the virtual necessity of emitting GHGs.

[48] Jamieson 2001b; see also Singer 2002. As far as I know, this idea was first advocated in print by Agarwal and Narain 1991.

the emissions to which people are entitled, either because historical patterns should be "grandfathered" or because past emissions count against present entitlements.[49] We do not need to resolve these disputes here.[50] My goal is simply to bring out some of the consequences of a view that sees emissions that are in excess of some baseline as constituting human rights violations.

Consider how the story might go on the equal per capita emissions approach.[51] Much of the world has coalesced around the idea that a 2°C warming of the earth's surface temperature would violate the FCCC, which commits parties to preventing "dangerous anthropogenic interference with the Earth's climate system."[52] While much remains unknown about climate sensitivity, the German Advisory Council on Global Change has estimated that in order to have a two-thirds chance of keeping the warming under 2°C, each person in the world must emit no more than 2.7 tons of carbon dioxide (or its equivalent) per year between now and 2050.[53] An individual exhausts this level of emissions by flying round-trip from San Francisco to New York or maintaining a typical single-family American home for one month. A year's driving by a typical American produces twice these emissions. If we adopt the standard of equal per capita emissions and conjoin it with some plausible assumptions about what total emissions we should allow, then virtually all Americans are human rights violators, as are most of those in the rest of the world who live middle-class (and beyond) lifestyles. Yet not only do most of these people not feel like human rights violators, many of them do not think that they have choices that would allow them to emit less. Many people in the United States say, after a trip to Paris, London, or New York, that they would willingly take public transport if it were available to them, but that it is not an option in their daily lives. On the view under consideration, billions of people around the world are human rights violators, yet it is not clear how they could refrain from being so, at least given the options that they see as being currently available to them. This does not sound like a view that is embedded in commonsense morality.

Another approach to identifying a plausible baseline would be to distinguish luxury from subsistence emissions.[54] On this view the idea is that everyone in the world is entitled to subsistence emissions but no one is entitled to luxury emissions. It is luxury emissions that violate human rights.

---

[49] Luc Bovens defends qualified grandfathering (2010).

[50] For a general review and critique of such views, see Caney 2012.

[51] This paragraph (indeed, the entire chapter) owes much to Kysar 2011.

[52] This target appears in various international documents and is enshrined in the Copenhagen Accord, available at http://unfccc.int/documentation/documents/advanced_search/items/3594.php?rec=j&priref=60000573#beg. Retrieved July 18, 2013.

[53] "Solving the Climate Dilemma: The Budget Approach," available at http://www.eeac-net.org/bodies/germany/german_wbgu.htm. Retrieved July 18, 2013.

[54] Shue 1993. Although I am discussing equal per capita emissions and the distinction between luxury and subsistence emissions in relation to human rights violations, these could alternatively be viewed as standards for fault liability.

There are clear cases of luxury and subsistence emissions. For example, Arnold Schwarzenegger driving his Hummer produces luxury emissions; a Kenyan farmer cooking her dinner on a dung fire produces subsistence emissions. However, for a large range of cases it is difficult to distinguish luxury and non-luxury, and subsistence and non-subsistence emissions.

The problem begins with the fact that people want the services that energy use provides but care relatively little about the sources that produce the energy. Most people in the developed world probably do not even know where their energy comes from. Except in rare cases, individuals are not presented with a cafeteria of options regarding energy sources from which they can select. It is true that some people have chronic concerns about some energy sources (e.g., oil, coal, and their relations to air pollution) and fears about some energy sources are brought to consciousness by particular episodes (e.g., an accident in a nuclear power plant). For the most part, however, what people care about are the services that energy use provides, such as transport, cooking, comfort, and convenience. Depending on where they live, transport might involve a gasoline-powered Hummer or a camel who feeds on dates, grass, wheat, and oats. Cooking a meal might depend on a dung fire or electricity from a coal-fired generating plant.

The quantity of emissions required to maintain a particular standard of living depends on differences in energy mix and other conditions across societies. For example, nearly 80% of the energy consumed in the United States comes from fossil fuels, compared to only 60% of the energy consumed in France. It is thus not surprising that France's per capita GHG emissions are lower than those of the United States (though it may still surprise that France's per capita emissions are less than half those of the United States). France's different energy mix and lower emissions are not simply a matter of luck or circumstance, though they may be experienced that way by some people. Policy choices regarding energy and transport go a long way toward explaining the differences between the United States and France. In any case, in both countries a large fraction of emissions might reasonably be regarded as luxury emissions, but it is not easy to be precise about what exactly the fraction is in each country.[55]

It is also difficult to say what fraction of emissions in poor countries are subsistence emissions. The quantity of emissions required for subsistence depends on what energy sources are available, as well as facts about social organization and the local environment. War and conflict matter, and so do other circumstances, such as whether necessities are imported or locally produced and under what conditions. As a result of these factors and others, Zimbabwe (for example) emits several times as much carbon per dollar of output as most comparable African countries.[56] Still, it is difficult to go from these observations to calculations about the extent to which

[55] For more on these themes, see Jamieson 2011.
[56] http://www.eia.gov/iea/carbon.html. Retrieved July 18, 2013.

Zimbabwe's emissions are subsistence emissions compared to those of other African countries.

A deeper problem in distinguishing luxury and subsistence emissions concerns how to regard various goods. Are the emissions associated with education, art-making, and religion subsistence emissions, luxury emissions, or something else? Each year about 3 million people visit Mecca for the Muslim *hajj*, most of them traveling by air or automobile.[57] How should we regard these emissions? While there are clear cases of luxury and subsistence emissions, it is hard to find an actionable principle for dividing emissions into these categories.[58]

Even if we had such a principle, it would still be a stretch to suppose that every luxury emission violates human rights. Unlike in the case of water-boarding, the relations between emissions and harms are just too complex and unknowable to make such a claim plausible. Given the non-linearities and buffers in the climate system, and the fact that other human and societal factors are implicated in producing the harmful effects of climate change, we cannot say exactly which emissions are causally active and in what way in producing climate change–related harms, much less that an agent should know the effects of her emissions. Standard human rights violations are not like this at all. Generally, a torturer knows what he is doing and the harm that he is causing: Indeed, that is why he is doing it.[59] There may be ignorance about a particular causal chain, but at least in principle it can be rectified. An electrode may fail or someone may intervene to prevent the suffering of a victim, but these possibilities are quite different from the cloud of uncertainty that surrounds slightly turning up a thermostat. While we might think that Arnold Schwarzenegger is selfish, thoughtless, or intemperate when he fires up his Hummer, it is difficult to see how he, or any individual engaged in producing luxury emissions, at least on this scale, can be seen as violating human rights. As is true of you and me as well, the relations between Schwarzenegger, his actions, and the twenty-second-century victims of climate change are different in important respects from the relations between the torturer, his acts, and his victim.

John Nolt (2011b) claims that, rather than violating human rights, anthropogenic climate change involves dominating posterity in a way that is analogous to historical instances of dominating racial, ethnic, or national minorities. He characterizes domination in the following way:

[57] This is about the same number of students who study abroad each year, according to the Institute of International Education. Do these involve luxury emissions? For attempts to "green" the *hajj* see http://www.greenprophet.com/2010/06/green-hajj-mecca/. Retrieved July 18, 2013.

[58] A more sophisticated version of this view would hold that there is a third category of emissions that could be grandfathered, auctioned, treated as excusable but not permissible, or in some other way, but this would still not help with knowing how to sort emissions into the proper categories.

[59] Parfit's (1984: ch.3) "harmless torturers" case is an exception that turns on imperceptible changes and thresholds. The relation between GHG emitters and harms is different from the relations in the harmless torturers case because there are shifts of scale involved in moving from emissions to harms. I return to these themes in the next section and in Section 6.2.

A subject is (harmfully) dominated by an agent if and only if:

    a)the agent wields superior power over the subject;

    b)the subject is not free to exit the relationship without incurring costs;

    c)the agent wields power over the subject in a way that harms the subject.[60]

Nolt argues that our relations with posterity satisfy this definition, so it follows that "our emissions of greenhouse gases constitute domination of posterity."[61] He goes on to anticipate a remarkable range of objections.

However, I am not satisfied. It is strange to think that a subject can be dominated by an agent when the subject does not exist at the time when the agent engages in the dominating actions and, indeed, would not exist at all if the agent did not engage in these actions. Nolt discusses something like this objection under the heading of "the non-identity objection." He asks us to consider a child born into slavery who would not otherwise have existed had there been no such institution. He claims that even so, slavery is an injustice to the child and concludes that "[l]ikewise it does not follow from the premise that future people owe their lives to our domination that the domination was not unjust" (2011b: 72).

I agree that once the child is born, living in slavery is an injustice to the child, but this observation does not bear on the objection that I want to raise. My concern is not with the question of whether our domination of posterity is unjust but whether the relationship between us and posterity constitutes domination in the first place.

Generations bring their successors into existence and bequeath to them, not just capital stock, but also the very conditions of their existence. Consider the case of Manhattan, where the harvest has always been rich but what is on offer has changed from nature to experience. Because of the legacy bequeathed by past generations, people in Manhattan today can enjoy walking on the Highline, visiting the Metropolitan Museum of Art, and soaking up the ambience of Greenwich Village. However, the same generations that bequeathed this legacy destroyed the wild green paradise that had been bequeathed to them with its oysters the size of dinner plates, dense flocks of birds that darkened the sky, and rivers so thick with fish that they could be pulled out by hand.[62] What should we say about them? We can be grateful for their legacy, castigate their short-sightedness, or assume a range of other attitudes. What we cannot say is that they dominate us. It is true that they determined the fact and conditions of our existence, but this is simply a consequence of how generations are temporally related and does not bear directly on the question of domination.

---

[60] This is my summary of Nolt's account, which he takes from Lovett 2001 and slightly revises.

[61] Nolt 2011b: 61. He does not say whether he thinks that we who live in the present are dominated by the emissions of our forebears.

[62] The very thought of Gowanus Bay oysters conjures up a starkly different image today than it once did. For more, visit http://books.google.com/books?id=6EjpxuZAsH0C&pg=PA189&dq=hudson+river+oysters&hl=en&ei=oLikTvXuO6X30gHN0s38BA&sa=X&oi=book_result&ct=result&resnum=10&ved=0CGUQ6AEwCQ#v=onepage&q=oysters&f=false. Retrieved July 18, 2013.

There are cases, however, in which a present generation can dominate posterity. Suppose that a present generation imposes a technology on posterity that would effectively eliminate people's ability to act freely, however exactly that concept is understood. A program written by people living in the present would determine everything that everyone in the future would do, regardless of their beliefs and desires. In this case it seems plausible to say that the present generation would be dominating posterity by depriving them of freedom. Once this point is granted, it might be said that we can imagine less draconian circumstances in which present generations might dominate posterity. Suppose that the present generation rigged a doomsday device that would explode in 2100. It would seem reasonable to say that this is an act of domination, since virtually all of life in the run-up to 2100 would be consumed by attempts to dismantle the device. There would be little space for those under threat to devote their time and energy to other projects.

What this brings out is the inadequacy of the definition with which Nolt is working. My examples are cases of domination, not because power is being wielded arbitrarily, but rather because of the extent to which present generations have power over posterity. The problem is not that the present generation brings posterity into existence and constrains its choices, but rather that it determines the content of its choices (or, in the second case, comes very close to determining them). Once we see that it is the extent to which an agent has power over a subject that matters, then we can see why anthropogenic climate change does not involve the domination of posterity by the present generation. The power that the present generation wields over posterity by changing climate, great as it is, is not sufficient for domination. Posterity will live in a very different world than we do as a result of climate change. People will suffer, and much that is of value will be lost. However, the losses will be more like the biological impoverishment of Manhattan than the elimination of free will.[63]

What this brief survey shows is that both the human rights and domination approaches face serious challenges. Neither provides an explanation of how individual actions that may contribute to climate change can be taken up by commonsense morality. Our everyday moral notions continue to strain to account for such behavior. The moral problem that some believe that climate change presents bursts out of our paradigm of individual responsibility.

5.5. DIFFERENCES THAT MATTER

Thus far I have tried to show that there are serious difficulties in bringing actions that may contribute to climate change under our commonsense notions of individual moral responsibility. In discussing these difficulties I have adverted to some of the features of the climate change problem that make this so. In this section I will

---

[63] See Section 6.5 for more on domination.

address some of these features explicitly. None of them are unique to climate change, though they are more extreme in this case than others, and no other problem displays all of these features.[64] Taken together, they go a long way in showing why climate change poses a unique challenge to our commonsense moral notions.

The first feature that makes climate change different from most other problems concerns the magnifying power of technology. Simple acts such as starting a car or adjusting a thermostat have broader and more extensive reach than previous forms of transportation and thermoregulation such as walking and fire-building. The growth and development of technology, especially in regard to the production and management of energy, is to a great extent responsible for this. While once people had the power to disrupt their local environments, now people have the power to alter the planetary conditions that allowed human life to evolve and that continue to sustain it. For the first time in human history we are now able to remove large amounts of carbon that are sequestered deep inside the earth and transfer it to the atmosphere, thus affecting global climate. This is part of what Revelle and Suess meant when they wrote in their landmark 1957 paper that "[h]uman beings are now carrying out a large scale geophysical experiment of a kind that could not have happened in the past nor be reproduced in the future."[65]

The spatial reach of climate change, especially in relation to the acts that contribute to it, is a second feature that helps to differentiate this problem from others. Climate change is a global phenomenon that is insensitive to the locations of the emissions that contribute to it, and has local effects that may bear no interesting relation to where these emissions occur.[66] The atmosphere does not care where GHG emissions occur. It responds in the same way whether they come from the poles, the equator, or somewhere in between. Some of the worst damages of climate change will occur in the Southern Hemisphere, while more than 90% of GHG emissions have occurred in the Northern Hemisphere.[67] It is as if millions of acts that occur very far from you, all over the world, in some way are associated with the pain in your foot.

A third difference between climate change and most other problems we face is the systematicity of the forces that give rise to it. People pay an enormous amount of attention to computing carbon footprints and arguing over responsibility for

[64] I cannot explore here the differences and similarities between climate change and other problems. However, I do want to say that the forces that I discuss in this section are bringing to life new problems that resemble climate change and have already transformed some old problems. The problem of global poverty, for example, now has characteristics that it did not have when Sidgwick was contemplating our duties to those who are remote in space.

[65] Revelle and Suess 1957: 19.

[66] This is because atmospheric mixing is rapid compared to the atmospheric residency times of GHGs. For details, see Wallace and Hobbs 2006.

[67] Dow and Downing 2006.

emissions, yet the fact is that the manipulation of the global carbon cycle is intrinsic to the existing global economy.[68] Consider a simple example. Coal is mined in Australia, then shipped to China where it is burned in electrical generating plants, which are used to power factories that produce products that are consumed in Europe and the United States. Virtually everyone is involved in some way in manipulating carbon, and it is unclear how to allocate responsibility among them. It is usually assumed (in the United States anyway) that China is responsible for these emissions, but everyone has an argument for off-loading responsibility to someone else. It is Australia that extracts the coal, it is China where the emissions occur, and it is the United States and Europe that consume the products with the embedded carbon.[69] One could argue that China's current "bad boy"image as the world's largest carbon emitter is simply a consequence of Europe and the United States outsourcing manufacturing to China.[70] This outsourcing has brought about some redistribution of income both across and within countries.[71] It is also likely that it has increased carbon emissions.[72]

In my opinion there is no clear winner in this argument: The assignment of responsibility seems arbitrary, at least within limits. Every nation implicated in this cycle benefits in some way, and every nation will also in some way suffer. Moreover, the process is dynamic. As the global economy changes, Australia may be replaced as the energy provider, China as the manufacturing site, and the United States and Europe as the consumers of finished products. But as long as the global economy is carbon-based, the problems we face will be the same, regardless of which countries and individuals are occupying which roles.

A fourth feature of climate change that makes it different from other problems is that it is the world's largest and most complex collective action problem. It is the largest, since everyone is a climate change actor and virtually everyone will be affected by climate change. It is the most complex for many reasons, including the high degree of connectivity in the climate system, the non-linear nature of many of the relationships, threshold effects, and buffers that exist in the system. What I want to emphasize here is the differences of scale that are involved in moving from human action to the climate system, and back to damages.

---

[68] What I say here of nations is true of individuals as well. Even so, there is enormous interest in calculating individual carbon footprints. For carbon calculators visit http://www.carbonfootprint.com/calculator.aspx. Retrieved July 18, 2013. For a skeptical view, see Michael Spector, "Big Foot," *The New Yorker*, February 25, 2008. For a thoughtful discussion, see Vandenbergh and Steinemann 2007.

[69] About one-third of China's carbon emissions occur in export industries (see Weber et al. 2008).

[70] For evidence of outsourcing emissions, see Peters et al. 2011.

[71] Given everything that we hear about China's rapid growth it is sobering to be reminded that it is now the 94th, 95th, or 100th richest country in the world in per capita GDP (according to the International Monetary Fund, the World Bank, and the CIA World Factbook, respectively), firmly ahead of Egypt but well behind Peru.

[72] Weber and Matthews 2007.

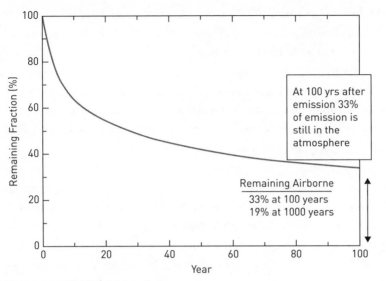

FIGURE 5.1 Decay of fossil fuel CO_2 emission.

Source: IPCC 2007 Science Technical.

Consider a radically oversimplified story that begins with me emitting some molecules of carbon dioxide.[73] As Figure 5.1 shows, these molecules may stay in the atmosphere for centuries or even longer, but what is most likely is that within several decades they will dissolve into the ocean or be taken up by the biosphere.

When carbon dioxide molecules dissolve in the ocean, they are usually replaced in the atmosphere by other molecules that radiate from the ocean. As the oceans warm, the velocity of these emissions increases, and it is likely that the original carbon will soon be returned to the atmosphere. However, a tiny fraction sinks to the ocean's depths and is eventually stored in carbonate rocks, where it may remain for tens of millions of years or more. The fate of carbon molecules in the terrestrial biosphere is even more various, but they are usually returned to the atmosphere within a decade or two.[74] The primary reason that carbon dioxide concentrations are increasing in the atmosphere is that people are mining carbon that is sequestered in mineral deposits (e.g., fossil fuels) and the biosphere (e.g., old-growth forests), transforming it into carbon dioxide and releasing it into the atmosphere. This change in the state of the carbon cycle produces a generalized warming, which affects the global climate system, which in turn affects the distribution, frequency, and intensity of various meteorological events. These events occur in environments that can result in anything from a heat wave or storm in an uninhabited part of the world, to an insurance claim for a

[73] Tyler Volk 2008 tells a fuller and more charming version of this story. The chart reproduced in Figure 5.1 is available on the web at http://onlyzerocarbon.org/uploads/CLONG.jpg. Retrieved October 23, 2013.

[74] Archer and Brovkin 2008.

BMW damaged in a hailstorm, or to the collapse of a government.[75] For my particular carbon emission to have a causal effect in producing these harms it must in some way be active at all of these levels, from increasing concentrations of atmospheric carbon dioxide, to producing untoward meteorological events that actually result in harms. The influence of my emission must travel upward through various global systems that affect climate, and then downwards, damaging something that we value. The sense of implausibility, ignorance, and downright confusion that such a scenario elicits can be illustrated by the following example.

I, along with many other people, toss an invisible smidgen of something into a blender. A man takes a drink of the resulting mixture. Am I responsible for the graininess of the texture, the chalkiness of the taste, the way it makes him feel after drinking it, his resulting desire for a Budweiser? You might think that I am a smidgen responsible, since a smidgen is the amount that I tossed into the blender. But I am tempted to say that I am not responsible even for a smidgen of the result because there are so many thresholds, non-linearities, and scalar differences that intervene between my action and the outcomes.

Even if I am wrong about this, it should still be clear that the problems with which climate change confronts us are importantly different from textbook collective action problems that have us trying to find solutions to an overgrazed commons or an overexploited fishery. In the climate change case, the distance from my particular acts to the damages that occur is far greater on several dimensions than in the cases that commonsense morality normally confronts.[76]

A fifth difference between climate change and other problems concerns the temporal reach of GHGs. These gases have different residence times in the atmosphere, ranging from a few years for methane, to millennia for some man-made gases such as tetrafluoromethane, which is used as a low-temperature refrigerant mainly in the manufacture of electronics (perhaps even in the fabrication of the computer that I am using to write these words). I will focus mainly on carbon dioxide.

Imagine that after reaching an atmospheric concentration of 450 ppm sometime in the next decade, we immediately stop all carbon dioxide emissions. By the year 3000, neither atmospheric concentrations of carbon dioxide nor global mean surface temperature would have returned to their pre-industrial baselines, and sea levels would still be rising.[77] It is as if someone steps on your foot, politely says excuse me, and then walks away, while the pain in your foot persists for the rest of your life.

The time horizons involved in climate change are simply flabbergasting. The idea that our contemporary way of life has left a mark on the planet that will persist for millennia is difficult to comprehend, much less to internalize in our

---

[75] For example, the 1973 collapse of the Ethiopian monarchy is often blamed on a drought-induced famine. There were of course other factors involved; there always are.

[76] Cf. Schelling (1995), who makes a similar point when he discusses the difficulties of mapping marginal abatement onto climate impacts.

[77] Solomon et al. 2009.

decision-making. When we blandly say that climate change poses problems of obligations to future generations we obscure the fact that commonsense morality was not built to respond to problems that involve such long time horizons.[78] There are future generations, and then there are those who will live centuries or millennia in the further future.

It is true that most of us care about many of those who are near us in time. This may be because our lives overlap with theirs, or because they are our children or grandchildren. Our concern may extend a little further into the future, in part because of something we might call "sentimental transitivity." We care about our children's children because we care about our children and they care about their children, or perhaps we care about our children's children because we see them as our own. The reach of this concern may extend another generation or two, but it rapidly gives out. Some abstract concern about the future may take its place, but that is not the same as caring about those who will live in the future. We cannot picture the people of the next millennium who will cope with the sea levels that will still be rising as a result of climate change. We have very little idea of what their lives will be like and what will matter to them. It is difficult for us to empathize with them. Whatever concern for the future remains is not as motivating nor as uniformly distributed as concern for one's children or grandchildren.[79]

There are philosophers who think that this presents no special problem because all generations, from the present to the further future, are linked by a "chain of love" or are part of an iterative "intergenerational community."[80] As we move through time, each generation cares for several generations into the future. Those who live in the further future will be cared for by their immediate predecessors, just as we were cared for by our immediate predecessors and we care for those who will immediately succeed us. This approach dissolves the problem of the further future, replacing it with the vision of a loving, temporally extended community.

Perhaps this picture would be true if the only damages that could be inflicted on future people were linear through time. However, damages can display many different temporal patterns. For example, they can crescendo much like a musical piece or they can erupt suddenly far in the future. Damages can be exported to the further future, largely bypassing the two or three generations that present people care most about. Cluster bombs, toxic waste dumps, and of course climate change all have this potential.[81]

[78] Nor is it clear that sophisticated moral theories do much better. This, I think, is one of the lessons of Lenman 2000.

[79] It is an amusing if mind-boggling exercise to read Lacey and Danziger 1999 and then try to imagine the people they describe imagining our lives today.

[80] The former expression is John Passmore's (1974); the latter is Avner de-Shalit's (1995).

[81] As we saw in Section 4.3, perhaps 90% or more of climate change damages will occur after 2200, according to the Stern Review (http://www.iie.com/publications/papers/paper.cfm?ResearchID=874). Retrieved July 18, 2013.

Part of the problem with motivating concern for those who will live in the further future is that reciprocity is at the center of commonsense morality.[82] Of course, reciprocity is not always demanded. Nor is it demanded from everyone at every stage in life. Nevertheless, the asymmetric nature of our relationship with those who will live in the further future is part of why it is difficult to motivate concern. In contrast, those who will live in the near future can stand in reciprocal relations with us. They can care for us when we are old as we care for them when they are young. They can complete our projects, fulfill our hopes, and make some of our dreams come true. Nothing very much like this can exist between us and those who will live in the further future.[83] We have enormous power over them, but they have very little, if any, power over us. This is one reason that, when faced with the time horizons that the problems of climate change present, commonsense morality is largely silent.[84]

A sixth difference between anthropogenic climate change and the problems that commonsense morality is used to confronting concerns the extent to which climate change is world-constituting.

It should be acknowledged at the outset that there is a sense in which any action is world-constituting. The world that results from my wearing a Hawaiian shirt to the Humane Society benefit is, in various subtle ways, different from the world that results from my wearing a sober blue suit. In addition to the brute difference between the two worlds, ripples radiate from my sartorial choices, affecting the world in a multiplicity of ways. However, unlike my sartorial choices, climate change will radically repopulate and remake the entire world.

It will radically repopulate the world because it is highly contingent on which particular individuals come into existence, and climate change will quickly affect on a very large scale who marries whom and what children are conceived. A warmer world may mean later bedtimes, which almost certainly would result in different sperm uniting with different eggs, bringing different people into existence than otherwise would have been born. As these climate change babies grow up and procreate, the fraction of people who owe their existence to climate change will steadily increase. In introducing this concern Derek Parfit rhetorically asks, "[H]ow many of us could truly claim, 'Even if railways and motor cars had never been invented, I would still have been born'?"[85] Similarly, the people of the future can ask (also rhetorically)

---

[82] For the importance of reciprocity to human cooperation generally, see Nowak and Highfield 2011.

[83] This is not to say that those in the further future cannot stand in moral relations with those in the past, at least from the perspective of some moral theories. For example, people in the further future may yet satisfy the prophet's desire (Amos 5:24) that "judgment run down as waters, and righteousness as a mighty stream." For an insightful discussion of these and related issues, see Scheffler 2013.

[84] The failure of commonsense morality to provide much guidance with respect to the further future is at the heart of the controversy over the discount rate discussed in Section 4.3.

[85] Parfit 1984: 361. The consideration that I am discussing here is of course related to Parfit's "non-identity problem."

whether they would have been born had the world not gone down the path of emitting more than 30 billion tons of carbon dioxide per year.[86]

Unlike some philosophers, I think this is an important consideration that marks a difference between this problem and many others.[87] Climate change will make millions of people worse off, but it will also produce a world stocked with a different population than otherwise would have existed, many of whom will have lives worth living, but less good than those of the people who would have existed had we not changed climate. Much or most of what we morally object to in everyday life is person-affecting in that it concerns actions that affect people who exist independently of the actions. Many of the climate change damages, on the other hand, will be suffered by people who would not otherwise have existed. This brings out an important difference between the challenge posed by climate change and the kinds of problems that are central to commonsense moral thinking. [88]

Climate change will remake the world as well as repopulating it. Climate change will produce a world that is radically different from the one that would otherwise have existed. Consider, again, my example of the transformation of Manhattan. Is it better or worse that Manhattan was transformed from a natural paradise to the city that it is today? This question is difficult to answer and it is relatively near. Consider another question which evokes an even longer time horizon. Is it better or worse that Christianity arose and became a world religion? The world that I know and can imagine is the world in which Christianity figured prominently in its history. I was educated in Christian schools. Most of the art, music, and architecture that I love are in some sense Christian.

The problem with these questions is not that we do not know the answers, but rather that they do not seem to admit of answers, at least from the perspective of commonsense morality. Asking these questions can seem like asking whether it is a good thing that there is an oscillation between glacial and inter-glacial periods. These are questions about the value of features that form the very structure of the world within which we make evaluations. Moral evaluations, at least those of the sort that we are generally prepared to make, arise within these structures rather than being about these structures. Commonsense morality operates within a horizon of possibility. It is not well-equipped to make judgments about the conditions that fix these possibilities.

---

[86] http://www.pbl.nl/en/publications/2010/No-growth-in-total-global-CO2-emissions-in-2009. Retrieved July 18, 2013.

[87] Shue (2010: 159, n.3) does not think it is an important consideration. See page 2006 for a good discussion of this consideration in the context of climate change.

[88] Other paradoxes discussed by Parfit 1984, Part 4 also bring out respects in which commonsense morality does not fare well with choices that result in different numbers of people brought into existence. A good introduction to the literature on the non-identity problem can be found by visiting http://plato.stanford.edu/entries/nonidentity-problem/. Retrieved July 18, 2013.

Thus far I have been emphasizing how grand and profound the problems are that are posed by anthropogenic climate change and how for that reason they outrun the responses that are characteristic of commonsense morality. However, it is also important to note that philosophical accounts of morality are often caricatures, overemphasizing, for example, the importance and centrality of harm causation to our ordinary moral concepts.[89]

Recent work by psychologists such as Daniel Gilbert and Jonathan Haidt has convincingly shown that our moral conceptions are only loosely associated with the infliction of harm. Many people are morally appalled by such apparently harmless acts as consensual gay sex or flag burning, but are completely unmoved by deaths caused in war or by environmental pollution. Jonathan Haidt and his colleagues have claimed that considerations involving fairness and reciprocity, in-group and loyalty, authority and respect, and purity and sanctity, in addition to considerations about the causation of harm, are at the foundation of morality as conceived by many people.[90] Since these considerations can come apart, people often deny that particular instances of harm-causing activity are within the moral domain while at the same time considering behavior that does not cause harm to be of moral import. Daniel Gilbert brings these considerations to bear on the question of climate change when he writes that

> [...] global warming doesn't [...] violate our moral sensibilities. It doesn't cause our blood to boil (at least not figuratively) because it doesn't force us to entertain thoughts that we find indecent, impious or repulsive. When people feel insulted or disgusted, they generally do something about it, such as whacking each other over the head, or voting. Moral emotions are the brain's call to action. Although all human societies have moral rules about food and sex, none has a moral rule about atmospheric chemistry. And so we are outraged about every breach of protocol except Kyoto. Yes, global warming is bad, but it doesn't make us feel nauseated or angry or disgraced, and thus we don't feel compelled to rail against it as we do against other momentous threats to our species, such as flag burning. The fact is that if climate change were caused by gay sex, or by the practice of eating kittens, millions of protesters would be massing in the streets.[91]

Climate change presents us with questions that display some of the marks of a paradigm moral problem but fail to exhibit others. To a great extent the difficulty of addressing these aspects of climate change as involving moral questions arises from the power and novelty of the problem, and the frailty of our moral consciousness.

---

[89] The centrality of harm to morality is a Millian idea, thoroughly developed in Joel Feinberg's magisterial four-volume work (1984–1988). Though criminal law is Feinberg's main concern, much of what he says applies to commonsense morality as well.

[90] For an introduction to this work, visit http://www.moralfoundations.org/. Retrieved July 18, 2013.

[91] http://articles.latimes.com/2006/jul/02/opinion/op-gilbert2. Retrieved July 18, 2013.

Viewing these aspects in moral terms would require revising our everyday under-standings of moral responsibility.

5.6. REVISING MORALITY

What I have been suggesting is that commonsense morality is not responsive to some important aspects of anthropogenic climate change. Theorists such as Simon Caney, Elizabeth Cripps, Steve Gardiner, Paul Harris, Avram Hiller, Marion Hourdequin, John Nolt, Henry Shue, Peter Singer, Steve Vanderheiden, and myself, who have argued that various actions relating to climate change are morally wrong, should be read as urging us to revise our conceptions of responsibility such that these actions would count as morally wrong. In other words, they (we) are engaged in "persuasive definition."[92] It is important to recognize this because how one argues for revising concepts is quite different from how one argues that particular acts fall under exist-ing concepts. Compare the task of revising our conceptions in this case with Peter Singer's arguments for famine relief and animal liberation.

In "Famine, Affluence, and Morality," Singer tried to show that a simple ethical principle that most of us accept has sweeping implications: If it is in our power to prevent something very bad from happening, without sacrificing anything morally significant, we ought, morally, to do it.[93] Singer does not, in this paper, try to per-suade us to accept new principles or to revise fundamental moral understandings. He simply tries to bring out the consequences of a principle to which we are already committed. Seeing the argument in this light helps to explain the power and influ-ence of the paper. The arguments that we considered in Section 5.4 for the claim that climate change violates human rights or involves present people in dominating posterity are similar in purpose. They try to show that we are committed to seeing actions that may contribute to climate change in this light, even though most of us do not normally see them in this way.

Singer's argument for animal liberation urges us to extend our principles rather than arguing that we should acknowledge a principle that we already tacitly embrace.[94] He argues that principles that we already hold that lead us to oppose racism, sexism, and unnecessary suffering should be extended so that they apply to non-human animals as well. Singer has arguments for extending these prin-ciples, but his opponents have arguments for what they consider principled stop-ping points.[95] The argument for animal liberation is directed toward leading us

---

[92] Stevensen 1938.

[93] Singer 1972. In unpublished work Avram Hiller has tried to do something similar for climate change.

[94] Singer 2009.

[95] See, for example, Williams 2009, Singer's reply in the same volume, and my discussion in Jamieson 2008: ch. 5.

to embrace a new commitment. While animal liberation is an instance of "the expanding circle," responding to famine is a matter of internal consistency.

My claim is that anthropogenic climate change is not like either of these cases and that is part of why it is so difficult for people to see important aspects of this problem in moral terms. Commonsense morality does not commit us to the views that climate ethicists say we should hold, and modest extensions of our principles will not do the trick either. Some new moral understandings are required if we are to moralize some important aspects of our climate-changing behavior.

Having drawn sharp distinctions between recognizing the consequences of our moral commitments, extending them, and revising them, I now want to soften them. There are borderline cases and interrelations between recognizing, extending, and revising. Moralizing can be a way of doing all three separately or together. The rhetoric of recognizing obligations is often used in an attempt to get people to extend their principles. Appeals to consistency are often deployed in attempts to recognize, extend, and revise. Moreover, revision is not replacement. Any revision of a domain must preserve enough connection to the domain of which it is a revision to be worthy of the name. Despite these complexities, drawing these distinctions helps us to see why it is so difficult to frame important aspects of climate change as presenting a moral problem.[96]

Still, revisions, even revolutions, in morality occur. One such revolution was associated with the rise of capitalism.[97] What had formerly been considered vices (e.g., selfishness) were redescribed and transformed into virtues. What might previously have been seen as harming others through competition came to be seen as simply a consequence of the rise of the new capitalist man whose pursuit of self-interest produces greater benefits overall. Climate ethicists who seek to moralize behavior that may in some way contribute to climate change are revolutionaries whether they see themselves in that way or not. Rather than viewing this work as consisting in failed attempts to report and innervate our common moral conceptions, we should see it instead as critiquing commonsense morality and recommending revisions. Conceptions of responsibility are pragmatic and context-sensitive, and so open to revision. They are for us to deploy and apply. It is not for them to tell us what we can think or say. What climate ethicists are claiming is that we should view such acts as needlessly driving and thoughtlessly jetting as wrong, even if most of us do not now see them in this way.

Commonsense morality is a complex tapestry of distinct threads. One thread sees morality as flowing out of special relationships and associative duties. Another regards moral and backward-looking causal linkages as closely tracking each other.

---

[96] For more on the themes of this paragraph, see Jamieson 2013a.

[97] Mandeville's *The Fable of the Bees* contributed to this revision in morality. The eighteenth century "luxury" debates provide a window on this transition (see Berg and Eger 2003). I owe this example to David Johnstone.

Yet another finds the ability to provide benefits and prevent harms as central. A great deal of moral theorizing involves pulling on these and other threads. Practitioners of climate ethics, on this view, are engaged in the practice of thread-pulling.

However, there are dangers. While commonsense morality may seem a ragtag collection of practices, beliefs, and attitudes, the elements are bound together in ways that are difficult to appreciate, much less untangle. Pull on a thread and the tapestry may unravel.

Those who want to revise morality in the face of climate change employ two main strategies. Some seek to collectivize responsibility. Others seek to reform responsibility so that it tracks the probability of outcomes. I will discuss these approaches in turn.

One consequence of conjoining commonsense morality and anthropogenic climate change is that together we may produce a world that is morally worse yet no one may have done anything that is morally wrong.[98] This seems strange because the loss of moral value seems to occur *ex nihilo*, even though we know that people have brought about this diminished state of affairs.

Non-consequentialist moral philosophers seem to accept small versions of this irony without blinking. They may agree, for example, that the world becomes morally worse when an additional person preventably starves while also asserting that no one acts wrongly in not feeding her. If the fit is too uncomfortable they have strategies for trying to escape this conclusion. For example, while they may admit that the world in which an additional person preventably starves is worse than the present world, they may deny that it is morally worse. Analogously, they may agree that the climate change world is worse than the climate stable world but deny that it is morally worse. It is difficult to understand the distinction between non-morally and morally worse changes, especially when in both of these cases they involve millions of lost lives. This exercise can quickly seem to become a dance in the service of a theory rather than an honest attempt to capture a moral insight.

The basic point here is simple. Only some consequentialists are committed to the idea that there is a necessary connection between morally worse outcomes and morally wrong actions. Other philosophers deny this connection at least in small doses. Perhaps climate change is in some way different from cases in which these philosophers deny the connection. Or perhaps what appears to be an implication of a theory begins to look like an objection if it occurs on a large enough scale. In any case many people find it strange that together we can kill many people without any of us doing something wrong.

When the problem is stated in this way the solution seems obvious: As individuals we have duties regarding how we act as members of collectives. As Derek Parfit

---

[98] "Today we face the possibility that the global environment may be destroyed, yet no one will be responsible" (Jamieson 1992: 149; revised version Jamieson 2012).

wrote, "Even if an act harms no one this act may be wrong because it is one of a set of acts that together harm other people."[99]

It is a challenge to precisely formulate and interpret this claim. Parfit's use of the word "may" suggests that this claim could be true even if on most occasions its particular instantiations are not. There are also difficulties in understanding what makes an act "one of a set of acts." The language is ambiguous between "this act" being itself a set of acts and "this act" being a member of a set of acts. Assuming that Parfit means the latter, anything that I do is a member of a set of acts that together harms other people if the other member of the set is the act of Brutus stabbing Caesar. Parfit rules out this kind of case by specifying that the group that produces the harm is "the smallest group of whom it is true that, if they had all acted differently, the other people would not have been harmed."[100]

Here is how this restriction works. Suppose that a set has two acts: DJ surfing, and Brutus stabbing Caesar. The smallest group of whom it is true that if they had all acted differently then the harm would not have occurred consists in Brutus alone, since I contributed nothing to Caesar's woe. In the climate change case there is also a smaller group which does not include me such that if it were to act differently then climate change would not occur. For climate change will occur whether or not I needless drive or thoughtlessly jet. Indeed, for virtually everyone there is such a group. Thus Parfit's criterion allows virtually all of us to escape moral responsibility for climate change.[101]

Whatever the difficulties of precisely formulating the view that among the duties we have as individuals are some regarding how we act together, there is a basic intuition that warrants further consideration. This intuition underlies the claim that when we needlessly drive and thoughtlessly jet, we violate duties that we have as members of collectives. This intuition has some support: It is one of the threads that make up the tapestry of commonsense morality. It can be seen as the basis for volunteer fire departments, parent-teacher associations, and faith-based social welfare programs. It supports the negative moral judgments that are sometimes made about those who do not contribute to such institutions.

However, the intuition seems to apply mainly to small, homogenous groups that think of themselves as acting together. In extraordinary circumstances for short periods of time it can be extended more broadly (e.g., to an entire nation during wartime). The extension of the intuition seems to require specific enemies (e.g., Nazis), goals (e.g., winning the war), and means (e.g., resource conservation). This model does not easily apply to climate change. There is no specific enemy, the goal is ill-defined, and the means are (too) many. Moreover, rather than extraordinary, the circumstances of life in a warming world are the "new normal." We are witnessing

[99] Parfit 1984: 70.

[100] Parfit 1984: 71–72.

[101] Here and elsewhere I have benefited from Sandberg 2011.

the harbingers of an emerging new relationship between humans and the planet, one in which as a matter of course humanity dominates nature (as we will see in Chapter 6). For these reasons the prospects for extending this model to behavior that may contribute to climate change seem bleak.

There is also a question about the philosophical basis for collectivizing duties.[102] Some accounts claim to be inspired by Kant but they can find no real foundation in his work. He was interested in the conditions under which our actions have moral worth, not in solving collective action problems. There may be many things that are wrong with Paris Hilton flying to Rome on a shopping trip but a contradiction in will is not among them.[103]

Rule utilitarians have sometimes specifically been interested in collective action problems.[104] However, they seem to face the following dilemma. Insofar as they are utilitarians their commitment to collective purposes threatens to collapse into individual calculation and defection, and insofar as they are committed to collective purposes they can be led to act wrongly from a utilitarian point of view. This is because when facing collective action problems there are instances when I would do best and indeed contribute the most to the world by defecting from collective purposes. While it may be better for no one to drive or fly than for everyone to engage in these activities, what may be best of all is for me to drive or fly while everyone else refrains. If despite this reasoning I refrain from driving or flying then I risk my utilitarian credentials, for I knowingly do what is less than the best. Even worse is the case in which I conform to some ideal set of rules to which there is not widespread conformity. In these cases I might find myself riding my bicycle through the snow while everyone else blows by me in their SUVs. In both cases the only difference my behavior makes is to reduce the general happiness by reducing my own happiness.[105]

One response to the difficulties in finding a compelling moral-theoretic foundation for collectivizing responsibility is to attempt to locate the foundation in moral psychology or the nature of agents. John Searle, for example, finds in us irreducible "we intentions."[106] Marion Hourdequin thinks that we need to adopt "a relational

---

[102] A great deal of important work that is relevant to this topic has been done by such writers as Michael Bacharach, Michael Bratman, Margaret Gilbert, Virginia Held, Christopher Kutz, Larry May, Christopher McMahon, Iris Marion Young, and others (for an overview, visit http://plato.stanford.edu/entries/collective-responsibility/#7, retrieved July 18, 2013). Elizabeth Cripps has worked on this topic specifically in relation to climate change (see her 2013). Unfortunately I cannot discuss this work here. In any case I do not believe that the details are important for the broad claims that I am making.

[103] I expand on this telegraphic remark and the themes of the next three paragraphs in Jamieson 2007b.

[104] See, e.g., Lyons 1965.

[105] The first objection was made years ago by David Lyons (1965). The second objection is made by many writers including Walter Sinnott-Armstrong (2005); see also Jamieson 2007b. Brad Hooker has developed a form of Rule Consequentialism (not Utilitarianism) that he believes is immune to these objections (visit http://plato.stanford.edu/entries/consequentialism-rule/, retrieved July 18, 2013).

[106] Searle 1983: ch. 3.

conception of persons...which...reconceptualize[s] collective action problems in a way that dissolves the sharp contrast between the individually and collectively rational."[107] In particular, she thinks that we need to adopt a more Confucian conception of the self. It is not just morality that needs revising on her view, but our very self-conception.

It would not be surprising if revising morality required revising our conception of what we are as persons, but it does raise the stakes. It also introduces another iteration of the collective action problem. How does a Confucian self survive in a world of non-Confucian selves? How can the Confucian self "go viral" and transform the community in such a way that effective action is taken against climate change? There are also questions about what duties a Confucian self has and specifically what duties in regard to climate change. In their open-endedness these questions seem to echo the question sometimes asked by evangelical Christians: "What would Jesus do?"

The other main strategy for revising morality is to reform responsibility so that it tracks the probability of outcomes rather than causal connections. This view has been most fully worked out by Avram Hiller, who endorses the following principle:

> (MP) It is *prima facie* wrong to perform an act which has an expected amount of harm greater than another easily available alternative.[108]

Hiller goes on to mobilize this principle in an argument showing that it is *prima facie* wrong to joyride in my '57 Chevy.[109] There are details to be filled in but it is pretty obvious that given MP, much of our driving and flying stands morally condemned. For instead of going for a joyride I could go for a bike ride. Instead of flying to Australia to deliver my climate change lecture I could deliver it via Skype. Whatever you think of two wrongs making a right, flying to Australia in order to joyride is certainly not going to survive moral scrutiny if MP is true! The most important question about Hiller's argument concerns the acceptability of MP, not the details of its application.

Even leaving climate change aside, much of what we do turns out to be *prima facie* wrong according to MP. If I buy a lottery ticket this increases the probability that someone's gambling habits will plunge them into misery since my action reduces the probability that they will win the lottery. Driving compared to bicycling increases the probability that someone will be hurt or late for work because of congestion, but bicycling also raises the probability of these harms compared to walking, and walking raises the probability of these harms compared to telecommuting.

---

[107] Hourdequin 2010.

[108] Hiller 2011: 352. The seeds of this idea can also be found in John Nolt 2011a and 2011b. I have heard other climate ethicists express general support for this sort of idea (e.g., Henry Shue).

[109] Hiller is referring to an example that I introduced in Jamieson 2007b. For more on joyriding in '57 Chevies, visit http://www.youtube.com/watch?v=2khhHpFWigc. Retrieved July 18, 2013.

Perhaps the only way that I can avoid acting in a way that is *prima facie* wrong is to stop immediately in my tracks and begin meditating.

The deep problem with MP is precisely the feature that gives it intuitive plausibility with respect to actions that may in some way contribute to climate change: It bypasses questions of causation. However, there are many things that we do that raise the probability of harms occurring that we do not think are morally wrong. In many cases we think this precisely because these actions do not cause the harms in question. Such actions may include having a child (someone may kill her), going for a walk (I may be run over), and opening a business (someone may become disastrously addicted to my vegan chocolate chip cookies). The fact that there is some probabilistic association between what I do and an increase in harm is not sufficient for my having acted wrongly.[110]

Hiller does not say that increasing the probability of harm is sufficient for an act to be wrong all things considered. Rather he says that increasing the probability of harm is sufficient for an act to be *prima facie* wrong. Perhaps none of the acts that I mentioned in the previous paragraph is wrong all things considered. However, this had better not be because of the lack of relevant causal relations. Otherwise, joyriding in my '57 Chevy may be able to escape moral condemnation after all. Even if plausible stories can be told for why the particular acts that I mentioned are not wrong all things considered, such explanations are not likely to be forthcoming in all such cases. Anyway, I find it hard to believe that going for a bicycle ride instead of a walk, or a walk instead of meditating in my room, or engaging in any of the other acts that I mentioned are even *prima facie* wrong.

An alternative approach, closer to existing practices, would be to specify a *de minimus* baseline. Only acts that increase the probability of harm above that baseline would count as *prima facie* wrongs. Increases that are far enough above the baseline could even count as imposing a risk that itself could be seen as causing a harm. The problem is that, on this account, joyriding in my '57 Chevy will almost certainly fall below the *de minimus* baseline. A variant of this alternative approach would be to say that wrongness occurs when the increase in the probability of expected harm is coupled with negligence or recklessness. However, in this case circularity looms, since we would need an argument for why needlessly driving and thoughtlessly flying are negligent or reckless behavior.

It is hard to know exactly what counts for or against proposed revisions in morality. That such proposals have counterintuitive consequences or would require revising related notions such as our conception of a person might be just what we

---

[110] Someone may claim that any probabilistic association between an action and a harm is sufficient for attributing causal influence to the action in bringing about the harm. While probabilistic association may be a necessary condition for such attribution, it is quite implausible to think of it as a sufficient condition, at least without serious qualification. For an introduction to some of the issues, visit http://plato.stanford.edu/entries/causation-probabilistic/. Retrieved October 25, 2013.

should expect in such cases. Moreover, by the very nature of the project we have only glimpses of what a revised morality would involve.

Nevertheless, there are important questions about both families of proposals. Some of these are obvious and familiar questions about to whom collective duties are owed and their relative stringency with respect to other duties. Others are deep questions about the relationships between these proposals and other values such as those embodied in classical liberalism.

A general commitment to the permissibility of harmless behavior is close to the heart of the classical liberal ideal.[111] The harm principle, as stated by John Stuart Mill, is "[t]hat the only purpose for which power can be rightfully exercised over any member of a civilized community, against his will, is to prevent harm to others."[112] As stated, this is fundamentally a legal principle and there are well-charted complexities in mapping the relations between law and morality.[113] Still, this principle (or something like it) should not be quickly jettisoned from the domain of morality. Hiller's idea that an agent can act wrongly simply by raising the probability of harm, even when there is no causal connection between the agent and the harm, should give liberals pause. Moreover, liberals should generally be concerned about collectivizing duties. Historically, societies that collectivize duties are not often paradigms of liberal societies (Confucian societies are a case in point). What I have said here is not dispositive but cautionary. While liberalism often takes a beating in dark times (such as wartime), it would be distressing if an adequate ethics of the Anthropocene required compromising liberal ideals.

The most fundamental challenge for those who want to revise morality is not in minding the deontic accounts but in determining what is in the domain of moral evaluation in the first place. As I pointed out in Section 5.2, most of our behavior that may affect climate is not regarded as being in the domain of morality at all.

Both moralization and non-moralization (called "amoralization" in the literature) are dynamic processes. Smoking was once seen as simply a personal preference but is increasingly morally freighted. Homosexuality and divorce were once widely seen as immoral but increasingly they are viewed as non-moral matters of preference, circumstance, or orientation.[114]

The process of moralization is not well understood, but it is clear that both cognitive and affective experiences can be important in this regard (e.g., reading

---

[111] See Feinberg 1984–1988 for a thorough discussion of this in the context of criminal law.

[112] Mill 1859: 21–22.

[113] E.g., lying is often morally wrong, may or may not cause harm, and should not generally be outlawed.

[114] Interestingly, those who want to continue to moralize homosexuality usually want to see it as a "lifestyle choice" while those who want to "amoralize" homosexuality often refer to it as an "orientation." Insofar as an orientation is not under an individual's control it is plausible to suppose that it should not be moralized. But much that is under an individual's control is not moralized either, such as the choice of a wide range of occupations or hobbies.

Animal Liberation, visiting a slaughterhouse). Moralization seems to occur most readily around health issues, matters that affect children, practices engaged in by stigmatized minorities, and behaviors for which there are multiple grounds for disapproval. Interestingly, moralization seems to thrive in periods of chaos and among Protestants.[115]

Whatever exactly the mechanisms of moralization, philosophers are unlikely to be their most effective practitioners. Journalists, writers, artists, celebrities, televangelists, and virtually everyone will be in on the act, and many of these people have much larger audiences and know better what to do with them than philosophers. Philosophers will have a role to play but much of it will be in retrospective reflection and systemization (Hegel's Owl of Minerva, mentioned in the epigraph, returns).

However, as I indicated earlier, revolutions in morality do occur. Just as people once considered the smell of pollution to be the smell of money, so we may come to see coal-fired power plants as the devil's furnaces. We may come to think of thermostats as ways of controlling carnage as much as temperature, and the choice between driving and flying as a decision between killing with a gun and killing with a knife. These changes may come, but for those who demand climate ethics and justice now, their eventual success is unlikely to provide much comfort.

5.7. CONCLUDING REMARKS

In Chapter 4 I showed that climate economics cannot give clear directives in its own terms because it rests on ethical commitments. What I have argued in this chapter is that commonsense morality cannot provide ethical guidance with respect to some important aspects of climate-changing behavior. I then discussed some of the challenges involved in revising morality. In light of these conclusions and given the difficult nature of the problem, it is not surprising that we have failed to act effectively in response to climate change. Still, we must go on. How do we live in the face of this silence? What progress can we hope to achieve in confronting the problems of climate change? These are the topics of the next two chapters.

---

[115] For more on moralization see Rozin et al. 1997; Rozin 1999; Markowitz and Shariff 2012; Lovett and Jordan 2010. For a popular account, see Steven Pinker, "The Moral Instinct," *New York Times Magazine*, January 13, 2008.

6 Living with Climate Change

Climate change is occurring and is effectively irreversible on timescales that are meaningful to us. Our failure to prevent or even to respond significantly reflects the impoverishment of our systems of practical reason, the paralysis of our politics, and the limits of our cognitive and affective capacities. None of this is likely to change soon. Many will find these conclusions depressing. Let us return to the beginning in an effort to find some consolation.

6.1. LIFE IN THE ANTHROPOCENE

The problem of climate change is often portrayed as the problem of atmospheric concentrations of carbon dioxide (and other greenhouse gases [GHGs]) increasing beyond their "pre-industrial" levels. This may suggest that there is a stable, "natural" background value for atmospheric carbon dioxide. However, atmospheric concentrations of carbon dioxide have varied radically throughout Earth's history. Fifty-five million years ago they exceeded 1,000 ppm.[1] About 200,000 years ago, when anatomically modern humans emerged, atmospheric carbon was about 225 ppm. Over the past 10,000 years, when almost everything we value about humanity and its creations came into existence, the Earth has been remarkably stable on a broad range of indicators. Until the last 250 years, when concentrations began to grow as a result of the industrial revolution, concentrations of atmospheric carbon dioxide have varied between 240 and 280 ppm. We have reached nearly 400 ppm as a result of human action, and if humans persist as long as the dinosaurs there is every reason to expect that much more extreme concentrations will occur.

In 1997 a distinguished group of scientists published an influential article in which they assessed the human impact on the Earth.[2] They calculated that between one-third and one-half of Earth's land surface had been transformed by human action; that carbon dioxide in the atmosphere had increased by more than 30% since the beginning of the industrial revolution; that more nitrogen had been fixed

---

[1] Unless otherwise noted, data in this paragraph are from www.epa.gov/climatechange/pdfs/print_ghg-concentrations.pdf. Retrieved July 18, 2013.

[2] Vitousek et al. 1997. For a recent review, see Running 2012.

by humanity than all other terrestrial organisms combined; that more than half of all accessible surface freshwater was being appropriated by humanity; and that about one-quarter of Earth's bird species had been driven to extinction. This led them to conclude that "it is clear that we live on a human-dominated planet."[3]

The challenge we face is not (only) to reduce or stabilize concentration of atmospheric carbon dioxide, but to live in productive relationship with the dynamic systems that govern a changing planet. This is a new challenge because humanity is young and now constitutes an important planetary force in a way that is unprecedented. Anthropogenic climate change is the harbinger of a new world in which humans have become a dominant force on Earth's natural systems. In recognition of the increasing human domination of the planet, some scientists propose that we have entered a new geological era, the Anthropocene.[4] Climate change may be the first challenge of the Anthropocene but it is not the last. What is needed is an ethic for the Anthropocene—not only a climate change ethics. For it is in the world of the Anthropocene that we and our descendants will have to live and find meaning.

6.2. IT DOESN'T MATTER WHAT I DO

Probably the greatest threat to meaning in such a world is the widespread perception that "it doesn't matter what I do." Environmentalists talk about "saving the earth" and websites tout "green consumerism," yet none of this seems to matter given the scale of the changes that are underway.

Indeed, it may be that the central reason that commonsense morality does not moralize needless driving and thoughtless flying is that whether or not I do these things makes no difference as to whether or not climate change will occur. Walter Sinnott-Armstrong (2005) seems to think that something like this is true.[5] He writes that

> my individual joy ride does not cause global warming, climate change, or any of the resulting harms, at least directly. (336)

He goes on to say that

> [w]e should not think that we can do enough simply by buying fuel-efficient cars, insulating our houses, and setting up a windmill to make our own electricity. That is all

---

[3] Vitousek et al. 1997: 494.

[4] For an influential statement of this view, see Crutzen 2002. The idea of the Anthropocene has become so influential that it figured in the title of the 2011 Geological Society of America meetings ("Archean to Anthropocene: The Past Is the Key to the Future"). See also Zalasiewicz et al. 2008. Priya Murthy has suggested to me that the idea of the Anthropocene may be implicit in the preface to Arendt 1998. In any case the claim that we have entered an era in which there are unprecedented ethical challenges does not rest on whether this proposed change in geological classification actually takes hold.

[5] See also Hale 2011; Johnson 2003; Hiller 2011; and Jamieson 2007b.

wonderful, but it does little or nothing to stop global warming and also does not fulfill our real moral obligations, which are to get governments to do their job to prevent the disaster of excessive global warming. It is better to enjoy your Sunday driving while working to change the law so as to make it illegal for you to enjoy your Sunday driving. (344)

There are some hedges here. Sinnott-Armstrong claims that his individual joyride does not cause climate change "at least directly" but nevertheless suggests that it should be "illegal." He says that the climate-friendly acts he mentions are not "enough," that they do "little or nothing" to stop global warming, yet he says that they are "wonderful." His main point seems to be that because these individual acts have little or no effect on producing harms, they are not in the domain of moral prescription. What is morally required is that we "get governments to do their job to prevent the disaster of excessive global warming."

In Section 5.5 I gave some reasons for why we should be skeptical about whether there is a causal relation between any particular act that emits GHGs (e.g., the Sunday drive) and climate change damages (e.g., a BMW dented in a hailstorm). The emissions that come from a Sunday drive are vanishingly small relative to the total GHG forcing, and intervening between the action and harms are various thresholds, non-linearities, and feedbacks that occur at different scales.

The most common models of collective responsibility discussed by philosophers do not fully capture the relations between individual emissions and climate change damages.[6] One common model is the Cumulative Model in which every relevant input produces a relevant output, though the inputs and outputs may be imperceptible. It is this model that is demonstrated by a case in which each of a thousand torturers turns a knob that imperceptibly increases the electric shock delivered to a victim. No single torturer is responsible for causing a perceptible increment of pain, but since the torturers together cause the pain, it is plausible to think of them as each causally responsible for some increment even if it is imperceptible. A second model is the Threshold Model in which no effect occurs unless a specific level of collective contribution is achieved (e.g., a car will not get out of the mud unless four people push). There are different ways of assessing the causal contributions of individuals in such cases, but what matters for our purposes is that on this second model, inputs produce outputs only when some particular threshold has been reached.

A cursory look at an introductory atmospheric science text shows how inadequate the Cumulative Model is to the complex relations between individual emissions and climate change damages. This model only seems plausible, I think, because of the seductiveness of the "bathtub" analogy that is often used in thinking about carbon emissions. On this analogy, emitting carbon is like running water into a bathtub and damages occur when the tub overflows. This is quite intuitive and can

---

[6] E.g., Sinnott-Armstrong 2005/; Parfit 1984, ch. 3; Glover 1975; and Kagan 2011.

be useful for pedagogical purposes but it is quite misleading if taken seriously. The carbon from individual emissions does not stack up, overflow the atmosphere, and cause damages. Rather, as mentioned in Section 5.6, the carbon emitted from joyriding in a '57 Chevy very slightly perturbs the global carbon cycle, affecting various fluxes and feedbacks, in ways that are difficult to quantify. The molecules themselves may stay in the atmosphere for centuries, be absorbed by the biosphere within a few years, or wind up in the oceans. In any case we will never know the fate of the particular molecules that were emitted.

The Threshold Model is somewhat more applicable because thresholds in the climate system actually exist. However, what this analogy does not capture is the dynamic nature of the climate system, the fact that there are vast numbers of differently structured processes that occur simultaneously, the differences in scale that are involved in moving from individual emissions to damages, and the fact that the system at each level is open to a vast number of influences, many of which are not causally active at other scales. In the end the relation between my emissions and climate-related harms is not at all like the relation between my pushing and the car getting out of the ditch in the threshold case.

In light of all this it is not clear that we can say that my Sunday drive in any way and to any extent caused a particular meteorological event, much less the socially mediated harms that may follow. The obstacles to making such claims are both epistemological and conceptual. In these kinds of cases we do not know and likely never will know whether some particular emission had any causal relevance for a particular harm. Even if we knew that a particular emission had some causal relevance, it would still remain a difficult conceptual question whether we would want to say that the emission caused the harm given the scalar differences between them. Having said this, however, I think that we are too ignorant and confused about both the climate system and the concept of causation to make Sinnott-Armstrong's categorical claim that an individual joyride "does not cause global warming, climate change, or any of the resulting harms, at least not directly," whatever exactly he may mean by this. Still, Sinnott-Armstrong has got it roughly right. Contributing to an outcome is not the same as causing it.[7] For all practical purposes, climate change damages are insensitive to individual behavior.[8]

However, I don't think the sting can be so easily balmed by transferring our supposed duties to the political domain as Sinnott-Armstrong suggests. For the same problem that arises with individual acts of emissions reduction arises for individual political acts, though perhaps not quite as sharply or always in the same ways. When it comes to voting, writing letters, making modest campaign contributions, or even occupying Wall Street, it is hard to feel that my individual act has much efficacy.[9]

---

[7] Julia Nefsky (2012) makes a similar point at the end of her paper.

[8] There are other reasons for being skeptical about the efficacy of individual behavior as well (e.g., the "rebound" effect). For discussion, see Csutora 2012.

[9] Hiller (2011) and Sandler (2010: 168) also make this point.

Rather than political action, the real alternative to green consumerism may be full-on conspicuous consumption, for that is something that may have identifiable, definitive consequences that matter to people (i.e., it seems to make some of them happy). But it is hardly a solution to our environmental problems.

However, this result is overly pessimistic. Our thought and action can inspire others, change their lives, and even affect the course of history. Indeed, reducing our own emissions as a demonstration of sincerity and commitment may be necessary for us to be effective in this way.

There are other things that we can do that would make a difference in the world. We can take action on adaptation and work to aid or compensate those who suffer from the effects of climate change. Individuals may be able to exert more influence in these ways than by working to affect macrolevel political decisions or in attempting to produce significant emissions reduction. Adaptation is inevitable and we can play a role in our own communities in trying to make sure that adaptation strategies are both fair and effective. Actions that aid or compensate those who are damaged by climate change would not be much different from those that assist people who are in need due to other causes. Indeed, climate change will increasingly make itself felt through the familiar scourges of poverty, disease, and insecurity, and the efficacy of our responses is not likely to depend much on the cause of the misery.[10]

6.3. IT'S NOT THE MEAT, IT'S THE MOTION

What we do matters because of its effects on the world, but what we do also matters because of its effects on ourselves. The balance and relations between what is world-affecting and self-affecting are important to determining life's meaning. I will not purport to provide a detailed account of such deep and personal matters but I will gesture toward a general view.

Let us begin with some questions. Did Lenin live a more meaningful life because the Bolshevik revolution succeeded? What would we think if Mandela had died in prison rather than becoming president of post-apartheid South Africa? Was it Plato who gave meaning to Socrates' life by memorializing his dialogues?

These examples elicit complicated responses. To some extent we do associate life's meaning with successfully achieving goals. Since Mandela's life was devoted to abolishing apartheid, it is hard not to feel that the meaning of his life would have been diminished had apartheid survived him or even if it had succumbed but not through his actions. Moreover, when assessing the meaning of a life, the value of what one is trying to do or how it actually turns out also seems to matter. We are less inclined to think that instigating the Bolshevik revolution gave Lenin's life meaning in the same way or to the same extent that abolishing apartheid gave meaning to

---

[10] This point has been made for decades by Michael Glantz and others in the climate impacts community. Visit http://www.ilankelman.org/glantz.html. Retrieved July 18, 2013.

Mandela's life. We think of a meaningful life as something that is good and so we do not fully separate our assessment of a life's meaning from our attitudes towards the goals towards which a life has been directed.[11] It also seems that a life's meaning can be affected by subsequent events that are not within the scope of an agent's intentions. We often speak as if the Arab Spring imbued meaning to the life of the Tunisian flower seller whose self-immolation ignited these events, even if his act was just a desperate suicide with no political motivation.[12]

What these examples show is that to some extent life's meaning depends on making a difference in the world and on the goodness of our goals. How should we understand these conditions and how far should we go in this direction?

Many Americans would say that what makes a life worth living is doing what is right, and doing what is right consists in obeying God's commandments. This idea was current in the Greek world as well (though the Greeks spoke of "the gods" rather than "God"). Plato (and perhaps Socrates) systematically discussed this view in his dialogue *Euthyphro*.[13] His conclusion was that anyone who held such a view was impaled on the following dilemma. If what makes an act right is that it is commanded by God, then any act, no matter how horrific (e.g., murder, rape, torture, etc.), would count as right so long as God commanded it. But this is the view of cultists and terrorists who commit horrifying acts of destruction in God's name. On the other hand, if what God commands is right, independent of his command, then we could do what is right and give meaning to our lives whether or not God exists.

Other ideas that have currency in contemporary America also had their analogues in the Greek world. The idea that success, fame, or celebrity is what is most important in life is reminiscent of the Greek idea that it is honor that gives life meaning. While honor is not the same as celebrity, fame, or success it is similar to them in one important respect. No one has it within themselves to be honored, famous, or successful. Whether one succeeds in achieving any of these goals depends on luck and the attitudes of other people. Thus, to suppose that the meaning of our life consists in such things is to take it out of our hands and make it contingent on luck or fate. Socrates, Jesus, and the Buddha were unanimous in rejecting the idea that the meaning of life should be held hostage entirely to fortune. Whether my life is worth living is to a great extent up to me. It does not primarily depend on the attitudes of others or the vicissitudes of fate.

---

[11] This helps to explain a debate that broke out in the United States about whether the 9/11 hijackers were courageous. While the discussion was innocent of much serious reflection, some separated the attribution of courage from the goals or character of the courageous person, while others thought that nothing good (e.g., courage) could be attributed to evil men who would perform such horrific acts.

[12] Thomas Nagel (1991) has wise things to say about these and related matters.

[13] Visit http://classics.mit.edu/Plato/euthyfro.html for an English translation. Retrieved July 18, 2013.

The idea that it is success, fame, or celebrity that makes life worth living is an instance of a more general view that is ubiquitous in American society. On this view, life is an instrument whose value consists in its contribution to achieving some goal. This is the attitude that underlies the slogan attributed to a widely admired football coach that "winning isn't the most important thing, it's the only thing." For people who see themselves as devoted to progressive projects that begin before they are born, that will persist long after they die, and whose outcome is very much in doubt, these are not the right metrics for evaluating lives. But because we live in a society that is dominated by such values it is easy to lose heart. Yet when these episodes are seen as part of a life that is engaged in valuable activities, they will not threaten the sense of meaningfulness that sustains us.

So what makes a life worth living? The views that I have been discussing see the value of life as contingent on the attitudes or approval of others, or on fate or fortune. The contrary view is that what makes a life worth living is primarily internal to each person. Of course we do not want to exaggerate the independence of life's meaning from the vicissitudes of fate. Under conditions of extreme material deprivation, when each day is dominated by the struggle for bare survival, questions about climate change are not at the forefront. But most of you who are reading this book are, like me, living in an affluent society in comfortable circumstances. Despite what we may sometimes say, life for us presents itself as a field for choice, decision, and action rather than as a set of imperatives required for survival. It is against this background that each of us must decide how to live.

In my view we find meaning in our lives in the context of our relationships to humans, other animals, the rest of nature, and the world generally. This involves balancing such goods as self-expression, responsibility to others, joyfulness, commitment, attunement to reality and openness to new (often revelatory) experiences. What this comes to in the conduct of daily life is the priority of process over product, the journey over the destination, and the doing over what is done.[14] This view is reminiscent of Aristotle's account that a life worth living is one that is devoted to valuable activities. Many of these activities are goal-directed, so insofar as they achieve their ends then so much the better. But the meaning of life fundamentally turns on engaging in these activities, not on reaching our ends. What I am responsible for is trying to make the world better. Whether or not I succeed is not entirely up to me.[15]

[14] Such thoughts are well expressed in various profound books and sappy (and not so sappy) pop songs. I personally recommend Kumar 2000 and John Lennon's "Watching the Wheel Go Round."
[15] For the philosophical underpinnings of this view, see Jamieson and Elliott 2009. A related view that emphasizes the importance of narrative structure to a worthwhile life has been developed by Alan Holland. See O'Neill et al. 2007; see also O'Neill 2008.

6.4. ETHICS FOR THE ANTHROPOCENE

The Anthropocene presents novel challenges for living a meaningful life. They begin with questions of ethics.

From the beginning of human morality, ethics has been primarily concerned with the proximate: what presents to our senses and causally interacts with us in identifiable ways. However, what is proximate is flexible. Stories, music, relics, sacred space, and even the establishment of a common language are all ways of bringing into view what would otherwise be remote. The expanding circle of ethics (which to a great extent coincides with globalization) has made the distal proximate through new living arrangements, forms of travel, and kinds of imagery enabled by technological innovation. However, there may be a limit to what can be made proximate.

The late philosopher Bernard Williams distinguished what he called "the morality system" from "ethics." Ethics concerns the generic question of how we should live and goes back to at least Homer and the ancient Greek dramatists. It is relatively universal and resilient, though flexible and revisable in its content. The morality system, on the other hand, is

> a particular development of the ethical, one that has a special significance in modern Western culture. It particularly emphasizes certain ethical notions rather than others, developing in particular a special notion of obligation, and it has some peculiar presuppositions.[16]

The mark of the morality system is the establishment of an inner deontic order that mirrors an external law.[17] It is characterized by an emphasis on purity, voluntariness, inescapability, and generalizability. According to Williams, the morality system has been enormously influential on "we moderns," though its underpinnings are largely illusory. He thinks that "we would be better off without"…this "peculiar institution."[18]

One does not have to accept Williams's entire story to wonder whether morality has more than met its match in the Anthropocene. Not everything that matters can be made proximate to creatures like us. Not all of contemporary life can be fruitfully modeled on eighteenth-century concepts. The morality system may have room for revision and may not disappear, but it may come to be seen as more like the

---

[16] Williams 1985: 6.

[17] This thought is explicit in the work of Williams's longtime colleague, G. E. M. Anscombe (see especially her 1958); to a great extent they share a common critique of modern moral philosophy, though their positive views are quite different.

[18] Williams 1985: 174. By artfully using an expression ("peculiar institution") that has traditionally been applied to American slavery, Williams indirectly references Nietsche's critique of Judeo-Christian morality as a slave morality. For Williams the morality system is basically a rationalized version of Judeo-Christian religious ethics, though so far as I know he never states this explicitly in his published writings.

"etiquette system," important for a particular domain, but hardly an oracle that can answer all of our most important questions.[19]

Ethics is a collective construction, like morality, but it seems to allow more individual variation. For this reason it may seem more revisable than morality, at least from the perspective of an individual. While ethics is fundamentally agent-centered, it leaves its mark on the world because it requires attunement to reality. While there is no guarantee or even much reason to believe that ethics and morality together can provide comprehensive guidance for life in the Anthropocene, we can hope that they can make some contribution to making the world better and enabling us to live meaningful lives.

An ethics for the Anthropocene would, in my view, rely on nourishing and cultivating particular character traits, dispositions, and emotions: what I shall call "virtues." These are mechanisms that provide motivation to act in our various roles from consumers to citizens in order to reduce GHG emissions and to a great extent ameliorate their effects regardless of the behavior of others. They also give us the resiliency to live meaningful lives even when our actions are not reciprocated.

My conception of the virtues does not rest on any deep metaphysical commitments about "natural goodness" or "the good for man." It flows from the general view that when faced with global environmental problems such as climate change, our general policy should be to try to reduce our contribution regardless of the behavior of others, and we are more likely to succeed in doing this and living worthwhile lives by developing and inculcating the right virtues than by improving our calculative abilities.[20]

The green virtues that would be part of an ethics for the Anthropocene would not be identical to classical or Christian virtues but neither would they be wholly novel. Much that mattered to humanity in the Pleistocene will matter in the Anthropocene as well. In writing a set of virtues for the Anthropocene we can draw on a great deal of traditional wisdom. However, some speculation is in order when we contemplate how to live meaningfully in a world that has not yet fully taken shape.

We can think of green virtues as falling into three categories: those that reflect existing values; those that draw on existing values but have additional or somewhat different content; and those that reflect new values. I call these three categories preservation, rehabilitation, and creation.[21] I will discuss each in turn, offering tentative examples of green virtues that might fall into these various categories.

---

[19] On the relationship between morality and etiquette, see Foot 1972.

[20] I defend these claims more fully in Jamieson 2007b. The instrumental attitude I take toward the virtues separates me from traditional virtue theorists and many of those who work in the tradition of environmental virtue theory. Cf. Sandler 2007; Cafaro and Sandler 2005.

[21] These strategies reflect the mechanisms of moral change discussed in Section 5.6. A fuller account would also have to provide an account of the vices (see, e.g., Thompson and Bendyk-Keymer 2012: Ch. 10–12).

Thomas Hill Jr. (1983) offers an example of preservation. He argues that the widely shared ideal of humility should lead people to a love of nature. Indifference to nature "is likely to reflect either ignorance, self-importance, or a lack of self-acceptance which we must overcome to have proper humility."[22] A person who has proper humility would not destroy redwood forests (for example) even if it appears that utility supports this behavior. If what Hill says is correct, humility is a virtue that ought to be preserved by greens.

Temperance may be a good target for the strategy of rehabilitation. Long regarded as one of the four cardinal virtues, temperance is typically associated with the problem of *akrasia* and the incontinent agent. But temperance also relates more generally to self-restraint and moderation. Temperance could be rehabilitated as a green virtue that emphasizes the importance of reducing consumption.[23]

A candidate for the strategy of creation is a virtue we might call mindfulness. Much of our environmentally destructive behavior is unthinking, even mechanical. In order to improve our behavior we need to appreciate the consequences of our actions that are remote in time and space. A virtuous green would see herself as taking on the moral weight of production and disposal when she purchases an article of clothing (for example). She makes herself responsible for the cultivation of the cotton, the impacts of the dyeing process, the energy costs of the transport and so on. Making decisions in this way would be encouraged by the recognition of a morally admirable trait that is rarely exemplified and hardly ever noticed in our society.

Cooperativeness would be another important characteristic of agents who could successfully address the problems of climate change. Surprisingly, this characteristic appears to be neglected by both ancient and modern writers on the virtues. Perhaps a virtue of cooperativeness is a candidate for creation; or perhaps, though not itself a virtue, cooperativeness would be expressed by those who have a particular constellation of virtues.[24]

There are other potential candidates for green virtues, some of which are related to those in the tradition and others that are not. Simplicity, for example, has a relatively long history, and the related virtue of conservatism has also been mentioned.[25] In what follows I discuss a virtue of particular importance in the Anthropocene.

---

[22] Hill 1983: 222.

[23] Another example of rehabilitation is exemplified in Jonathan Lear's 2006 story of how courage came to take on new meaning in the life of Crow Chief Plenty Coups after his people were virtually destroyed and confined to a reservation. For its application to climate change, see A. Thompson 2010.

[24] Hume is an exception in the tradition in noting the importance of cooperativeness. For further discussion of the importance of cooperativeness to morality, see Hinde 2002.

[25] For simplicity, see Elgin 2010 and Cafaro 2005; generally, see Jamieson 1992 and 2012.

6.5. RESPECT FOR NATURE

Respect for nature has been celebrated at various places and times to different degrees.[26] It is a persistent if not universal value. There are at least precursors of this idea in Kant and strong assertions of it in the Romantic tradition.[27] It is frequently attributed to indigenous peoples and found in various Asian traditions. While it is difficult to say exactly what this virtue consists in, it is relatively easy to give examples of the failure to express it.

As we saw in Section 6.1, according to some eminent scientists "it is clear that we live on a human-dominated planet."[28] If we dominate our planet, then surely we can be said in an important sense to dominate nature. Dominating something can be one way of failing to respect it, so it is plausible to say that in virtue of our domination of nature we fail to respect it.[29] But what exactly does it mean to dominate nature?

In Section 5.4 I claimed that domination is related to the extent to which an agent has power over a subject. When an agent's power is of a certain kind or extremity, it can compromise a subject's autonomy to the extent that the agent can be said to dominate the subject. In the literature of environmental ethics, nature is often seen as autonomous in the sense of self-determining.[30] Rather than being autonomous (i.e., governed by its own laws and internal relations) nature is increasingly affected by human action. While humans (and other forms of life) have always influenced their environments, what makes the present human relationship to nature one of domination is the degree and extremity of human influence. Human influence on nature is now so throughgoing that it constitutes domination.[31]

Domination can be expressed attitudinally in the ways in which we think and feel about nature as well as substantively. We often treat nature as "mere means," as if it did not have any value or existence independent of its role as a resource for us. As a society we seem to treat the Earth and its fundamental systems as if they were toys

---

[26] Respect for nature can be thought of as a duty as well as a virtue, which is how Paul Taylor (1986/2011) understands it, and also how I regarded it in Jamieson 2010b. See also Wiggins 2000.

[27] On Kant, see Wood 1998; for an expression of respect for nature in Romantic poetry, see Coleridge's poem "The Rhyme of the Ancient Mariner."

[28] Vitousek et al. 1997: 494.

[29] There is a sense of "domination" in which it does not imply a lack of respect (e.g., one team can be said to dominate another in a game) but for reasons that are given below (e.g., that our lack of respect for nature expresses attitudinally as well as substantively) and for others that are obvious it is not this sense that is in play here.

[30] See, for example, Katz 1997; the essays collected in Heyd 2005; and Turner 1996. What Turner means by "wildness" is related to what I mean by "autonomy." For reservations, see O'Neill et al. 2007: 134–137.

[31] This is why Vitousek (1997) used the language of domination. These are also the sorts of reasons why McKibben (1989) took climate change to mark "the end of nature." While this was an exaggeration, McKibben was making an important point: Though it does not mark the end of nature climate change is a mark of the Anthropocene. For more on these themes, see Jamieson 2008: 166–168 and Jamieson 2002: 190–196.

that can be treated carelessly, as if their functions could easily be replaced by a minor exercise of human ingenuity. It is as if we have scaled up slash-and-burn agriculture to a planetary scale.[32]

One of the insights of the social movements of the 1960s was that a vicious circle can take hold with subordinated groups.[33] Mistreatment diminishes respect, which leads to further mistreatment, which further diminishes respect, and so on. The same vicious circle can take hold with nature. Dominating nature both expresses and contributes to a lack of respect, which in turn leads to further domination.

Respecting nature, like respecting people, can involve many different things. It can involve seeing nature as amoral, as a fierce adversary, as an aesthetic object of a particular kind, as a partner in a valued relationship, and perhaps in other ways. These attitudes can exist simultaneously within a single person.

When nature is seen as amoral it does not constitute a moral resource in any way. Moral concepts arise, on this view, either from divine commandment, as in the case in the Hebrew Bible, from reason (as in Kant), the emotions (as in Hume), or are artificial human constructions laboriously created and maintained to provide us with refuge in an otherwise heartless world (as in the story told by Thomas Hobbes). One memorable statement of nature as amoral occurs in chapter 5 of the *Tao Te Ching*, attributed to the Taoist sage Lao-Tse: "Heaven and Earth are impartial; they treat all of creation as straw dogs." In ancient Chinese rituals, straw dogs were burned as sacrifices in place of living dogs. What is asserted here is that the forces that govern the world are as indifferent to human welfare as humans are to the fate of the straw dogs they use in ritual sacrifice. On this view we should respect nature because of its blind, unpurposing force and power.

Seeing nature as amoral can easily slip into seeing nature as an immensely powerful even malevolent adversary, and humanity as weak, vulnerable, and in need of protection.[34] If humanity and its projects are to survive and thrive, nature must be subdued and kept at bay. Nature, on this view, is the enemy of humanity.

Amoral nature can be respected for its radical "otherness" that cannot be assimilated to human practices. Nature as an adversary can be respected for its power and abilities in pursuing its ends, which are fundamentally at odds with those of humanity. Seeing nature as amoral or as an adversary can provide grounds for respecting nature but can also provide a rationale for dominating nature.[35]

A third way of respecting nature sees profound aesthetic significance in its overwhelming power. This thought is powerfully developed in Edmund Burke's 1757 work *A Philosophical Enquiry into the Origin of our Ideas of the Sublime and Beautiful.*

---

[32] I owe this image to Jeremy Waldron.

[33] This theme was especially prominent in the work of Franz Fanon and Malcom X.

[34] Werner Herzog's *Grizzly Man* is a wonderful film on this and related themes.

[35] Mill is an interesting case of someone who saw nature as amoral but maintained a fundamental respect for nature, in part for its otherness, but also because of its aesthetic qualities and the ways it contributes to human life.

The human experience of the sublime is, according to Burke, a "delight," and one of the most powerful human emotions. Yet, perhaps paradoxically, the experience of the sublime involves such "negative" emotions as fear, dread, pain, and terror, and can occur when we experience deprivation, darkness, solitude, silence, or vacuity. The experience of the sublime arises when we feel we are in danger but it is actually not so. Immensity, infinity, magnitude, and grandeur can cause this experience of unimagined eloquence, greatness, significance, and power. The sublime is often associated with experiences of mountains or oceans. Such experiences may occasion wonder, awe, astonishment, admiration, or reverence. In its fullest extent, the experience of the sublime may cause total astonishment.

The idea of the sublime was profoundly influential on nineteenth-century American culture, notably through painters such as Thomas Cole and Frederic Church. It went on to be an important influence on American environmentalism through the writings of John Muir and, more recently, Jack Turner (1996), Dave Foreman (1991), and other advocates for "the big outside." Indeed, the case for wilderness preservation is often made in the language of the sublime.

Finally, there is the idea of nature as a partner in a valuable relationship. People often speak of particular features of nature as if they were friends, lovers, or even parents. People who see elements of nature as friends often feel that they learn from nature as they do from other companions. Some speak of nature in language that is usually reserved for lovers.[36] Indeed, we often speak of those who want to protect nature as "nature lovers." In some people, nature elicits feelings of filial devotion. John Muir wrote that "[t]here is a love of wild nature in everybody, an ancient mother-love."[37] Many of us also associate nature with a feeling of being home. I grew up in San Diego, California, and the sights, smells, breezes, and quality of light that I experience when I am there are transformative, especially when I step onto the beach at Torrey Pines, just north of the city.

This idea of nature as a partner in a valuable relationship makes itself felt in economic language when people talk about "natural capital" or "ecosystem services." On this view protecting nature returns monetized benefits. Damaging nature damages ourselves.

These different ways of respecting nature support somewhat different attitudes toward nature and reasons for respecting it. Rather than discussing the details, I will mention three reasons for respecting nature that seem quite robust across times and cultures. Respect for nature can be grounded in prudence, can be seen as a fitting response to the roles that nature plays in giving our lives meaning, and can also spring from a concern for psychological wholeness.

---

[36] There is even a blog "52 Ways to Fall in Love With the Earth" which can be viewed at http://52ways.wordpress.com/. Retrieved July 18, 2013.

[37] http://www.goodreads.com/author/quotes/5297.John_Muir. Retrieved July 18, 2013.

One reason for respecting nature is that it is in our interests to do so. The geo-scientist Wallace Broecker (2012: 284) compares our climate-changing behavior to poking a dragon with a sharp stick. Angering the dragon of climate is not likely to be a good business plan for maintaining human life on Earth. Versions of this argument are ubiquitous in the environmental literature and something like this view is implicit in slogans such as Barry Commoner's (1971) "third law of ecology" which states that "nature knows best." It can also be seen as providing the foundation for the precautionary principle.

A second reason for respecting nature is that, for many people and cultures, nature provides important background conditions for lives having meaning. It is easy to think of examples from history, literature, or contemporary culture. Blake's idea of England as a "green and pleasant land" is important in English literature, history, and identity. The cherry orchard in Chekhov's play of the same name defines the life of everyone in the community. Think of the role that landscape plays in the lives of indigenous peoples. For that matter, think of how the "flatirons" define Boulder, Colorado.[38]

An analogy may help to bring the point out more clearly. Representational painting is not the only kind of valuable painting but it is one very important kind. Indeed, it may be the mother from which other forms of valuable painting emerged. Representational painting exploits the contrast between foreground and background. What is in the foreground gains its meaning from its contrast with the background. What I want to suggest is that nature provides the background against which we live our lives, providing us with an important source of meaning. It is thus not surprising that we delight in nature and take joy in its operations, and feel grief and nostalgia when familiar patterns are disrupted and natural features destroyed.[39] In these respects, meaning and mourning are closely related concepts.[40]

A third reason for respecting nature flows from a concern for psychological integrity and wholeness. As Kant (and later Freud) observed, respecting the other is central to knowing who we are and to respecting ourselves. Indeed, the failure to respect the other can be seen as a form of narcissism. Some work in environmental psychology gestures toward a story in which the recognition of nature as an "other" beyond our control is at the root of our self-identity and communal life.[41]

Many of these same reasons for respecting nature apply to respecting those who have gone before and those who will come after. Seeing ourselves as related to others in these ways is important to respecting ourselves and knowing who we are. It is

---

[38] http://en.wikipedia.org/wiki/Flatirons#A_symbol_of_Boulder. Retrieved July 18, 2013.

[39] For an articulate example of these feelings regarding the devastation of Utah's red rock canyon country by the creation of Lake Powell, see Lee 2006 and Abbey 1985. A similar sense of loss and nostalgia can be engaged by urban projects such as Robert Moses's plan to build a highway though Manhattan's Washington Square Park (see Caro 1975).

[40] I owe this thought to Sebastiano Maffetone.

[41] See, e.g., Clayton and Opotow, 2003.

also central to giving meaning to our lives. Such respect is also likely to help us from destroying ourselves.

The idea of respect for nature may seem in tension with another thought that is often articulated by environmentalists. On this view the ultimate source of our environmental problems is our separation from nature. The solution is to see humans as part of nature. From this perspective, nature is inside of us and we are part of nature. Our skin is a permeable membrane that is itself part of the natural world.[42] How can we respect nature when we ourselves are part of nature?

Such claims can be irritating because it is easy to hear them as trivial, false, pernicious, or mystical. For a naturalist such claims seem trivial. Of course we are part of nature. What else is there for us to be part of? Yet in another sense it is clear that we distinguish people from nature in much the same way that we distinguish artifacts from natural objects. Someone who cannot make such distinctions, at least in the ordinary case, either does not know how to speak the language or has some serious psychological deficiency or disorder. The claim that we are part of nature can also seem pernicious since it seems to imply that there is no moral difference between a human being killed by an earthquake and one who is killed by another human being. Of course those who claim that humans are part of nature typically want to deny this implication, but this is where the mysticism sets in.

Nevertheless, I think there is important truth in the claim that humans are part of nature. We can take many different perspectives on the relationship between ourselves and nature. For example, we can see nature as a set of cycles and from within this single perspective there are multiple views. From the point of view of biogeochemistry, nature is the carbon cycle, the nitrogen cycle, and so on. On this view we, like other natural objects, are instances of these cycles. At another level of analysis we can say that breathing and respiration are instances of the same cycles that govern the atmosphere; our circulatory system as well as various cellular processes are instances of the hydrological cycle; digestion and metabolism recapitulate the soil cycle; and we are as subject to the laws of thermodynamics as any planet or star. We could go on acknowledging other perspectives and various points of view within them. From these perspectives we are not separate from nature. Not only has nature brought us into existence and sustains us, but it also constitutes our identity.

This may seem hopelessly abstract or romantic but it is because of these perspectives from which we see ourselves as part of nature that we cannot fully reduce nature to competing baskets of distributable goods, at least not without radically changing our own self-understandings. We are hesitant about markets in kidneys and more than hesitant about markets in brains, in part because we see these organs as partly constitutive of who we are. Even if we allow such markets we will not be tempted to think that everything that is important about a kidney or a brain is expressed by its market value. It would be strange for someone to do a benefit-cost

---

[42] These themes are suggested by Suzuki and McConnell (1997).

analysis of a brain as if its value in a shadow market were its most important feature. The same sort of strangeness attaches to attempts to assess in market terms "the value of the world's ecosystem services and natural capital."[43] A residue remains of our relation to nature that cannot be fully expressed in the language of economics. This dimension is primordial, and occurs in various traditions around the world. It cannot easily be dismissed.[44]

Much that I have said in this section is sketchy and unsatisfactory. The important points, which surely need fuller development and deeper reflection, are these. Respect for nature is an important virtue that we should cultivate as part of an ethics for the Anthropocene. Respect can be manifest in many different ways within a single person, sometimes simultaneously. Nature itself is not a single thing and we can respect elements or dimensions of nature while expressing contempt for others. Respecting nature is respecting ourselves.

6.6. GLOBAL JUSTICE

One aspect of the dream that dies hard is the view that anthropogenic climate change is fundamentally a problem of global justice that can be assimilated to other such concerns. This view holds out the hope that climate change can be solved by a global deal. On this view an international group of adults, acting as agents of states or of other powerful institutions, pursuing national and institutional interests but constrained by considerations of justice, meeting behind closed doors somewhere like Breton Woods, can put the world back together. Indeed, it is their responsibility to do so. Exactly what the deal should or could be is a matter of some dispute. What happens if they fail is something people do not like to think about.

There are important differences among people who have such views. Some just want to make a deal; they care very little about justice. Others care passionately about justice and argue that justice matters practically because nations will not agree to deals that they see as fundamentally unfair. What these people have in common is a state-centric view of how the climate change problem can be solved.

Some of those who are committed to this view have been shaken in recent years by the failure of world leaders to respond adequately to climate change. Increasingly they worry that there are no adults left in the world or that the few who remain have been exiled to cushy sinecures where they can be safely ignored. The politics of some countries seem to have been seized by resentful adolescents engaged in never-ending popularity contests. In other countries it really does seem like the lunatics are running the asylum.

---

[43] This is the title of Constanza et al. 1997. According to the authors, the value in question is in the range of $16–54 trillion per year. For a critical discussion, see Sagoff 2004: ch. 6.

[44] Sagoff (1991) and Dworkin (1993: ch. 3) argue points that are similar to this—Sagoff when he distinguishes nature from the environment, and Dworkin when he talks about species as sacred.

Still, this view remains influential. Some academics find it attractive because they think that we know what we are talking about when it comes to global justice or rational choice theory. Climate ethics and justice appear to be special cases of these broader concerns or in any case an underdeveloped and undisciplined field. They dismiss collisions with reality as involving questions of "non-ideal" theory, which is not their subject.

Many activists and world leaders share the view that climate change is at heart a problem of justice between states. For those who suffer from the existing global order or speak for those who do, the language of global justice provides a kind of soft power. Despite the seductiveness of this view, some complications become apparent upon reflection.

Activists and leaders from developing countries often speak of climate change as an injustice that rich countries inflict on poor countries. For example, Ugandan President Yoweri Museveni has been quoted as saying that climate change is "an act of aggression by the rich against the poor."[45] At Copenhagen in 2009 Lumumba Stanislaus-Kaw Di-Aping, the chief negotiator for the G-77, upped the ante when he compared the Copenhagen Accord to the Holocaust.[46]

There is reason to see climate change as an injustice that rich countries inflict on poor countries. Rich countries have done most of the emitting, but most of the climate change–related suffering is likely to occur in poor countries, just as poor countries suffer most today from climate variability and extreme events.[47] Honduras suffers more from hurricanes than Costa Rica, Ethiopia suffers more from drought than the United States, and probably no country is more affected by floods than Bangladesh. Generally, 96% of disaster-related deaths in recent years have occurred in developing countries.[48]

Some would deny that poor countries are more vulnerable, pointing to the long history of mutual accommodation between indigenous peoples and their environments. However, underdevelopment is not the same as lack of development. In some regions of the world people are less able to feed themselves and to manage their environments than they were in the distant past.[49] In some cases contact with the Northern-dominated global economy has brought the risks of capitalism without the benefits. Traditional ways of coping have been lost or driven out, while modern approaches are not available. From this perspective underdevelopment should be thought of as something that has been produced by the global economy rather than as some point of origination from which development proceeds. To say this,

---

[45] *The Economist* (2007): 123.

[46] http://www.youtube.com/watch?v=s0_wvZw0fOU. Retrieved July 18, 2013.

[47] From 1850 to 2002 more than three-fourths of all CO_2 emissions came from developed countries (Baumert et al. 2005: 32). For a review of the health impacts, see Patz et al. 2007.

[48] See African Development Bank et al. 2003 and the sources cited therein for documentation of the claims made in this paragraph,

[49] Davis 200l.

however, is not to endorse any "myth of merry Africa" in which all was paradisiacal before European contact. No doubt, in many regions "capitalist scarcity [has simply] replaced precapitalist famine."[50]

Whatever is true about the details of these speculations, the vulnerability of poor countries to climate change has been widely recognized in international reports and declarations, including the 2007 Intergovernmental Panel on Climate Change (IPCC) report. The Johannesburg Declaration, issued on the tenth anniversary of the 1992 Rio Earth Summit, declared that "the adverse effects of climate change are already evident, natural disasters are more frequent and more devastating and developing countries more vulnerable."[51] When we look at particular countries, the case for this view is even more compelling.

Even without climate change, Bangladesh suffers enormously from extreme events. In a "normal" year about a quarter of the country is inundated by floods.[52] In an "abnormal" year things are often worse. In 1998 68% of Bangladesh's landmass was flooded, displacing 30 million people and killing more than a thousand, and this was only one of seven major floods that occurred over a 25-year period.

Climate change will make things worse. By the end of the century global mean sea level rise may be a meter or more.[53] An 80-centimeter sea level rise would put about 20% of Bangladesh permanently under water, creating about 18 million environmental refugees.[54] Climate change may also intensify cyclones, which generally occur about every three years. Saline water will intrude even farther inland during storm surges, fouling water supplies and crops, and harming livestock.

In recent years Bangladesh has made significant progress in reducing vulnerability to extreme events by developing early warning systems, building cyclone shelters, and implementing other disaster-preparedness measures. The mortality figures show the results. In 1970 Cyclone Bhola killed 500,000 people, in 1991 Cyclone Gorky killed 140,000 people, and in 2007 Cyclone Sidr killed 3,500 people. Even though mortality has been greatly reduced, extreme events still result in widespread damage to houses, crops, livestock, and other assets.

---

[50] Iliffe 1987: 3.

[51] http://www.un-documents.net/jburgdec.htm. Retrieved August 2, 2013.

[52] For more on Bangladesh's vulnerability to natural disasters and climate change see "Assessing the Evidence: Environment, Climate Change and Migration in Bangladesh," International Organization for Migration (IOM) Regional Office for South Asia, Dhaka, Bangladesh, 2010. Also visit http://www.washdiplomat.com/index.php?option=com_content&view=article&id=8456:as-ground-zero-of-climate-change-bangladesh-braces-for-the-deluge&catid=1491&Itemid=428. Retrieved July 18, 2013.

[53] See Grinsted et al. 2009; Rignot et al. 2011. For a review, see National Research Council 2010: 243–250.

[54] P. Roy, Climate refugees of the future. *ALRD Newsletter on Land, Water and Forest,* issue 3, January 2010. See also the five-part *Scientific American* account on Bangladesh and climate migration that begins at http://www.scientificamerican.com/article.cfm?id=climate-change-refugees-bangladesh. Retrieved July 18, 2013.

In 2008 Bangladesh published a Climate Action Plan.[55] Implementing the first phase would involve constructing embankments, cyclone shelters, roads, and other infrastructure; strengthening disaster research and knowledge management; and building capacity and creating public awareness programs. To fully fund the first five years of this plan required $5 billion, a figure that is more than half of Bangladesh's 2008 total annual budget. The plan launched with a contribution of about $125 million from the United Kingdom, but aid to Bangladesh has been volatile and has generally been declining in constant dollars and as a percentage of GDP.[56] Bangladesh will only succeed in adapting to climate change if others provide the financial support that was promised in the Framework Convention on Climate Change (FCCC).

Bangladesh will suffer enormously from climate change, yet its contribution to the problem is minuscule. Its total carbon dioxide emissions are less than .2 of 1% of the global total.[57] On a per capita basis, Bangladesh's emissions are about 1/20th of the global average and about 1/50th of American emissions.[58] Several small island states (e.g., Seychelles, Maldives) whose national emissions are even more negligible are even more at risk. They may literally cease to exist as their landmass is swallowed by rising seas.

It is these sorts of considerations that support the conclusion that anthropogenic climate change is an act of aggression by the rich countries of the North against the poor countries of the South. However, it is also important to recognize that global climate change fails to display some of the central features of an injustice between states.

The first difference is that paradigm injustices between states, such as aggressive war, involve the intentional infliction of damages, while this is not the case with global climate change. GHGs are a by-product of a nation's economic and other activities, and climate change damages are a by-product of these (and other) emissions. Virtually every nation would be happy if their economic and other activities continued as they are while their emissions ceased. They would also be happy if their emissions occurred but did not cause damages. When it comes to an unjust war, on the other hand, the whole point is to deprive other states of what is rightfully theirs. The difference between emitting GHGs and fighting unjust wars can be reduced to

---

[55] MoEF, 2008. Bangladesh Climate Change Strategy and Action Plan 2008. Ministry of Environment and Forests, Government of the People's Republic of Bangladesh, Dhaka, Bangladesh.

[56] http://www.indexmundi.com/facts/bangladesh/net-official-development-assistance-received (retrieved July 18, 2013). Generally see Overseas Development Institute, Bangladesh Case Study for the MDG Gap Task Force Report, May 2010. See also http://www.washdiplomat.com/index.php?option=com_content&view=article&id=8456:as-ground-zero-of-climate-change-bangladesh-braces-for-the-deluge&catid=1491&Itemid=428. Retrieved July 18, 2013.

[57] http://co2now.org/Know-GHGs/Emissions/. Retrieved July 18, 2013.

[58] This is calculated from World Bank data available here: http://data.worldbank.org/indicator/EN.ATM.CO2E.PC/countries/BD-8S-US?display=graph. Retrieved July 18, 2013.

a familiar adage. The purpose of a military is to smash things and kill people while the purpose of emitting GHGs is to become rich and enjoy life.

Second, many people and even some political leaders in nations that have high levels of emissions at least claim ignorance about the effects of GHG emissions. Other nations admit to the damages and undertake policies to reduce emissions or to aid those who suffer from climate change. But if this is to be understood on the model of an injustice between states this is weird in its own way. It is as if one nation unjustly invades another but does not know that it has invaded, or seeks to alleviate the harm it unjustly causes while continuing to cause it as a matter of policy.

The third and most important difference is the fact that since the atmosphere does not attend to national boundaries and a molecule of carbon has the same effect on climate wherever it is emitted, climate change is largely caused by rich people, wherever they live, and is suffered by poor people, wherever they live. Thus the people who contribute most to climate change and will suffer the most from it are distributed throughout all the countries of the world though in different proportions.

One way of thinking about those who contribute most to climate change is to focus on the 500 million people who emit half of the world's carbon.[59] Who are these people and where do they live? The shape of the climate change problem would be very different if they (we) did not exist. Although I know where to find some of the high-emitters (e.g., me and my readers), it is not easy to identify and locate all of those who emit most of the carbon. One way of trying to find them is through the use of a proxy.

In 2010 there were a little over 700 million registered cars in the world.[60] Anyone who owns a car is quite likely to be one of the 500 million who emit half the world's carbon (or equivalent to them in terms of emissions). This is not only because of the emissions from their automobile, but also because someone who owns a car is able to command relatively large amounts of energy to use for heating, cooling and other purposes.

Here are some examples of where these 700 million cars are registered.

United States 119 million
Japan 58 million
Germany 42 million
Italy 37 million
China 35 million

[59] This is the approach of Chakravartya et al. 2009.

[60] There is probably a fewer number of car owners since some people own more than one car. I have rounded off numbers supplied by Ward's Automotive Group. The numbers are obviously increasing rapidly and the calculations can be updated from data found on the following sites: wardsauto. com/ar/worlds_vehcicle_population_110815; http://dc.streetsblog.org/2013/07/05/car-ownership-may-be-down-in-the-u-s-but-its-soaring-globally/; http://data.worldbank.org/indicator/IS.VEH. PCAR.P3/countries/1W?display=default. Retrieved October 25, 2013.

Russia 35 million

France 31 million

United Kingdom 31 million

Brazil 26 million

Spain 22 million

Mexico 21 million

Canada 20 million

Poland 17 million

India 13 million

South Korea 13 million

Australia 12 million

South Africa 5 million

Switzerland 4 million

Saudi Arabia 4 million

New Zealand 3 million

Iran 3 million

Ireland 2 million

Israel 2 million

Slovenia 1 million

Afghanistan 600,000

Ecuador 300,000

Viet Nam 170,000

Papua New Guinea 38,000

Vanuatu 9,000

Central African Republic 2,000

The differences in car ownership between some countries are enormous, while car ownership is widely distributed over many countries. The extremity of the differences is indicated by the fact that car ownership in the United States is greater by four orders of magnitude than car ownership in the Central African Republic. China and Russia have more than 17 times as many cars as Ireland and more than all but two EU countries. The broad and sometimes surprising distribution of car ownership is shown by the fact that only six of the top ten countries in automobile ownership are among those countries required to fund the climate change activities of developing countries under the FCCC, while some of the 24 countries that are required to fund these activities are not among the top 24 countries in car ownership. What this means is that rich people who live in countries such as China and Russia escape obligations that attach to poor people who live in countries such as Ireland and Spain.

Even more troubling than the fact that poor countries suffer more from climate-related impacts than rich countries is the fact that poor people wherever they live suffer more from such impacts than rich people. This pattern of the poor suffering most from extreme climatic events has been documented as far back as the "little ice age" that occurred in Europe from 1300 to 1850.[61] A more recent example is the Chicago heat wave of July 14–20, 1995. In a fascinating book, Klinenberg (2002) documents in detail the victims of this event; they were disproportionately low-income, elderly, African-American males living in violence-prone parts of the city. A total of 739 people died in the heat wave, more than four times as many as in the Oklahoma City bombing that occurred three months earlier, although it received much less media attention. This pattern of the poor suffering disproportionately from climate-related impacts, even in rich countries, occurred once again in the wake of Hurricane Katrina, which struck the Gulf Coast of the United States in August, 2005.

The societal factors that made Hurricane Katrina so devastating in New Orleans—high levels of inequality, large populations living in poverty, poor public services, and so on—will lead to similar consequences in the future in otherwise rich countries that have such features. Indeed, something like this is more likely to happen again in the United States, if not in New Orleans, than perhaps in Houston, Atlanta, Miami, or Baltimore. Indeed, there is reason to suppose that poor people in the United States will suffer more from climate change than similarly situated people in a country such as Cuba, which has less inequality and a public sector that is more effective in responding to climate- and weather-related disasters than the United States.[62]

The fact that the high-emitting 500 million as well as the potential victims of climate change are distributed around the globe is awkward for those who want to assimilate climate change to traditional notions of global justice. It is as if the army of the aggressor includes citizens from the victimized country and the aggressor's victims include residents of both countries. Something like this may be true to some extent in some unjust wars, but in nothing like the degree to which it will be true in the case of climate change.[63]

I want to be clear that I am not denying that climate change poses questions of global justice. Rather, my points are these. First, like questions of individual moral responsibility, the problems that climate change presents stray from the paradigm of global justice. A nation's emitting a large quantity of GHGs is not, in several important respects, like unjustly invading another country. Second, the nation-state is not a particularly good vehicle for collecting high GHG emitters or even perhaps potential victims of climate change. A picture that views individual people in their

---

[61] Fagan 2001.

[62] Mas Bermejo 2006.

[63] There is more to say about these matters. Steve Gardiner (2011) thinks there's more to the analogy between war and carbon emitting than I do. Shue 1996 and Pogge 2002 provide materials for supposing that states can act unjustly with respect to other states short of war by violating negative duties not to harm. There is also a growing literature on complex forms of injustice that bears on these questions (see, e.g., Young 2013). See also Jamieson and Di Paolo 2013.

various roles and relationships as the primary bearers and beneficiaries of duties and obligations is one that comports more naturally with the climate change problem than a picture that views nations as fundamental.[64] Specific normative relationships emerge from a network of considerations. People and their values and commitments matter as they manifest in their gender, ethnic, class, and religious identities, and in their roles as parents, students, members of NGOs, citizens, stockholders, consumers, patrons of the arts, sports fans, home owners, commuters, and so on. Each of us occupies multiple roles, and different responsibilities and powers attach to them. We do not have to choose between these roles or privilege some particular level of analysis when it comes to ascribing actionable duties.[65] To a great extent the nation-state matters when it does because people care about it and it is a causally efficacious institution.

6.7. CONCLUDING REMARKS

We live in a post-Nietzschean world in which the gods are not available to give meaning to our lives, nor can nature provide transcendental grounding in a human-dominated world. The authority of reason, which according to the thinkers of the Enlightenment was supposed to replace obedience to the gods and subservience to nature, has turned out to be tenuous and under sustained attack. Still we can find meaning in the Anthropocene. Climate change threatens a great deal but it does not touch what ultimately makes our lives worth living: the activities we engage in that are in accordance with our values. The green virtues are not an algorithm for solving the problems of the Anthropocene, but they can provide guidance for living gracefully in a changing world while helping to restore in us a sense of agency. Acting individually and collectively in the various roles we occupy gives us the power to blunt the force of climate change while living meaningful lives. Reasonable people can make a difference while living well. In the final chapter I describe what can be achieved even within the limits of these modest but hopeful aspirations.

---

[64] Such a view is, I guess, a version of Cosmopolitanism, but there are so many undercharacterized versions of Cosmopolitanism in circulation that it is not clear that it is a useful concept. In any case see Pogge 2002: ch. 7 for an attempt to provide some order.

[65] Related views have been put forward by Kuper (2000) and Sen (2002); see also Jamieson (2005a and 2005b).

7 Politics, Policy, and the Road Ahead

I have argued that the dream of the 1992 Rio Earth Summit came to an end in Copenhagen in 2009. In this chapter I trace a path through this world littered with empty words and failed dreams and focus on what we might reasonably hope to accomplish in the next few years.

Rather than a global deal rooted in a conception of global justice, climate policy for the foreseeable future will largely reflect the motley collection of policies and practices adopted by particular countries. There will be climate-relevant action, but it will be different in different countries and it will be pursued under different descriptions and with different objectives. Some countries will adopt emissions trading, others carbon taxes, and others technology-forcing policies. Some countries will alter their energy mix, others their transportation systems, and others will focus on buildings. Some countries will do a lot and others will do a little. In some countries there will be a great deal of subnational variation, while other countries will nationalize and even to some extent internationalize their policies. These policies, in different proportions depending on the country, will reflect a mix of self-interest and ethical ideals constructed in different ways in different countries.

In order to understand this new world of overlapping consensus rather than comprehensive doctrines, of portfolios of responses rather than simple sweeping solutions, we should start at the beginning, and in the beginning was the word.[1]

7.1. THE RECTIFICATION OF NAMES

Early on in the climate change discussion there was a tripartite division of possible responses: prevention, mitigation, and adaptation.[2] In those halcyon days

---

[1] For the distinction between overlapping consensus and comprehensive doctrines, see Rawls 2005.

[2] Matthews 1987. The doctrine of the rectification of names is associated with the sixth-century BCE philosopher Confucius and especially his third-century follower Xunzi. It can be summarized in this passage from The *Analects*: "If names be not correct, language is not in accordance with the truth of things. If language be not in accordance with the truth of things, affairs cannot be carried on to success" (http://www.analects-ink.com/mission/Confucius_Rectification.html, retrieved July 18, 2013). Similar sentiments can be found in the Western philosophical tradition from Plato to Logical Atomism.

"prevention" referred to the possibility of preventing climate change. We now know that it was not possible to prevent climate change even then, much less now. However, we can still envision preventing "dangerous anthropogenic interference with the climate system" (depending on how "dangerous" is defined) or at least preventing some of the worst consequences of climate change.[3] Despite the range of possible uses, the language of prevention has largely dropped out of the climate change discussion. The tripartite division now in play is between mitigation, adaptation, and geoengineering.

The fact that the language of prevention can be repurposed brings out an important point. There is no uniquely correct way of categorizing the range of possible responses to climate change, any more than there is a uniquely correct way of mapping the world. The Mercator Projection is useful for some purposes, which is why virtually all Internet mapping sites including Google use a variant of it. For other purposes it is disastrous which is why some geography associations have sought to ban it and the *New York Times* has editorialized against it.[4]

For some important purposes the language that is used to discuss climate change is not useful and should be reformed. Whether we reform it or not we need to be sensitive to what the language obscures and presupposes, and the associations that it drags along.

The least problematic term in the standard vocabulary, though in many ways vague, is "adaptation." "Adaptation" as used in the climate change discussion refers to a wide range of responses from building floating houses to migration. People can adapt to climate change, but so can plants and animals. On one influential account,

…adaptation refers to adjustments in ecological-social-economic systems in response to actual or expected climate stimuli, their effects or impacts.[5]

There are many different dimensions on which adaptations can be distinguished, but for present purposes I will mark only three.

First, adjustments can be directed toward coping with climate change or toward reducing vulnerability to climate change.[6] For example, building sea walls is a way

---

[3] The quoted words are from Article 2 of the Framework Convention on Climate Change, which states the ultimate objective of the convention. California, which is the American state most active in addressing climate change, speaks of "climate change prevention" on its website (http://www.climatechange.ca.gov/, retrieved July 18, 2013).

[4] For the proposed ban visit http://www.scribd.com/doc/76953700/Projections (retrieved July 18, 2013); the *New York Times* editorial is mentioned in John Snyder's very illuminating book (1997: 157).

[5] Smit et al. 2000: 225. For other accounts of adaptation, see, for example, Abramovitz et al. 2002, Smithers and Smit 1997, Kates 2001, Kelly and Adger 2000, and Reilly and Schimmelpfennig 2000. The Intergovernmental Panel on Climate Change (IPCC) defines "adaptation" as "adjustment in natural or human systems in response to actual or expected climatic stimuli or their effects, which moderates harm or exploits beneficial opportunities" (Parry et al. 2007: 27).

[6] For Working Group III of the 2007 IPCC report, adaptation is necessarily vulnerability-reducing (Metz et al 2007: 809); for Working Group II of the 2007 report, it is not (Parry et al. 2007: 869).

of coping with sea level rise, while "managed retreat," which involves moving people and infrastructure out of harm's way, is directed toward reducing vulnerability.[7]

Second, adaptations can be conscious or they can be non-conscious. Plans that are currently underway to evacuate low-lying Pacific islands are conscious adaptations, while adaptations by plants, animals, and ecosystems, as well as those by farmers who incrementally respond to what they see as climate variability and changes in growing season, are non-conscious adaptations. The "managed relocation" of plants and animals that would involve people physically moving plants and animals from climate change–compromised habitats to more favorable habitats would be an example of conscious adaptation.[8] Intuitively, the distinction between conscious and non-conscious adaptations is a distinction between cases in which we are aware that we are adapting to climate change and those cases in which the adaptations are autonomous or automatic.

On another dimension, some adaptations are anticipatory while others are reactive. Bangladesh's Climate Action Plan includes many examples of anticipatory adaptations. Migration in response to an extreme climate-related event (e.g., the permanent evacuation of New Orleans by a sizable fraction of its residents in response to Hurricane Katrina) is an example of a reactive adaptation. This dimension marks the intuitive distinction between adaptations based on foresight and those that are responses to immediate events.

Taking these dimensions together, we can say that adaptations are directed toward coping with change or reducing vulnerability, that they are driven by policy or are autonomous responses, and that they are based on predictions or stimulated by immediate events. Adaptations can vary independently on the three dimensions that I have identified but they will probably cluster (e.g., policy-driven, conscious, and vulnerability-reducing are likely to go together). What adaptations have in common is that they are responses directed toward reducing the negative impacts of climate change.[9]

One distinction that is important but difficult to draw precisely concerns the directness of the link between climate and the adaptation it engenders. For example, adopting new seed varieties, creating irrigation systems, and migrating from an area of climate-driven economic, political, or social upheaval are all adaptations to climate change, yet they are very different from one another. In the first case (adopting new seed varieties) the link between climate change and the adaptation seems

---

[7] For more on managed retreat, visit http://coastalmanagement.noaa.gov/initiatives/shoreline_ppr_retreat.html. Retrieved July 18, 2013. These ideas descend from the work of the father of floodplain management, Gilbert White. See his early paper, White, G. F. 1945. *Human Adjustment to Floods*. Department of Geography Research Paper no. 29. Chicago: The University of Chicago, which can be downloaded from http://www.colorado.edu/hazards/gfw/vita.html. Retrieved October 25, 2013.

[8] For discussion, see Schwartz et al. 2012.

[9] The term "adaptation" is typically used positively in opposition to the negative term "maladaptation."

more direct than in the third case (migration) in which the effects of climate change are mediated through a broad range of social, economic, and political institutions. However, it is difficult to make this distinction precise because it is difficult to distinguish climate (which is after all an abstraction) from its effects. Hovering in the background is the further (muddy) distinction between adapting to climate change and adapting to the effects of climate change. What should be clear from this discussion is that a great deal more work needs to be done to adequately conceptualize adaptation.

"Geoengineering" is a term whose origins are difficult to trace, but the idea has been in circulation for decades and perhaps centuries.[10] In a 1961 address to the United Nations General Assembly, President John Kennedy declared his intention to "propose further cooperative efforts between all nations in weather prediction and eventually in weather control."[11] As we saw in Section 2.2, when four years later President Johnson's Science Advisory Committee produced the first US government report discussing climate change, the only responses that were considered were those that brought about "countervailing climate changes."[12] Specifically mentioned was the possibility of covering thousands of square miles of ocean with reflective particles. Not a word was said about reducing carbon emissions.

Geoengineering began to be seriously discussed in the 1990s.[13] Recently, the momentum has grown. A rush of new books and official reports urges us to think seriously about addressing climate change by painting roofs white, injecting reflective aerosols into the atmosphere, or even by launching space shields that would protect us from solar radiation.[14] This newfound interest in geoengineering is partly a reaction to the steady increase in greenhouse gas (GHG) emissions, which has continued despite scientific consensus, international treaties, and solemn declarations. In the background is the fact that many of us find technological solutions to urgent problems almost irresistibly attractive.

A recent report from the Royal Society of London defined "geoengineering" as the "deliberate large-scale manipulation of the planetary environment to counteract

---

[10] Fleming 2010.

[11] http://www.state.gov/p/io/potusunga/207241.htm. Retrieved July 31, 2013.

[12] Available on the web at http://dge.stanford.edu/labs/caldeiralab/Caldeira%20downloads/PSAC,%201965,%20Restoring%20the%20Quality%20of%20Our%20Environment.pdf. Retrieved July 18, 2013.

[13] An influential moment was a 1994 symposium convened as part of the annual meeting of the American Association for the Advancement of Science. The papers were subsequently published in *Climatic Change*, 1996.

[14] Shepherd et al. 2009, Goodell 2010, Kintisch 2010, https://www.ametsoc.org/policy/2013geoengineeringclimate_amsstatement.html (retrieved August 2, 2013), http://www.publications.parliament.uk/pa/cm200910/cmselect/cmsctech/221/22102.htm (retrieved August 2, 2013), http://www.agu.org/sci_pol/positions/geoengineering.shtml (retrieved August 2, 2013), http://www.gao.gov/products/GAO-10-903 (retrieved August 2, 2013).

anthropogenic climate change" and discussed at least 16 different techniques, including afforestation, ocean upwelling, and space-based reflectors.[15]

There are obvious problems with defining "geoengineering" in this way. Two interventions can have identical effects, yet one may be considered an instance of geoengineering while the other is not. A "deliberate large-scale manipulation of the planetary environment" undertaken for some other purpose than counteracting anthropogenic climate change would not count as geoengineering even if in fact it had that effect.

The Royal Society counts afforestation as geoengineering (presumably only if it is undertaken with the right intention) while the IPCC considers afforestation to be a form of mitigation. The IPCC defines "mitigation" as:

> An anthropogenic intervention to reduce the anthropogenic forcing of the climate system; it includes strategies to reduce greenhouse gas sources and emissions and enhancing greenhouse gas sinks.[16]

This way of defining "mitigation" has the important virtue of expressing an earth system perspective on the problem of climate change. On this view the problem is not the emission of GHGs but the forcing of the climate system. Since it is the forcing of the climate system that is the problem, the impact of GHGs can be mitigated by enhancing sinks as well as by reducing or eliminating emissions.

Despite its elegance, there are at least four important problems with this definition. First, there are important differences between reducing emissions and enhancing sinks. Reducing emissions reduces flows while enhancing sinks reduces stocks. Carbon that is not emitted remains sequestered in stable geological formations where it will remain virtually forever; carbon that has been emitted and stored in biomass is likely to return to the atmosphere relatively quickly. Second, it is much more difficult to reliably quantify sink enhancement than emissions reduction.[17] Third, this definition seems to count as mitigation various forms of what is usually called geoengineering (e.g., air capture of carbon by artificial trees). Finally, in popular and even policy discussions, "mitigation" is normally used to refer to emissions reductions and is rarely used to refer to sink enhancements.

The term is used in this way, I think, because the official conception of mitigation was introduced and championed by scientists and expresses an Earth systems view that does not neatly cohere with the pollution paradigm that has become dominant in the policy discourse. NGOs and political leaders talk about global warming pollution, not disequilibrium in the carbon cycle.[18] In 2007 the US Supreme

---

[15] Shepherd et al. 2009.

[16] Parry et al. 2007: 809

[17] Ballantyne et al. 2012.

[18] http://www.environmentamerica.org/news/ame/president-obama-reaffirms-commitment-tackling-global-warming. Retrieved July 18, 2013.

Court ruled that carbon dioxide was a pollutant under the Clean Air Act.[19] In the policy discourse the term that is normally used for reducing emissions of pollutants is "abatement" while "mitigation" is normally used to refer to policies that moderate the severity of the effects of the pollution.[20] For example, we abate air pollution by installing catalytic converters on cars or prescribing "no drive" days, and we mitigate pollution by installing air purifiers or house plants in our houses. My hypothesis is that when people came to see climate change as a pollution problem they began to use "mitigate" for "abate," since the term "mitigate" was already deeply entrenched in the climate change discussion. The effect of this has been to marginalize sink enhancement or leave it out of the conversation altogether.

Although there is serious disagreement about exactly what technologies count as geoengineering, the distinction between carbon dioxide removal (CDR) and solar radiation management (SRM) has become increasingly well-established.[21] CDR technologies would reduce atmospheric concentrations of carbon dioxide by increasing sinks (e.g., by fertilizing the ocean with iron) or by capturing carbon directly from the air ("air capture"). The use of these technologies is in principle no different from other attempts at enhancing sinks. Like other such attempts at reducing atmospheric concentrations of GHGs, these CDR techniques should be thought of as mitigation strategies. SRM strategies would affect Earth's mean surface temperature by affecting albedo (e.g., painting surfaces white), blocking solar radiation (e.g., sun shields), or reflecting solar radiation back into space (e.g., stratospheric aerosol injection, space mirrors). These approaches are importantly different from abatement or mitigation since they are not directed toward reducing either stocks or flows of GHGs. Instead they are directly aimed at altering the Earth's energy balance. They are thus in a class of their own.

Geoengineering is a contested category of questionable coherence in part because scientists and engineers from different research traditions and disciplinary backgrounds have forwarded proposals that reflect their own interests. Oceanographers, biologists, chemists, physicists, and engineers have all found something to advocate under this rubric. What these proposals have in common, if anything, is that they are "global, intentional, and unnatural."[22] What Schelling is gesturing at by "unnatural"

---

[19] http://www.supremecourt.gov/opinions/06pdf/05-1120.pdf). Retrieved July 18, 2013.

[20] Clare Heyward (who is British) tells me that she has only heard the term "abatement" used by Americans I speculate this is because she does not spend enough time hanging around with lawyers (barristers, soliciters, or whatever), but perhaps this is another example of "two nations separated by a common language." Schelling has been using the term in this way in the climate change context since at least his 1995 article. In any case this section has greatly benefited from correspondence with Heyward. For her typology, visit http://www.academia.edu/2369574/Situating_and_Abandoning_Geoengineering_A_Typology_of_Five_Responses_to_Climate_Change. Retrieved July 18, 2013.

[21] http://www.gao.gov/products/GAO-10-903 (retrieved August 2, 2013); Parson and Keith 2013.

[22] Schelling 1996: 303.

is, I think, that these are new, untried technologies or technologies that would be put to new, untried uses. I think the most plausible view is that "geoengineering" does not mark a specific category of response to climate change but simply alerts us to the fact that the approach under discussion is viewed as novel, weird, exotic, unfamiliar, or untested. So long as we see the use of "geoengineering" as an attitudinal marker of suspicion and do not confuse it with a term that delineates a distinct category of responses, then it may still have a role to play in the climate policy debate. The use of this term alerts us to the fact that a proposed intervention in the climate system is one that, in the opinion of the speaker, requires a heightened level of scrutiny.

What I have suggested in this section is that the prevailing tripartite vocabulary for classifying responses to climate change is confused and that it would be better to replace it with the four-part division of adaptation, abatement, mitigation, and solar radiation management. Adaptation includes a wide range of policies that are directed toward reducing the negative consequences of climate change. Abatement refers to any measure that reduces GHG emissions. Mitigation applies to measures that reduce concentrations of GHGs in the atmosphere. Solar radiation management includes those approaches that address climate change by directly altering the Earth's energy balance.

I am not the only person to suggest that linguistic reform is a good first step toward improving policy, and there are others who have made suggestions about how the vocabulary of climate policy should change. For example, some have suggested that "geoengineering" be replaced by "climate restoration" or "climate remediation."[23] The thought is that geoengineering techniques are meant to restore climate to its previous state or to remediate climate by correcting a deficiency introduced by human action. Neither of these will do. A geoengineered climate will not be the climate of the Holocene but an engineered climate of the Anthropocene. Geoengineering may reduce the earth's temperature, but there is no guarantee that regional climates will return to their previous states. Nor does geoengineering remediate climate, since there is nothing defective about the climate of the Anthropocene that needs fixing. Both the new climate equilibrium and the transition may be hostile to humanity, but that does not mean it is in any way defective. The pre-industrial climate was not always conducive to human interests. We heat and cool houses, not because there is anything wrong with the climate, but to make ourselves more comfortable. The fact that humanity is now one of the drivers of the climate from which we want protection does not mean that the climate has now become defective and needs to be remediated.[24]

The distinctions that I have suggested can be challenged on various grounds. Abatement and mitigation in the sense that I have characterized them are, like

---

[23] Bipartisan Policy Center, Task Force on Climate Remediation Research 2011. Other terms that have been used include "climate engineering."

[24] This paragraph has been influenced by Hale 2009.

adaptations, directed toward reducing the negative impacts of climate change. Yet I do not count them as adaptations. This is because they mark different kinds of interventions that occur at different points. Abatement and mitigation are directed toward flows and stocks of GHGs, while adaptation concerns responses to the resulting climate change.

Still, it must be recognized that there are complicated relationships among these categories and the climate change to which they are a response. For example, one possible adaptation to a warmer world is more extensive use of air-conditioning, which itself contributes to greater warming. Painting roofs white, which is an adaptation to increased warming, is also an example of SRM.[25]

Despite overlapping categories and in some cases the lack of sharp distinctions, my preferred vocabulary is more illuminating than the standard vocabulary. Still, however elegantly austere reality may be, our vocabularies seem irredeemably schlumpy no matter how we try to scrub them up. Nor do I have any illusions that clarity will trump habit and that we will immediately begin to speak with the angels.

7.2. ADAPTATION: THE NEGLECTED OPTION?

For many years it has been clear that the primary global response to climate change will be adaptation.[26] Despite this, there have been those who have regarded adaptation as a neglected option.[27] They have constructed a history in which there was supposed to have been a kind of taboo against talk of adaptation.[28] To a great extent this narrative has been driven by an attempt to privilege adaptation over abatement and mitigation. This preference for adaptation has been grounded in suspicion about whether climate change is really occurring, whether abatement and mitigation are possible, or whether abatement and mitigation are really needed in order for people to cope with whatever changes are ahead.

Some who have forwarded this view have their roots in the climate and weather impacts community and have been influenced by those who study natural hazards. The intellectual father of this community, Gilbert White, came of age during the Dust Bowl of the 1920s. Reflecting on his experiences, he argued that many societies are not well adapted to predictable environmental hazards that occur infrequently.[29] Every flood in a hundred-year floodplain comes as a surprise, as does the blizzard of the decade. Michael Glantz and others in the climate impacts community argued that people are not even well adapted to climate variability and that this maladaptation

---

[25] I owe this point to Steve Gardiner.

[26] See, e.g., Schelling's contribution to the 1983 NAS report.

[27] Pielke Jr. 1998. See also Rayner and Malone 1997, Parry et al. 1998, and Sarewitz and Pielke Jr. 2000.

[28] Pielke Jr. et al. 2007.

[29] For more on Gilbert White, see Kates 2011. For more still, consult Hinshaw 2006.

occurs around the world.[30] Researchers pointed to ongoing failures to adapt to such predictable features of a stable climate regime as droughts, storms, and hurricanes. For people who suffer from these events, it matters little if they are part of normal variability, associated with various long-term natural cycles, or consequences of anthropogenic climate change. What people experience is weather, not the statistical abstractions of climatologists. There are many reasons that people are maladapted to normal variability, including the structure of our cognitive and affective systems and how they affect our discount rates and utility functions. Other reasons are institutional and policy-driven, and concern how liability is assigned and property rights distributed. The main point, from this perspective, is that an unrelenting focus on abatement and mitigation distracts people from confronting the widespread maladaptation to weather and climate that exists independent of climate change.

Another community that views adaptation as a neglected option comes from a quite different place. Beginning with a commitment to a kind of functionalism that was extremely influential in the social sciences during the last century, they see societies as basically well-adapted to their environments. This community, composed mainly of anthropologists and those influenced by the social movements of the 1960s, are opposed to what they see as scientistic, top-down, managerial approaches to human problems. Their concern is that focusing primarily on abatement and mitigation transforms problems of human survival and livelihood into technical problems of carbon management that are best approached by scientists with their formal methods of prediction and economists with their quantitative approaches to evaluating policy options. What drops out is the perspective of ordinary people such as subsistence farmers in the developing world. Most of these people would do better by adjusting and adapting to changing environmental conditions based on their indigenous knowledge than waiting for the right sort of policy to emerge in New York, Geneva, or Washington, and then filtering down through a panoply of national institutions, subject to who knows what kinds of distortions and revisions.

When climate change became a salient but contested issue, it provided an opportunity for people from both of these camps to argue for the importance of adaptation. From one perspective an increasing focus on adaptation would help vulnerable people whether or not climate change was occurring. From the other perspective a focus on adaptation would help illuminate the resources available in traditional societies for coping with change and variability. Whatever the cause of the particular climate anomalies that were threatening people, the answer was the same: focus on adaptation.

It may come as a surprise given the influence of the story of "adaptation as a neglected option" that concern for adaptation is both explicit and implicit in the Framework Convention on Climate Change (FCCC). The objective of the FCCC

---

[30] Some of Glantz's work is accessible through this website: http://www.ilankelman.org/glantz.html. Retrieved July 18, 2013.

as stated in Article 2 is "stabilization of greenhouse gas concentrations in the atmosphere at a level that would prevent dangerous anthropogenic interference with the climate system."[31] The sentence that follows this statement tells us that "such a level should be achieved within a time frame sufficient to allow ecosystems to adapt naturally to climate change, to assure that food production is not threatened, and to enable economic development to proceed in a sustainable manner." Article 4 of the FCCC, which specifies the commitments undertaken by the parties to the Convention, mentions adaptation on several occasions. The parties agree to implement national or regional adaptation measures, to cooperate in preparing for adaptation to the impacts of climate change, and to take adapting to climate change into account in their relevant social, economic, and environmental policies and actions. In 1994 the IPCC published technical guidelines to assist nations in performing "vulnerability and adaptation assessments," and in 1995 at the first Conference of the Parties (COP 1) explicit guidance was provided on adaptation planning and measures. The second IPCC report, published in 1996, observed that many societies are poorly adapted to climate and emphasized the importance of adopting "no-regrets" policies to better adapt to both the prevailing climate regime and what may come next. In July 2003, the strategic plan of the United States Government's Climate Change Science Program listed, as one of its goals, understanding "the sensitivity and adaptability of different natural and managed ecosystems and human systems to climate and related global changes.[32] No comparable goal regarding abatement or mitigation figured in the plan.

Further examples can be given, but the point is that once it became clear that prevention was not possible, it became crystal clear that adaptation had to be part of the portfolio of responses. The logic of the US government's *Climate Action Report 2002* is unassailable: "[B]ecause of the momentum in the climate system and natural climate variability, adapting to a changing climate is inevitable."[33] The adaptations may be clumsy, inefficient, inequitable, or inadequate, but it has been clear for some time that human beings and the rest of the biosphere will have to adapt to climate change or they will perish. What is in question is not whether a strategy of adaptation should and will occur, but whether there will be any serious attempt to abate or mitigate.

7.3. WHY WE NEED MORE THAN ADAPTATION

The claim that adaptation was a neglected option began to become influential around the time that the Kyoto Protocol was adopted in 1997. Some of those who

---

[31] Available at http://unfccc.int/essential_background/convention/background/items/1353.php. Retrieved July 18, 2013.

[32] http://www.climatescience.gov/Library/stratplan2003/vision/. Retrieved July 31, 2013.

[33] http://www.epa.gov/oppeoeeI/globalwarming/publications/car/ch6.pdf. Retrieved July 18, 2013.

made this claim wanted to stop any agreement or policy that would restrain GHG emissions. They advocated an "adaptation only" policy in response to the climate change that they did not believe was occurring.[34] Now some of these same figures favor research in geoengineering.[35]

Even people who do not share this ideological agenda might reasonably wonder what could be the point of abatement and mitigation at this stage.[36] The "ultimate objective" of the FCCC, to achieve "stabilization of greenhouse gas concentrations in the atmosphere at a level that would prevent dangerous anthropogenic interference with the climate system," is unlikely to be achieved. In order for it to be likely that the warming will remain below 2°C from the pre-industrial baseline (the threshold that the parties to the Convention have effectively acknowledged for "dangerous anthropogenic interference") carbon dioxide concentrations in the atmosphere must be stabilized at no more than 468 ppm.[37] In 1750 (the stipulated pre-industrial baseline) the atmospheric concentration of carbon dioxide was 280 ppm. In 1992, when the FCCC was signed, the concentration was 356 ppm. It is now nearing 400 ppm. Every day there are fewer emissions for an abatement regime to allocate if the "ultimate objective" of the FCCC is to be achieved.

Abatement and mitigation matter for several reasons. First, as we saw in Chapter 4, there is a consensus among economists that it is economically rational to invest in abatement. Significantly abating or mitigating GHGs will reduce the costs of adaptation by limiting the extent of the warming. It is also likely that it will ease the burden of adaptation by reducing the rate of the warming as well as giving us more time to adapt to the full extent of the warming. Second, significant abatement and mitigation will also help to limit the extent of irreversible losses that climate change will bring to animals, plants, and ecosystems, as well as people. Third, even successful adaptation may not be morally cost-free. Increasingly, we may come to see people and other living things who are compelled to adapt as morally wronged in virtue of the fact that this has been forced upon them. Indeed, I speculate that even now, many people are attracted to the idea that those who are forced to adapt are morally wronged, even though (as I discussed in Chapter 5) our prevailing morality does not distribute responsibilities in a way that allows us to successfully ascribe wrongdoing to particular individuals.

---

[34] E.g., Okonski 2003.

[35] http://www.guardian.co.uk/environment/2010/sep/13/geoengineering-coalition-world-climate. Retrieved July 18, 2013.

[36] Some, such as contributors to the Copenhagen Consensus (http://www.copenhagenconsensus. com/, retrieved August 3, 2013), may ask why we should be concerned about weather and climate at all. Why not focus directly on global poverty? For replies, see Gardiner 2010, Jamieson 2005b.

[37] "Likely" here means a greater than 66% probability. See Rogelj et al. 2011. For the 2°C threshold and 1750 as the pre-industrial baseline see Copenhagen Accord, para. 1, UNFCCC Decision 2/CP.15, Dec. 18, 2009, UN Doc. FCCC/CP/2009/11/Add.1; Cancun Agreements: Outcome of the Work of the AWG-LCA, para. 4, UNFCCC Decision 1/CP.16, Dec. 10, 2010, UN Doc. FCCC/CP/2010/7/ Add.1.

It is also widely believed that abatement and mitigation reduce the probability of abrupt climate change. A 2002 report from the National Academy of Sciences states that

> [i]n a chaotic system, such as the earth's climate, an abrupt change could always occur. However, existence of a forcing greatly increases the number of possible mechanisms. Furthermore, the more rapid the forcing, the more likely it is that the resulting change will be abrupt on the time scale of human economies or global ecosystems.[38]

An influential 2003 review article states that

> the models show that forcing increases the probability of a threshold crossing. If human activities are driving the climate system toward one of these thresholds it will increase the likelihood of an abrupt climate change in the next hundred years or beyond."[39]

A more recent review simply asserts that

> Anthropogenic climate change likely increases the threat of major abrupt climate change and also likely increases the severity of some abrupt change impacts. . . . Reducing anthropogenic greenhouse gas forcing will likely reduce the probability of several high-impact types of abrupt climate change."[40]

The claim has intuitive plausibility but it is hard to find a convincing argument. The problem is that the relation between a set of mechanisms that could produce a result and the probability of actually producing the result depends on the probabilities of each member of the set (perhaps in combination with other members of the set) producing the result. The fact that one state has a larger number of mechanisms that could produce the result than another state does not in itself show that the result is more probable in the first state than in the second. Consider an example. There are more ways that I might become President of the United States than Chair of my department. I can become President by receiving the greatest number of votes in the Electoral College or by being Vice President when the President is removed from office. The only way that I can become Chair of my department is by being appointed by my Dean. Yet it is far more likely that I will become Chair of my department than President of the United States. This is because the probability of my becoming President by each of the possible mechanisms is vanishingly small, while the probability of my becoming Chair through the only possible mechanism is very high. In order for us to be sure that more mechanisms lead to higher probabilities in

[38] National Academy of Sciences 2002: 107.

[39] Alley et al. 2003: 2008.

[40] Overpeck and Cole 2006.

a particular case, we would need to know something about the probability of each mechanism producing the effect (singly and in combination).

The picture that some may have is that there is some set of possible mechanisms for how abrupt change can occur in a chaotic system and each member of the set has some fixed probability of producing the result. When we create a new set by adding a mechanism then we add another fixed probability. If we sum over the probabilities of each set, then the probability of producing the result is greatest in the set that contains all of the members of the other set and an additional member. However, there is no reason to think that chaotic systems work in this way. A forcing may well change the probabilities of mechanisms producing particular results.

There is a second reason that people may have this view. They begin with the thought that we are ignorant about the probability of any particular mechanism causing an abrupt change. A forcing introduces some additional mechanisms that could cause abrupt change to which we cannot assign probabilities. All we know is that there is some probability that each mechanism could cause abrupt change. In such a state of ignorance it is tempting to believe that the probabilities of each mechanism producing abrupt change are equal but this would be a mistake. It is fallacious to infer that two mechanisms have the same probability of producing an effect from the fact that we are ignorant about the probability of each mechanism producing the effect.

There may be features of the climate system that support the claim under consideration, but we would need to know the details. The nature of the fear is obvious. An extreme, rapid forcing may suddenly drive the climate system into some unanticipated, radically different state to which it is virtually impossible to adapt. Such a catastrophic climate surprise could occur through a changing climate setting off a series of positive feedbacks—for example, warmer temperatures leading to lower albedo (surface reflectancy), leading to warmer temperatures, leading to lower albedo, and so on. Another possibility concerns the flipping of a climate "switch." We know that the current climate regime depends on regular circulation systems in the oceans and atmosphere that at various times have turned on, shut down, or been radically different. At the end of the Younger Dryas, about 11,500 years ago, global temperatures rose as much as 8°C in a decade and precipitation doubled in about three years.[41]

Indeed, there is some evidence that abrupt change may already be underway. In recent years we have witnessed the greatest contraction of Arctic sea ice since modern measurements began, and perhaps much longer if anecdotal and anthropological reports are to be believed.[42] The summer of 2012 saw an all-time low in Arctic sea ice cover.[43] Already in the summer of 2000 a Canadian ship succeeded in transiting

---

[41] National Academy of Sciences 2002: 27.

[42] Thompson and Wallace 2001.

[43] http://thinkprogress.org/climate/2012/08/26/745571/why-the-arctic-sea-ice-death-spiral-matters/. Retrieved July 31, 2013. http://www.climatecentral.org/news/astonishing-arctic-sea-ice-melt-may-lead-to-extreme-winter-weather-14989. Retrieved July 31, 2013.

the legendary, once impassable Northwest Passage, the elusive goal of mariners since the sixteenth century. The 2004 Arctic Climate Impact Assessment, sponsored by the Arctic Council, a high-level intergovernmental forum that includes the United States, found that the warming in the Arctic is much more extreme than that in the mid-latitudes, with some Arctic regions having warmed 10 times as much as the mid-latitude average.[44] A recent paper tells us that "[t]he perception of present danger is such that the Arctic Council is already discussing regional geoengineering options."[45]

Even without abrupt climate change, an "adaptation only" policy runs serious moral risks. For such a policy is likely to be an application of the "polluted pay" principle rather than the "polluter pays" principle. Some of the victims of climate change will be driven to extinction (e.g., some small island states and endangered species) and others will bear the costs of their own victimization (e.g., those who suffer from more frequent and extreme climate-related disasters). The moral risk of a policy of "adaptation only" is that it will hit the poorest people hardest, yet it is they who have done the least to bring about climate change. They will suffer the worst impacts and they have the least resources for adaptation.

One response to the fact that it is poor countries that will suffer most from climate change would be to internationalize the costs of adaptation. This is favored by many of those in the research community who have championed adaptation and was also envisioned in Article 4.4 of the FCCC, which commits developed countries to "assist the developing country Parties that are particularly vulnerable to the adverse effects of climate change in meeting costs of adaptation to those adverse effects." Discussions about providing such assistance began at COP 1 in Berlin in 1995, and in 2001 the Marrakech Accords established three new funds to assist developing countries with adaptation. The Least Developed Countries Fund and the Special Climate Change Fund are both instruments of the FCCC and are financed by donors. The Special Climate Change Fund assists all developing countries with adaptation projects and technology transfer. The Adaptation Fund is an instrument of the Kyoto Protocol and is resourced by a levy placed on transactions under the Clean Development Mechanism, the program under which GHG reductions are traded between firms in the developed and developing world. This fund was supposed to begin operation in 2005 but was stalled at the COP 10 meeting in December 2004, in part due to demands by Saudi Arabia that it receive compensation if the world turns away from the use of fossil fuels. The Adaptation Fund was finally launched in 2009. While it is difficult to get reliable statistics about total disbursals, it is clear that funding through these mechanisms has been inadequate.[46] They also suffer from the

---

[44] http://www.acia.uaf.edu/. Retrieved July 31, 2013.

[45] Duarte et al. 2012.

[46] For further information, visit http://www.climatefundsupdate.org. Retrieved July 18, 2013.

fact that, except for the Adaptation Fund, they rely on voluntary donations, and the United States does not contribute to the Adaptation Fund because it is not a party to the Kyoto Protocol.

The adaptation funding action has turned to the Copenhagen Accord and subsequent agreements. These agreements established a Green Climate Fund as an instrument of the FCCC that is supposed to launch in 2014 and have $100 billion per year in funding by 2020. In order to get started, the parties to the Copenhagen Accord agreed to pledge $30 billion for 2010–2012 as "fast-start finance." All of these funds are supposed to be "new and additional" (i.e., not renamed or reprogrammed funds) and provide a "balanced allocation between adaptation and mitigation." It is difficult to assess the success of "fast-start finance" because the only real information comes from individual donors, and they are not uniformly transparent. What appears to be the case is that the donors have pledged the full amount but have been slow in delivering funds, and that much of the funding is not new and additional and most of it is going to mitigation (abatement) rather than adaptation.[47]

One way of appreciating the difficulties involved in funding and implementing adaptation is by looking at responses to natural disasters that occur in poor countries, since climate change will make itself felt by increasing the frequency and perhaps intensity of these events. When such events occur, large amounts of aid are often pledged and commitments made to provide both humanitarian assistance and support for transforming the society in order to reduce its vulnerability to future disasters. Often, however, little change actually occurs.

In 1998 Hurricane Mitch struck Honduras, killing at least 6,500 people and causing $2–4 billion in damage, an amount equivalent to 15–30% of gross domestic product (GDP). [48] At the height of the emergency, donors pledged $72 million to the World Food Program for immediate humanitarian assistance. More than a year later, less than one-third of the promised funds had been delivered. At a donors' conference convened in Stockholm in 1999, $9 billion was pledged for the reconstruction and transformation of Central America. The conference report stated that "the tragedy of Hurricane Mitch provided a unique opportunity to rebuild not the same, but a better Central America."[49] Much of the promised aid was not delivered in any form. Many of the resources that were provided were reprogrammed funds or "in-kind" contributions. Still, a significant amount of aid did find its way into the

[47] Cuming, Victoria, "Have developed nations broken their promise on $30bn 'fast-start' finance?" Bloomberg New Energy Finance White Paper, www.bnef.com/WhitePapers/download/47. Retrieved July 31, 2103. See also http://www.wri.org/publication/summary-of-developed-country-fast-start-climate-finance-pledges. Retrieved July 18, 2013.

[48] The following discussion is based on Glantz and Jamieson 2000.

[49] Summary report of proceedings: InterAmerican Development Bank Consultative Group meeting for the reconstruction and transformation of Central America (May 1999), Stockholm, Sweden, available at http://www.iadb.org/regions/re2/consultative_group/summary.htm. Retrieved July 18, 2013).

country, especially compared to pre-Mitch levels of assistance. Despite some success stories trumpeted by various governments and NGOs, Honduras remains extremely poor and vulnerable to climate-related disasters. A 2006 World Bank assessment reports that "poverty in Honduras has hardly changed since 1998."[50]

Tragically, the same story had occurred 25 years previously. In 1974, Hurricane Fifi swept through Honduras, killing about 8,000 people and causing about $1 billion in damages. Shortly after this event, studies showed that the destruction was exacerbated by various social, economic, and political conditions. These included deforestation, as well as the displacement of *campesinos* into isolated valleys and onto steep hillsides by foreign-owned banana plantations and large-scale beef ranches.

After Hurricane Mitch, studies again implicated these same factors. The report of the 1999 donors' conference stated that the tragedy "was magnified by man-made decisions due to poverty that led to chaotic urbanization and soil degradation."[51] A local observer wrote that

[o]n the North Coast, the Aguan River flooded big after Fifi. It is a closed basin and dumps huge amounts of water straight into the ocean. Not only did the same flooding occur with Mitch, but it carried the village of Santa Rosa de Aguan out to sea, drowning dozens. There was no effort in the headwaters to do something to avoid this repeat catastrophe.[52]

Sadly, the cycle of vulnerability continues.

...after Mitch, we see many environmentally bad habits on replay. People are moving back into high-risk zones, farming practices degrade upper watersheds, illegal logging damages forests. trash dumping and sediment stop up storm drains (50 percent are out of order...). new buildings weaken river channels, lack of educational campaigns, poor emergency readiness, forest burning.[53]

On the tenth anniversary of Hurricane Mitch, heavy rains again caused severe flooding, affecting 200,000 people and forcing 20,000 people from their homes.

---

[50] Available at http://web.worldbank.org/WBSITE/EXTERNAL/COUNTRIES/LACEXT/0, conte ntMDK:20990670~pagePK:146736~piPK:146830~theSitePK:258554,00.html. Retrieved July 18, 2013.

[51] Summary report of proceedings: InterAmerican Development Bank Consultative Group meeting for the reconstruction and transformation of Central America (May 1999), Stockholm, Sweden, available at http://www.iadb.org/regions/re2/consultative_group/stockholm.htm. Retrieved October 25, 2013.

[52] *Honduras This Week* (May 29, 2000) (http://www.marrder.com/htw/special/environment/70. htm. Retrieved April 23, 2003. For some firsthand accounts of the impact of Hurricane Mitch on this village see http://environmentalmigration.blogspot.com/feeds/posts/default?alt=rss. Retrieved July 18, 2013.

[53] *Honduras This Week* (May 29, 2000) (http://www.marrder.com/htwjspecial/environmentf70. htm). Retrieved July 18, 2013.

Some may think that pressure will build to internationalize the costs of adaptation as climate change becomes increasingly palpable. I am skeptical. As we saw in Chapter 4, a conservative estimate of climate change damages is 1.5–2% of global GDP with some developing countries suffering losses an order of magnitude greater. Globally, this amounts to $1–1.4 trillion in 2011 dollars.[54] It is unclear what it would cost to adapt in a way that avoids damages on this scale, but it seems obvious that the amount would be many times greater than what was put forward in the Copenhagen Accord. We can get a sense of the resources involved by reflecting on the fact that the United States spent $14 billion on New Orleans alone to try to protect it from another Hurricane Katrina–style disaster.[55] It is difficult to believe that rich countries would invest anything like this amount to protect 100 million or more threatened Bengalis, Egyptians or inhabitants of disappearing island nations, especially since so much will have to be spent domestically to adapt to the warming that is underway.[56]

We have been down this road before. In 1992 former Vice President Gore proposed a "Global Marshall Plan" aimed at "heal[ing] the global environment."[57] While his book was a best-seller, the idea of a Global Marshall Plan had almost no traction. Even if there were popular support for such an idea it would still be a difficult challenge. Rich countries, perhaps especially the United States, have the political equivalent of attention deficit disorder. A Global Marshall Plan or even a conscientious effort to finance adaptation to climate change on a global scale would require a level of sustained commitment that most Western societies seem incapable of maintaining. If we had the moral and political resources to internationalize the costs of adaptation, it seems likely that the attempt to control emissions would succeed. A reasonable approach to adaptation is not really an alternative to a reasonable approach to abatement and mitigation for it would mobilize the same resources of respect and reciprocity that are so clearly in short supply.

An exclusive focus on adaptation, on the other hand, is likely to be an instance of the "polluted pays" principle. Those who suffer from climate change will bear the costs of coping with it. It is the poor who suffer most from climate-related disasters, and in the end they will be largely on their own. International assistance is likely to be inadequate, and many of the changes required to reduce vulnerability can be made

---

[54] The calculation is based on World Bank figures.

[55] http://takingnote.blogs.nytimes.com/2012/08/29/we-built-it-flood-control-edition/. Retrieved July 18, 2013. The National Oceanic and Atmospheric Administration estimates that Hurricane Sandy cost about $50 billion (http://www.nhc.noaa.gov/data/tcr/AL182012_Sandy.pdf. Retrieved July 18, 2013).

[56] Generally on climate change and migration, visit http://www.boell.org/web/138-Climate-Migration-Security.html, http://publications.iom.int/bookstore/index.php?main_page=product_info&products_id=503, and http://www.iisd.org/publications/pub.aspx?pno=954 All retrieved on August 3, 2013.

[57] Schelling 1997 also used the Marshall Plan as an analogy to the way that we should think about an adequate response to climate change.

only by affected communities themselves in conjunction with their governments. In addition to their own problems, local, regional, and national decision-makers are often constrained by the economic and political realities of the global order. There is little reason to expect this pattern to shift as a changing climate increasingly makes itself felt in climate-related disasters.

Indeed, in some respects successful abatement seems easier to deliver than successful adaptation. If adaptation were easy we would already be well-adapted to climate variability. Yet, as we have seen, many countries, even some that are rich, are not well-adapted to climate variability even though resources for adaptation are available within the country itself. One problem is epistemological. Climate models are more reliable about the global response to GHG forcings than they are with respect to regional impacts.[58] Yet successful adaptation planning requires disaggregated regional information.[59] There are also incentive issues. A country that abates and mitigates can do well by doing good. Providing funds for adaptation to those who will suffer seems closer to an act of altruism. For example, Denmark's transition to renewable energy and greater efficiency has clear benefits for the country, but it is much more difficult to say what national interests are served by overseas development aid that helps poor countries adapt to climate change.[60] Finally, implementing abatement and mitigation policies is difficult, but doing so is largely under the control of national governments, at least in the developed world. When it comes to supporting adaptation, however, a benevolent donor can provide resources but to a great extent policy and behavior change must occur where the suffering exists. For these reasons it is easier to imagine (for me, anyway) that people in rich countries can be convinced to spend more to reduce emissions than to finance adaptation in other countries. I can imagine, for example, Americans funding alternative energy programs and even perhaps adopting a carbon tax, but I cannot imagine anything like the same level of resources deployed to fund adaptation in developing countries.

This, I think, is all true as a first approximation. There are bright lights hard at work in the world of climate finance trying to overcome these problems and to align knowledge and incentives in a way that will mobilize capital to help alleviate climate change–driven suffering. Nevertheless, there is a clear conclusion from this discussion. Just as we must acknowledge the necessity of adaptation, so any reasonable approach to climate change cannot escape the reality of abatement and mitigation. In addition to the benefits that I discussed earlier in this section, abatement and mitigation, if carried out properly, can provide a form of moral education. Abatement, as envisioned by the FCCC, embodies aspects of the "polluter pays" principle. By

---

[58] Orsekes et al. 2010.

[59] Some in the climate impacts community have been struggling with this problem for decades. See, e.g., Glantz 1989.

[60] http://blogs.worldwatch.org/revolt/denmark%E2%80%99s-road-to-a-low-carbon-energy-efficient-economy/. Retrieved July 18, 2013.

bearing some costs to reduce GHG emissions, those who have contributed the most to climate change bear some of the burdens.

7.4. THE CATEGORY FORMERLY KNOWN AS GEOENGINEERING

Adaptation to climate change will occur, and so to some extent will abatement and mitigation. None of this will be enough and pressure is already building for other approaches, especially those that promise gain without pain. To many, this is the promise of proposals discussed under the rubric of "geoengineering."[61] But even people who see such proposals as attractive in this way tend to see them as a last resort.

In Section 7.1 I argued that geoengineering is not a well-defined concept. However, I grudgingly accepted the term so long as we see it as an attitudinal marker of suspicion rather than as delineating a distinct kind of response. To call an approach geoengineering is to mark it as novel, weird, exotic, unfamiliar, or untested. The reason that it is important to "deconstruct" this category is that this grab bag of technologies is often thought to have special powers and privileges.

The picture many people have is that deploying geoengineering would be like giving an experimental drug to a dying patient—the usual norms and ethical principles would not apply. Geoengineering has even been called Plan B, as if it were the "morning after pill" for societies that do not practice safe consumption.[62] Geoengineering is supposed to be the "backstop" that is going to gather up all those errant carbon molecules.[63] Because geoengineering is typically treated as nearly cost-free and only to be used in the "bottom of the ninth," there may be a tendency to exempt proposals that are classed in this way from the critical scrutiny that we give to other proposals for responding to climate change (e.g., building nuclear power plants).[64] After all, when it comes to preventing the explosion of a "ticking bomb," we are allowed to take steps that would not otherwise be justified.

If metaphors were arguments, geoengineering would be home free. What these metaphors have in common is that they exploit a distinctive role that geoengineering is supposed to play in contrast to those technologies classed as abatement, mitigation, and adaptation. They invite us to see geoengineering as a categorical rival to these other approaches to climate change. In my opinion this view is entirely wrong. The real problem we face is not in choosing the right class of responses to climate change but rather in selecting and implementing a portfolio of specific strategies for

---

[61] Nordhaus 1992, Barrett 2008.

[62] Goodell 2010: 110.

[63] See, for example, the National Research Council 2011.

[64] Nordhaus 1992.

responding to a problem that is urgent, multidimensional, and extended in space and time.

It is important to interrogate each particular proposal—whether considered geoengineering or not—for efficacy and for ethical, political, social, and economic acceptability in the same way that we examine other proposals for responding to climate change. There is no particular set of norms that specifically apply to proposals that are introduced in the language of geoengineering. Nor should such proposals be exempted from norms that would otherwise apply simply because they have been introduced to the discussion in the language of this weedy category.

In what follows I discuss various worries that have been expressed about the uses of some technologies that are often considered forms of geoengineering. Some of these worries are broader than geoengineering, some specifically involve solar radiation management (SRM) or carbon dioxide removal (CDR) strategies, while others are specific to specific instances of these proposals. I do not discuss all the worries that have been expressed about these or other proposals that are considered by some to be in the domain of geoengineering.

Even under very optimistic assumptions and a capacious notion of what counts as geoengineering, there are no "silver bullets" (to use another metaphor) for addressing climate change. Deploying particular technologies could help to address some problems associated with GHG emissions while neglecting or exacerbating others.

Sulfate aerosol injection has received a great deal of attention.[65] It would involve injecting sulfate aerosols into the stratosphere where they would scatter sunlight back into space. Even if this approach were successful in reducing mean surface temperatures, it would likely produce substantial regional variations in temperature, precipitation, and intensity of the hydrological cycle, even perhaps disrupting the Indian monsoon.[66] The 1991 eruption of Mount Pinatubo, which many consider a "natural experiment" in sulfate aerosol engineering, produced a substantial decrease in precipitation over land and brought drought to some parts of the tropics.[67] In any case sulfate injection would do nothing to address problems such as ocean acidification.[68] Managing solar radiation through sulfate aerosol injection would pose an enormous societal challenge since the particles would have to be replenished frequently, perhaps on an annual basis.[69] If we were to embark on any SRM program while continuing to increase the atmospheric concentration of carbon dioxide, we would risk catastrophic climate change if we were to lose the capacity or will to

---

[65] This is the approach discussed by Crutzen in his influential 2006 paper.

[66] Robock et al. 2008; Brovkin et al. 2009; Bala 2008.

[67] Trenberth and Dai 2007.

[68] As a result of anthropogenic carbon dioxide emissions the acidity of seawater has increased about 30% since the industrial revolution. While the effects are not well-understood, they are expected to be deleterious. Visit http://www.pmel.noaa.gov/co2/story/Ocean+Acidification/. Retrieved July 18, 2013.

[69] Bengtsson 2006.

manage solar radiation anytime during the next millennium or beyond. There are few precedents in human history of such successful millennium-scale management.[70]

CDR strategies avoid some of these risks, but depending on the rate of removal could have unpredictable climate effects.[71] Moreover, it would be difficult and expensive to create the infrastructure for a program that would be on a scale large enough to affect global climate. Extracting, transferring, and sequestering carbon for centuries or millennia would be like running the global fossil fuel industry in reverse. In addition to affecting local ecosystems, if such a system failed the result could be catastrophic.

Many people think that geoengineering technologies should be developed but only deployed (notice the military word) in case of a climate emergency.[72] Sometimes climate emergencies are thought of in terms of crossing tipping points, but in any case similar questions arise: How do we know when we are experiencing a climate emergency? Who has the authority to declare such an emergency? Could geoengineering technologies be deployed in a timely way to save us from the threat once an emergency was declared?

The first problem with knowing whether we are in a climate emergency is that one person's emergency is another person's bad day at the office. When Hurricane Sandy struck New York and New Jersey in 2012 it was regarded as an emergency, but hurricanes and tropical cyclones with much greater proportional impacts are familiar facts of life in parts of the Caribbean and South Asia.[73] Moreover, there are people living today in drought-stricken parts of the world under conditions that we might reasonably say constitute an ongoing climate emergency. On the other hand, rich people in fortunate regions may be able to cope fairly successfully with even relatively extreme climate change. Claims of emergency are value-laden and can be quite relative.

Recognizing this, Bart Gordon (2010), former Chair of the House Committee on Science and Technology, said that "the global climate science and policy communities should work towards consensus on what constitutes a 'climate emergency.'"[74]

---

[70] Perhaps the Great Wall of China, which was functional from the fifth century BCE through the sixteenth century CE, is one.

[71] Preston 2012.

[72] E.g., Goodell 2010, Victor et al. 2009.

[73] Pielke Jr. and Pielke Sr. 1997.

[74] Gordon was succeeded by 89-year-old Ralph Hall, who in a rare December 2011 interview expressed the following view when asked about whether climate change is causing the Earth to become warmer: "I don't think we can control what God controls." When asked about a report in the *Proceedings of the National Academies of Science* that indicated that 97 percent of scientists were in consensus that human activities lead to global warming, Hall replied that "they each get $5,000 for every report like that that they give out." See http://news.sciencemag.org/scienceinsider/2011/12/ralph-hall-speaks-out-on-climate.html. Retrieved July 18, 2013. Hall has showed very little interest in science during his 30 years in Congress, but has been one of the largest recipients of oil money. He was succeeded by another Texan, Lamar Smith, a Christian Scientist with no apparent background in science.

Noble sentiments perhaps, but when it comes to such a profound issue on which so much hinges, a consensus between global climate science and policy communities will be difficult to achieve. Even if such a consensus were achieved, it is unlikely to represent the views of all the peoples of the world. Despite these difficulties we do sometimes seem to reach consensus around value-laden notions such as "dangerous anthropogenic interference with the climate system."[75] While the value-ladenness of claims about a climate emergency is not sufficient to forestall consensus it does make matters more difficult, especially since climate is abstract and many of its most dramatic effects are indirect.

A more serious problem for knowing when we are in a climate emergency is that the effects of climate change occur over centuries and even millennia. Were we able to see clearly from here all the effects of the GHGs that we have already emitted, perhaps we would agree that a climate emergency is already upon us. The problem is that we cannot see all the effects of our emissions because they are so dissociated (temporally and otherwise) from their causes. Not only does this make it difficult for us to know whether we are in a climate emergency but it leads to a further problem. By the time we might come to an agreement that we are in a climate emergency, there may be little to do but watch it unfold. Or perhaps at that stage the appropriate response would be attempts at radical adaptation and survival rather than trying to exert control over climate. It is often said that some SRM technologies such as sulfate injection could be rapidly deployed, but it is not clear exactly what "rapidly" means in a real-world context.[76] Even if in principle sulfate injection could be deployed and affect climate in less than a decade, there are human and social factors that could dramatically affect the pace of deployment.

An even more troubling question concerns who has the authority to declare a climate emergency. There is a great deal of talk in the geoengineering community about the importance of "governance." At the same time there is concern that any truly inclusive governance process would not be able to act decisively in the face of a climate emergency (the glacial pace of negotiations under the FCCC is evidence for this). It might be said (perhaps unfairly) that many in the geoengineering community think that governance is good so long as it rapidly comes to the right decisions. Of course many of us are tempted to think the same about democracy.

There are very serious issues at stake here. Intentionally changing climate is a way of exerting power on a global scale in a context in which relevant norms, conventions, and treaties barely exist, are highly ineffectual, or are very controversial. In 1955 John Von Neumann predicted:

> Intervention in atmospheric and climatic matters....will unfold on a scale difficult to imagine at present...[T]his will merge each nation's affairs with those of every other, more thoroughly than the threat of a nuclear or any other war would have done." (pp. 108, 151)

---

[75] Oppenheimer 2005.
[76] Shepherd et al 2009.

Climate change, whether inadvertent or intentional, involves winners and losers at many different scales. Even countries that would benefit from geoengineering value their autonomy and right to engage in decision-making. Any attempt by any individual or nation to assume the authority to intentionally change climate without broad international agreement would be extremely divisive and even disruptive.[77] Indeed, outside the geoengineering community, suspicion about these activities is already very great. In Nagoya, Japan, in the fall of 2010 the parties to the Convention on Biological Diversity (a treaty that the United States has signed but not ratified) declared a moratorium on geoengineering research that would affect biodiversity.

It is difficult even to imagine what would be the correct principles of justice to invoke in cases in which the intention was to change global climate. Every living thing on Earth (and perhaps even those who will live in the future) would be affected by such an action. Yet it is surely too much to require that everyone who is affected must participate in a decision for it to be legitimate.[78] I am affected by your opening a donut shop across the street from mine, but I have no right to participate in your decision to open the shop (except perhaps in the most general and indirect way, e.g., in background decisions about zoning, property rights, etc.). Even if we assume that nations are the proper decision-makers for attempts to change the global climate, it leaves open the question of the threshold of agreement that is required (majority? consensus?) and the institutional location of the decision-making process. It is sometimes suggested that the UN Security Council would be the most appropriate institution for authorizing intentional climate change, but the moral authority of the Security Council is itself in question and it is not clear that under the UN Charter it has competence over such matters.

One possibility would be to restructure the FCCC so that it incorporates two bodies, one that mirrors the Security Council and another that mirrors the General Assembly. The Conference of the Parties of the FCCC, mirroring the General Assembly, would operate according to majority vote rather than by consensus as it does currently. A new body would be composed of the world's largest nations. Mirroring the Security Council, it would have the authority to take strong action, but unanimous consent would be required. Such a picture both reflects the vision of a reasonable reform of the UN Security Council and expresses the idea that decisions regarding climate change are of the same gravity as those regarding military intervention. Too bad it has little chance of adoption.[79]

One plausible conclusion that can be drawn from this miasma of uncertainty is that the more likely a procedure is to be legitimating, the less likely it is that

---

[77] It is often argued that the US or the US and Britain should develop geoengineering capability in case a rogue state or other actor decides to geoengineer on their own. It is not entirely clear how this would deter such imagined rogues, and in any case the people I hear talking about developing such a capability are mainly Britons and Americans and recently the Chinese.

[78] Cf. Hale and Dilling 2011, Nozick 1974: 268–271, Caney 2005: 158.

[79] I am grateful to conversation with Harold Mooney on this point.

intentional climate change would be authorized. As a result, if geoengineering technologies are deployed, they are likely to be deployed without moral authority by the same countries that have caused a large share of inadvertent climate change and have evaded the difficult decisions that would be required to reduce emissions. In other words, the same people who brought you climate change will be here to save you from it.[80]

Many people, even some prominent proponents, have expressed concern that geoengineering research will distract us from the basic challenge of reducing carbon emissions.[81] I believe that talk about geoengineering has already to some extent contributed to dampening our willingness to abate. Only months after the Rio Earth Summit, the adoption of the FCCC, and the promise by the United States and other developed countries to stabilize their GHG emissions, the economist William Nordhaus wrote:

> [G]eoengineering, would introduce a hypothetical technology that provides costless mitigation of climate change. This could occur, for example, if one of the geoengineering options proved technically feasible and environmentally benign. Two interesting proposals include shooting smart mirrors into space with 16-inch naval rifles or seeding the oceans with iron to accelerate carbon sequestration.[82]

The dream of "costless mitigation of climate change" has been a constant if ghostly presence in the climate change debate for the last half century and I believe has already functioned as a moral hazard with respect to GHG emissions reduction.[83] We prefer certain, decisive action free of politics to messy, indeterminate responses that affect the way we live. We will avert our eyes from reality as long as a simple solution seems just over the horizon.

My fear is that speculations about intentional climate change will increasingly become a moral hazard with respect to adaptation as well, driving out funding especially for the poorest populations who have done the least to cause climate change. SRM and CDR technologies are increasingly being discussed as technologies that will primarily benefit the poor, precisely because they will suffer most from climate change.[84] On Plan B, rather than spending trillions to curb our emissions, adapt, or compensate victims, the rich countries will give their own scientists billions in an effort to reverse climate change. It is this emerging vision that presents the

---

[80] The problem of legitimizing the use of geoengineering is extensively discussed in Jamieson 1996b.

[81] Keith et al. 2010.

[82] Nordhaus 1992: 1317.

[83] But cf. Hale 2012.

[84] This sentiment is often expressed at conferences and on list-serves and I predict will soon be turning up in print.

second and currently most threatening moral hazard posed by speculation about geoengineering.

The very idea of intentionally changing climate strikes many people as arrogant, both because it fails to show respect for nature and because it is of a piece with attitudes that have been implicated in causing the problem it purports to solve. Indeed, many of our environmental problems flow from attempts to manipulate nature in order to make it conform to our desires rather than shaping our desires in response to nature. We have "improved" nature in many ways—bringing water to places where people want to live, exterminating animals who prey on animals we raise for food, dredging harbors and filling wetlands so towns and cities can be developed, and so on. Although it is not possible or desirable for humans always to "let nature take its course," there is a growing sense that modern societies have erred on the side of excessive intervention; that we have become arrogant and intrusive in attempting to manage all elements of nature.

A view that one often hears in conversation is that whatever arrogance would be involved in intentionally changing climate is already expressed in our current climate-changing behavior. Some even say that there is no difference of intentionality in these cases since we have been aware of the climate-changing impacts of our actions since at least 1992. On this view deploying a geoengineering technology would be undertaking intentional climate change in response to the intentional climate change that is now underway.[85] This view is mistaken, however. Many of the actions that cause climate change are intentional but climate change is not their intended effect, and thus the climate change they produce cannot be said to be intentional.

This distinction is important because many people believe that there is a moral asymmetry between what is brought about intentionally and what is an inadvertent result of an action. While I do not believe that this view in its strongest forms can be maintained, it is surely not generally true that intentionally performing some act is morally equivalent to inadvertently performing the same act. Indeed, when trying to evade responsibility for an action, people often claim that what happened was not what they intended ("I didn't mean to do it"). In some cases intentionality is crucial even to how acts are classified. Intentionally running down a pedestrian is murder; inadvertently killing the pedestrian is an accident. Intentional deception is lying; inadvertent deception is leaving a false impression. There is much more to say here, but the simple thought that whatever arrogance there would be in intentionally

---

[85] If arrogance is not an issue then why not "optimize" climate rather than returning to some historical baseline that itself was just a moment in the long history of the Earth? Paul Ehrlich has suggested to me in response that we should try to maintain the present climate because what is primarily disruptive is changing from one climate regime to another. This point has force but, if that is all there is to it, then all that follows is that if there is some climate regime that is better overall than the current one we should manage the transition to the optimal regime gradually and carefully.

changing climate is already present in our current pattern of behavior because such acts are morally equivalent or identical cannot be sustained.

What drives the view that intentionally changing climate would be an act of human arrogance is the idea that geoengineering would disrupt a relationship that is as old as humanity. Until relatively recently human lives were lived against the background of natural events that were beyond human control. But rather than providing the background against which human lives unfold, nature is increasingly becoming another human artifact. The idea that even climate could become a human creation is seen by many as a deep rupture in the fabric that brought humanity into existence and over millennia given meaning to human lives.[86]

Most geoengineering advocates say what they want is not deployment but a dedicated research program. The program would start small, but could gear up to the scale of the Manhattan Project. They claim that there is a bright line between research and deployment.

Bright lines, however, have a way of fading, particularly when it comes to dedicated research programs. In 1983, President Reagan created the Strategic Defense Initiative, a program devoted to developing technologies that would protect the American homeland from nuclear attack. Despite large costs and widespread opposition from many of the nation's leading scientists, Reagan's initiative has survived in some form for three decades, focusing on different technologies and wrapping itself in different purposes. It led to the US withdrawal from the Anti-Ballistic Missile Treaty in 2002, increased international tensions on numerous occasions, and siphoned money away from valuable uses toward technological fantasies.

Large research initiatives can be tougher to kill than vampires: They feed fortunes, careers, and reputations. As with the Strategic Defense Initiative, a dedicated geoengineering research program risks creating a self-amplifying cycle of interest groups and lobbies, building momentum toward eventual deployment as a way of justifying the research.

A dedicated geoengineering research program is especially dangerous in the current unstable policy environment in which there is a large amount of goodwill backed by large sums of money in a context in which there is little regulation. At least one entrepreneur has set sail in an attempt to fertilize the ocean, hoping to profit from the carbon offset market.[87] Successful attempts to appeal to this market could eventually lead to being part of a regulated offset market potentially worth billions.

---

[86] For more on this theme see Section 6.5 and Jamieson 2010a and 2013b. For an interesting historical overview of human perceptions of weather and climate, see Behringer 2010. For a discussion of similar issues in the context of ecological restoration, see Elliot 1997 and Katz 1997.

[87] In 2008 Russ George attempted to do this under the auspices of Planktos but was stopped by international outrage. In July 2012, he succeeded in dumping 200,000 pounds of iron sulfate into the Pacific Ocean under the auspices of Haida Salmon Restoration Corporation, a "for profit" partnership with a Canadian indigenous community. The voluntary offset market has been valued at more than $700 million. See Peters-Stanley et al. 2011.

It is not too difficult to imagine that something like the medical/pharmaceutical complex could emerge in which research, deployment, marketing, and government policy are closely linked and mutually reinforcing. Given the large potential sums at stake, it is not surprising that the push for a dedicated government-supported research program is strong and comes from many different directions.

What is often ignored is that the United States government already spends upward of $50 million per year in geoengineering-related research, this in addition to private spending.[88] There is a case for better coordination and perhaps for increased funding, but it matters enormously how the research is conceptualized, what agencies lead, and whether it is regarded as mission-driven or basic research. Indeed, in some geoengineering-related areas (e.g., ocean fertilization), it is basic research that is most needed.

7.5. THE WAY FORWARD

The dream of Rio was that states, motivated at least in part by a sense of justice, would make binding commitments to limit emissions and transfer resources in an effort to protect the global environment and bring the benefits of modernity to less developed countries. We have awakened instead to a world of "pledge and review."[89] While binding commitments may eventually tag along as an advertisement for what is already being done for other reasons, it is reviewable public pledges regarding emissions reductions and climate finance that is where the action is now and for the foreseeable future. The hope is that the publicity of this process will motivate states to make pledges that are fair and adequate to addressing climate change, and then to live up to them.

Thus far things do not look good. Many of the pledges made under the Copenhagen Accord are contingent rather than categorical, creating an additional level of uncertainty about what actually will be delivered. Assuming that existing pledges are kept, we will experience a warming of 2.5–5°C.[90] Since, as we have seen, 2°C is the widely accepted threshold for "dangerous…interference with the climate system," this means that if the nations of the world actually do what they say and live up to their pledges then they will violate their obligations under the FCCC.

However, failure can come in degrees, and there is an enormous difference between a 2.5°C warming and a 5°C warming. Which world we live in will largely be a function of the policies and practices adopted by particular countries. What countries do (and fail to do) will reflect their internal politics, values, fears, ambitions, hopes, and national priorities. What happens may actually be quite volatile.

[88] http://www.gao.gov/products/GAO-10. Retrieved July 18, 2013.
[89] Schelling (1992) advocated pledge and review because he thought that carbon taxes or cap and trade were either politically impossible, would have trivial effects, or would stimulate a race for benefits, attempts to shift costs, and further distortions that would require taxes elsewhere.
[90] UNEP 2011: 16.

An election may transform a leader into a laggard or a laggard into a leader. This will be a world of "small ball" climate politics rather than large schemes and big dreams. Any international agreement will be a matter of an overlapping consensus, largely acknowledging existing realities. No comprehensive doctrine has a chance in this fragmented world.

This does not mean that there is no point in preserving the FCCC. It is important to keep the institutions of cooperation alive and functional for the role they might play in the future. They also have an expressive function and can affect the internal politics of particular nations. The FCCC in particular will continue to be a site at which policy at all levels is discussed and a platform for whatever moral suasion can be brought to bear against recalcitrant actors.

In the United States climate policy over the next few years will be driven by the effectiveness and resiliency of laws, policies, and institutions such as California's climate change legislation (e.g., AB 32 California Global Warming Act of 2006), the Northeastern states' Regional Greenhouse Gas Initiative, attempts to regulate carbon dioxide under the federal Clean Air Act, and the vast amount of litigation slowly working its way through the courts.[91]

The result in the United States and globally will be a portfolio of policies without a single, effective portfolio manager. Many different kinds of actions will be taken and traded off against each other and many different agents will be decision-makers. The choices available to the CEO of Duke Power will not be the same as those available to the citizens of Seattle or the students of Ann Arbor. What is acceptable in China or New York may not fly in Germany or Texas. The good news is that this fragmentation and decentralization create an array of spaces in which action can be taken. As I noted previously, we are agents who occupy multiple roles, and we have a shot at making a difference in what enters the portfolio. A lot could happen, though it may all seem rather drunk and disorderly.

Given such uncertainty and decentralization it is fatuous to try to sketch an optimal portfolio for addressing climate change over the next half century. Still, for readers who have come this far, I feel that I owe you some account of what can be done that would make a difference. What I suggest are different kinds of policies that could be implemented in different ways by different kinds of decision-makers. These proposed policies have different degrees of urgency and express different temporal horizons. What follows is a list of seven broad policy priorities, three principles for how to pursue them, and one suggestion for immediate action. I present them in no particular order.

The first priority is to integrate adaptation with development. As we have seen, climate change and extreme events have enormous and increasing impacts on developing countries, yet very little has been done to integrate these considerations

---

[91] You can track these developments at http://www.law.columbia.edu/centers/climatechange. Retrieved July 18, 2013.

with overall development objectives.[92] At the United Nations Millennium Summit in September 2000, the world's governments committed themselves to eight Millennium Development Goals (MDGs), the achievement of which is supposed to result in a 50% reduction in global poverty by 2015. Despite the fact that one of these goals is "ensuring environmental sustainability," the MDGs make no mention of climate change or climate-related disasters as threats to environmental sustainability or to the overall goal of poverty reduction. Yet a report from the African Development Bank et al. (2003) states that "climate change is a serious threat to poverty reduction and threatens to undo decades of development effort." A similar conclusion was reached in a review of the United Nations International Decade for Natural Disaster Reduction: "[M]illennium development targets cannot be reached unless the heavy human and economic toll of disasters is reduced."[93] It is clear that climate change and variability should be thought of not only as environmental problems but also as major influences on the development process itself, yet it is still the case that these concerns tend to be promoted by different agents each working in their own silo.[94]

One reason it is difficult to integrate climate change concerns with development is that the FCCC defines climate change as a "change of climate which is attributed directly or indirectly to human activity that alters the composition of the global atmosphere and which is in addition to natural climate variability observed over comparable time periods."[95] Adaptation to climate change thus refers only to actions taken in response to a "change of climate which is attributed directly or indirectly to human activity." Consistent with this understanding, the FCCC has required a successful applicant for adaptation funds to identify the incremental risk posed by climate change over and above natural variability and to show that the benefit that the proposed project would provide would address only this increment. This is beginning to change but not quickly and dramatically enough, and the language of the FCCC is a straitjacket that makes change more difficult. Part of what lies behind this requirement is the fact that developed countries have been concerned not to allow the climate regime to become a mechanism for redressing global inequality.

---

[92] The desire to integrate them has been the motivation for the greenhouse development rights concept promoted by Tom Athanasiou, Paul Baer and colleagues (visit http://www.ecoequity.org/about/theme of ecoequity, retrieved July 18, 2013). This has also been a consistent theme of Schelling's work.

[93] http://www.id21.org/society/SIOaisdrlg1.html. Retrieved July 18, 2013.

[94] For a recent report on this theme, visit www.adpc.net/v2007/downloads/2010/oct/mdgproofing.pdf. Retrieved July 18, 2013. It is heartening to note that there are organizations working to integrate environment and development including Oxfam, the Mary Robinson Foundation—Climate Justice, and the International Institute for Sustainable Development.

[95] Article 1.2 of the FCCC available at http://unfccc.int/essential_background/convention/background/items/1349.php. Retrieved July 18, 2013. The IPCC has a different definition of climate change which does not make reference to human activity (visit http://www.ipcc.ch/publications_and_data/ar4/syr/en/mains1.html, retrieved July 18, 2013).

Hence any funds made available under the FCCC must be quite specific responses to climate change and not to the background conditions of poverty and inequality.[96]

It is also worth noting that even in developed countries infrastructure is often sited and built without reference to climate change. During Hurricane Sandy the New York subway system was shut down due to saltwater intrusion and two major hospitals were evacuated because backup generators flooded. More than 16 million people in the United States now live in coastal floodplains and this number is increasing.[97] Despite the threats posed by the colliding trends of increasing coastal migration and sea level rise, in many regions there is little interest in the sort of planning that would be required to address them. Remarkably, a recent law passed in North Carolina effectively forbids planners from taking future projections regarding sea level rise into account in their planning decisions.[98]

A second priority should be to protect, encourage, and increase terrestrial carbon sinks while honoring a broad range of human and environmental values. One reason the terrestrial biosphere is important is that over the last 150 years about 33% of anthropogenic carbon emissions has come from changes in land use and land-cover such as deforestation. This has declined to about 12.5% over the last decade, not because emissions related to land use changes have decreased but because total anthropogenic emissions have increased.[99] Some land use changes such as reforestation and leaving crop residue on agricultural lands after planting can increase carbon sequestration.

Despite the importance of the terrestrial biosphere to carbon emissions and sequestration, there have been few incentives for agents to preserve tropical forests. Individuals, corporations, and governments can capture large economic benefits through deforestation and exploitation while the costs are externalized to everyone who will live on the planet for at least the next millennium. Mechanisms must be created for rewarding people for protecting forests and other carbon sinks.

However, a single-minded focus on carbon sequestration can lead to compromising other values. There is no reason to think that if engineers were to design the optimal system for storing carbon that they would come up with the Amazon rain forest (for example). The Amazon rain forest is important for other reasons in addition to its role in storing carbon. For example, it is the site of an enormous range of biological diversity and complexity as well as the home of endemic, rare, and endangered species. Moreover, each of these individuals has moral value in the

---

[96] For further discussion, see Pielke Jr. 2005. Henry Shue, Paul Baer, Simon Caney, and others have also argued that climate change concerns should be integrated with concerns about poverty and underdevelopment.

[97] http://stateofthecoast.noaa.gov/pop100yr/welcome.html. Retrieved July 18, 2013.

[98] http://abcnews.go.com/US/north-carolina-bans-latest-science-rising-sea-level/story?id=16913782#.UGl5d0SRLV0. Retrieved July 18, 2013.

[99] Houghton 1999; Friedlingstein et al. 2010; Denman et al. 2007. For a recent review, see Houghton et al. 2012.

eyes of some people. The Amazon is also one of the few parts of the planet where one can feel the forces that produced life on Earth operating according to their own imperatives relatively uninhibited by the "hand of man." The forests are also the homes of indigenous peoples whose cultures are themselves rare and endangered. Newly minted PhDs in "carbon management" may be able to manage forests for optimal carbon sequestration, but the forest peoples and other inhabitants have moral claims that must be respected. The challenge is to protect and extend carbon sinks while protecting these other important values.

A third priority is full-cost energy accounting that takes into account the entire life-cycle of producing and consuming a unit of energy. This involves taking into account the costs of obtaining the raw material, processing and delivering it to users, and the costs entailed by waste and waste disposal. When subsidies or exemptions from regulations are granted for purposes of economic or geographical equity, national energy independence, or because the industry has captured a regulator, politician, or even an entire political party, market prices are unlikely to reflect full costs. Some of these subsidies or exemptions may be justified, but their desirability should not affect the evaluation of the costs.

Part of the reason that people can get away with endorsing full-cost accounting in principle but evading it in practice is that notions like "full-cost" and "life-cycle" are vague. The boundaries of the costs that should be attributed to a unit of energy are not clear. For example, some would say that a fraction of US military spending should be counted as a cost of oil since one of the main functions of the US military is to ensure a reliable supply from the Middle East and elsewhere. Instruments such as subsidies, tax credits and regulation can all be used to try to reflect such hidden costs or to subvert the entire enterprise. Given the nature of existing energy markets, the call for full-cost accounting does not lead to the categorical denunciation of any particular instrument. Despite the complications, it is clear that taking market values at face value radically understates the costs of coal and nuclear energy.

This leads to the fourth priority: the importance of raising the price of emitting GHGs to a level that roughly reflects their costs. Both carbon taxes and cap and trade have fierce advocates who argue for their efficiency and political feasibility. These instruments can take many different forms and display a wide range of properties. Under some conditions they are virtually equivalent.[100] Cap and trade sets a ceiling on emissions and allocates permissions to emit among firms that can trade these permissions in a market. The cap provides certainty about the quantity of GHGs that will be emitted and trading ensures efficiency. A carbon tax fixes a price for emitting carbon and the government captures the revenue, which it can use to benefit those who are worst off, invest in green energy research, or for other purposes. It is true that in many cases effective carbon pricing schemes are likely to disadvantage those who are already badly off. The proper response to this is to provide benefits to

---

[100] Stavins 2008.

those who will be further damaged through transfer payments or other mechanisms that are not directly tied to energy usage or pricing.

Many jurisdictions have already implemented cap and trade systems including the European Union, Australia, New Zealand, South Korea, California, Quebec, and several regions in China, and such systems are under active consideration in other jurisdictions.[101] Some EU countries that are governed by the European emissions trading system also have carbon taxes, as do several other countries around the world and several US and Canadian jurisdictions. Carbon pricing schemes are now operating in jurisdictions that encompass about 30% of the global economy and produce about 20% of global emissions.[102] The challenge for jurisdictions that already price carbon is to improve their systems so that they better represent the cost of emissions, are more efficient, introduce fewer and less damaging market distortions, address problems such as leakage, and institutionalize them in a way that is consonant with other values and priorities. In countries such as the United States and China the challenge is to create effective national mechanisms in the first place.

A fifth priority is to force technology adoption and diffusion. In a classic paper Princeton scientists Steve Pacala and Robert Socolow (2004) show how it is possible for us to get through the next 50 years on a course that would stabilize concentrations of atmospheric carbon at 500 ppm by employing only technologies that have passed beyond the laboratory bench and are more than demonstration projects. While the details are debatable, there is no question that there is an enormous range of technologies that are on the shelf. The problem is the gap between technological development, and diffusion and adoption. It is sobering to be reminded that the first hybrid was invented in 1901.

One of the lessons from the first generation of American environmental law is that technological diffusion and adoption can be forced by regulation and legislation, often at relatively low cost. This approach has been enormously successful in the automobile industry, and also with appliances and building standards.

Technological innovation is also important, so the sixth priority should be substantial increases in research. Economic theory explains why generally there is an underinvestment in basic research. Basic research is a public good, so taxpayers of a single country who invest in research are benefiting other people, some of whom are their competitors. Still, there are large differences among countries in how much they invest in research, as Figure 7.1 indicates.

---

[101] See The State and Trends of the Carbon Market 2012, available at http://web.worldbank.org/WBSITE/EXTERNAL/TOPICS/ENVIRONMENT/EXTCARBONFINANCE/0,, contentMDK:232 06428~menuPK:5575595~pagePK:64168445~piPK:64168309~theSitePK:4125853~isCURL:Y,00. html. Retrieved July 31, 2013.

[102] The Critical Decade: International Action on Climate Change, available at http://www.sbs.com. au/news/article/1492651/Factbox-Carbon-taxes-around-the-world. Retrieved July 18, 2013.

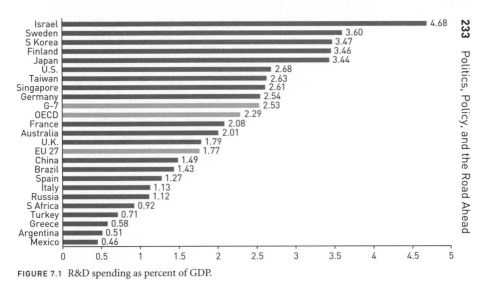

FIGURE 7.1 R&D spending as percent of GDP.

Source: Science and Engineering Indicators 2010, National Science Board.

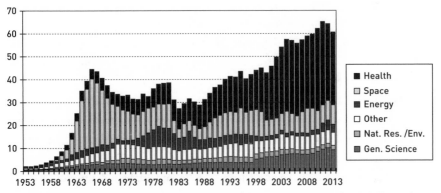

FIGURE 7.2 Trends in nondefense R&D by function (outlays for the conduct of R&D, billions of constant FY 2012 dollars).

Note: Some energy programs shifted to general science beginning in FY 1998.

Source: AAAS, based on OMB Historical Tables in *Budget of the United States Government FY 2013*. FY 2013 is the President's request.

There are two areas in particular where investment is important in dealing with climate change: carbon-free energy production, and capturing carbon dioxide from the air.

US investment in energy has been inversely proportional to the increase of atmospheric carbon dioxide. The more these investments have been needed, the less likely they have been to occur, as Figure 7.2 indicates.

Technologies already exist that remove carbon dioxide from the air but they face two serious problems. The first is cost. Even at relatively high concentrations, carbon dioxide is a trace gas. A large volume of air must be processed in order to remove a significant amount of carbon and this requires an enormous amount of energy. Moreover, it is difficult to fully assess these technologies since they are proprietary.[103] The second concerns what to do with the carbon once it is removed. Basically what would be required is something like the current fossil fuel industry running in reverse. Instead of removing sequestered carbon and injecting it into the atmosphere, it would remove carbon from the atmosphere and sequester it in the Earth. At this point it is unclear where this carbon would be stored and how exactly it would get there.

In neither case do we need a "Manhattan" or "Apollo" project.[104] Remaking the energy system, even on the back of a new technology, would be a massive undertaking involving challenges of diffusion and adoption as well as innovation, unlike the Manhattan and Apollo projects, which had clearly defined, simple goals and a single customer. We will have elevated levels of atmospheric carbon dioxide for centuries or millennia because of the carbon dioxide that we have already emitted. Even if air capture technologies do not become viable until the twenty-third century they will still have an important role to play in restoring the planet and delivering humanity from centuries of climate change–induced suffering and risk.

Some may think that research on large-scale solar radiation management should also be a priority. Launching space mirrors, for example, has the potential to enable a planetary manager to turn down the global thermostat very quickly. This possibility is part of the problem with this technology. If successful, it concentrates too much power in too few hands and thus becomes an invitation to abuse and military exploitation. For these reasons it is difficult to imagine the problems of global governance related to this technology ever being worked out. The alternative is for a nation, firm, individual, or coalition to go it alone, and this would introduce another risk into an already extremely risky situation.[105]

The seventh priority, to plan for the Anthropocene, has wide applicability. As we discussed in the previous chapter, we are now living in a new world in which humanity is a dominant force on the fundamental systems that govern life on Earth. The recognition of this fact should bring with it new ways of thinking about the human project and its relations to the natural systems that sustain it. The old picture of stable natural systems that humanity can choose to interfere with or not should be replaced by the picture of a restless planet on which humanity is a constant and enduring force. Human influence on this planet must be accepted; what matters are

---

[103] For an overview of such technologies, see Lackner et al. 2012. For discussion of the economics, see House et al. 2012.

[104] Yang and Oppenheimer 2007.

[105] For more, see Jamieson 1996b. Other problems with SRM technologies are discussed earlier in this chapter and in Preston 2012.

the scale and consequences of the influence. Population size and the scale and structure of consumption are key, as are questions about how we distribute ourselves in space and how we relate to supply chains and the means of survival. We need to think about the resiliency of the human project and its relations to the threat of disaster, which are as natural as death and extinction. Climate change, ozone depletion, and nuclear holocaust are not bolts from the blue that disrupt the providential order of things, but rather threats that we pose to ourselves. Planning for the Anthropocene will require new forms of decision-making, institutionalized in different ways, that will give us the flexibility to deal with change while enhancing our ability to commit to projects that extend far into the future. We need to develop institutions and capacities that would allow us to retreat from vulnerable places and reverse our steps, even when the reasons for this have been forgotten.

In addition to these seven priorities, there are three principles for how they should be applied.

First, in this world of a portfolio of responses with no single portfolio manager, everything should compete against everything else. What this means in practice is that particular projects, policies, and investments that express priorities should compete against each other on their individual merits. There is no single category of response to climate change that has precedence over all others nor any privileged policies that must be enacted no matter the alternatives. There are only better and worse responses at different temporal and spatial scales, each of which must stand on its own feet in a way that complements other efforts that are underway.

A second principle is that actions that address climate change should piggyback on other actions, policies, and regimes whenever possible. Such an approach is likely to produce a greater range of benefits than focusing only on actions that specifically target climate change. They are also likely to have greater support if they have more than a climate leg to stand on. A good example of this is the ozone regime. Since the chlorofluorocarbons (CFCs) that figure in ozone destruction are also GHGs, the Montreal Protocol and the successor agreements that phase out such gases have had a greater impact on limiting global warming than the Kyoto Protocol.[106] Even more can be done by restricting gases that have been introduced as substitutes. Another example would be to work for policies that reduce black carbon, which is a local air pollutant that causes health problems and also contributes to climate change. Black carbon tends to be produced in processes that also have a cooling effect but there is little doubt that reducing black carbon would have a substantial effect on reducing global warming.[107] There are also opportunities to adopt climate-sensitive policies linked to regimes governing trade, immigration, human rights, currency, and capital flows.

---

[106] Velders et al. 2007.
[107] Ramanathan and Carmichael 2008.

A third principle that we should adopt is to stop arguing about what is optimal and instead focus on doing what is good.[108] There is a great deal of support for significant action on climate change but too often it is dissipated in highly public disagreements about exactly what should be done. Those who think we should both abate and adapt argue about which is more important, and champions of cap and trade and carbon taxes have it out publicly even when they agree that either is better than nothing. It is time to stop letting the perfect (as if we know what that is anyway) be the enemy of the good. People should work to implement as many good responses as possible.

Finally, I want to suggest one focus of immediate action. The use of coal should be discouraged, limited, and phased out as soon as possible.[109] Coal production and consumption causes enormous damages. Coal contains mercury, lead, cadmium, arsenic, manganese, beryllium, chromium, and other toxic and carcinogenic substances. Coal crushing, processing, and washing releases tons of particulate matter and chemicals that contaminate water, harm public health, and damage ecological systems. Burning coal results in emissions of nitrogen oxides, sulfur dioxide, particulates and mercury, all of which affect air quality and damage public health. A recent review suggests that the price of coal would at least double if all the costs were taken into account.[110]

Discouraging, limiting, or phasing out coal will mean different things in different countries. In developing countries it may mean that some new coal-fired generating plants will be built as part of a larger plan for limiting their role and eventually phasing them out. In the United States and Europe it will mean no new coal-fired plants and the phasing out of existing ones. In Australia and other countries it means planning for the end of coal-mining. This will create hardship for some people, regions, and countries but this should be addressed by the familiar mechanisms that are available in modern welfare states. There is no justification for putting the Earth's climate at risk in order to generate jobs in rich countries that could do without them. Supposing otherwise is like arguing for war, genocide, and police states on the grounds of the employment opportunities they present. While what I say may sound extreme in our present political context, I have little doubt that these words will seem obvious and restrained to our descendants.

The priorities, principles, and immediate action that I suggest are practical and actionable. They do not require comprehensive agreements across large diverse populations in order to implement. Even so, the list should be up for constant revision as new opportunities present themselves and options that had once been attractive

---

[108] Actually I think this is related to a fundamental principle of morality. See Jamieson and Elliott 2009.

[109] Many environmentalists are diligently working on this now, including Jim Hansen and Bill McKibbon.

[110] Epstein et al. 2011.

shut down. Modest and tentative though it is, this list provides a road map for how we might be less stupid in our immediate responses to climate change.

7.6. CONCLUDING REMARKS

In this book I have argued that the climate change narrative that prevailed from 1992 to 2009, from Rio to Copenhagen, is now at an end. It foundered because of the obstacles to action sketched in Chapter 3, and the failure of our systems of decision-making discussed in Chapters 4 and 5. There have been attempts to reframe climate change as an issue about energy, green jobs, or concern for our children, but thus far none of these frames has gained much traction.[111] A narrative may come along in the future that will move people and organize our thoughts and feelings about climate change in a way that will be effective. In the meantime we live in the wreckage of the old story.

Climate change is important for many reasons. It brings out the pace, gravity, and voraciousness of the anthropogenic change that is remaking the planet, and highlights the weakness of our institutions in responding effectively to our own behavior, especially when it is magnified by technology and population. Survival in any recognizable form requires that we moderate the extent and velocity of the changes that are now underway, or that we manage our responses and contributions to these changes in a more rational manner. We can hope that the challenge will bring us together and that we will develop new conceptions of responsibility that are robust over the long term. In the meantime we will latch on to whatever features we can, and a broad range of actors will be mobilized to help us respond with everything at our disposal. This messiness reflects the fact that, as we discussed in Section 3.8, evolution did not build us to address or even to recognize this kind of problem.

One cause for optimism is that while the global environmental movement has not succeeded in motivating the countries of the world to adopt an effective global climate regime, it has insinuated itself into the political fabric of virtually every country, even those such as the United States that have been the most recalcitrant on climate change. In the sober light of these new realities, old stereotypes about Northern environmentalism in conflict with Southern development priorities are no longer viable. In elections held in 2010, the Green Party candidate for President of Brazil drew nearly 20% of the vote while the Green Party in Great Britain captured only about 1% of the vote. Much can be said to try to show that these numbers do not really mean what they seem to mean. Nevertheless, it is clear that seismic changes are underway in the configuration of global environmentalism. This is part of the reason that the global struggle to stabilize climate is now primarily within

---

[111] Hoffert et al. 1998, Shellenberger and Nordhaus 2007, and Mary Wood (http://law.uoregon.edu/faculty/mwood/publications/, retrieved July 31, 2013), respectively. Generally on framing, see Hulme 2009.

countries rather than among them. The old slogan "think globally, act locally" has never been more relevant.

Whatever happens, it is clear that we will have to live with climate change and find meaning and joy in a world that increasingly fails to resemble the one in which we came to consciousness. The biota will change, diversity will diminish, weather will be less stable, skies will be different, and it will become increasingly difficult to relate to the old stores and tales. We will have to live in the knowledge that this was not caused by "an asteroid from space" but is the result of a pattern of human action. For some, this will mean grief, guilt, and nostalgia. For others it will mean suffering. For still others, it will be just another day at the office.

Despite the unprecedented nature of the challenge, human life will have meaning as long as there are people to take up the burden. It matters what we do and how we live. We can cope with change even when our resources are thin. This does not mean that we will "solve" the "problem" of climate change any time soon. Rather than a problem, climate change will increasingly present as an array of challenges that we will have to manage and live with as best we can, and hope that the darkest scenarios do not come to pass. We will have to abandon the Promethean dream of a certain, decisive solution and instead engage with the messy world of climate politics sprawling across jurisdictions. This is life in the Anthropocene. Climate change will trouble us but there is no magic bullet solution. John Wayne is dead, and there is no Colt 45 peacemaker in sight. What remains is the human spirit, and its enduring quest to survive and flourish on a changing planet.

References

Abbey, Edward. 1985. *The Monkey Wrench Gang*. Salt Lake City: Dream Garden Press.

Abrahamson, Dean, ed. 1989. *The Challenge of Global Warming*. Washington, DC: Island Press.

Abramovitz, J., T. Banuri, P. O. Girot, B. Orlando, et al. 2001. "Adapting to Climate Change: Natural Resource Management and Vulnerability Reduction." Background paper to the Task Force on Climate Change, Adaptation and Vulnerable Communities. World Conservation Union (IUCN), Worldwatch Institute, International Institute for Sustainable Development (IISD), Stockholm Environment Institute/Boston (SEI-B).

Abram, David. 1996. *The Spell of the Sensuous: Perception and Language in a More-Than-Human World*. New York: Vintage Books.

Ackerman, Frank, and Lisa Heinzerling. 2005. *Priceless: On Knowing the Price of Everything and the Value of Nothing*. New York: New Press.

Ackerman, Frank. 2009. *Can We Afford the Future? The Economics of a Warming World*. London: Zed Books.

Ackerman, Frank, Stephen J. DeCanio, Richard B. Howarth, and Kristen Sheeran. 2009. "Limitations of Integrated Assessment Models of Climate Change." *Climatic Change* 95: 297–315.

Adger, J. et al., eds. 2006. *Fairness in Adaptation to Climate Change*. Cambridge MA: The MIT Press.

African Development Bank, Asian Development Bank, Department of International Development, United Kingdom, Directorate-General for International Cooperation, The Netherlands, Directorate General for Development, European Commission, Federal Ministry for Economic Cooperation and Development, Germany, Organisation for Economic Development, United Nations Development Programme, United Nations Environment Programme, and the World Bank. 2003. *Poverty and Climate Change: Reducing The Vulnerability of the Poor Through Adaptation*. Washington, DC: The World Bank.

Agarwal, Anil, and Sunita Narain. 1991. *Global Warming in an Unequal World: A Case of Environmental Colonialism*. New Delhi: Centre for Science and Environment.

Agrawala, Shardul. 1998. "Context and Early Origins of the Intergovernmental Panel on Climate Change." *Climatic Change* 39(4): 605–620.

Aichele, Rahel, and Gabriel Felbermayron. 2012. "Kyoto and the Carbon Footprint of Nations." *Journal of Environmental Economics and Management* 63(3): 336–354.

Alley, R. B., J. Marotzke, W. D. Nordhaus, et al. 2003. "Abrupt Climate Change." *Science* 299(5615): 2005–2010.

Anderegg, W. R. L., et al. 2010. "Expert Credibility in Climate Change." *Proceedings of the National Academy of Sciences* 107: 12107–12109.

Ångström, Knut. 1900. "Über die Bedeutung des Wasserdampfes und der Kohlensäure bei der Absorption der Erdatmosphäre." *Annalen der Physik* 4(3): 720–732.

Anscombe, G. E. M. 1958. "Modern Moral Philosophy." *Philosophy* 33(124): 1–19.

Archer. David. 2009. *The Long Thaw: How Humans Are Changing the Next 100,000 Years of Earth's Climate*. Princeton: Princeton University Press.

Archer, David, and V. Brovkin. 2008. "The Millennial Atmospheric Lifetime of Anthropogenic CO2." *Climatic Change* 90: 283–297.

Archer, David, and Ray Pierrehumbert, eds. 2011. *The Warming Papers: A Compendium of Classic Scientific Papers on Human-Driven Climate Change*. Oxford: Wiley-Blackwell.

Archer, David, and Stefan Rahmstorf. 2010. *The Climate Crisis: An Introductory Guide to Climate Change*. New York: Cambridge University Press.

Arendt, Hannah. 1998. *The Human Condition*. Chicago: University of Chicago Press.

Arrow, Kenneth J. 2007. "Global Climate change: A Challenge to Policy." *The Economists' Voice* 4(3) ISSN (Online) 1553–3832.

Baer, Paul. 2010. "Adaptation to Climate Change: Who Pays Whom?" In Stephen Gardner, Simon Caney, Dale Jamieson, Henry Shue, eds., *Climate Ethics: Essential Readings*. New York: Oxford University Press: 247–262.

Bala, G., P. B. Duffy, and K. E. Taylor. 2008. "Impact of Geoengineering Schemes on the Global Hydrological Cycle." *Proceedings of the National Academy of Sciences* 105: 7664–7669.

Ballantyne, A. P., C. B. Alden, J. B. Miller, P. P. Tans, and J. W. C. White. 2012. "Increase in Observed Net Carbon Dioxide Uptake by Land and Oceans during the Past 50 Years." *Nature* 488: 70–72.

Barrett, Scott. 2003. *Environment and Statecraft*. Oxford: Oxford University Press.

Barrett, Scott. 2008. "The Incredible Economics of Geoengineering." *Environmental and Resource Economics* 39:45–54.

Baumert, Kevin A., Tim Herzog, and Jonathan Pershing. 2005. "Navigating the Numbers: Greenhouse Gas Data and International Climate Policy." World Resources Institute. http://www.wri.org/publication/navigating-the-numbers.

Baums, Iliana B. 2008. "A Restoration Genetics Guide for Coral Reef Conservation." *Molecular Ecology* 17(12): 2796–2811.

Bean, Jonathan J. 2000. " 'Burn, Baby, Burn': Small Business in the Urban Riots of the 1960s." *The Independent Review* 5: 165–187.

Beck, Ulrich. 1992. *World Risk Society*. Malden, MA: Blackwell Publishers.

Behringer, Wolfgang, trans. Patrick Camiller. 2010. *A Cultural History of Climate*. Cambridge: Polity Press.

Beitz, Charles R. 2009. *The Idea of Human Rights*. Oxford: Oxford University Press.

Bell, Derek. 2013. "Does Anthropogenic Climate Change Violate Human Rights?" *Critical Review of International Social and Political Philosophy* 14(2): 99–124.

Benedick, Richard Elliot. 1991. *Ozone Diplomacy: New Directions in Safeguarding the Planet*. Cambridge, MA: Harvard University Press.

Bengtsson L. 2006. "Geo-Engineering to Confine Climate Change: Is It At All Feasible?" *Climatic Change* 77: 229–234.

Berg, Maxine, and Elizabeth Eger, eds. 2003. *Luxury in the Eighteenth Century: Debates, Desires and Delectable Goods*. Basingstoke: Palgrave.

Biagioli, Mario. 2002. "From Book Censorship to Academic Peer Review." *Emergences: Journal for the Study of Media & Composite Culture* 12(1): 11–45.

Bipartisan Policy Center, Task Force on Climate Remediation Research. 2011. "Geoengineering: A National Strategic Plan for Research on the Potential Effectiveness, Feasibility, and Consequences of Climate Remediation Technologies."

Bodansky, Daniel. 1993. "The U.N. Framework Convention on Climate Change: A Commentary." *Yale Journal of International Law* 18: 451–558.

Bodansky, Daniel. 2001. "The History of the Global Climate Change Regime." In Urs Luterbacher, Detlef F. Sprinz, eds., *International Relations and Global Climate Change*. Cambridge, MA: MIT Press: 23–39.

Bodansky, Daniel. 2010. "The Copenhagen Climate Change Conference: A Post-Mortem." *American Journal of International Law* 104(2): 230–240.

Bolin, Bert. 2008. *A History of the Science and Politics of Climate Change: The Role of the Intergovernmental Panel on Climate Change*. Cambridge: Cambridge University Press.

Bolin, Bert, and Erik Eriksson. 1959. "Changes in the Carbon Dioxide Content of the Atmosphere and Sea Due to Fossil Fuel Combustion." In Bert Bolin, ed., *The Atmosphere and the Sea in Motion*. New York: Rockefeller Institute Press: 130–42.

Bolin, Bert, et al., eds. 1986. *The Greenhouse Effect, Climatic Change, and Ecosystems*. SCOPE Report No. 29. Chichester: John Wiley.

Boonin, David. 2003. *A Defense of Abortion*. Cambridge: Cambridge University Press.

Born, Max. 2004. *The Born - Einstein Letters: Friendship, Politics and Physics in Uncertain Times*. New York: Palgrave Macmillan.

Bovens, Luc. 2010. "A Lockean Defense of Grandfathering Emissions Rights." In Denis G. Arnold, ed., *Ethics and Climate Change*. Cambridge: Cambridge University Press: 124–144.

Bowen, Mark. 2005. *Thin Ice: Unlocking the Secrets of Climate in the World's Highest Mountains*. New York: Henry Holt and Company.

Bowen, Mark. 2007. *Censoring Science: Inside the Political Attack on Dr. James Hansen and the Truth of Global Warming*. New York: Dutton.

Brekke, Kjell Arne, and Olof Johansson-Stenman. 2009. "The Behavioural Economics of Climate Change." In Dieter Helm and Cameron Hepburn, eds., *The Economics and Politics of Climate Change*. Oxford: Oxford University Press: 107–125.

Broecker, Wallace S. 1975. "Climatic Change: Are We on the Brink of a Pronounced Global Warming?" *Science* 189(4201): 460–463.

Broecker, Wallace S. 2012. The Carbon Cycle and Climate Change: Memoirs of My 60 Years in Science. *Geochemical Perspectives* 1, 2: 221–340.

Broome, John. 1978. "Trying to Value a Life." *Journal of Public Economics* 88(352), 778–787.

Broome, John. 1991. *Weighing Goods: Equality, Uncertainty and Time*. Malden, MA: Blackwell.

Broome, John. 1994. "Discounting the Future." *Philosophy and Public Affairs* 23(2): 128–156.

Broome, John. 2012. *Climate Matters: Ethics in a Warming World*. New York: W. W. Norton and Company.

Brovkin, Victor, Vladimir Petoukhov, Martin Claussen, Eva Bauer, David Archer, Carlo Jaeger. 2009. "Geoengineering Climate by Stratospheric Sulfur Injections: Earth System Vulnerability to Technological Failure." *Climatic Change* 92: 243–259.

Bruce, J. P., H. Lee, and E. F. Haites, eds. *Climate Change 1995: Economic and Social Dimensions of Climate Change, Contribution of Working Group III to the Second Assessment Report of the Intergovernmental Panel on Climate Change*. Cambridge: Cambridge University Press.

Bryson, Reid A. April 1, 1967. "Is Man Changing the Climate of the Earth?" *Saturday Review*: 52–55.

Buchner, Barbara. 2001. *What Really Happened at the Hague*. Milan: Fondazione Eni Enrico Mattei, 2001.

Burnett, D. Graham. 2012. *The Sounding of the Whale: Science and Cetaceans in the Twentieth Century*. Chicago: University of Chicago Press.

Burnham, John C. 1990. "The Evolution of Editorial Peer Review." *Journal of the American Medical Association* 263(10): 1323–1329.

Cafaro, Philip. 2005. "Thoreau, Leopold, and Carson: Toward an Environmental Virtue Ethics." Reprint in Cafaro and Sandler 2005: 31–44.

Cafaro, Philip, and Ronald Sandler, eds. 2005. *Environmental Virtue Ethics*. Lanham, MD: Rowman and Littlefield Publishers.

Callendar, Guy S. 1938. "The Artificial Production of Carbon Dioxide and Its Influence on Temperature." *Quarterly Journal of Royal Meteorological Society* 64(275): 223–240.

Callicott, J. Baird. 1987. "Just the Facts, Ma'am." *The Environmental Professional* 9: 279–288.

Cameron, A. R., E. Green, M. Bakkenes, L. J. Beaumont, Y. C. Collingham, B. F. N. Erasmus, M. F. de Siqueira, A. Grainger, L. Hannah, L. Hughes, B. Huntley, A. S. van Jaarsveld, G. F. Midgley, L. Miles, M. A. Ortega-Huerta, A. T. Peterson, O. L. Phillips, and S. E. Williams. 2004. "Extinction Risk From Climate Change." *Nature* 427: 145–148.

Caney, S. 2005. *Justice Beyond Borders: A Global Political Theory*. Oxford: Oxford University Press.

Caney, Simon. 2009. "Human Rights, Responsibility, and Climate Change." In Charles R. Beitz and Robert E. Goodin, eds., *Global Basic Rights*. Oxford: Oxford University Press: 227–247.

Caney, Simon. 2010a. "Cosmopolitan Justice, Responsibility, and Global Climate Change." Reprinted in Stephen Gardner, Simon Caney, Dale Jamieson, Henry Shue, eds., *Climate Ethics: Essential Readings*. New York: Oxford University Press: 163–180.

Caney, Simon. 2010b. "Climate Change, Human Rights, and Moral Thresholds." In Stephen Humphreys, ed., 2010. *Human Rights and Climate Change*. Cambridge: Cambridge University Press: 69–90.

Caney, Simon. 2012. "Just Emissions." *Philosophy and Public Affairs* 40(4): 255–300.

Caro, Robert A. 1975. *The Power Broker: Robert Moses and the Fall of New York*. New York: Vintage Books.

Carson, Rachel. 1962. *Silent Spring*. Boston: Houghton Mifflin.

Cass, Loren R. 2006. *The Failures of American and European Climate Policy: International Norms, Domestic Politics, and Unachievable Commitments*. Albany: State University of New York Press.

Cerulo, Karen. 2006. *Never Saw It Coming: Cultural Challenges to Envisioning the Worst*. Chicago: University of Chicago Press.

Chakrabarty, Dipesh. 2009. "The Climate of History: Four Theses." *Critical Inquiry* 35(2): 199–222.

Chakravarty, Shoibal, Ananth Chikkatur, Heleen de Coninck, Stephen Pacala, Robert Socolow and Massimo Tavoni. 2009. "Sharing Global CO2 Emission Reductions among One Billion High Emitters." *Proceedings of the National Academy of Sciences* 106: 11885–11888.

Chichilnisky, Graciela. 1996. "An Axiomatic Approach to Sustainable Development." *Social Choice and Welfare* 13: 231–257.

Christianson, Gale E. 1999. *Greenhouse: The 200-Year Story of Global Warming*. Vancouver, CA: Greystone Books.

Clayton, Susan and Susan Opotow, eds. 2003. *Identity and the Natural Environment: The Psychological Significance of Nature*. Cambridge, MA: MIT Press.

Cline, William R. 1992. *The Economics of Global Warming*. Washington, DC: Peterson Institute.

Cole, Daniel H. 2008. "The Stern Review and Its Critics: Implications for the Theory and Practice of Benefit-Cost Analysis." *Natural Resources Journal* 48(1): 53–90.

Cook, John et al. 2013. "Quantifying the Consensus on Anthropogenic Global Warming in the Scientific Literature." *Environmental Research Letters* 8(2).

Collins, William J., and Robert A. Margo. 2007. "The Economic Aftermath of the 1960s Riots in American Cities: Evidence from Property Values." *The Journal of Economic History* 67: 849–883.

Commoner, Barry. 1971. *The Closing Circle: Nature, Man, and Technology.* New York: Knopf.

Converse et al. 1969. "Continuity and Change in American Politics: Parties and Issues in the 1968 Election." *American Political Science Review* 63(4): 1083–1105.

Costanza, Robert, Ralph D'Arge, Rudolf de Groot, Stephen Farberi, Monica Grasso, Bruce Hannon, Karin Limburg, Shahid Naeem, Robert V. O'Neill, Jose Paruelo, Robert G. Raskin, Paul Sutton, and Marjan van den Belt. 1997. "The Value of the World's Ecosystem Services and Natural Capital." *Nature* 387: 253–260.

Cowen, Tyler, and Derek Parfit. 1992. "Against the Social Discount Rate." In Peter Laslett and James S. Fishkin, eds., *Justice Between Age Groups and Generations.* New Haven: Yale University Press: 144–161.

Cripps, Elizabeth. 2013. *Climate Change and the Moral Agent: Individual Duties in an Interdependent World.* Oxford: Oxford University Press.

Crutzen, Paul J. 2002. "Geology of Mankind." *Nature* 415(6867): 23.

Crutzen, Paul J. 2006. "Albedo Enhancement by Stratospheric Sulfur Injections: A Contribution to Resolve a Policy Dilemma?" *Climatic Change* 77(3–4): 211–220.

Csutora, Maria. 2012. "One More Awareness Gap? The Behavior-Impact Gap Problem." *Journal of Consumer Policy* 35(1): 145–163.

D'Arge, R. C., and K. C. Kogiku. 1973. "Economic Growth and the Environment." *The Review of Economic Studies* 40(1): 61–77.

Dasgupta, Partha. 2007. "Comments on the Stern Review's Economics of Climate Change." *National Institute Economic Review* 199: 4–7.

Davis, M. 2001. *Late Victorian Holocausts: El Nino Famines and the Making of the Third World.* London: Verso.

DeCanio, Stephen J. 2003. *Economic Models of Climate Change.* New York: Palgrave Macmillan.

Denman, K. L., G. Brasseur, A. Chidthaisong, et al. 2007. "Couplings Between Changes in the Climate System and Biogeochemistry." In S. Solomon, D. Qin, M. Manning, et al., eds., *Climate Change 2007: The Physical Science Basis. Contribution of Working Group I to the Fourth Assessment Report of the Intergovernmental Panel on Climate Change.* Cambridge: Cambridge University Press.

Depledge, Joanna. 2006. "The Opposite of Learning: Ossification in the Climate Change Regime." *Global Environmental Politics* 6(1): 1–22.

de-Shalit, Avner. 1995. *Why Posterity Matters.* London: Routledge.

Desmond, Adrian, and James Moore. 2009. *Darwin's Sacred Cause: How a Hatred of Slavery Shaped Darwin's Views on Human Evolution.* Boston: Houghton Mifflin Harcourt.

Dessai, S. 2001. "Why Did The Hague Climate Conference Fail?" *Environmental Politics* 10(3): 139–144.

Dewey, John. 1910. "The Need for Training Thought?" Chapter 2 in *How We Think.* Lexington, MA: D.C. Heath.

Dickinson, J. L. 2009. "The People Paradox: Self-Esteem Striving, Immortality Ideologies, and Human Response to Climate Change." *Ecology and Society* 14(1): 34.

Dickson, David. 2000. "Deadlock in The Hague, But Hopes Remain for Spring Climate Deal." *Nature* 408: 503–504.

Dietz, S., C. Hepburn, and Nicholas Stern. 2009. "Economics, Ethics and Climate Change." *Arguments for a Better World: Essays in Honour of Amartya Sen* (Volume 2: *Society, Institutions and Development,* Kaushik Basu and Ravi Kanbur, eds.). Oxford: Oxford University Press.

Dimitrov, Radoslav S. 2010. "Inside Copenhagen: The State of Climate Governance." *Global Environmental Politics* 10(2): 18–24.

Dotto, Lydia, and Harold Schiff. 1978. *The Ozone War*. Garden City, NY: Doubleday.

Dow, Kirstin, and Thomas Downing. 2006. *The Atlas of Climate Change: Mapping the World's Greatest Challenge*. Berkeley: University of California Press.

Duarte, Carlos M., Timothy M. Lenton, Peter Wadhams, and Paul Wassmann. 2012. "Abrupt Climate Change in the Arctic." *Nature Climate Change* 2: 60–62.

Dunlap, Riley E, and Aaron M. MacCright. 2011. "Organized Climate Change Denial." In *Oxford Handbook of Climate Change and Society*. John Dryzek, Richard Norgaard, and David Schlosberg, eds. New York: Oxford University Press: 144–160.

Dworkin, Ronald. 1993. *Life's Dominion: An Argument about Abortion, Euthanasia, and Individual Freedom*. New York: Vintage Books.

Edwards, Paul N. 2010. *A Vast Machine: Computer Models, Climate Data, and the Politics of Global Warming*. Cambridge, MA: The MIT Press.

Elgin, Duane. 2010. *Voluntary Simplicity: Toward a Way of Life That Is Outwardly Simple, Inwardly Rich*. New York: Harper.

Elliot, R. 1997. *Faking Nature*. London: Routledge.

Epstein, Paul R., et al. 2011. "Full Cost Accounting for the Life Cycle of Coal." *Annals of the New York Academy of Science* 1219: 73–98.

Etzkowitz, Henry, and Loet Leydesdorff. 2000. "The Dynamics of Innovation: From National Systems and 'Mode 2' to a Triple Helix of University–Industry–Government Relations." *Research Policy* 29: 109–123.

Fagan, Brian. 2001. *The Little Ice Age: How Climate Made History 1300–1850*. New York: Basic Books.

Fan, S., et al. 1998. "A Large Terrestrial Carbon Sink in North America Implied by Atmospheric and Oceanic Carbon Dioxide Data and Models." *Science* 282(5388): 442–446.

Farber, Daniel. 2013. "Carbon Leakage Versus Policy Diffusion: The Perils and Promise of Subglobal Climate Action." *Chicago Journal of International Law* 13(2).

Feinberg, Joel. 1970. "Nature and Value of Rights." *Journal of Value Inquiry* 4: 243–257; reprinted in his *Rights, Justice, and the Bounds of Liberty* (Princeton: Princeton University Press, 1980).

Feinberg, Joel. 1984–1988. *The Moral Limits of the Criminal Law*, 4 volumes. New York: Oxford University Press.

Feinberg, M., and R. Willer. 2011. "Apocalypse Soon? Dire Messages Reduce Belief in Global Warming by Contradicting Just World Beliefs." *Psychological Science* 22: 34–38.

Feygina I. et al. 2010. "System Justification, the Denial of Global Warming, and the Possibility of 'System-Sanctioned Change.'" *Personality and Social Psychology Bulletin* 36: 326–338.

Fleming, James R. 1998. *Historical Perspectives on Climate Change*. Oxford: Oxford University Press.

Fleming, James. 2007. *The Callendar Effect: The Life and Work of Guy Stewart Callendar (1898-1964), The Scientist Who Established the Carbon Dioxide Theory of Climate Change* (Historical Monographs). Boston: American Meteorological Society.

Fleming, James. 2010. *Fixing the Sky*. New York: Columbia University Press.

Fleurbaey, Marc, and Stephanie Zuber. 2013. "Climate Policies Deserve a Negative Discount Rate." *Chicago Journal of International Law* 13(2): 565–595.

Foley, Duncan. 2009. "The Economic Fundamentals of Global Warming." In Jonathan M. Harris and Neva R. Goodwin, eds., *Twenty-First Century Macroeconomics: Responding to the Climate Challenge*. Edward Elgar Publishing: 115–126.

Foreman, Dave. 1991. *Confessions of an Eco-Warrior*. New York: Crown Publishing Group.

Foot, Philippa. 1972. "Morality as a System of Hypothetical Imperatives." *Philosophical Review* 81(3): 305–316.

Foot, Philippa. "Moral Arguments," reprinted in her collection of essays *Virtues and Vices*. Oxford: Basil Blackwell, 1978.

Freeman, Myrick. 2000. "Economics." In Dale Jamieson, ed., *A Companion to Environmental Philosophy*. Malden, MA: Blackwell.

Friedlingstein, P., R. A. Houghton, G. Marland, et al. 2010. "Update on CO_2 Emissions." *Nature Geoscience* 3: 811–812.

Friedman, Milton. 1966. *Essays in Positive Economics*. Chicago: University of Chicago Press.

Funtowicz, S. and J. Ravetz. 1993. "Science for the Post-Normal Age." *Futures* 25(7 September): 739–755.

Gardiner, Steve. 2011. "Is No One Responsible for Global Environmental Tragedy? Climate Change as a Challenge to Our Ethical Concepts." In Denis G. Arnold, ed., *The Ethics of Global Climate Change*. Cambridge: Cambridge University Press: 38–59.

Gardiner, Stephen et al., eds. 2010. *Climate Ethics: Essential Readings*. New York: Oxford University Press.

Gardiner, Steve. 2010. *A Perfect Moral Storm*. Oxford: Oxford University Press.

Gelbspan, Ross. 1998. *The Heat Is On*. Boston: Addison-Wesley.

Gibbons, Michael, et al. 1994. *The New Production of Knowledge: The Dynamics of Science and Research in Contemporary Societies*. Thousand Oaks, CA: Sage.

Gilbert, Daniel T. 1991. "How Mental Systems Believe." *American Pscyhologist* 46(2): 107–119.

Gladwell, Malcolm. 2000. *The Tipping Point: How Little Things Can Make a Big Difference*. Boston: Little, Brown and Company.

Glantz, M. H., J. Robinson, and M. E. Krenz. 1985. "Recent Assessments." In R.W. Kates et al., eds., *Climate Impact Assessment: Studies of Interaction of Climate and Society*. SCOPE 27, International Council of Scientific Unions. Chichester: Wiley: 565–598.

Glantz, M. H., ed. 1989. *Societal Responses to Regional Climate Change: Forecasting by Analogy*. Boulder: Westview Press.

Glantz, M. H., and D. Jamieson. 2000. "Societal Responses to Hurricane Mitch and Intra-Versus Intergenerational Equity Issues: Whose Norms Should Apply." *Risk Analysis* 20(6): 869–882.

Glover, J. 1975. "'It Makes No Difference Whether or Not I Do It.'" *Proceedings of the Aristotelian Society* Supplementary Volumes 49: 171–209.

Gonzalez, Patrick, et al. 2010. "Global Patterns in the Vulnerability of Ecosystems to Vegetation Shifts Due to Climate Change." *Global Ecology and Biogeography* 19(6): 755–768.

Goodell, Jeff. 2010. *How to Cool the Planet: Geoengineering and the Audacious Quest to Fix Earth's Climate*. Boston: Houghton Mifflin Harcourt.

Gordon, Bart. 2010. *Engineering the Climate: Research Needs and Strategies for International Coordination*. Committee on Science and Technology, US House of Representatives, One Hundred Eleventh Congress, Second Session.

Gore, Albert. 1992. *Earth in the Balance: Ecology and the Human Spirit*. Boston: Houghton Mifflin.

Graham, Carol. 2012. *Happiness Around the World: The Paradox of Happy Peasants and Miserable Millionaires*. Oxford: Oxford University Press.

Graves, Dan. 1996. *Scientists of Faith*. Grand Rapids, MI: Kregel Resources.

Griffin, James. 2008. *On Human Rights*. Oxford: Oxford University Press.

Grinsted, Aslak, John C. Moore, and Svetlana Jevrejeva. 2010. "Reconstructing Sea Level from Paleo and Projected Temperatures 200 to 2100AD." *Climate Dynamics* 34(4): 461–472.

Grubb, Michael, and Farhana Yamin. "Climatic Collapse at The Hague: What Happened, Why, and Where Do We Go from Here?" *International Affairs* 77(2): 261–276.

Halberstam, David. 1972. *The Best and the Brightest*. New York: Random House.

Hale, Ben. 2009. "Remediation and Respect: Do Remediation Technologies Alter Our Responsibility?" *Environmental Values* 18: 397–415.

Hale, Ben. 2011. "Nonrenewable Resources and the Inevitability of Outcomes." *The Monist* 94(3): 369–390.

Hale, B. 2012. "The World That Would Have Been: Moral Hazard Arguments Against Geoengineering." In Christopher Preston, ed. *Reflecting Sunlight: The Ethics of Solar Radiation Management*. Lanham, MD: Rowman and Littlefield: 113–131.

Hale, B., and Dilling L. 2011. "Carbon Sequestration, Ocean Fertilization, and the Problem of Permissible Pollution." *Science, Technology, and Human Values* 36(2): 190–212.

Hansen, James. 2010. *Storms of My Grandchildren: The Truth about the Coming Climate Catastrophe and Our Last Chance to Save Humanity*. New York: Bloomsbury.

Hare, Caspar. 2009. *On Myself, and Other, Less Important Subjects*. Princeton: Princeton University Press.

Harrison, Chris. 2004. "Peer Review, Politics and Pluralism." *Environmental Science & Policy* 7(5): 357–368.

Harrod, Roy. 1948. *Towards a Dynamic Economics: Some Recent Developments of Economic Theory and Their Application to Policy*. New York: Macmillan.

Harsanyi, John C. 1955. "Cardinal Welfare, Individualistic Ethics, and Interpersonal Comparisons of Utility." *Journal of Political Economy* 63(4): 309–321.

Harsanyi, John C. 1976. *Essays on Ethics, Social Behaviour and Scientific Explanation*. New York: Springer.

Hart, Herbert Lionel Adolphus, and Tony Honoré. 1985. *Causation in the Law*, 2nd ed. Oxford: Clarendon.

Haworth, Lawrence. 1955. "Common Sense Morality." *Ethics* 65(4): 250–260.

Hays, J. D., et al. 1976. "Variations in the Earth's Orbit: Pacemaker of the Ice Ages." *Science*. 194(4270): 1121–1132.

Heal, Geoffrey. 2007. "Discounting: A Review of the Basic Economics." *The University of Chicago Law Review* 74: 59–77.

Hegel, F. W., trans. T. M. Knox. 1952. *Hegel's Philosophy of Right*. Oxford: The Clarendon Press.

Heinzerling, Lisa, and Frank Ackerman. 2002. "Pricing the Priceless Cost-Benefit Analysis of Environmental Protection." Georgetown University Law and Policy Institute.

Hepburn, Cameron, Stephen Duncan, and Antonis Papachristodoulou. 2010. "Behavioural Economics, Hyperbolic Discounting and Environmental Policy." *Environmental and Resource Economics* 46(2): 189–206.

Herrick, Charles, and Dale Jamieson. 1995. "The Social Construction of Acid Rain." *Global Environmental Change* 5(2): 105–112.

Herrick, Charles, and Dale Jamieson. 2001. "Junk Science and Environmental Policy: Obscuring Public Debate with Misleading Discourse." *Philosophy and Public Policy Quarterly* 21(2/3): 11–17.

Heyd, Thomas, ed. 2005. *Recognizing the Autonomy of Nature: Theory and Practice*. New York: Columbia University Press.

Hill, Thomas, Jr. 1983. "Ideals of Human Excellence and Preserving the Natural Environment." *Environmental Ethics* 5(3): 211–224.

Hiller, Avram. 2011. "Climate Change and Individual Responsibility." *The Monist* 94(3): 349–368.

Hinde, Robert A. 2002. *Why Good Is Good: The Sources of Morality*. London: Routledge.

Hinshaw, R. E. 2006. *Living with Nature's Extremes: The Life of Gilbert Fowler White*. Boulder: Johnson Books.

Hoffert, M. I., K. Caldeira, A. K. Jain, et al. 1998. "Energy Implications of Future Stabilization of Atmospheric CO2 Content." *Nature*, Vol. 395: 881–884.

Hoffman, J. S., et al. 1983. "Projecting Future Sea Level Rise: Methodology, Estimates to the Year 2100, and Research Needs." Office of Policy and Resource Management, US EPA 230-09-007.

Hofstadter, Richard. 1963. *Anti-intellectualism in American Life*. New York: Knopf.

Hofstadter, Richard. 1965. *The Paranoid Style in American Politics, and Other Essays*. New York: Knopf.

Hoggan, James. 2009. *Climate Cover-Up*. Vancouver: Greystone Books.

Holdaway, R. N., and C. Jacomb. 2000. "Rapid Extinction of the Moas (Aves: Dinornithiformes): Model, Test, and Implications." *Science* 287(5461): 2250–2254.

Houghton, J. T., L. G. Meira Filho, B. A. Callander, et al., eds. 1996. *Climate Change 1995: The Science of Climate Change, Contribution of Working Group I to the Second Assessment Report of the Intergovernmental Panel on Climate Change*. Cambridge: Cambridge University Press.

Houghton, R. A. 1999. "The Annual Net Flux of Carbon to the Atmosphere from Changes in Land Use 1850–1990." *Tellus* B, 51: 298–313.

Houghton, R. A, G. R. van der Werf, R. S. DeFries, et al. 2012. "Chapter G2 Carbon emissions from land use and land-cover change." *Biogeosciences Discuss* 9: 835–878.

Hourdequin, Marion. 2010. "Climate, Collective Action and Individual Ethical Obligations." *Environmental Values* 19(4): 443–464.

House, K. Z., A. C. Baclig, M. Ranjan M, et al. 2012. "Economic and Energetic Analysis of Capturing CO_2 from Ambient Air." *Proceedings of the National Academy of Sciences* 108(51): 20428–20433.

Hulme, Mike. 2009. *Why We Disagree about Climate Change: Understanding Controversy, Inaction and Opportunity*. Cambridge: Cambridge University Press.

Humphrey, Hubert. 1962. "A Magna Carta for the Social and Behavioral Sciences." *American Behavioral Scientist* February 5(6):11–14.

Humphreys, Stephen, ed. 2010. *Human Rights and Climate Change*. Cambridge: Cambridge University Press.

Hunter, David, and James Salzman. 2007. "Negligence in the Air: The Duty of Care in Climate Change Litigation." *University of Pennsylvania Law Review* 155: 1741–1794.

Iliffe, John. 1987. *The African Poor: A History*. Cambridge: Cambridge University Press.

Jaeger, Jill. April 1988. "Developing Policies for Responding to Climatic Change: A Summary of the Discussions and Recommendations of the Workshops Held in Villach (28 September – 2 October 1987) and Bellagio (9–13 November 1987), under the Auspices of the Beijer Institute, Stockholm." WMO/TD-No. 225.

Jamieson, Dale. 1990. "Managing the Future: Public Policy, Scientific Uncertainty, and Global Warming," in D. Scherer, ed., *Upstream/Downstream: Essays in Environmental Ethics*. Philadelphia: Temple University Press: 67–89.

Jamieson, Dale. 1991. "The Epistemology of Climate Change: Some Morals for Managers." *Society & Natural Resources: An International Journal*. Special Issue: Global Climate Change: A Social Science Perspective 4(4): 319–329.

Jamieson, Dale. 1992. "Ethics, Public Policy, and Global Warming." *Science, Technology, & Human Values* 17(2): 139–153.

Jamieson, Dale. 1996a. "Scientific Uncertainty and the Political Process," *The Annals of the American Academy of Political and Social Sciences* 545 (May 1996): 35–43

Jamieson, Dale. 1996b. "Ethics and Intentional Climate Change." *Climatic Change* 33: 323–336.

Jamieson, Dale. 2001a. "Method and Moral Theory." In Singer P., ed. *A Companion to Ethics*. Malden, MA: Blackwell: 476–486.

Jamieson, Dale. 2001b. "Climate Change and Global Environmental Justice." In P. Edwards and C. Miller, eds., *Changing the Atmosphere: Expert Knowledge and Global Environmental Governance*. Cambridge, MA: The MIT Press: 287–307.

Jamieson, Dale. 2002. *Morality's Progress: Essays on Humans, Other Animals, and the Rest of Nature*. Oxford: Oxford University Press.

Jamieson, Dale. 2005a. "Duties to the Distant: Aid, Assistance, and Intervention in the Developing World." *The Journal of Ethics* 9: 151–170.

Jamieson, Dale. 2005b. "Adaptation, Mitigation, and Justice." In Walter Sinnott-Armstrong and Richard B. Howarth, eds., *Perspectives on Climate Change: Science, Economics, Politics, Ethics. Advances in the Economics of Environmental Resources*, Volume 5. Amsterdam: Elsevier: 217–248.

Jamieson, Dale. 2007a. "The Moral and Political Challenges of Climate Change." In S. Moser and L. Dilling, eds., *Creating a Climate for Change: Communicating Climate Change and Facilitating Social Change*. New York: Cambridge University Press: 475–482.

Jamieson, Dale. 2007b. "When Utilitarians Should Be Virtue Theorists." *Utilitas* 19(2): 160–183.

Jamieson, Dale. 2008. *Ethics and the Environment: An Introduction*. Cambridge: Cambridge University Press.

Jamieson, Dale. 2010a. "Ethics, Public Policy, and Global Warming." In Stephen Gardiner, Simon Caney, Dale Jamieson, Henry Shue, eds., *Climate Ethics: Essential Readings*. New York: Oxford University Press: 77–86.

Jamieson, Dale. 2010a. "Climate Change, Responsibility, and Justice." *Science and Engineering Ethics* 16(3): 431–45.

Jamieson, Dale. 2010b. "The Question of the Environment." In *Trattato di Biodiritto*, diretto da S. Rodota and P. Zatti, *Ambito e Fonti del Biodiritto*, a cura di S. Rodota and M. Tallacchini. Milano: Giuffre Editore: 37–50.

Jamieson, Dale. 2011. "Ethics, Energy, and the Transformation of Nature." In Denis G. Arnold, ed., *The Ethics of Global Climate Change*. Cambridge: Cambridge University Press: 16–37.

Jamieson, Dale. 2012. "Ethics, Public Policy, and Global Warming." In Allen Thompson and Jeremy Bendik-Keymer, eds., *Ethical Adaptation to Climate Change: Human Virtues of the Future*. Cambridge: The MIT Press: 187–202.

Jamieson, Dale. 2013a. "Jack, Jill, and Jane in a Perfect Moral Storm." *Philosophy and Public Issues* 2(2).

Jamieson, Dale, 2013b. "Some Whats, Whys and Worries of Geoengineering." *Climatic Change*.

Jamieson, Dale and Marcello Di Paolo. 2013. "Climate Change and Global Justice: New Problem, Old Paradigm?" *Global Policy*.

Jamieson, Dale, and Robert Elliot. 2009. "Progressive Consequentialism." *Philosophical Perspectives* 23(1): 241–251.

Jasanoff, Sheila. 1990. *The Fifth Branch: Science Advisors as Policymakers*. Cambridge, MA: Harvard University Press.

Jerolmack, Colin. 2008. "How Pigeons Became Rats: The Cultural-Spatial Logic of Problem Animals." *Social Problems* 55(1): 72–94.

Johnson, Baylor. 2003. "Ethical Obligations in a Tragedy of the Commons." *Environmental Values* 12(3): 271–287.

Joireman, J., et al. 2010. "Effect of Outdoor Temperature, Heat Primes and Anchoring on Belief in Global Warming." *Journal of Environmental Psychology* 30: 358–367.

Jordan, Andrew, and Tim Rayner. 2010. "The Evolution of Climate Policy in the European Union: A Historical Overview." In Jordan et al., eds. *Climate Change Policy in the European Union: Confronting the Dilemmas of Mitigation and Adaptation?* Cambridge: Cambridge University Press: 52–80.

Kagan, Shelly. 2011. "Do I Make a Difference?" *Philosophy and Public Affairs* 39(2): 105–141.

Kahan, Dan M., et al. 2012. "The Polarizing Impact of Science Literacy and Numeracy on Perceived Climate Change Risks." *Nature Climate Change* 2: 732–735.

Kahneman, Daniel. 2011. *Thinking Fast and Slow.* New York: Farrar, Straus and Giroux.

Kates, R. W. 2001. "Cautionary Tales: Adaptation and the Global Poor." *Climatic Change* 45: 5–17.

Kates, R. W. 2011. *Gilbert F. White, 1911–2006, A Biographical Memoir.* Washington, DC: The National Academies.

Katz, Eric. 1997. *Nature as Subject: Human Obligation and the Natural Community.* Oxford: Rowman & Littlefield.

Keith D., E. Parson, and M. Morgan. 2010. "Research on Global Sun Block Needed Now." *Nature* 463: 426–427.

Kelemen, R.D., and D. Vogel. 2010. "Trading Places: The Role of the United States and the European Union in International Environmental Politics." *Comparative Political Studies* 43(4): 427–456.

Keller, Evelyn Fox. 2011. "Stick to Your Guns." *New Scientist* 8: 22–23.

Kelly, P., and W. N. Adger, 1999: "Assessing Vulnerability to Climate Change and Facilitating Adaptation." Working Paper GEC 99–07, Centre for Social and Economic Research on the Global Environment, University of East Anglia, Norwich, UK.

Kincer, Joseph B. 1933. "Is Our Climate Changing? A Study of Long-Time Temperature Trends." *Monthly Weather Review* 61: 251–259.

Kintisch, Eli. 2010. *Hack the Planet: Science's Best Hope—or Worst Nightmare—for Averting Climate Catastrophe.* Hoboken, NJ: John Wiley and Sons.

Klinenberg, Eric. 2002. *Heat Wave: A Social Autopsy of Disaster in Chicago.* Chicago: University of Chicago Press.

Knill, Christoph, and Duncan Liefferink. 2007. *Environmental Politics in the European Union Policy-Making, Implementation and Patterns of Multi-Level Governance Issues in Environmental Politics.* Manchester, UK: Manchester University Press.

Knobe, Joshua. 2003. "Intentional Action in Folk Psychology: An Experimental Investigation." *Philosophical Psychology* 16: 309–324.

Krutilla, John. 1967. "Conservation Reconsidered." *The American Economic Review* 57(4): 777–786.

Kuhn, Thomas S. 2012. *The Structure of Scientific Revolutions,* fiftieth anniversary edition. Chicago: University of Chicago Press.

Kumar, Satish. 2000. *No Destination: An Autobiography.* Cambridge: UIT Cambridge Ltd.

Kuper, A. 2000. "Rawlsian Global Justice: Beyond the Law of Peoples to a Cosmopolitan Law of Persons." *Political Theory* 28(5): 640–674.

Kurzban, Robert. 2011. *Why Everyone (Else) Is a Hypocrite: Evolution and the Modular Mind.* Princeton, NJ: Princeton University Press.

Kysar, Douglas A. 2007. "Discounting on Stilts." *The University of Chicago Law Review* 74(1): 165–187.

Kysar, Douglas A. 2010. *Regulating from Nowhere: Environmental Law and the Search for Objectivity.* New Haven: Yale University Press.

Kysar, Douglas. 2011. "What Climate Change Can Do About Tort Law." *Environmental Law* 41: 1–71.

Lacey, Robert, and Danny Danziger. 1999. *The Year 1000: What Life Was Like at the Turn of the First Millennium, An Englishman's World*. London: Little Brown and Company.

Lackner, K. S., S. Brennan, J. M. Matter, et al. 2012. "The Urgency of the Development of CO_2 Capture from Ambient Air." *Proceedings of the National Academy of Sciences* 109(33): 13156–13162.

Lahsen, Myanna. 1999. "The Detection and Attribution of Conspiracies: The Controversy Over Chapter 8." In George E. Marcus, ed., *Paranoia Within Reason: A Casebook on Conspiracy as Explanation*. Chicago: University of Chicago Press: 111–136.

Lahsen, Myanna. 2005. "Technocracy, Democracy and U.S. Climate Science Politics: The Need for Demarcations." *Science, Technology, and Human Values* 30(1): 137–169.

Lahsen, Myanna. 2008. "Experiences of Modernity in the Greenhouse: A Cultural Analysis of a Physicist 'Trio' Supporting the Conservative Backlash Against Global Warming." *Global Environmental Change* 18(1): 205–219.

Lahsen, Myanna. 2013. "Climategate: The Role of the Social Sciences." *Climatic Change* 119 (3–4): 547–558.

Lamont, Michele. 2009. *How Professors Think: Inside the Curious World of Academic Judgment*. Cambridge, MA: Harvard University Press.

Lanchester, John. 2007. "Warmer, Warmer." *London Review of Books* 29(6): 3–9.

Lane, Robert E. 2001. *The Loss of Happiness in Market Democracies*. New Haven: Yale University Press.

Layard, Richard. 2005. *Happiness: Lessons from a New Science*. New York: The Penguin Press.

Lear, Jonathan. 2006. *Radical Hope: Ethics in the Face of Cultural Devastation*. Cambridge MA: Harvard University Press.

Lee, Katie. 2006. *Glen Canyon Betrayed: A Sensuous Elegy*. Flagstaff, AZ: Fretwater Press.

Leggett, Jeremy. 2001. *Carbon War: Global Warming and the End of the Oil Era*. New York: Routledge.

Leiserowitz, A., Maibach, E., Roser-Renouf, C., Smith, N., and Dawson, E. 2013. "Climategate, public opinion, and the loss of trust." *American Behavioral Scientist* 57(6): 818–837.

Leitenberg, M. 2006. *Death in Wars and Conflicts in the 20th Century*. 3rd ed. Ithaca, NY: Cornell University, Peace Studies Program.

Lenman, James. 2000. "Consequentialism and Cluelessness." *Philosophy & Public Affairs* 29(4): 342–370.

Lewis, John M. 1993. "Meteorologists from the University of Tokyo: Their Exodus to the United States Following World War II." *Bulletin of the American Meteorological Society* 74(7): 1351–1360.

Lewis, John M. 2008. "Smagorinsky's GFDL: Building the Team." *Bulletin of the American Meteorological Society* 89(9): 1339–1353.

Lichtenberg, Judith. 2009. "Are There Any Basic Rights?" In Charles R. Beitz and Robert E. Goodin., eds., *Global Basic Rights*. Oxford: Oxford University Press: 71–91.

Lomborg, Bjorn. 2001. *The Skeptical Environmentalist: Measuring the Real State of the World*. Cambridge: Cambridge University Press.

Long, M., and A. Iles. 1997. "Assessing Climate Change Impacts: Co-Evolution of Knowledge, Communities, and Methodologies." Kennedy School of Government, Harvard University ENRP Discussion Paper E-97–09.

Lorenz, Edward N. 1963. "The Predictability of Hydrodynamic Flow." *Transactions of the New York Academy of Sciences*, Series II, 25(4): 409–432.

Lorenz, Edward N. 1968. "Climatic Determinism." *Meteorological Monographs* 8: 1–3.

Lorenz, Edward N. 1969. "The Predictability of a Flow which Possesses Many Scales of Motion." *Tellus* 21(3): 289–307.

Lovett, Francis. 2001. "Domination: A Preliminary Analysis." *Monist* 84(1).

Lovett, B.J., and A. H. Jordan. 2010. "Levels of Moralisation: A New Conception of Moral Sensitivity." *Journal of Moral Education* 39(2): 175–189.

Lyons, David. 1965. *The Forms and Limits of Utilitarianism*. Oxford: Oxford University Press.

MacDonald, Gordon J. 1982. The *Long-Term Impacts of Increasing Atmospheric Carbon Dioxide Levels*. Cambridge: Ballinger.

MacKenzie, Donald. 1990. *Inventing Accuracy: A Historical Sociology of Nuclear Missile Guidance*. Cambridge: The MIT Press.

Maibach, Edward, et al. 2011. "'Climategate' Undermined Belief in Global Warming Among Many American TV Meteorologists." *Bulletin of the American Meteorological Society* 92: 31–37.

Manabe, Syukuro, and Kirk Bryan. 1969. "Climate Calculations with a Combined Ocean-Atmosphere Model." *Journal of Atmospheric Sciences* 26: 786–789.

Manabe, Syukuro, and Richard T. Wetherald. 1967. "Thermal Equilibrium of the Atmosphere with a Given Distribution of Relative Humidity." *Journal of Atmospheric Sciences* 24: 241–259.

Mann, Michael. 2012. *The Hockey Stick and the Climate Wars*. New York: Columbia University Press.

Marglin, S. A. 1963. "The Social Rate of Discount and the Optimal Rate of Investment." *Quarterly Journal of Economics* 77: 95–111.

Markowitz, Ezra M. 2012. "Is Climate Change an Ethical Issue? Examining Young Adults' Beliefs about Climate and Morality." *Climatic Change* 114(3–4): 479–495.

Markowitz, Ezra, and Azim Shariff. 2012. "Climate Change and Moral Judgement." *Nature Climate Change* 2: 243–247.

Mas Bermejo, P. 2006. "Preparation and Response in Case of Natural Disasters: Cuban Programs and Experience." *Journal of Public Health Policy* 27: 13–21.

Matthews, Jessica Tuchman. 1987. "Global Climate Change: Toward a Greenhouse Policy." *Issues in Science and Technology* 3: 57–68.

McCright, Aaron M., and Riley E. Dunlap. 2011a. "From Polarization on Global Warming." *The Sociological Quarterly* 52:155–194.·

McCright, Aaron, and Riley E. Dunlap. 2011b. "Cool Dudes: The Denial of Climate Change Among Conservative White Males in the United States." *Global Environmental Change* 21: 1163–1172.

McGinnis, Joe. 1969. *The Selling of the President*. New York: Trident Press.

McKibben, Bill. 1989. *The End of Nature*. New York: Random House.

McKinnon, Catriona. 2012. *Climate Change and Future Justice*. New York: Routledge.

Mendelsohn, Robert. 2011. "Economic Estimates of the Damages Caused by Climate Change." In John S. Dryzek, Richard B. Norgaard, and David Scholsberg, eds., *The Oxford Handbook of Climate Change and Society*. Oxford: Oxford University Press: 177–189.

Merchant, Carolyn. 1994. *Ecology: Key Concepts in Critical Theory*. Amherst, NY: Humanity Books.

Merton, Robert K. 1968. "The Matthew Effect in Science." *Science* 159(3810): 56–63.

Metz, B., O. R. Davidson, P. R. Bosch, R. Dave, and L. A. Meyer, eds. 2007. *Contribution of Working Group III to the Fourth Assessment Report of the Intergovernmental Panel on Climate Change, 2007*. Cambridge: Cambridge University Press.

Migeotte, M. V. 1948. "Methane in Earth's Atmosphere." *Journal of Astrophysics* 107: 400–403.

Mikhail, John. 2011. *Elements of Moral Cognition: Rawls' Linguistic Analogy and the Cognitive Science of Moral and Legal Judgment*. New York: Cambridge University Press.

Mill, John Stuart. 1859. *On Liberty.* Oxford: Oxford University Press.

Miller, Jon D. 2010. "The Conceptualization and Measurement of Civic Scientific Literacy for the Twenty-First Century." In Jerrold Meinwald and John G. Hildebrand, eds., *Science and the Educated American: A Core Component of Liberal Education.* Cambridge: American Academy of Arts and Sciences.

Monbiot, George. 2006. *Heat.* London: Allen Lane.

Munk, Walter H. 1997. "Tribute to Roger Revelle and His Contribution to Studies of Carbon Dioxide and Climate Change." *Proceedings of the National Academy of Sciences* 94(16): 8275–8279.

Nagel, Thoman. 1991. "Death." Reprinted in *Mortal Questions.* Cambridge: Cambridge University Press: 1–10.

Nash, Roderick 2001. *Wilderness and the American Mind*, fourth edition. New Haven: Yale University Press.

National Academy of Sciences, Carbon Dioxide Assessment Committee. 1983. *Changing Climate.* Washington, DC: National Academy of Sciences.

National Academy of Sciences. 2002. *Abrupt Climate Change: Inevitable Surprises.* Washington, DC: National Academy Press.

National Research Council. 2011. *America's Climate Choices, Advancing the Science of Climate Change.* Washington, DC: The National Academies Press.

Nefsky, Julia. 2012. "Consequentialism and the Problem of Collective Harm: A Reply to Kagan." *Philosophy and Public Affairs* 39(4): 363–395.

Neumann J. 1985. "Climatic Change as a Topic in the Classical Greek and Roman Literature." *Climatic Change* 7(4): 441–454.

Neumayer, Eric. 2007. "A Missed Opportunity: The Stern Review on Climate Change Fails to Tackle the Issue of Non-Substitutable Loss of Natural Capital." *Global Environmental Change* 17 (3/4): 297–301.

Nierenberg, Nicolas, et al. 2010. "Early Climate Change Consensus at the National Academy: the Origins and Making of Changing Climate." *Historical Studies in the Natural Sciences* 40(3): 318–349.

Nolt, John. 2011a. "How Harmful Are the Average American's Greenhouse Gas Emissions?" *Ethics, Policy and Environment* 14(1): 3–10.

Nolt, John. 2011b. "Greenhouse Gas Emission and the Domination of Posterity." In Denis Arnold, ed., *The Ethics of Global Climate Change.* Cambridge: Cambridge University Press: 60–76.

Nordhaus, W. 1992. "An Optimal Transition Path for Controlling Greenhouse Gases." *Science* 258: 1315–1319.

Nordhaus, William R. 1994a. *Managing the Global Commons: The Economics of Climate Change.* Cambridge, MA: The MIT Press.

Nordhaus, William R. 1994b. "Expert Opinion on Climate Change." *American Scientist* 82(1): 45–51.

Nordhaus, William D. 2007. "A Review of the Stern Review on the Economics of Climate Change." *Journal of Economic Literature* 45(3): 686–702.

Nordhaus, William, 2008. *A Question of Balance: Weighing the Options on Global Warming Policies.* New Haven: Yale University Press.

Nordhaus, William. 2010. "Economic Aspects of Global Warming in a Post-Copenhagen Environment." *Proceedings of the National Academy of Sciences* 107(26): 11721–11726.

Norgaard, Kari. 2011. "The Psychology and Sociology of Denial." In John Dryzek, Richard Norgaard, and David Schlosberg, eds., *Oxford Handbook of Climate Change and Society.* New York: Oxford University Press: 399–413.

Norton, Bryan. 1991. *Toward Unity Among Environmentalists.* New York: Oxford University Press.

Nowak, Martin, and Roger Highfield. 2011. *SuperCooperators: Why We Need Each Other to Succeed*. New York: Simon & Schuster.

Nowotny, Helga. 2001. *Re-Thinking Science: Knowledge in an Age of Uncertainty*. Cambridge UK: Polity.

Nozick, R. 1974. *Anarchy, State, and Utopia*. New York: Basic Books.

Nussbaum, Martha. 2011. *Creating Capabilities: The Human Development Approach*. Cambridge, MA: Harvard University Press.

Nuzzo, Regina. 2005. "Profile of Stephen H. Schneider." *Proceedings of the National Academy of Sciences* 102(44): 15725–15727.

Oberthür, Sebastian, and Marc Pallemaerts. 2010. "The EU's Internal and External Climate Policies: An Historical Overview." In Sebastian Oberthür and Marc Pallemaerts, eds., *The New Climate Policies of the European Union: Internal Legislation and Climate Diplomacy*. Brussels: VUB Press: 27–63.

Okonski, Kendra, ed. 2003. *Adapt or Die: The Science, Politics and Economics of Climate Change*. London: Profile Books Ltd.

O'Neill, John. 2008. "Happiness and the Good Life." *Environmental Values* 17(2): 125–144.

O'Neill, John, Alan Holland, and Andrew Light. 2007. *Environmental Values*. New York: Routledge.

Oppenheimer, Michael. 1989. "Climate Change and Environmental Pollution: Physical and Biological Interactions." *Climatic Change* 15(1–2): 255–270.

Oppenheimer, M. 2005. "Defining Dangerous Anthropogenic Interference: The Role of Science, the Limits of Science." *Risk Analysis* 25(6): 1399–1407.

Oreskes, Naomi, et al. 2008. "From Chicken Little to Dr. Pangloss: William Nierenberg, Global Warming, and the Social Deconstruction of Scientific Knowledge." *Historical Studies in the Natural Sciences* 38(1): 109–152.

Oreskes, Naomi, et al. 2010. "Adaptation to Global Warming: Do Climate Models Tell Us What We Need to Know?" *Philosophy of Science* 77(5): 1012–1028.

Oreskes, Naomi, and Erik M. M. Conway. 2010. *Merchants of Doubt: How a Handful of Scientists Obscured the Truth on Issues from Tobacco Smoke to Global Warming*. New York: Bloomsbury Press.

Overpeck, Jonathan T., and Julia E. Cole. 2006. "Abrupt Change in Earth's Climate System." *Annual Review of Environment and Resources* 31: 1–31.

Pacala, S., and Socolow R. 2004. "Stabilization Wedges: Solving the Climate Problem for the Next 50 Years with Current Technologies." *Science* 305(5686): 968–972.

Packard, Vance. 2007. *The Hidden Persuaders*. Brooklyn NY: Ig Publishing.

Page, Edward, 2006. *Climate Change, Justice and Future Generations*. Cheltenham, UK: Edward Elgar.

Palmer, Geoffrey. 1992. "Earth Summit: What Went Wrong at Rio." *Washington University Law Quarterly* 70(4): 106.

Parfit, Derek. 1984. *Reasons and Persons*. Oxford: Oxford University Press.

Parfit, Derek. 1997. "Equality and Priority." *Ratio* 10(3): 202–221.

Parkinson, Claire. 2010. *Coming Climate Crisis? Consider the Past, Beware the Big Fix*. Lanham, MD: Rowman and Littlefield.

Parmesan, Camille, and Gary Yohe. 2003. "A Globally Coherent Fingerprint of Climate Change Impacts Across Natural Systems." *Nature* 421(6918): 37–42.

Parry, M. L., O. F. Canziani, J. P. Palutikof, P. J. van der Linden, and C. E. Hanson, eds. 2007. *Climate Change 2007: Impacts, Adaptation and Vulnerability. Contribution of Working Group II to the Fourth Assessment Report of the Intergovernmental Panel on Climate Change*. Cambridge: Cambridge University Press.

Parry, Martin, Nigel Arnell, Mike Hulme, Robert Nicholls, and Matthew Livermore. 1998. "Adapting to the Inevitable." *Nature* 395: 741.

Parson, Edward. 2004. *Protecting the Ozone Layer: Science and Strategy*. New York: Oxford University Press.

Parson, Edward A., and David W. Keith. 2013. "End the Deadlock on Governance of Geoengineering Research." *Science* 339(6125): 1278–1279.

Passmore, John. 1974. *Man's Responsibility for Nature*. London: Duckworth.

Patz, Jonathan A., Holly K. Gibbs, Jonathan A. Foley, Jamesine V. Rogers, and Kirk R. Smith. 2007. "Climate Change and Global Health: Quantifying a Growing Ethical Crisis." *Ecohealth* 4(4): 397–405.

Pearce, Fred. 2010. *The Climate Files*. London: Guardian Books.

Peters, Glen P., Jan C. Minx. Christopher L. Weber, and Ottmar Edenhofer. 2011. "Growth in Emission Transfers via International Trade from 1990 to 2008." *Proceedings of the National Academy of Sciences* 108: 8903–8908.

Peters-Stanley, M., K. Hamilton, T. Marcello, and M. Sjardin. 2011. "Back to the Future State of the Voluntary Carbon Markets 2011, A Report by Ecosystem Marketplace & Bloomberg New Energy Finance." Washington, DC, and New York.

Peterson, T. C., et al. 2008. "The Myth of the 1970s Global Cooling Scientific Consensus." *Bulletin of the American Meteorological Society* 89(9): 1325–1337.

Pielke, Jr., Roger, and Roger Pielke, Sr. 1997. *Hurricanes: Their Nature and Impacts on Society*. Oxford: John Wiley and Sons.

Pielke, Jr., Roger. 1998. "Rethinking the Role of Adaptation in Climate Policy." *Global Environmental Change* 8: 159–170.

Pielke, Jr., Roger. 2000a. "Policy History of the U.S. Global Change Research Program: Part I. Administrative Development." *Global Environmental Change* 10: 9–25.

Pielke Jr., Roger. 2000b. "Policy History of the U.S. Global Change Research Program: Part II. Legislative Process." *Global Environmental Change* 10: 133–144.

Pielke, Jr., Roger A. 2005. "Misdefining 'Climate Change': Consequences for Science and Action." *Environmental Science & Policy* 8: 548–561.

Pielke Jr., Roger. 2007. *The Honest Broker: Making Sense of Science in Policy and Politics* Cambridge: Cambridge University Press.

Pielke Jr., Roger. 2010. *The Climate Fix: What Scientists and Politicians Won't Tell you About Global Warming*. New York: Basic Books

Pielke Jr., Roger, G. Prins, S. Rayner, and D. Sarewitz. 2007. "Lifting the Taboo on Adaptation." *Nature* 445: 597–598.

Plass, Gilbert N. 1956a. "Carbon Dioxide and the Climate." *American Scientist* 44: 302–316.

Plass, Gilbert N. 1956b, "Effect of Carbon Dioxide Variations on Climate." *American Journal of Physics* 24: 376–387.

Pogge, Thomas. 2002. *World Poverty and Human Rights*. Cambridge: Polity.

Ponte, Lowell. 1976. *The Cooling: Has the Next Ice Age Already Begun? Can We Survive It?* Englewood Cliffs, NJ: Prentice-Hall.

Posner, Richard A. 2005. *Catastrophe: Risk and Response*. Oxford: Oxford University Press.

Postman, Neil. 1985. *Amusing Ourselves to Death*. New York: Penguin Books.

Preston, C. 2012. "Ethics and Geoengineering: Reviewing the Moral Issues Raised by Solar Radiation Management and Carbon Dioxide Removal." WIREs Climate Change. DOI: 10.1002/WCC.198; available at http://wires.wiley.com/WileyCDA/WiresArticle/wisId-WCC198.html.

Quiggin, John. 2008. "Stern and His Critics on Discounting and Climate Change: An Editorial Essay." *Climate Change* 89(3–4): 195–205.

Ramanathan, V., and G. Carmichael. 2008. "Global and Regional Climate Changes Due to Black Carbon." *Nature Geoscience* 1: 221–227.

Ramsey, Frank. 1928. "A Mathematical Theory of Saving." *Economic Journal* 38: 543–549, reprinted in his *Foundations: Essays in Philosophy, Logic, Mathematics and Economics*, edited by D. H. Mellor. London: Routledge and Kegan Paul, 1978: 261–281.

Randall, David A., ed. 2000. *General Circulation Model Development: Past, Present, and Future*. San Diego: Academic Press.

Rapp, Geoffrey Christopher. 2008. "The Wreckage of Recklessness." *Washington University Law Review* 86(1): 111–180.

Rasool, S. I., and H. I. Schneider. 1971. "Atmospheric Carbon Dioxide and Aerosols: Effects of Large Increases on Global Climate." *Science* 173: 138–141.

Rawls, John. 1971. *A Theory of Justice*. Cambridge, MA: Harvard University Press.

Rawls, John. 2005. *Political Liberalism: Expanded Edition*. New York: Columbia University Press.

Rayner, Steve, and E. Malone. 1997. "Zen and the Art of Climate Maintenance." *Nature* 390: 332–334.

Read, Daniel. 2001. "Is Time-Discounting Hyperbolic or Subadditive?" *Journal of Risk and Uncertainty* 23(1): 5–32.

Reilly, John, and David Schimmelpfennig. 2000. "Irreversibility, Uncertainty, and Learning: Portraits of Adaptation to Long-Term Climate Change." *Climatic Change* 45: 253–278.

Reitze, Arnold W. 1999. "The Legislative History of U.S. Air Pollution Control." *Houston Law Review* 36: 679–741.

Rennie, Drummon. 1986. "Guarding the Guardians: A Conference on Editorial Peer Review," *JAMA* 256(17): 2391–2392.

Repetto, Robert, and Duncan Austin. 1997. *Costs of Climate Protection: A Guide for the Perplexed*. Washington, DC: World Resources Institute, Climate Protection Initiative.

Revelle, Roger. 1978. "The Purpose of Pugwash: Past and Future." *Bulletin of the American Academy of Arts and Sciences* 31(5): 4–8.

Revelle, Roger, and Hans E. Suess. 1957. "Carbon Dioxide Exchange Between Atmosphere and Ocean and the Question of an Increase of Atmospheric CO_2 During the Past Decades." *Tellus* 9: 18–27.

Revesz, Richard L., and Matthew R. Shahabian. 2011. "Climate Change and Future Generations." *Southern California Law Review* 84(5): 1097–1180.

Rignot E., I. Velicogna, M. R. van den Broeke, A. Monaghan, and J. Lenaerts. 2011. "Acceleration of the Contribution of the Greenland and Antarctic Ice Sheets to Sea Level Rise." *Geophysical Research Letters* 38 (5).

Roberts, J. Timmons, and Bradley C. Parks. 2007. *A Climate of Injustice: Global Inequalitiy, North-South Politics, and Climate Policy*. Cambridge MA: The MIT Press.

Roan, Sharon. 1990. *Ozone Crisis: The 15-Year Evolution of a Sudden Global Emergency*. New York: Wiley.

Robock, A., L. Oman, and G. L. Stenchikov. 2008. "Regional climate responses to geoengineering with tropical and Arctic SO2 injections." *Journal of Geophysical Research* 113, D16101, doi:10.1029/2008JD010050.

Rogelj, Joeri, Hare William, Lowe Jason, van Vuuren Detlef P., Riahi Keywan, Matthews Ben, Hanaoka Tatsuya, Jiang Kejun, and Meinshausen Malte. 2011. "Emission Pathways Consistent with a 2°C Global Temperature Limit." *Nature Climate Change* 1(8): 413–418.

Rozin, Paul. 1999. "The Process of Moralization." *Psychological Science* 10(3): 218–221.

Rozin, Paul, Maureen Markwith, and Caryn Stoess. 1997. "Moralization and Becoming a Vegetarian: The Transformation of Preferences into Values and the Recruitment of Disgust." *Psychological Science* 8(2): 67–73.

Ruddiman, William. 2005. *Plows, Plagues and Petroleum: How Humans Took Control of Climate*. Princeton: Princeton University Press.

Running, Steven W. 2012. "A Measurable Planetary Boundary for the Biosphere." *Science* 337(6101): 1458–1459.

Sælen, Håkon, et al. 2009. "Siblings, Not Triplets: Social Preferences for Risk, Inequality and Time in Discounting Climate Change." *Economics: The Open-Access, Open-Assessment E-Journal* 3(2009-26). http://dx.doi.org/10.5018/economics-ejournal.ja.2009-26.

Sagoff, Mark. 1988/2008. *The Economy of the Earth: Philosophy, Law, and the Environment*. Cambridge: Cambridge University Press.

Sagoff, Mark. 1991. "Nature Versus the Environment," *Report from the Institute for Philosophy & Public Policy* 11(3): 5–8.

Sagoff, Mark. 2004. *Price, Principle, and the Environment*. Cambridge: Cambridge University Press.

Sandberg, Joakim. 2011. "'My Emissions Make No Difference': Climate Change and the Argument From Inconsequentialism." *Environmental Ethics* 33(3): 229–248.

Sandel, Michael. 2012. *What Money Can't Buy: The Moral Limits of Markets*. New York: Farrar, Straus and Giroux.

Sandler, Ronald L. 2007. *Character and Environment: A Virtue-Oriented Approach to Environmental Ethics*. New York: Columbia University Press.

Sandler, R. 2010. "Ethical Theory and the Problem of Inconsequentialism: Why Environmental Ethicists Should Be Virtue Oriented Ethicists." *Journal of Agricultural and Environmental Ethics* 23: 167–183.

Sarewitz, D. 2004. "How Science Makes Environmental Controversies Worse." *Environmental Science and Policy* 7: 385–403.

Sarewitz, D. and R. A. Pielke, Jr. 2000. "Breaking the Global Warming Gridlock." *The Atlantic Monthly* (July): 54–64.

Satz, Debra. 2010. *Why Some Things Should Not Be for Sale: The Moral Limits of Markets*. New York: Oxford University Press.

Scheffler, Samuel 2013. *Death and the Afterlife*, Niko Kolodny, ed. New York: Oxford University Press.

Schelling, Thomas. 1968. "The Life You Save May Be Your Own." In Samuel B. Chase, Jr., ed., *Problems in Public Expenditure Analysis*. Washington, DC: The Brookings Institution: 122–176.

Schelling, Thomas C. 1992. "Some Economics of Global Warming." *The American Economic Review* 82(1): 1–14.

Schelling, Thomas C. 1995. "Intergenerational Discounting." *Energy Policy* 23(4/5): 395–401.

Schelling, Thomas C. 1996. "The Economic Diplomacy of Geoengineering." *Climatic Change* 33(3): 303–307.

Schelling, Thomas C. 1997. "The Cost of Combating Global Warming: Facing the Tradeoffs." *Foreign Affairs* 76: 8–14.

Schimel, David, et al. 2000. "Contribution of Increasing CO_2 and Climate to Carbon Storage by Ecosystems in the United States." *Science* 287(5460): 2004–2006.

Schmidt, Gavin, and Joshua Wolfe. 2009. *Climate Change: Picturing the Science*. New York: W. W. Norton.

Schneider, Stephen H. 1989. *Global Warming: Are We Entering the Greenhouse Century?*, San Francisco: Sierra Club Books.

Schneider, Stephen H. 2009. *Science as a Contact Sport: Inside the Battle to Save Earth's Climate*. Washington, DC: National Geographic.

Schoenbrod, David, et al. 2010. *Breaking the Logjam: Environmental Protection That Will Work*. New Haven, CT: Yale University Press.

Schuldt, Jonathon P., et al. 2011. "'Global Warming' or 'Climate Change'?: Whether the Planet Is Warming Depends on Question Wording." *Public Opinion Quarterly* 75(1): 115–124.

Schwartz, M. W., J. J. Hellmann, J. M. McLachlan, D. F. Sax et al. 2012. "Managed Relocation: integrating the scientific, regulatory and ethical challenges." *Bioscience* 62: 732–743.

Scitovsky, Tibor. 1976. *The Joyless Economy: The Psychology of Human Satisfaction.* Oxford: Oxford University Press.

Searle, John. 1983. *Intentionality: An Essay in the Philosophy of Mind.* Cambridge: Cambridge University Press.

Seidel, Stephen, and Dale L. Keyes. 1983. "Can We Delay a Greenhouse Warming?: The Effectiveness and Feasibility of Options to Slow a Build-up of Carbon Dioxide in the Atmosphere." 2nd ed. (corr.) Strategic Studies Staff, Office of Policy Analysis, Office of Policy, Planning, and Evaluation.

Sen, Amartya 2002. "Justice across borders." In: P. de Greiff and C. Cronin, eds. *Global Politics and Transnational Justice.* Cambridge, MA: The MIT Press: 14–27.

Sen, Amartya. 2012. *The Idea of Justice.* Cambridge, MA: Harvard University Press.

Shellenberger, Michael, and Ted Nordhaus. 2007. *Break Through: From the Death of Environmentalism to the Politics of Possibility.* Boston: Houghton Mifflin.

Shepherd, J., K. Caldeira, P. Cox, et al. 2009. "Geoengineering the Climate: Science, Governance, and Uncertainty." *The Royal Society,* Policy Document 10/09.

Shue, Henry. 1988. "Mediating Duties." *Ethics* 98(4): 687–704.

Shue, Henry. 1993. "Subsistence Emissions and Luxury Emissions." *Law & Policy* 15(1): 39–60.

Shue, Henry. 1996. *Basic Rights.* 2nd ed. Princeton: Princeton University Press (first ed. 1980).

Shue, Henry. 2010. "Global Environment and International Inequality." In Stephen Gardiner, Simon Caney, Dale Jamieson, and Henry Shue, eds., *Climate Ethics: Essential Readings.* New York: Oxford University Press: 146–162.

Sidgwick, Henry. 1907. *The Methods of Ethics.* Cambridge: Hackett Publishing.

Simon, Steven L. et al. 2006. "Fallout from Nuclear Weapons Tests and Cancer Risks." *American Scientist* 94(1): 48–57.

Singer, Peter. 1972. "Famine, Affluence, and Morality." *Philosophy and Public Affairs* 1(3): 229–243.

Singer, Peter. 2002. *One World.* New Haven: Yale University Press.

Singer, Peter. 2009. *Animal Liberation.* New York: Harper Perennial Modern Classics.

Sinnott-Armstrong, Walter. 2005. "It's Not My Fault: Global Warming and Individual Moral Obligations." In Walter Sinnott-Armstrong and Richard B. Howarth, eds., *Perspectives on Climate Change: Science, Economics, Politics, Ethics Advances in the Economics of Environmental Research* 5: 293–315. Reprinted in Gardiner et al. 2010: 332–346.

Sinnott-Armstrong, Walter, ed. 2008. *Moral Psychology,* Volume 2, *The Cognitive Science of Morality: Intuition and Diversity.* Cambridge MA: The MIT Press.

Sitarz, Dan. 1993. *Agenda 21: The Earth Summit Strategy to Save Our Planet.* Hauppauge, NY: Nova Publishing.

Slaughter, Sheila, and Larry L. Leslie. 1999. *Academic Capitalism: Politics, Policies and the Entrepreneurial University.* Baltimore: Johns Hopkins University Press.

Slovic, Paul. 2007. "'If I Look at the Mass I Will Never Act': Psychic Numbing and Genocide." *Judgment and Decision Making* 2(2): 79–95.

Smit, Barry, Ian Burton, Richard Klein, and J. Wandel. 2000. "The Anatomy of Adaptation to Climate Change and Variability." *Climatic Change* 45: 223–251.

Smith, V. Kerry. 2010. "Reflections—Legacies, Incentives, and Advice." *Review of Environmental Economics and Policy* 4(2): 309–324.

Smithers, J., and Barry Smit. 1997. "Human Adaptation to Climatic Variability and Change." *Global Environmental Change* 7(2): 129–146.

Snow, C. P. 1960. *The Two Cultures.* Cambridge: Cambridge University Press.

Snyder, John. 1997. *Flattening the Earth: Two Thousand Years of Map Projections.* Chicago: University of Chicago Press.

Solomon, Susan, et al. 2009. "Irreversible Climate Change Due to Carbon Dioxide Emissions." *Proceedings of the National Academy of Sciences* (106): 1704–1709.

Solomon, Susan, et al. 2010. "Persistence of Climate Changes Due to a Range of Greenhouse Gases," *Proceedings of the National Academy of Sciences* 107(43): 18354–18359.

Spash, Clive L. 2002. *Greenhouse Economics: Value and Ethics.* London: Routledge.

Spash, Clive L. 2007. "The Economics of Climate Change Impacts à la Stern: Novel and Nuanced or Rhetorically Restricted?" *Ecological Economics* 63(4): 706–713.

Speth, Gustave. 2012. *America the Possible.* New Haven: Yale University Press.

Spier, Raymond. 2002. "The History of the Peer-Review Process." *Trends in Biotechnology* 20(8): 357–358.

Robert N. Stavins. 2008. "Addressing Climate Change with a Comprehensive US Cap-and-Trade System." *Oxford Review of Economic Policy* 24(2): 298–321.

Stavins, Robert N. 2011. "The Problem of the Commons: Still Unsettled after 100 Years." *American Economic Review* 101: 81–108.

Sterman, J. D. 2008. "Risk Communication on Climate: Mental Models and Mass Balance." *Science* 322: 53–533.

Stern Nicholas. 2007. *The Economics of Climate Change: The Stern Review.* Cambridge: Cambridge University Press.

Stern, Nicholas. 2010a. *A Blueprint for a Safer Planet.* London: Vintage.

Stern, Nicholas. 2010b. "The Economics of Climate Change." In Stephen Gardiner et al., eds. *Climate Ethics: Essential Readings.* New York: Oxford University Press: 39–76.

Stern, Nicholas. 2013. "The structure of economic modeling of the potential impacts of climate change: grafting gross underestimation of risk onto already narrow science models." *Journal of Economic Literature* 51(3): 838–859.

Stern, Nicholas. Forthcoming. "Ethics, Equity and the Economics of Climate Change." *Economics and Philosophy.*

Sterner, T., and U. M. Persson. 2008. "An Even Sterner Review: Introducing Relative Prices into the Discounting Debate." *Review of Environmental Economics and Policy* 2 (1): 61–76.

Stevensen, C. L. "Persuasive Definitions." *Mind* 47 (July 1938): 331–350.

Summers, Lawrence, and Richard Zeckhauser. 2008. "Policymaking for Posterity." *Journal of Risk and Uncertainty* 37(2):115–140.

Sunstein, Cass R. and David A. Weisbach. 2009. "Climate Change and Discounting the Future: A Guide for the Perplexed." *Yale Law and Policy Review* 27(2): 433.

Suomi, Verner E. 1979. In *Report of an Ad Hoc Study Group on Carbon Dioxide and Climate,* Woods Hole, Massachusetts, July 23–27, to the Climate Research Board, Assembly of Mathematical and Physical Sciences, National Research Council, Carbon Dioxide and Climate: A Scientific Assessment. Washington, DC: National Academy of Sciences Press.

Suzuki, David, and Amanda McConnell. 1997. *The Sacred Balance: Rediscovering Our Place in Nature.* Vancouver: Greystone Books.

Tannenwald, Julia. 2006. "Nuclear Weapons and the Vietnam War." *Journal of Strategic Studies* 29: 675–722.

Tasioulas, John. 2007. "The Moral Reality of Human Rights." In Thomas W. M. Pogge, ed., *Freedom from Poverty as a Human Right: Who Owes What to the Very Poor?* Oxford: Oxford University Press: 75–101.

Taylor, Paul. 1986/2011. *Respect for Nature: A Theory of Environmental Ethics.* Princeton: Princeton University Press.

Thomas, Chris D., et al. 2004. "Extinction Risk from Climate Change." *Nature* 427: 145–148.

Thomson, Judith Jarvis. 1971. "A Defense of Abortion." *Philosophy & Public Affairs* 1(1): 47–66.

Thompson, Allen. 2010. "Radical Hope for Living Well in a Warming World." *Journal of Agricultural and Environmental Ethics* 23(1): 43–59.

Thompson, Allen, and Jeremy Bendik-Keymer, eds. 2012. *Ethical Adaptation to Climate Change: Human Virtues of the Future.* Cambridge, MA: The MIT Press.

Thompson, D. W. J., and J. M. Wallace. 2001. "Regional Climate Impacts of the Northern Hemisphere Annular Mode." *Science* 293(5527): 85–89.

Thompson, Lonnie G. 2010. "Climate Change: The Evidence and Our Options." *The Behavior Analyst* 33(2): 153–170.

Tol, R. S. J. 2006. "The Stern Review of the Economics of Climate Change: A Comment." *Energy & Environment* 17(6): 977–981.

Torrance, Wendy. 2006. "Science or Salience: Building an Agenda for Climate Change." In Ronald B. Mitchell et al., eds., *Global Environmental Assessment: Information and Influence.* Cambridge: The MIT Press: 29–56.

Trenberth, K. E., and A. Dai. 2007. "Effects of Mount Pinatubo Volcanic Eruption on the Hydrological Cycle as an Analog of Geoengineering." *Geophysical Research Letters* 34: L15702.

Turner, Jack. 1996. *The Abstract Wild.* Tucson: University of Arizona Press.

Tyndall, John. 1863. "On Radiation through the Earth's Atmosphere." *Philosophical Magazine*, Series 4(25): 200–206.

UNEP. 2011. *Bridging the Emissions Gap.* Nairobi, Kenya: United Nations Environment Programme.

Vandenbergh, Michael, and Anne Steinemann. "The Carbon Neutral Individual." *New York University Law Review* 82: 1673–1745.

Velders, Guus J. M., et al. 2007. "The Importance of the Montreal Protocol in Protecting Climate." *Proceedings of the National Academy of Sciences* 104 (12): 4814–4819.

Victor, D., M. Morgan, J. Apt, J. Steinbruner, and K. Ricke. 2009. "The Geoengineering Option: A Last Resort Against Global Warming?" *Foreign Affairs* 88(2): 64–76.

Villar, Ana, and Jon A. Krosnick. 2011. "Global Warming vs. Climate Change, Taxes vs. Prices: Does Word Choice Matter?" *Climatic Change* 105: 1–12.

Vitousek, Peter M., Harold A. Mooney, Jane Lubchenco, and Jerry M. Melillo. 1997. "Human Domination of Earth's Ecosystems." *Science* 277(5325): 494–499.

Volk, Tyler. 2008. *Carbon Rising.* Cambridge MA: The MIT Press.

Von Neumann, John. 1955. "Can We Survive Technology?" *Fortune Magazine* 15: 106–108, 151–152.

Von Storch, Hans, and Nico Stehr. 2006. "Anthropogenic Climate Change: A Reason for Concern since the 18th Century and Earlier." *Geografiska Annaler: Series A, Physical Geography* 88(2): 107–113.

Wallace, John, and Peter Hobbs. 2006. *Atmospheric Sciences, An Introductory Survey.* 2nd ed. San Diego: Academic Press.

Watson, R. T., M. C. Zinyowera, and R. H. Moss, eds. 1996. *Climate Change 1995: Impacts, Adaptations and Mitigation of Climate Change: Scientific-Technical Analyses, Contribution* of *Working Group II to the Second Assessment Report of the Intergovernmental Panel on Climate Change*. Cambridge: Cambridge University Press.

Weart, Spencer R. 2008. *The Discovery of Global Warming: Revised and Expanded Edition* (New Histories of Science, Technology, and Medicine). Cambridge, MA: Harvard University Press.

Weber, Christopher, and H. Scott Matthews. 2007. "Embodied Emissions in U.S. International Trade: 1997–2004." *Environmental Science and Technology* 41(14): 4875–4881.

Weber, Christopher L., Glen P. Peters, Dabo Guan, and Klaus Hubacek. 2008. "The Contribution of Chinese Exports to Climate Change." *Energy Policy* 36(9): 3572–3577.

Weitzman, Martin L. 1998. "Why the Far-Distant Future Should Be Discounted at Its Lowest Possible Rate." *Journal of Environmental Economics and Management* 36(3): 201–208.

Weitzman, M. L. 2007. "A Review of the Stern Review on the Economics of Climate Change." *Journal of Economic Literature* 45(3): 703–724.

Weitzman, M. L., and Christian Gollier. 2010. "How Should the Distant Future Be Discounted When Discount Rates Are Uncertain?" *Economic Letters* 107(3): 350–353.

White, Theodore. 1961. *The Making of the President: 1960*. New York: Atheneum.

Wiggins, David. 2000. "Nature, Respect for Nature, and the Human Scale of Values," *Proceedings of the Aristotelian Society* 100(1): 1–32.

Williams, Bernard. 1985. *Ethics and the Limits of Philosophy*. Cambridge, MA: Harvard University Press.

Williams, Bernard. 2009. "The Human Prejudice." In Jeffrey A. Schaler, ed., *Peter Singer Under Fire: The Moral Iconoclast Faces His Critics*. Chicago: Open Court Publishing: 77–96.

Winks, Robin W. 1997. *Laurance S. Rockefeller: Catalyst for Conservation*. Washington, DC: Island Press.

Wood, Allan. 1998. "Kant on Duties Regarding Nonrational Nature." *Proceedings of the Aristotelian Society* Supplementary Volume 72(1): 189–210.

Woods, R. W. 1909. "Note on the Theory of the Greenhouse." *The London, Edinburgh and Dublin Philosophical Magazine and Journal of Science* 17: 319–320.

Woolner, David B., and Henry L. Henderson, eds. 2005. *FDR and the Environment*. New York: Palgrave Macmillan.

World Commission on Environment and Development. 1987. *Our Common Future*. New York: Oxford University Press.

Yang, C.-J., and M. Oppenheimer. 2007. "A 'Manhattan Project' for Climate Change?" *Climatic Change* 80: 199–204.

Yeager, Phil, and John Stark. "Mystery of the Warming World." *Washington Sunday Star*, 26 Jan. 1958, p. A26.

Young, E. J. et al. 2008. "Attributing Physical and Biological Impacts to Anthropogenic Climate Change." *Nature* 453: 353–357.

Young, Iris Marion. 2013. *Responsibility for Justice*. Chicago: University of Chicago Press.

Zalasiewicz, Jan, Mark Williams, Alan Smith, et al. 2008. "Are We Now Living in the Anthropocene?," *GSA Today*, http://www.geosociety.org/gsatoday/archive/18/2/.

Ziff, Paul. 2004. *Moralities: A Diachronic Evolutionary Approach*. Dordrecht, The Netherlands: Springer.

Ziman, John. 1995. *Of One Mind: The Collectivization of Science*. Melville, NY: American Institute of Physics.

Ziman, John. 2000. *Real Science. What It Is, and What It Means*. Cambridge: Cambridge University Press.

Zuckerman, Harriet, and Robert Merton. 1971. "Patterns of Evaluation in Science: Institutionalisation, Structure and Functions of the Referee System." *Minerva* 9(1): 66–100.

Index